NIGHTMARE
ALONG
PENNSYLVANIA
AVENUE

PERRY STONE

A STRANG COMPANY

NIGHTMARE ALONG PENNSYLVANIA AVENUE by Perry Stone
Published by FrontLine
A Strang Company
600 Rinehart Road
Lake Mary, Florida 32746
www.strangbookgroup.com

Cover design by Justin Evans
Design Director: Bill Johnson

Library of Congress Cataloging-in-Publication Data:

Stone, Perry F.
  Nightmare along Pennsylvania Avenue / Perry Stone. -- 1st ed.
      p. cm.
  Includes bibliographical references.
  ISBN 978-1-59979-860-8
  1. Bible--Prophecies--United States. 2. Christianity--Influence. 3. United States-
-History. 4. United States--History--21st century. 5. United States--Forecasting. 6.
End of the world. I. Title.
  BS649.U6S76 2010
  277.3'08--dc22

                                    2009032826

First Edition

10 11 12 13 14 — 9 8 7 6 5 4 3 2 1
Printed in the United States of America

This book is dedicated to all truth-seeking, God-fearing, and freedom-loving Americans. It is you who can set the course of the direction America will follow in the prophetic climax of the great American Empire.

CONTENTS

••• Introduction •••
AMERICA'S MAIN STREET

IN OUR NATION'S capital, Washington DC, there is a seven-mile-long street, nicknamed *America's Main Street*, where cheering crowds of people filled with hopeful dreams have stood to wave red, white, and blue banners as they welcomed each newly elected American president. That street—Pennsylvania Avenue, laid out by Pierre-Charles L'Enfant—has felt the footprints of all forty-four elected United States presidents, from George Washington to Barack Obama. A 1.5-mile strip of this street links two major houses—the White House and the United States Capitol building—and the individuals who live and work in these two houses and the buildings lining this 1.5-mile strip control the laws and decisions that impact the citizens of America.

Throughout America's political history, the name Pennsylvania Avenue has brought memories of the legacy of the American Dream and the efforts of elected leadership to work diligently to build a nation "of the people, by the people, and for the people." Yet even as the embryo of American society was being formed in the womb of the republic, the Founding Fathers warned future generations of the possibility that the republic could take a wrong turn from the path of the Constitution and destroy the original intent of the founders. Today we may be experiencing a government that our fathers warned about.

Nightmare Along Pennsylvania Avenue

The great American Dream has become the great American Nightmare. The slippery hands of legislators have reached into the pockets of hardworking citizens to fund more pork than can be found on the nation's pig farms. For years, liberal professors from Ivy League universities have poured their Marxist-Socialist agendas into the young minds of students who today are leading the nation. In 1962, during the Cuban missile crisis, Americans feared a nuclear attack from the evil Communist empire of the Soviet Union. The founder of Communism, Karl Marx, would be smiling in his grave if he knew how closely we are following his *Manifesto of the Communist Party.*

Today there is a nightmare along Pennsylvania Avenue. The great American Dream is being interrupted as Americans sleepwalk their way into a moral, economic, and spiritual abyss that begins in the heart of the nation—Washington DC. Our Founding Fathers chose the bald eagle to be America's emblem, symbolizing their vision of American greatness and strength. But today the mighty eagle of the United States is being plucked feather by feather, bringing the nation down from her once mighty heights of prestige, power, and influence.

The whole world is watching to see what becomes of America. Groups of Americans are forming committees and conferences to strategize how to continue to provide every American with the opportunity to succeed and to prosper in their pursuit of the American Dream. Others, like Igor Panarim, a Russian diplomat and dean at Russia's Foreign Ministry's school for future diplomats, have predicted that we are witnessing "the end of the American Dream." He has predicted that "the United States will break up into six autonomous regions and Alaska will revert to Russian control." He believes that "Russia and China would emerge from the economic turmoil stronger and said the two nations should work together, even to create a new currency to replace the U.S. dollar."[1]

Years ago I was having lunch with the personal secretary of one of President Bush's top appointees in his administration, a young woman who had served during the early days of the war on terror. She made an unusual observation about those making the laws and working in the Washington beltway. She commented: "Having lived and worked inside of Washington, I can tell you that there are *two Washingtons.* One segment believes in the principles of the founders and base their actions and work ethic on the Constitution. Many members of this group have a personal faith in God and the Scriptures. There is, however, another large group that is totally opposite and would not hesitate to see a socialistic-type nation controlled by liberal thinking in America."

At the time I was uncertain just what she meant by "a socialistic-type nation" and did not pursue more comments. I now understand what she was speaking about. A recent cover story in *Newsweek* magazine was titled, "We Are All Socialists Now." The article stated: "Whether we like it or not—or even whether many people have thought much about it or not—the numbers clearly suggest that we are headed in a more European direction."[2]

Socialism—defined as a centrally planned economy in which the government controls all means of production—begins with a major crisis, including but not limited to an economic crisis. Storms in the financial institutions are often followed by the rise of a messianic-type figure the masses believe can solve their problems. However, the problems are always blamed on others, and, eventually, a *class warfare* begins, identified as the tug-of-war between the wealthy and the poor, between the rich and the middle class. Soon an image is etched in the minds of the populace—rich brokers, bankers, and business class members have abused the common people, and it is time to take from them and redistribute the wealth.

Many of the "isms" of history—including Socialism—were formed by leaders who knew how to exploit the lower-income-class masses and turn them against the rich, demanding a redistribution of the money supply. This was often done when the national workers (and unions) were facing an economic crisis or meltdown. A four-phase plan enabled them to accomplish this goal. The phases are as follows:

- Phase 1: Teach the lower-income masses that the government is corrupt and that you will change it.
- Phase 2: Plant the seed in their minds that the rich (Wall Street, the bankers) are the bad guys.
- Phase 3: Promise to redistribute the wealth of a few to those less fortunate.
- Phase 4: Raise up the youth to support you and to take your plan before the people continually.

Several well-known leaders have used this four-phase plan very effectively and were able to take charge of their nations and turn things around…for the worse! They are:

- Lenin—who produced Communism
- Hitler—who produced Nazism
- Mussolini—who became the dictator of Italy
- Castro—who became the dictator of Cuba

We can see this happening today in the Middle East, as Hamas in the Gaza Strip and Hezbollah in Lebanon are promising help but bringing nothing but war to those Middle East regions.

Socialism was the root cause of the Communist revolution. In fact, major economic crises often lead to class warfare and the rise of a dictatorial type of leader, something our founders warned us about. We see the following examples:

- The crisis in France led to the rise of Napoleon.
- The crisis in Russia led to the Russian Revolution and Communism.
- The economic crisis in Germany led to the Third Reich and Fascism.
- The crisis in Cuba led to the rise of Fidel Castro.
- The crisis in Venezuela led to the rise of Hugo Chavez.

These leaders—most of whom became dictators—who rose to prominence were placed there by the masses who were seduced into the belief that these men would solve all their problems and bring in prosperity. Communism banned faith in God and created an iron curtain and poverty. Hitler slaughtered six million Jews and left much of Eastern Europe in smoke and rubble. Cuba, a once prosperous tourist destination with flowing wealth, was seized by a Communist rebel, and the freedom-loving Cubans who could, fled. Today Cuba is, in many places, a third-world country. Venezuela is also experiencing severe poverty at the hands of a powerful dictator.

Why would any nation—including America—choose a socialistic-type of government? As each powerful leader rose to prominence, he recognized and understood the unrest among the people in his nation and saw that they demanded *change*. Each leader was able to use that knowledge to make the move to government control.

Today in America, *change* may be all that you have left after the tax collectors finish reaching into your paycheck—if you still have one.

Nightmare of My Fathers

In 1848, Karl Marx published his *Manifesto of the Communist Party*, which included a long list of complaints against the *bourgeoisie* or rich, wealthy upper class. Two items stand out:

- "Centralization of credit in the banks of the state, by means of a national bank with state capital and an exclusive monopoly."
- "Centralization of the means of communication and transport in the hands of the state."[3]

America's Founding Fathers warned against just such a crisis happening within the borders of America. On May 23, 1857, Lord Macaulay wrote a letter to H. S. Randall, Esq., in which Macaulay made predictions of America's future troubles:

> ...your Republic will be as tearfully plundered and laid waste by the barbarians in the twentieth century as the Roman Empire was in the fifth, with the difference that the Huns and Vandals who ravaged the Roman Empire came from without, and that your Huns and Vandals will have been engendered within your country by your own institutions.[4]

In 1888, the managing editor of a New York daily paper, David Goodman Croly, wrote a book titled *Glimpses of the Future*, in which he made a series of predictions, many of which have now come to pass:

- Concentration of wealth in the hands of a few
- Abuse of power by giant corporations
- Promiscuous sex relations with easy divorce
- New York subways
- Public works administration (PWA) to solve unemployment
- Reforestation and public rehabilitation projects
- Premarital health examinations
- Adoption of many socialistic policies by the Democratic Party
- Antilabor bias of the press
- A global war started by Germany
- Humiliation of the United States by a weaker power
- An electrical age
- Aerial navigation by ships made from aluminum
- Annexation of islands by USA for defense
- Illustrated color magazines
- Color inks used on colored paper
- Sound motion pictures
- Motion pictures used in education[5]

As you can read, all of Mr. Croly's predictions have come to pass. It is these final three predictions we should observe:

- Capture of our coast cities by foreign powers
- Acceptance of polygamy by many nations
- Possessors of great wealth forced to disburse their wealth to people employed[6]

Before you read further, take a minute to take the following quiz to see if you can identify the world leader being described:

Who Am I?
• The nation was a democracy.
• The nation had spent billions during the war before his election.
• Before being elected, he was a relative unknown.
• Before his election, many did not know what he believed or stood for.
• He became famous for his charisma and his speeches.
• He wrote a best-selling book that was read across the nation.
• Women would often scream, people cry, and some pass out when he spoke.
• Large crowds followed him, and people waited for hours just to see him.
• The people of the country wanted a major political change.
• The country at the time was in an economic crisis.
• He promised to restore the economy, bring jobs, and rebuild the infrastructure.
• When elected, he was considered a messiah or savior to many people.
• He was accused by some of having thugs in his life and background.
• It was the youth vote that got him into power.
• He made a famous speech in Berlin.
• Certain records about his past were hidden from the public.
• People were bullied and harassed if they spoke against him.[7]
The answer: Adolf Hitler

Adolf Hitler is just one example of this truth: *Using the discontent of the PEOPLE and the CRISIS in the WORKPLACE brings a revolution!* And revolution may birth destruction and devastation such as that nation has never experienced. The Russian Revolution brought in Marxism and Communism. The German economic crash brought in Hitler's Third Reich. And America's current economic crisis has the potential for birthing a new order in America—Socialism.

Today, many believe that our forty-fourth president, Barack Obama, leans toward a more socialistic form of government where government is the *big brother* who provides for all your needs—as long as you follow the regulations and guidelines of Big Brother! Notice some of the goals and the aggressive agenda the Obama administration has introduced since his inauguration:

1. Attempt to revive the Fairness Doctrine[8]
2. Take control of the census[9]
3. Nationalize the banks[10]
4. Take away the secret vote at unions[11]
5. Restrict the availability of firearms[12]
6. Redistribute the wealth from the rich to the poor[13]
7. Nationalize health care[14]
8. Enlarge government[15]
9. Support dictatorships (Iran)[16]
10. Give up sovereignty to global laws[17]

Many Americans now agree that the forty-fourth president's agenda is pushing America closer to a more socialistic form of government. Continually, greedy corporate bankers, investors, and Wall Street brokers are blamed for the world's problems, and the solution is to seize control from the private sector, raise taxes on the rich, and redistribute personal wealth.

What Can We Do?

What has caused this nightmare, and how do we wake a nation from sleepwalking before it walks into a pit of no return? First, we can keep a *balance* by electing those to office who will *oppose* Marxist ideas. We have believed that if we elected the *right* person, that person will be able to change things. But history has not always proven this to be correct. Our culture is corrupted and perverted by the professors, media voices, and entertainment and Internet professionals who head these industries. Abortion has still not been overturned in America, even though both Presidents Reagan and Bush stood against it.

This book will take an in-depth look at our dynamic history, including significant prophetic patterns of the past and future of America. It is a manifesto for the American Dream. But even more than that, it stands as proof that although we may not always be able to change the culture, *we can change a person's heart and lifestyle* by bringing the gospel to the people in our homes, communities, nation, and world.

••• Chapter 1 •••

THE AMERICAN PRESIDENT

Experience teaches us that it is much easier to prevent an enemy from posting themselves than it is to dislodge them after they have got possession.

—GEORGE WASHINGTON

O UR FIRST PRESIDENT, George Washington, understood thoroughly the sacred trust placed in the hands of the individual chosen to the office of the president of the United States. That office holds within its powers the potential for helping—or hindering—every citizen of this great nation to reach his or her own "great American Dream." In his farewell address of 1796, President Washington reflected on this sacred trust by saying:

> In looking forward to the moment which is intended to terminate the career of my public life, my feelings do not permit me to suspend the deep acknowledgment of that debt of gratitude which I owe to my beloved country for the many honors it has conferred upon me; still more for the steadfast confidence with which it has supported me; and for the opportunities I have thence enjoyed of manifesting my inviolable attachment, by services faithful and persevering, though in usefulness unequal to my zeal. If benefits have resulted to our country from these services, let it always be remembered to your praise, and as an instructive example in our annals, that under circumstances in which the passions, agitated in every direction, were liable to mislead, amidst appearances sometimes dubious, vicissitudes of fortune often discouraging, in situations in which not unfrequently want of success has countenanced the spirit of criticism, the constancy of your support was the essential prop of the efforts, and a guarantee of the plans by which they were effected. Profoundly penetrated with this idea, I shall carry it with me to my grave, as a strong incitement to unceasing vows that heaven may continue to you the choicest tokens of its benefi-

cence; that your union and brotherly affection may be perpetual; that the free Constitution, which is the work of your hands, may be sacredly maintained; that its administration in every department may be stamped with wisdom and virtue; that, in fine, the happiness of the people of these States, under the auspices of liberty, may be made complete by so careful a preservation and so prudent a use of this blessing as will acquire to them the glory of recommending it to the applause, the affection, and adoption of every nation which is yet a stranger to it.[1]

Every four years, Americans observe the finished product of an emerging president. After nonstop campaigning, countless telemarketing-type of television interviews, and twelve to eighteen months of seemingly endless advertisements that are more like a publicity marathon, a finely tuned, silver-tongued politician walks his companion along Pennsylvania Avenue and up the White House steps, packaged like a set of Ken and Barbie dolls. Some men become president because of name recognition (such as the name Bush), others due to military records, and still others as a result of political clout or unbalanced media reporting that prevents negative reports from surfacing during a campaign.

A Sovereign Calling

Others enter the presidential arena believing that they have a sovereign calling from a higher power to fulfill a specific role in history. One such man was former President Ronald Reagan. Few Americans are aware of a personal prophecy given to Ronald Reagan while he was governor in California, revealing his future destiny as president. According to the book *Reagan Inside Out*, the story begins in California on a beautiful October day in 1970. Herbert E. Ellingwood, Governor Reagan's legal affairs secretary, had invited several guests to visit the governor. Among them were celebrity Pat Boone, Harald Bredesen, and a minister named George Otis. Boone was a longtime friend of the Reagans, and the governor at that time was running for reelection.

According to those present that day, the conversations included a discussion on Bible prophecy and the Holy Spirit's moving in the last days. After a series of interesting discussions, Ellingwood finally led the group toward the front door, and the final good-byes were being said. One of the ministers spoke up and asked, "Governor, do you mind if we take a moment and pray for you and Mrs. Reagan?"

Immediately, Governor Reagan replied, "We would appreciate that," as his countenance turned rather serious. Then the group joined hands forming a circle. Reagan bowed his head rather sharply, and the others tilted theirs a bit. Prayer was immediately offered asking for God's blessings. Suddenly in the middle of the prayer, the unexpected occurred. George Otis recalled what transpired:

> The Holy Spirit came upon me, and I knew it. In fact, I was embarrassed. There was this pulsing in my arm, and my hand—the one holding Governor Reagan's hand—was shaking. I didn't know what to do. I just didn't want this to be happening. I can remember even as I was speaking, tensing my muscles trying to get the shaking to stop.

As this was transpiring, the prayer of Otis changed completely from the basic prayer of blessing to a more steady and intent word. The Holy Spirit–inspired words coming from Otis's mouth spoke directly to Reagan, addressing him as "My son," and recognizing his role as leader in a state that was the size of many nations on earth. His "labor" was described as "pleasing." Suddenly the following words were spoken: "*If you walk uprightly before Me, you will reside at 1600 Pennsylvania Avenue.*" Everyone knew that 1600 Pennsylvania Avenue was the address of the White House, the home of America's presidents.[2]

Ten years passed, and in 1980, Governor Reagan, against all odds, ran for president. He was on the bottom of the pile of ten other Republican candidates, all seeking their party's nomination. The major factor against him was his age: near the time of the election he was approaching his seventieth birthday. Political analysts were critical, saying he was "too old to make correct decisions and could die while in office." Others said he was incompetent and just an actor. Despite the objections, Reagan won, and then was reelected for a second term. He not only lived to be seventy-eight, but he passed the age of ninety!

In November 1980, upon hearing Reagan had been elected, Pat Boone telephoned the Reagans at their Pacific Palisades home to congratulate Ronald. After Boone spoke with Nancy, Reagan came to the phone. During the conversation, Boone inquired if Reagan remembered the prayer in Sacramento ten years earlier. Reagan said, "Of course I do."

Ten years before his election as president, God revealed His will for Ronald Reagan. Mr. Reagan was a dedicated Christian and loved the Bible. He was familiar with biblical prophecy and at times privately consulted key ministers to ask for input on how certain world events would play into the prophetic scenarios of Scripture.

Another president who perceived his presidency was appointed by sovereignty was George W. Bush. His wife, Laura, recalls him saying, "I believe that God wants me to be president, but if that doesn't happen, its OK." In his book, *A Charge to Keep*, we read that Bush's inspiration to run for president came after he heard Pastor Mark Craig of Highland Park United Methodist Church deliver a sermon in which he spoke of the reluctance of Moses to serve as a leader and how people were "starved for leadership..." The pastor continued, and as he did, Bush felt a "call," a sense that God was directing him to run for president. After the sermon, Bush's mother, Barbara, turned to him and said, "He was talking to you."[3] Not long after, Bush called James Robison and told him, "I've heard the call. I believe God wants me to run for president."[4]

Bill Clinton may also have recognized a sovereign calling to the presidency.

Having been to President Bill Clinton's hometown of Hot Springs, Arkansas, and having spoken with former classmates of the president, I can tell you they were all impressed with him as a young man in high school. Even as a teenager, he would speak to business leaders who were amazed at his knowledge and ability to craft words that created powerful mental images among the listeners. One woman described him as a studious, intelligent young man with high goals, which his friends knew would take him to the top.

It remains to many a mystery of how Bill Clinton managed to accomplish the political feats he did with the background he had as a young man. Insiders in Arkansas believe that his mother, Virginia, played a major role through the people with whom she developed close friendships and relationships, including an Arkansas senator, James Fulbright. The former senator, who served from 1945 to 1974, was a mentor to young Bill Clinton. In 1963, Clinton was a Hot Springs delegate to Boys State, where, while attending Boys Nation in Washington DC, he shook hands with President Kennedy. Clinton served as an intern for Fulbright from 1966 to 1967. Older insiders from Hot Springs state that Virginia, and her close relationship to Fulbright, assisted in Bill's early trend to politics.

After losing his reelection bid for governor, Bill Clinton took a trip to Israel. After this Israeli tour, he returned to Arkansas where his pastor was in the hospital. Clinton's pastor related to him that he believed one day Clinton would become president in a time when Israel needed a friend, and he must stand with Israel. If the time came that Clinton rejected Israel, then God would reject him.[5]

Barack Obama

No American president has amazed the general public more than the forty-fourth president, Barack Obama. Obama made history by becoming the first black president—and one of the youngest (age forty-seven at his inauguration) in history, following Ulysses S. Grant (1869, age forty-six), Grover Cleveland (1885, age forty-seven), Theodore Roosevelt (1901, age forty-two), and John F. Kennedy (1960, age forty-three). What is even more astonishing is how he was elected president with such a record of *political inexperience*, having only served in the United States Senate from 2004 to 2008.

Throughout the primaries and the campaign, many people were trying to discover his family history, his personal political beliefs, and those beliefs linked to his life that molded his thinking. Voters knew he was from Chicago and learned that he had been a member of Pastor Jeremiah Wright's church for twenty years. Wright's church was distinguished by its message of Black Liberation Theology, which includes the following:

1. It has its roots in Latin and African theology.
2. It is the new interpretation of Christian reality.
3. It thrives on perpetuating a class struggle.
4. It encourages revolution against whites if necessary.
5. It rejects traditional scriptural interpretations—"The experience of the community determines the understanding and the interpretation of the Scripture... normally what is normative for interpretation is not historical research but the hermeneutic of history experienced in the community or the political group."
6. It is radically Marxist—"The world must be interpreted in terms of class struggle and that the only choice is between capitalism and Marxism..."
7. It makes the Bible subject to a Marxist view of history.[6]

Months prior to the election, when supporters were asked on live television to name one thing of political significance that Barack Obama had done during his career, over and over again they could not name one thing, but they would respond with answers such as, "He makes a great speech," or "He makes me feel good," or "He gives me hope for the future."

After Obama's father left his mother, she remarried and moved to Indonesia, where Obama (called Barry at the time), attended a Catholic school. He later returned to Hawaii to live with his mother's parents and finish high school.[7]

In Obama's book he speaks of attending Socialist conferences and seeing Marxist literature. Some of his political opponents have made statements about his Marxist leanings, including:

- Alan Keyes, his 2004 opponent in the senatorial race, went so far as to accuse Obama of being a "hard-core, academic Marxist."[8]

- Former Senator Tom Delay stated, "I have said it publicly, and I will again, that unless he proves me wrong, [Barack Obama] is a Marxist."[9]

- Joe Lieberman, a conservative Independent senator from Connecticut, was asked on FOX News if he believed Obama was a Marxist. Lieberman answered, "I've learned some things about him, about the kind of environment from which he came ideologically. And I wouldn't...I hesitate to say he is a Marxist, but he's got some positions that are far left of me and I think of mainstream America."[10]

Men Who Influenced Obama

Part of the reason that many conservative thinkers believe Obama has a strong socialistic, academic mind-set is because of his past associations during the early days of his education. In this section we will consider the influence some of these associates may have had on Obama.

Frank Marshall Davis

Obama's childhood mentor was a man named Frank Marshall Davis. Davis publicly admitted that he was a member of the Communist Party USA (CPUSA). In 1951, the Commission on Subversive Activities to the Legislature of the Territory of Hawaii identified Davis as a member of the CPUSA, and several anticommunist congressional committees accused him of involvement in several communist-front activities.[11] While Obama was in Hawaii (1971–1979), he developed a close relationship—almost like a son, with Davis, listening to his "poetry" and getting advice. In his book *Dreams From My Father*, Obama mentions Davis several times simply as "Frank."

Professor Gerald Horne (a contributing editor for a Communist Party USA magazine) spoke at a reception at the Communist Party archives in March 2007, noting that Davis moved from Kansas to Hawaii in 1948 at the suggestion of his good friend Paul Robeson, where he came into contact with Barack Obama and his family, becoming the young man's mentor and influencing Obama's sense of identity and career moves.[12] Robeson, of course, was the well-known black actor and singer who served as a member of the CPUSA and an apologist for the Soviet Union. Davis had known Robeson from his time in Chicago.

Saul Alinsky

Saul Alinsky was born January 30, 1909, in Chicago, Illinois. A Marxist, he is considered the founder of modern community organizing. In 1971, Alinsky published *Rules for Radicals*, revealing his views for organizing for mass power.[13] The book included the concept of how to change the world from what it was to what Alinsky and his Marxist associates believed it should be, including how the "have-nots" can take away from the "haves." In the prologue of his book, he writes:

> Any revolutionary change must be preceded by a passive, affirmative, non-challenging attitude toward change among the mass of our people. They must feel so frustrated, so defeated, so lost, so futureless in the prevailing system that they are willing to let go of the past and change the future. This acceptance is the reformation essential to any revolution. To bring on this reformation requires that the organizer work inside the system, among not only the middle class but the 40 percent of American families—more than seventy million people—whose incomes range from $5,000 to $10,000 a year [in 1971]....If we fail to communicate with them, if we don't encourage them to form alliances with us, they will move to the right. Maybe they will anyway, but let's not let it happen by default.[14]

One well-known person who was familiar with Alinsky's writings, once a student at Wellesley College, would one day be the head of the State Department: Hillary Clinton. As a student she wrote a senior honor thesis on Alinsky's efforts. In her book *Living History*, Mrs. Clinton acknowledged that Alinsky offered her a job after her graduation. However, she moved on to attend Harvard.[15]

It is interesting to note that the writings of Alinsky and his ideas of community organizing also influenced a young Barack Obama when he worked on Chicago's South Side. It was Alinsky who taught that shareholders should share their power with the disenfranchised working poor. This influence may explain why Obama has promoted many rather *new* ideas to bring about *change* in America's social system.

Chicago Connections

Why did Barack Obama leave Hawaii and end up in Chicago, becoming a community organizer? His contacts in Chicago become more interesting in light of his past. He became acquainted with the Democratic Socialists of America (DSA), which maintains ties to European socialists.

It was the DSA that pushed Obama as a senator! *The Socialist Viewpoint*, a Marxist publication, has stated:

> The capitalist ruling class of the United States exercises a virtual dictatorship not only over American society but also over the entire world. This capitalist class rule is the basic cause of the poverty, wars and the degradation of the natural environment.[16]

> After being expelled from Socialist Action in 1999, we formed Socialist Workers Organization in an attempt to carry on the project of building a nucleus of a revolutionary party true to the historic teachings and program of Marx, Engels, Lenin and Trotsky.[17]

Obama also met and befriended two former members of Students of a Democratic Society, William Ayers and Carl Davidson. This group led a siege on college campuses in the 1960s, protesting the Vietnam War. Ayers was also linked to the Weather Underground, which bombed several government buildings, killing innocent people. He received no jail time due to a technicality and later became a professor.[18]

It was Carl Davidson who would later organize a Chicago antiwar rally in 2002, where Obama spoke out against the war in Iraq.[19] It is important to remember that Communism and Socialism both trace their roots to Karl Marx, the coauthor of the *Manifesto of the Communist Party*. Karl Marx also coined the slogan: "From each according to his ability, to each according to his needs!"[20]

The King of a New Global Order?

As we have already demonstrated, there are interesting links between biblical prophecy—the ability of holy men to see into the future and predict events thousands of years before they transpire—and worldwide events happening in our world today. These predictions are so clear that they are not open to private interpretation. One of the amazing predictions relates to the formation and order of empires that will rise and fall, eventually leading to one final empire that will impact the entire world.

The order of empires was revealed more than twenty-six hundred years ago in the Book of Daniel, written by the prophet Daniel in ancient Babylon. About six hundred years later, John recorded additional insights in the Book of Revelation, revealing the rise of a seventh and eighth empire prior to the return of the Messiah to Jerusalem (Rev. 17:10–12). The first six empires as revealed in biblical prophecy are:

1. The Egyptian Empire
2. The Assyrian Empire
3. The Babylonian Empire
4. The Media-Persia Empire
5. The Grecian Empire
6. The Roman Empire

In Daniel 2, King Nebuchadnezzar experienced a dream of a large metallic image of a man with a head of gold, representing ancient Babylon; chest and two arms of silver representing Media and Persia; and thighs of brass, an allusion to the Grecian Empire led by Alexander the Great. The image changed from brass to two legs of iron, representing the Western and Eastern portions of the Roman Empire (Rome and Constantinople). Eventually the East and West legs evolve into two feet of iron and clay (an east and west division) and conclude at the very end of days with ten toes of miry clay and iron (Dan. 2:41–43).

Having studied the Scriptures for more than forty-two thousand hours, I believe we are in the formation of the two feet. We have not seen evidence of ten kings, which would be identified with the ten toes. Since these two feet are a mixture of clay and iron and are a division between East and West, the clay (West) is the government of democracy, and the iron (East) is an allusion to the *iron curtain* of Communism. Although Communism has fallen in the Soviet Union, the countries of China, North Vietnam, and North Korea are all Communist nations, and the people are living under an iron fist that holds them in political, spiritual, and economic bondage and control.

According to Daniel, this iron and clay will merge but will not hold together, forming a kingdom that has a mix of strength and weakness (Dan. 2:42–44). It is interesting that although China is a Communist nation, it mixes in dealings with democratic nations like America. However, when it comes to things like freedom of speech, freedom to assemble, and freedom of religion, China's iron fist of Communism does not mix with the clay of democratic freedoms.

After the sixth (Roman Empire), there is a seventh empire that will continue for a "short space." The seventh empire will be a continuation of the sixth; however, it will not have the power, influence, or destructive nature of the final eighth empire, which is identified in prophetic Scriptures as the kingdom of the beast. The concluding eighth kingdom will delegate authority to ten kings who, during a one-hour meeting, will submit their nations into the hands of the Antichrist (Rev. 17:12). For forty-two months, all buying and selling will be under the control of this final empire. Those who reject the system will be executed (Rev. 13:17–18; 20:1–4). Many scholars believe that the seventh empire, which will exist before the final kingdom of the beast, will be a global government under the direction of one man.

For many centuries Bible scholars have mused upon who or what will represent this seventh. For the past sixty years, it has been commonly taught that the nations of the Imperial Roman Empire will unite under one name, with one currency and under one leader. This interpretation received widespread acceptance with the formation of the European Union (EU).

Many scholars believe a final seven-year government will come on Earth that will dominate Europe and the Middle East, and that eventually an Islamic leader will emerge who will take control of much of Israel and lead the world into a final battle known as Armageddon (Rev. 16:16). This seven-year period, called the Great Tribulation, is divided into two sections of forty-two months each. It appears that the seventh empire controls the first part and the eighth kingdom swallows up the seventh kingdom and will rule for the final forty-two months.

Both Daniel and John saw this beast "rise up out of the sea" (Dan. 7:1–3; Rev. 13:1), which alludes to the sea of nations. However Daniel saw four beasts rise out of the "Great Sea," which is identified as the Mediterranean Sea. If the final kingdoms emerge from the regions of the previous, then how is America involved in the preparation and promotion of this kingdom? Here are the questions:

- Will *America* or *Europe* pave the road as the initiator of a seventh global empire?
- Will the American president *now* or in the *future* be the premier leader of a new order?

- Will this new order carve the road for a final kingdom with a final kingdom dictator?

Time and events are the indicators of prophetic fulfillment. Men may prepare plans, but all purposes are eventually determined by the will of God. When the timing is right for the complete formation of the seventh empire, which precedes the appearing of the biblical Antichrist, then the restraining force that is holding back wickedness, evil, and the man of sin will be removed (2 Thess. 2:7), and the leaders of the world will have unrestrained power and authority to set up a system that will eventually lead to the mother of all battles, Armageddon (Rev. 16:16), and the return of the Messiah.

Looking for the Right Man

I am a student of American history—not a scholar, but a student. I have more than fifteen thousand books in my library, including the biographies of many of the U.S. presidents. From George Washington to George W. Bush, all presidents have stressed the importance of life, liberty, and the pursuit of happiness. Each president considered Christianity as his faith or wrote positively of the Christian faith and the Bible.

However, from the beginning, not one president would have been popular enough in the eyes of foreign nations to be the leader of a new global order that would create a United States of Europe—until the election of the forty-fourth president, Barack Hussein Obama.

During the past one hundred years there have been too many opposing ideologies to prevent a merging of nations. Communism was divided against capitalism. The Nazi regime was an enemy to the Allies of Europe. Islam would not accept a Western leader for fear of disrupting the cultural traditions of the Islamic world. The world is divided in the arenas of religion, culture, and ethnicity. Any global king of a seventh empire would need to be received as a *unifier* in religion, culture, and among ethnic groups. It would require a worldwide economic crisis to introduce a new form of currency or a more unified system. For this seventh empire to emerge, there must arise, at some point of time, a person whose background, charisma, and views are popular with much of the world. Throughout history, there have been many possible candidates—all of whom have failed. Now we may see another candidate in President Barack Obama.

During his candidacy, President Obama claimed to be a Christian, which appealed to many Christians in America. He had a Muslim father and grandfather and attended school as a child in Indonesia, the world's largest Islamic nation. Although for many years he was called by his nickname, Barry, while in college he began to insist on being addressed by his formal name, Barack Hussein Obama, established Muslim names in the Islamic world. He is loved and received by the masses of Muslims living in the Islamic world. Thus he is seen by some as a *unifier* of the more *progressive* Christians and moderate Muslims.

Because Obama has a black African father from Kenya, he also appeals to the black community throughout the world, and especially among blacks living in Africa. When he was elected, there was dancing in the streets throughout Africa, especially among the Kenyans, since his father was from Kenya and many relatives still reside in Kenya.

While many Europeans detested President Bush because he went after terrorists without the stamp of approval of many European nations and leaders, Europeans are now enamored with both Obama and his wife. Large crowds greeted him during a European tour, with few if any negative protests. Canada and most of Western Europe operate on a Socialist form of government. Within the first one hundred days of the Obama administration, it became clear that he was directing the United States economically into a form of nationalization and Socialism, which was a thrill to the European nations already operating in this form of government. It meant that America would no longer be viewed as a superpower superior to Germany, France, and England but would now be placed on a level playing field with the majority of European nations.

In an interview in the *Economist Magazine* in November 2008, famed politician Henry Kissinger stated: "Now that the clay feet of the economic system have been exposed, the gap between a global system for economics and the global political system based on the state must be addressed as a dominant task..."[21]

Obama Patterns and Symbolism

Obama not only has the favor of the majority of nations outside of America (at the present), but he also has several patterns that run parallel to a previous U.S. president. From the outset, it was clear that Senator Obama understood the power of symbolism. Abraham Lincoln is recognized as the president who helped to break the back of slavery following the Civil War. Lincoln was born in another state (Kentucky), but he won the Republican Senate seat in Illinois. Obama too was elected senator in Illinois. Obama stood at the same courthouse in Springfield, Illinois, to announce his run for president as Lincoln did 143 years earlier.[22] On his way to his inauguration, President-elect Obama followed the same route as Lincoln did by taking the train from Illinois to the train station in Washington. He was sworn in with his hand on the same Bible that Abraham Lincoln used (Lincoln's Bible) and dined on some of Lincoln's favorite foods served on replicas of the plates from Lincoln's inauguration.[23]

The patterns and unique symbolism linked from his administration to those of Abraham Lincoln are not the only symbolism or patterns we can see. By examining an Islamic tradition handed down from the time of Muhammad, we can find symbolism linking him to Islamic traditions.

Muhammad, the founder of Islam, claimed to have received numerous revelations from an angel of God. After his death, these messages were placed in a book called the Quran, containing 114 chapters called surahs. Other books were written, compiled by the followers of Muhammad, that contained the statements, procedures, and comments that his followers recalled while Muhammad was alive. These books, called the *hadith*, also hold information related to numerous predictions and signs of the last days. Islam has seventy signs of the last days, classified as major and minor signs.

One of the more famous predictions that Muhammad left his followers, penned in the hadith, has spread throughout Arabia and the Middle East. This prediction involved the West:

> Allah's Apostle said, "The Hour will not be established...till the sun rises from the West. So when the sun will rise and the people will see it (rising from the West) they will all believe (embrace Islam) but that will be the time when: (As Allah said,) 'No good will it do to a soul to believe then, if it believed not before, nor earned good (by deeds of righteousness) through its Faith.'"[24]
>
> —*Sahih Bukhari*

There are basically three interpretations by Islamic scholars as to the meaning of this hadith. The first, and a very common interpretation among Middle East Muslims, is that the literal sun will one morning rise in the west instead of the east as a sign to those living on Earth. Years ago some Muslims stated that the planet Mars had shifted and the sun was now rising on Mars' western side. However, this prediction says nothing about Mars. Obviously to take this literally would mean that if it did occur on Earth, it would mean instant death to every person on Earth.

A second meaning is that before the end of the age, Islam will spread its message and influence and be received and accepted in the nations of the West. Traditionally, Islam has been strong in the eastern part of the world, especially from Egypt eastward toward Iraq, Iran, Pakistan, and Afghanistan, along with the southern Russian states that were once a part of the ancient Roman Empire. According to this interpretation, the sun rising indicates the *light* of Islam from the east to the west, which included Spain and Britain, but now includes the United States and Canada.

While ministering in 2001 in Pensacola, Florida, I heard a third interpretation of the sun rising in the west from Minister Louis Farrakhan, the head of the Nation of Islam, who was teaching on television about the spread of Islam. At the conclusion of his televised message, he quoted the Islamic prediction that the "sun would rise in the west." His interpretation was that a new messenger would arise in the West (America) who would help to spread the light of Islam into the darkened minds of the American population. At that time he inferred that he might be that messenger.[25]

As far back as the early 1990s I heard of this prediction from Muslim friends who live in the Middle East. The statement by Louis Farrakhan only renewed my interest in the subject. In 2008, after researching the background of Senator Obama, something occurred that caught my attention. In the month of June, a new seal for Senator Obama was placed on the front of a podium where he was speaking. This seal was similar to the presidential seal but not identical due to changes in the design. This seal caused so much controversy that it was dropped from public presentation. A second seal, the official Obama seal, piqued my curiosity, especially since Senator Obama was friends with Farrakhan and had received support from the black organization Nation of Islam as senator and as a presidential candidate. The seal of Obama was a large "O" with the sun rising in the center. Here is the explanation of the first seal that also contained the second seal:

> A new seal debuted on Obama's podium Friday, sporting iconography used in the U.S. presidential seal, the blue background, the eagle clutching arrows on left and olive branch on right, but with symbolic differences. Instead of the Latin "E pluribus unum" (Out of many, one), Obama's says "Vero possumus," rough Latin for "Yes, we can." Instead of "Seal of the President of the United States," Obama's Web site address is listed. And instead of a shield, Obama's eagle wears his "O" campaign logo with a rising sun representing hope ahead.[26]

The rising sun was in the center of the O. If the president-elect did not have an Islamic name, a Muslim father and grandfather, and had not attended school in Indonesia, then a rising sun within the letter *O* of his name would have little if any significance. However, the seal, created in Chicago, and the fact that Muslims were a part of Obama's campaign staff indicate that this symbol could have served as a rather *cryptic* message to *knowledgeable Muslims* in the Nation of Islam and throughout the world that the "sun" was about to rise in the west.

When Senator Obama made his bid for the presidency, there were two people who had been close associates and friends from whom he distanced himself. The first was his former pastor, Reverend Jeremiah Wright, the controversial minister whose brief excerpts were aired worldwide. The second but lesser-known separation was the link with Louis Farrakhan, who had publically endorsed Obama, but whose endorsement Obama immediately played down, noting he did not agree with Farrakhan's teaching. However, Farrakhan made a very unusual comment about Obama when addressing a group of young people before the election:

> You are the instruments that God is going to use to bring about universal change. And this is why that Barack has captured the youth. And he has involved young people in a political process that they didn't care anything about. That's a sign. When the Messiah speaks, the youth will hear. And the Messiah is absolutely speaking.[27]

Why would a Muslim leader identify a presidential candidate as the "Messiah"? Farrakhan does not accept that Christ was the Messiah. But being a Muslim, he knows (as stated on television) the Islamic hadith that says the sun would rise in the west. He also knows the teaching about the *Mahdi*—the future Islamic leader who will convert the world to Islam, destroy the Jews, and tear down the crosses.

Because the sun rising in the west is a twelve-hundred-year-old prediction, and because there is an Islamic family link and political link with Islam in South Chicago, then it would be a crafty political move to use the sun rising not just as a picture of "rising on a new day," as the news article states, but also as a cryptic message to Muslims that a man has now come who will be friendly, acceptable, and open to Islam in the West. It is interesting that Obama spoke to Muslims on television, traveled to Turkey (an Islamic nation) to speak, and conducted a third meeting in Egypt to address the Islamic world, all within the first 140 days in office. Why would one man make such a continual effort to speak to the Islamic world, when there are more than 5.5 billion other people who are not Muslims?

There is another unique link between Obama and traditional Islamic beliefs. The name *Barack* is both a biblical name and an Islamic name. In the Scriptures, Barak was a military commander in Israel who, at the request of Deborah, a judge in Israel, waged a war against Jabin (Judg. 4). The Hebrew meaning of *Barak* is "lightning, or a flash of light."

In Islam it is taught that in the year 621, at age fifty-one, Muhammad rode a white-winged horse named *Buraq*, meaning "Lightning," to what Muslims believe was Jerusalem.[28] Today Muslims believe that inside the Dome of the Rock in Jerusalem, where Muhammad came on his night journey, is the foot-print left by Muhammad as he ascended to heaven.[29] This story is inbred in Islamic teaching to the point that the Jewish Western Wall, a retaining wall from the second temple, is called by Arab Muslims the *Al-Buraq wall*, believed to be the tying post for Muhammad's horse.[30]

Thus, in the Islamic world, the name *Barack* is always identified with the white-winged stallion that Muhammad allegedly rode on his night journey from Mecca to Jerusalem (although Jerusalem is not mentioned in the Quran), where Muslims teach he met the prophets and Isa (Jesus).[31] A white horse is important in the traditions of the Shiite Muslims in regard to the Imam Hussein, who was leader of the Shiite branch of Islam and was martyred at Karbala (Iraq) in the seventh century, where he is said to have ridden a white horse.[32]

The white horse imagery is interesting for several reasons. The Book of Revelation predicts that a rider on a white horse will appear, going forth conquering: "And I looked, and behold, a white horse. He who sat on it had a bow; and a crown was given to him, and he went out conquering and to conquer" (Rev. 6:2). According to the traditional Christian interpretation, this unnamed rider is the leader of the final kingdom, which is identified with the Antichrist. Oddly, according to some Islamic scholars, this verse is identified with a coming leader known as the *Mahdi*, who also appears on a white horse.

> It is clear that this man the Mahdi who will ride the white horse and judge by the Qur'an (with justice) and with whom will be men with marks of prostration on their foreheads [Marks on their forehead from bowing down from bowing in prayer with their heads to the ground five times a day].[33]

Islam expects the Mahdi to ride upon a white stallion when he emerges as the new leader of the Islamic world. There are several Islam leaders in the Middle East who own white horses, including Muammar Qaddafi of Libya and the late Saddam Hussein. Even the son of Osama bin Laden, Omar bin

Laden, rides a stallion and has been quoted that he would like to help bring peace. Thus, the imagery of a white stallion is linked in the minds of knowledgeable Muslims to the "awaited and enlightened one."

Only two president-elects made their acceptance speeches in outdoor stadiums: John Kennedy in 1960 in the Los Angeles Coliseum, and Barack Obama in Denver, Colorado. While the following may be a complete coincidence, in light of these Islamic predictions it is interesting—at least.

While the rest of the Democratic National Convention was held in the Pepsi Center, on the night of August 28, 2008, Barack Obama made his acceptance speech to an estimated crowd of eighty-four thousand cheering supporters at Mile High Stadium, home of the Denver Broncos NFL football team. The Broncos have a mascot that is a large white stallion named Thunder II. The first mascot, Thunder I, was a white Arabian stallion. During the acceptance speech, what many people did not see on television, but was seen to thousands in the stadium, was that just above the head of speaker Obama was a huge metal white stallion, Thunder II. Barack's name is linked with Muhammad's white horse and the future Mahdi, who allegedly appears on a white horse according to Muslim traditions. Since Denver was chosen as the convention location in January 2007, the speech at the stadium and the white horse would merely be a coincidence. However, the "symbolism" is quite interesting.

Obama's Muslim Connections

Anyone who accesses Obama's official campaign site will find a page titled, "Obama Has Never Been a Muslim, and Is a Committed Christian." That page states: "Obama never prayed in a mosque. He has never been a Muslim, was not raised a Muslim, and is a committed Christian who attends the United Church of Christ."[34]

But the *Israel Insider* staff compiled a report, dated March 27, 2008, and made available on their Web site, that gives compelling information from accumulated research from primary sources that indicate Obama was a devout Muslim, the son of a devout Muslim, the stepson of a devout Muslim, and the grandson and namesake (*Hussein*) of a devout Muslim. Let's consider some of this information.[35]

- On January 1, 1968, he entered the Roman Catholic Franciscus Assisi Primary School in Jakarta, Indonesia, registered under the name Barry Soetoro, an Indonesian citizen whose religion was listed as Islam.

- Three years later, in 1971, Obama enrolled in the Besuki Primary School, a government school, as Barry Soetoro, Muslim.

- All Indonesian students are required to study religion at school, and young Barry Soetoro, being a Muslim, would have been required to study Islam daily in school.

- According to Tine Hahiyary, one of Obama's teachers and the principal from 1971 through 1989, Barry actively took part in Islamic religious studies and "studied 'mengaji' (recitation of the Quran)" during his time at the school. Mengaji indicates learning to recite the Quran in the Arabic language rather than the native tongue.

- Classmate Rony Amiris describes young Barry as "being a very devout Muslim." Amiris, now the manager of Bank Mandiri, Jakarta, recently said: "Barry was previously quite religious in Islam."

- Emirsyah Satar, CEO of Garuda Indonesia, was quoted as saying, "He was often in the prayer room wearing a 'sarong' at that time. He was quite religious in Islam but only after marrying Michelle, he changed his religion."

- Barack Obama's brother Roy, who was, Obama said, "the person who made me proudest of all," converted to Islam over Christianity, arguing that the black man must "liberate himself from the poisoning influences of European culture."

- While a senator, Obama stumped for his cousin Raila Odinga, who was seeking election as president of Kenya. Raila Odinga and Sheikh Abdullah Abdi, chairman of the National Muslim Leaders Forum of Kenya, signed a Memorandum of Understanding in which Raila agreed, if elected president, "within 6 months rewrite the Constitution of Kenya to recognize Shariah as the only true law sanctioned by the Holy Quran for Muslim declared regions [and] within one year to facilitate the establishment of a Shariah court in every Kenyan divisional headquarters...and to popularize Islam, the only true religion...by ordering every primary school in Kenya in the regions to conduct daily Madrassa classes."

- An American Expat in Southeast Asia blog, written by an American who has lived in Indonesia for twenty years and has met with both the Taliban and al Qaeda, contains the following: "Barack Hussein Obama might have convinced some Americans that he is no longer a Muslim, but so far he has not convinced many in the world's most populous Muslim country who still see him as a Muslim and a crusader for Islam and world peace."

As this report concludes, "Obama wants it both ways, has always wanted it both ways. Black and white, Indonesian and American, Muslim and Christian. He is a changeling, a veritable chameleon, adapting and amending his life story to fit the circumstances."[36]

Written before his election, this report seems even more important in light of President Barack Obama's visits to Middle Eastern countries since his election. In an interview before his speech at Cairo University, Obama told a reporter: "I think that the United States and the West generally, we have to educate ourselves more effectively on Islam. And one of the points I want to make is, is that if you actually took the number of Muslim Americans, we'd be one of the largest Muslim countries in the world."[37] According to statistics, less than 3 percent of the U.S. population, 5 to 8 million, are Muslims. At least twenty-three countries have more Muslims than America.[38] So it is rather obvious that we are not a Muslim country.

The Soles of Your Feet

In June of 2009, a White House photograph, taken by photographer Pete Sousa, was released of President Obama speaking on the phone with his feet on his desk. Both soles of his feet were facing the camera. Americans viewing the picture would say, "He's just chilling out; we all put our feet up when we are relaxing at home." In the Middle East, however, showing the soles of your shoes, or your feet, is the worst form of insult imaginable. This is why the Iraqi threw both shoes during President Bush's final visit, to express his disgust of the American leader. What made the White House picture so controversial was that the president at that moment was on the phone with the Israeli prime minister Benjamin Netanyahu!

When the photo was released in Israel, the *Jewish Tribune* titled an article, "Osama's Chutzpah: Dictating to Bibi and the Jewish State." The word *chutzpah* means "insolence or audacity," often alluding to someone who brazenly and with arrogance oversteps their boundaries. "Bibi" is the Israeli nickname for

Benjamin Netanyahu. The article said the act was sending a message of disrespect toward the prime minister. The Hebrew-language newspaper *Haaretz* noted:

> The president is seen with his legs up on the table, his face stern and his fist clenched, as though he were dictating to Netanyahu: "Listen up and write 'Palestinian state' a hundred times. That's right, Palestine, with a P." As an enthusiast of Muslim culture, Obama surely knows there is no greater insult in the Middle East than pointing the soles of one's shoes at another person. Indeed, photos of other presidential phone calls depict Obama leaning on his desk, with his feet on the floor.[39]

As pointed out by an Israeli diplomat in Washington, "The president has 'total control' of the photographs that are issued by the White House and that he [the diplomat] has no doubt that either Obama or a top staffer like White House Chief of Staff Rahm Emanuel approved the picture's dissemination."[40]

Perhaps the president was relaxing. However with his knowledge of Islamic culture and the fact he was speaking to an Israeli leader, to release the photo was read by Muslims as Obama disrespecting the Israeli leader. Was this a coincidence? Or was this picture released on purpose to show the Palestinians that the president is "pro-Palestinian" and not supportive of Netanyahu?

There are many unanswered questions at this point in Obama's presidency regarding his Muslim connections and his push toward Socialism. But there are further indications that help us "read" the "signals" he is giving, as we will see in the rest of this chapter and throughout the book.

President Obama and the People of the World

Some suggest that President Obama is going out of his way to receive acceptance, approval, and popularity among Islamic nations. I recall that during the 2008 campaign, the opposing party used his full name—Barack Hussein Obama—in public. The secular media immediately criticized this as a "scare tactic" to paint the Illinois senator as a "secret Muslim." People tagged use of his middle name as "Islamaphobia."

However, some within his own party, including Hillary Clinton, were asked about the possibility that he was a Muslim, and it was alleged that the Clinton campaign released a photo of a younger Obama outfitted in a traditional African outfit, thus implying some type of African-Islamic link.[41]

After winning the election, he was sworn in (as are all presidents) using all three names, Barack Hussein Obama. President Obama uses *Barack Obama* in America, but when he is interviewed on Islamic television on Al Arabiya, in Egypt, or was introduced in Turkey, he is introduced as Barack Hussein Obama, with the emphasis on *Hussein*. The name Hussein was the name of the second leader of the Islam religion after Muhammad died. In fact, it was his name that excited much of the Islamic world prior to his election. In his interview, the president said:

> Now, my job is to communicate the fact that the United States has a stake in the well-being of the Muslim world, that the language we use has to be a language of respect. I have Muslim members of my family. I have lived in Muslim countries.... The largest one, Indonesia. And so what I want to communicate is the fact that in all my travels throughout the Muslim world, what I've come to understand is that regardless of your faith—and America is a country of Muslims, Jews, Christians, nonbelievers—regardless of your faith, people all have certain common hopes and common dreams.[42]

Another interesting point was when the president made his first visit to Saudi Arabia. Saudi Arabia is the world headquarters for the Islamic religion. The founder, Muhammad, is buried in an elaborate mosque in Medina, and the famous black stone in the Ka'aba is located in Mecca. I personally have numerous Arab friends and know that the highest compliment a man can give another man is to kiss the right, then the left, cheek of the fellow when shaking hands or hugging. This is a worldwide custom in the Arab world among both Christians and Muslims. It is a custom to bow when greeting a person from Japan, as this is their normal custom of greeting.

As President Obama greeted the Saudi king, he bowed before him. The White House staff denied that it was a bow, but he was *bending down* to greet him. If this was a bow, it was read in America as a simple gesture of respect, and the issue was dropped. However, in the Islamic world it is reported: "If one meets an elderly Muslim, one should stand up and greet with salaam, shake hands or hug.... According to the holy Quran, it is unlawful in the eyes of Allah if one bows before anyone, excluding him."[43] According to Islamic sources, a person bows only if they are seeking a blessing from the elders. So, was Obama not informed of the Islamic customs, even though he was raised in an Islamic country and has Islamic members of his family? Or, as some suggest, was he seeking the blessing of the king of Arabia?

The President and American Christians

The symbolic meaning of the sun rising in his seal, the white horse stadium mascot, the use of his middle name, Hussein, and the bow before the king are all subject to speculation and are possibly just *chance* and *coincidence*. However, two other events that occurred within weeks of each other add more fuel to the fire of speculation that the leader was more concerned about Islamic opinions and popularity than with the religious feelings of the majority of Christians in America.

Covering up the name of Jesus

On April 14, 2009, President Obama was invited to speak at Georgetown University, a respected Catholic school. In the room where the speech was to be made there were several large, stained-glass windows. Black curtains were placed in front of the windows. However, there were several places where the monogram, a cross and the letters IHS, symbolizing the name of Jesus Christ, could be seen. According to the university, the White House requested that these letters be covered with black-painted plywood. It was apparent that the White House wanted to prevent offending anyone of a different religion who would be watching the televised speech.[44]

However, unless a person is a Catholic or a traditional Christian, the majority of people would never know what these letters represent. No Catholic or religious student in the audience would be offended, since they attend this university and understand what they represent. So who was the president concerned about offending? I suggest there are four groups that may be offended at the IHS symbol: atheists, agnostics, progressive liberals, and strict Muslims. Why would a Muslim be offended? Muslims do not believe that Jesus was crucified, and the cross is an offense to them. In fact, one Islamic teaching reveals that in the last days, when the Mahdi arrives, he will "break the cross…and kill the swine" (an allusion to the Jews) and convert men to Islam.[45] These types of occurrences, combined together, provide speculation for a wide range of theories, suggesting the president is oversensitive to Muslims or is seeking special popularity and favor with the Islamic world.

National Day of Prayer

Perhaps the most discouraging event, at least for evangelical Christians, was during the National Day of Prayer. This special day was established by Congress in 1952. In 1982, the first Thursday in May was designated as the *National Day of Prayer*, and President Ronald Reagan issued a proclamation that signed into law that day each year as the National Day of Prayer.[46] Early in 1983, Reagan had issued another proclamation establishing 1983 as the Year of the Bible.[47] Each year the president signs a proclamation recognizing the National Day of Prayer. During the eight years of President George W. Bush, he invited religious leaders, both Christians and Jews, to the White House for a meal and a time of prayer.

In May of 2009, President Obama signed the declaration but expressed that he would not have ministers at the White House for a meal or for prayer.[48] This, of course, is his own personal choice. However, with the economic crisis; loss of jobs; threats from North Korea, Pakistan, and Iran looming; and flu bugs spreading from state to state, most Americas who believe in prayer (80 percent) would appreciate honoring God at least by allowing prayer in the "people's house" on a day set aside for prayer.

Based upon these circumstances and statements made in Turkey, Mexico, and on Arabic television, I believe the president is attempting to avoid any form of controversy abroad, especially among Europeans and Muslims, in an effort to prepare himself to be either the leader or the respected spokesperson for a possible new global order. In my opinion, if the person is not Obama, he is the best choice I have seen in my lifetime to fulfill a role of preparing or moving America toward a new order linked to Europe and the Middle East, instead of America being the lone superstar on the block of nations.

Islam Has a Plan for America

America is a melting pot and a mixed multitude of nations. Prior to 1963 and the influence of atheist Madalyn Murray O'Hair, anyone immigrating to America understood us to be a "Christian nation," with our moral and spiritual values based upon the Bible. Even today, in most overseas countries America is identified as a Christian nation.

Since 1963–1964, native Americans and immigrants pouring into the nation no longer know the history of America with its Christian roots or the influence of the godly covenant that established our nation when the cross was planted on the shores at the founding of the Jamestown colony. Thus they continue to follow their own religious indoctrinations.

One of the possible dangers to America is the same crisis that Great Britain, France, and Germany are experiencing. By opening the doors wide to immigration, these nations have seen millions of Muslims settle in their nations who refuse to merge into the culture of the nation and who introduce their own customs, laws, and religion upon those living in and around them. It can be proven that in some instances the reason to come to the West is not about freedom and prosperity—but about an agenda to spread the light of Islam, either by choice or by force.

One such person is Washington DC imam Abdul Alim Musa, who has stated that he is working to replace the U.S. government with an Islamic state by 2050. He has stated he will establish a complete way of Islamic life in the United States.[49]

Omar Ahmad, the former board chairman of the Council on American-Islamic Relations (CAIR), told a Muslim audience in 1998: "Islam isn't in America to be equal to any other faith, but to become dominant.... The Koran, the Muslim book of scripture, should be the highest authority in America, and Islam the only accepted religion on Earth." CAIR spokesman Ibrahim Hooper also said: "I wouldn't want to create the impression that I wouldn't like the government of the United States to be Islamic sometime in the future."[50]

For many years, only a small minority of Muslims lived in the United States. But today, it is one of the fastest-growing religions in the country. "It is estimated that there are between 6 to 7 million Muslims in America, roughly 2 percent of the entire population. The first official mosque was built in Cedar Rapids, Iowa, in 1934. Today, according to the Council on American-Islamic Relations (CAIR) based in Washington DC, there are more than 1,209 known mosques throughout America. The majority of mosques were established since the 1980s with a 25 percent increase in the number of mosques in the past eight years. In addition to these there are hundreds of Islamic cultural centres and schools."[51]

Having traveled to Israel more than thirty-two times, and having spent hundreds of hours with Jewish guides, I have a rather clear understanding as to the importance of Islam setting up a strong base in the West. The West is the last stronghold of Christianity, the heart of democracy, and the economic center for the world. There are numerous religions and religious freedom in America. There are Hindus, Buddhists, and others who have their religious centers in America, and they have no plan to take over the United States. However, if you study, as I have, the Islamic religion, there is a strong teaching that they alone will be the global religion in the end of days. Thus, when any major leader rises to the forefront in America who is a friend of, or has a background in, the Islamic religion, he or she will have favor globally.

Biblical prophecies predict a time of false peace that will engulf the world. Paul wrote: "For when they say, 'Peace and safety!' then sudden destruction comes upon them..." (1 Thess. 5:3). Someone will assist in laying the foundation of a Middle East peace that will eventually be interrupted by a major war, leading the world into the final storm.

John also wrote in Revelation of a religious leader, identified as a beast with "two horns like a lamb" (Rev. 13:11), who would unite two major religions under his control. I believe these two are apostate Christianity and Islam. While I do not believe President Obama is a part of the final predictions mentioned in Revelation, he may well become a forerunner to unlock events that will eventually lead to the fulfillment of many of the predictions in Scripture. Since the seventh empire is a global entity, and America is speaking of a new currency and nationalization, we may see the early formation of such an empire within the next few years.

The Future

While we see signs of nationalization, which is government-controlled Socialism, only time will tell how far the forty-fourth president will take this new "change" and this socialist agenda. It is also unclear if the president is the man whom the world system has waited for and the person who fits the bill of the "sun rising" in the eyes of the moderate Islamic world. Many things can suddenly change and prevent or accelerate prophetic events. A new president in 2012 could prevent or delay certain agendas of a new world order.

But this book will not focus only on the future of the American presidency. We are taking a bigger look at our nation—America, home of the free! We will take a close look at the amazing history of America. There is much that we can learn from our Founding Fathers and from the biblical parallels and patterns we can find in our past.

We will also consider carefully the perils of America's present. America is facing the destruction of her families, chaos in her cities, and trouble on her coastlines. America is facing an identity crisis, and how we respond—as a president, as a government, as a people, and as individuals—will lay the groundwork for where we will find ourselves in the future.

Finally we will take a look at the prophetic revelations in Scripture about America's future. We will discover that the future of the West was foretold twenty-five hundred years ago. As we close this book, I will remind you there is much more that we can do than sit back and wait for the events in America's future—and end—take place. It is impossible to know the exact time frame for many of these events, but we are able to discern the signs of the times, and we do have instructions from God to help us understand what our response should be.

I don't think, friends, that I need to deal with the question of when all this is going to happen. You know as well as I that the day of the

Master's coming can't be posted on our calendars. He won't call ahead and make an appointment any more than a burglar would. About the time everybody's walking around complacently, congratulating each other—"We've sure got it made! Now we can take it easy!"—suddenly everything will fall apart. It's going to come as suddenly and inescapably as birth pangs to a pregnant woman.

But friends, you're not in the dark, so how could you be taken off guard by any of this? You're sons of Light, daughters of Day. We live under wide open skies and know where we stand. So let's not sleep-walk through life like those others. Let's keep our eyes open and be smart. People sleep at night and get drunk at night. But not us! Since we're creatures of Day, let's act like it. Walk out into the daylight sober, dressed up in faith, love, and the hope of salvation.

God didn't set us up for an angry rejection but for salvation by our Master, Jesus Christ. He died for us, a death that triggered life. Whether we're awake with the living or asleep with the dead, we're alive with him! So speak encouraging words to one another. Build up hope so you'll all be together in this, no one left out, no one left behind. I know you're already doing this; just keep on doing it.

—1 THESSALONIANS 5:1–11, THE MESSAGE

Believers are not in darkness. We can sense coming storms and hear the pealing sound of thunder over the horizon. A storm is building in America. The date 9/11 is etched in our minds forever. But another 9/11, even more dramatic, is being planned.

Chapter 2

THE THUNDER OVER AMERICA

Like the fascism our nations defeated six decades ago, terror-ism is designed to make us afraid of today, afraid of tomorrow, and afraid of each other. It is a battle based not on territory, but on ideology—on freedom versus fear, on tolerance versus tyranny. Once again, freedom is at stake.... The struggle will be hard fought, and hard won—but it will be won. Our aim, in the words of Winston Churchill, is "victory at all costs, vic-tory in spite of all terror, victory, however long and hard the road may be."[1]

—ROBERT S. MUELLER,
DIRECTOR, FEDERAL BUREAU OF INVESTIGATION

THERE ARE LESSONS we can learn from history—and one of the most powerful ones for us to review as we begin to consider the future of America is the ancient empire of Babylonia. In 605 B.C., Nebuchadnezzar II became ruler and reigned for forty-three years. Under him the Babylonian Empire reached its greatest strength. It was during his reign that Jerusalem was captured and its inhabitants taken to Babylon to live in exile. Using the treasures that he took from other nations, Nebuchadnezzar built Babylon, the capital city of Babylonia, into one of the leading cities of the world. The famous hanging gardens of Babylon were known to the Greeks as one of the Seven Wonders of the World. The city of Babylon was the global mili-tary and economic headquarters of the ancient world. Fortified with massive walls and protected by a skilled army, it was considered the Titanic of cities—impregnable.

Nebuchadnezzar and his kingdom were at the pinnacle of their glory! They were the most powerful nation in the world. Life was good! After Nebuchad-nezzar's death, his son Belshazzar, the king, planned an impressive banquet for a thousand of his political leaders. Not one political leader in the kingdom knew that the party was about to be over.

On the fateful night, the best wine in the world was being drunk from gold chalices. The people gathered in the opulent banquet hall and dined on a scrumptious feast as thousands of trained musicians played their instruments. The room was filled with the thunderous noise of merriment and laughing. We read the account of this massive party in Daniel 5:

> Belshazzar the king made a great feast for a thousand of his lords, and drank wine in the presence of the thousand. While he tasted the wine, Belshazzar gave the command to bring the gold and silver vessels which his father Nebuchadnezzar had taken from the temple which had been in Jerusalem, that the king and his lords, his wives, and his concubines might drink from them. Then they brought the gold vessels that had been taken from the temple of the house of God which had been in Jerusalem; and the king and his lords, his wives, and his concubines drank from them. They drank wine, and praised the gods of gold and silver, bronze and iron, wood and stone.
>
> —DANIEL 5:1–4

But suddenly, within seconds, the drunken revelry came to a screeching halt. The thunderous noise of laughing was silenced as a massive hand appeared near the candlestick.

> In the same hour came forth fingers of a man's hand, and wrote over against the candlestick upon the plaister [plaster] of the wall of the king's palace: and the king saw the part of the hand that wrote. Then the king's countenance was changed, and his thoughts troubled him, so that the joints of his loins were loosed, and his knees smote one against another.
>
> —DANIEL 5:5–6, KJV

It is important to note that the hand appeared "against the candlestick." In the Jewish temple that had been destroyed by Nebuchadnezzar, the golden menorah, or candlestick, was the place where the high priest stood to inquire of the Lord. Using his gold breastplate of twelve stones, he would ask God a question, and the light from the candlestick would illuminate the individual Hebrew letters that were carved on the stones. By looking at the letters, he would spell out the answer from the Lord.

It was more than sixty-five years earlier that the Babylonians had invaded Jerusalem, seizing the gold and silver vessels from the sacred temple of the Jews. On that fateful night, the king of Babylon was drinking wine from those same sacred vessels. It is very possible that the very menorah that once stood in the temple was brought out along with the holy vessels. On the wall where the candlestick stood, God sent a warning to the Babylonian leaders!

The words that appeared were, "Mene, Mene, Tekel, Upharsin" (v. 25). These words were unknown to the Babylonians, but a Hebrew prophet, Daniel, was called from his home to interpret the meaning. The words meant: "God has numbered your kingdom, and finished it....You have been weighed in the balances, and found wanting....Your kingdom has been divided, and given to the Medes and Persians" (vv. 26–28). The drunken king was unaware that at that very moment an invading army was sneaking through an underground tunnel and would soon make its move. Before the sun rose in the morning, the city of Babylon and the government were in the control of the king of the Medes, Darius.

The overthrow of Babylon happened within twenty-four hours. No leader in the kingdom saw it coming, except for the Hebrew prophet Daniel.

Sudden Changes Within Twenty-four Hours

On the night of September 10, 2001, three men were overheard expressing anti-American sentiments in a bar in Daytona Beach, Florida. According to the manager of the bar, "They were talking about what a bad place America is. They said, 'Wait 'til tomorrow. America is going to see bloodshed.'" Those near them assumed they had too much to drink and ignored their comments.[2]

In Baton Rouge, Louisiana, where I was preaching a few weeks after 9/11, a young girl told me how a young Muslim man had pressed her to marry him, and she refused. Shortly before September 11, 2001, he called her to tell her he could not give her an explanation, but he was on his way to New Jersey and would have to leave the car in the parking lot of the church she attended. On September 11, he was missing, and the car was in the parking lot. He returned weeks later, without any explanation.

Long before sunrise on the morning of September 11, something strange was happening. As a local pastor in a northern eastern city told me after 9/11, on the morning of September 11 he observed something he had never seen before. He knew that Friday was the Muslim holy day, and the mosque near where he lived was always filled with worshipers. But why was there activity this early on a Tuesday morning? Cars were at the mosque. A meeting was going on. The pastor had never seen this before. He felt something strange was up, but he had no clue what it could be. Apparently those attending the mosque knew something was coming within a few hours.

I met and spoke with a man who attends a large Assembly of God church in

Florida who was returning home from an overseas business trip. On September 11, he had a long layover in Boston's Logan Airport and would take an early flight back to Pensacola. Sitting alone at the gate in the early hours of the morning, he observed a young Middle Eastern woman sitting alone with a purse and a cell phone. From her seat she could see the airport tower. She made continual phone calls as she peered back and forth from the tower to the runway. Long before passengers arrived at the gate, three men, wearing identical shirts with a travel company logo, approached the girl. He heard one say, "How long must you stay here?"

She replied, "Just a little longer." The men spoke Arabic then left. Moments later she exited the area and was not seen again. Hours later, after arriving in Pensacola, he watched on the airport TV as the planes hit the towers and heard the news that they came from Logan Airport. Convinced that the woman and three men had been aware of the plan, he reported the information about what he had seen and heard.

The following was briefly reported in a local Florida paper but was never reported again. I heard the information from a woman who lived in Florida near the school where President Bush spoke on the morning of September 11. That morning, a white van with two Middle Eastern–looking men pulled up to a security entrance near the school where Bush was going to speak. They informed the security personnel that they were a television crew that had a scheduled meeting with President Bush following his speech and desired to set up the equipment for the interview. The security personnel checked with the Secret Service, who forbade the men to enter because there was no record of them or of any preapproved interview. Upon hearing this, the men drove the van away from the gate.[3]

After they were some distance from the school, an eyewitness reported seeing men in a white van shake their fists out the window and scream something about "death to America and Bush." The van fled away, and hours later, the president was being whisked away from the school to an underground bunker for his protection.[4]

Only days earlier in Afghanistan, the head of the Afghan Northern Alliance had been killed by several men posing as journalists who had filled their *cameras* with deadly explosives.[5] It is possible that the alleged men in the van were highly trained terrorists who believed they could conduct an on-location assassination by taking out the president at the same time as the towers were falling in New York City. Of course, this would have been captured on tape while other network cameras were filming.

On September 10, 2001, life was going as usual with no national interruptions. Planes were filled with travelers and tourists, schools were safe as children sat at their desks, and in mid-afternoon, fifty thousand people in and around the twin towers of the World Trade Center in New York City were conducting routine global business. Yet within twenty-four hours, the handwriting was on the wall, and from place to place strange warning signs had been visible, *but no one could decipher them.*

Three months prior to 9/11, I was informed of a Web site where bin Laden had announced in June of 2001 that he would hit America within two weeks. The date he had set was July 4, America's Day of Independence.[6] When July 4 passed without a conflict, few people paid much attention to the bits and pieces of information that had been forming the handwriting on America's wall.

Warning: Serpent in the Eagle's Nest

During the early part of the new millennium, I had stepped off the platform after ministering at Free Chapel Worship Center in Gainesville, Georgia. Immediately a young woman approached me and requested a few moments of time. She told me her name was Fatima. As we engaged in conversation, I learned that her religious background was Muslim and her native home was France. She was serving as an English teacher in a public school in the United States. Her conversion to Christianity had been dramatic—she experienced a vision of Christ on a cross telling her that He was the only way to heaven. This experience led her to a personal relationship with Christ; however, it was an ominous vision that she had experienced later that continued to trouble her.

She related seeing a large eagle and a huge nest. Hidden within the nest, unseen to the keen eyes of the eagle, was a dangerous serpent that had managed to slip unnoticed into the nest of the giant eagle. She heard these words: "The serpent is in the eagle's nest." Just as years earlier she had understood the vision of Christ to be God speaking to her, she discerned this vision of the eagle and serpent to be a spiritual warning of some sort for America. She asked me, "What do you think the vision represents, and what do the words mean?"

Immediately I replied, "The eagle is a symbol for the United States of America. The nest is the home and the security of the eagle, or our homeland— the place where we live, rest, and should feel secure. In the Bible, a serpent always alludes to Satan, evil, or an enemy (Gen. 3:1; Rev. 12:9). The vision means that America's enemies are no longer on the outside of our nation, but they are now hidden within our borders in the very nest of our nation."

Since that vision, and after 9/11, the term *sleeper cells* became synonymous with small groups of predominantly Islamic terrorists who were hiding like rats in a large house, waiting for the cover of darkness to sneak from their secret places and initiate another attack within the United States.

Americans have short-term memories! Do you remember the scene from the smoldering pile of bent metal, with President George W. Bush, his arm resting on a New York City fireman, gripping a bullhorn and blasting a message through the gaping hole at the World Trade Center? He asserted that the American people had heard the message from New Yorkers impacted by the tragedy, and that those who attacked the World Trade Center would soon hear from the United States. Shouts and cheers flowed across the ruins, and the nation, united in spirit, was thrust into a war we did not initiate, did not expect, and did not want.

At that moment, the nation immediately forgot about the 2000 election controversy in Florida and the belief among some that Bush was an invalid president. Suddenly, he was the man of the hour, and his unwavering backbone of steel and powerful words, "Bin Laden, wanted, dead or alive," brought a chill of pride. We were Americans—how dare nineteen men from a desert in the Middle East, and a maniac living like a bear in a cave, dare to disrupt our lives and the American Dream?

As President George W. Bush's approval ratings jumped to 92 percent approval, the House and Senate willingly hopped on the political bandwagon of America's new feeling of unity and, while standing on the steps of the Capitol, performed a rather out-of-pitch rendition of "God Bless America." Musty flags were pulled out of closets in thousands of homes and proudly displayed from porches or waving from poles outside of businesses from coast to coast. We felt angry at the attack, fearful of what may follow, yet proud to be Americans. We could not get enough of the images—two planes flying into the twin towers, the terrifying screams of thousands of fleeing New Yorkers, the gray pillars of smoke rising like tornadoes and blanketing the landscape like a massive gray carpet. As the dusty debris fell from the sky and blanketed the people on the streets of New York, they appeared like gray clay statues from a fantasy movie.

We would snuff out those "thugs" and chase them to the ends of the earth and the gates of hell, if necessary, for taking the lives of nearly three thousand innocent, hardworking moms, dads, brothers, and sisters. America had not experienced such unity in Washington DC since the attack on Pearl Harbor.

We carried war against the terrorists outside our borders in order to prevent more *serpents of evil* from slithering their way through our porous northern and southern borders. The United States military took the battle to the heart of the beast in Afghanistan. Bombs from a coalition of troops targeted the Taliban and followers of Osama bin Laden. To prevent the possibility of terrorists laying hold of weapons of mass destruction, America initiated a war in Iraq against the Butcher of Baghdad. As bombs fell, guns fired, and the death toll increased, it was clear that America and her coalition forces were initiating a defeat to terrorists on their own turf. The days turned into weeks, the weeks become months, and the months turned to years.

And then America began to forget.

From September 11, 2001, until the final year of the Bush administration, there were no terrorist attacks on American soil. The twisted metal from the Trade Center complex was cleared, and the Pentagon was repaired. The economy, which took a dip in 2001, began recovering, and Americans went back to work feeling safer as the years passed.

By the year 2008, the wars in Afghanistan and Iraq had become unpopular. They became the nails in the coffin of a president whom Americans were ready to bury in the ground of time, placing RIP over his tomb. Bush's rating had dropped from 90 percent in the days following 9/11 to a mere 37 percent—the lowest for any president since ratings have been studied. It seemed that many Americans had forgotten the burden the president had carried to keep our nation safe. Few of them knew, as I did, that every morning the president received a special intelligence briefing about the dangers America faced at home and abroad. Few knew the information I received from a former senator and personal friend of Bush, listing *thirty-five* different actual attacks or planned attacks that were prevented by Homeland Security and the anti-terror laws passed during the Bush administration. Dangerous and suspected terrorists were captured, interrogated, and taken to the edge of Cuba to a U.S. prison called *Gitmo* (Guantanamo Bay). Evidence released reveals that important information was collected that assisted in the prevention of other planned attacks on American soil and American interests abroad.

And America's memory began to fade as life went on. America's fading memories of 9/11 can be seen in:

- The desire to shut down Gitmo and return the terrorists to their home countries or bring them to the United States
- The idea that we must stop listening in on calls from possible terror cells and potential terrorists
- The pressure to pull all troops out of Iraq and end the *occupation*
- The pressure to get out of Afghanistan as soon as possible
- The political concept that *we* should talk to dictators

Strange ideas emerge from the Washington think tanks when we forget. Even the Almighty warned His ancient people Israel of the dangers of forgotten memories:

> So it shall be, when the LORD your God brings you into the land of which He swore to your fathers, to Abraham, Isaac, and Jacob, to give you large and beautiful cities which you did not build, houses full of all good things, which you did not fill, hewn-out wells which you did not dig, vineyards and olive trees which you did not plant—when you have eaten and are full—then beware, lest you forget the LORD who brought you out of the land of Egypt, from the house of bondage.
> —DEUTERONOMY 6:10–12

What We Didn't Know

If there was one weakness in the Bush administration, it may have been that it did not go before the public and occasionally reveal who and what the terrorist attacks were that it had prevented. I can only speculate why there was little information released, but secular, liberal journalists seem most concerned with how terrorists are treated, how their plots were discovered, and what methods the government used to obtain their information.

This brings up the question about Saddam's alleged weapons of mass destruction. Those who believe that Saddam Hussein's weapons were moved and hidden in Syria include Ali Ibrahim al-Tikriti, a former general and personal friend of Saddam, who defected but remained in contact with Iraqis. In an interview posted on *World Net Daily*, Tikriti stated that Saddam had contacts on the black market and contacts in Russia who could provide him with the munitions he desired. Ali stated that he knew Saddam's weapons were in Syria because of Saddam's contingency plans in the event either Damascus or Baghdad were taken over by enemy forces. Ali remained in contact with some of Saddam's key scientists and released his information to the U.S. government prior to the war in 2003.[7]

A second Iraqi general, Georges Sada, a strong Christian, released information that six weeks before the war began, Saddam's arsenal was banned under UN sanctions, including weapons that could be used for mass destruction and that were transported out of Iraq using Iraqi Boeing jets with the seats removed and converted into cargo planes. Sada stated that fifty-six flights were made, and the transfer went unnoticed by the intelligence community because they were civilian planes. Saddam used the cover of a Syrian dam that had collapsed in 2002 and did the transfers under the heading of relief for the Syrians.[8]

A third source who revealed details of the transfer was Syrian journalist Nizar Nayouf, who had defected to France, where he was dying of cancer. He revealed some amazing information given to him by a Syrian military official. In a letter to the Dutch newspaper *De Telegraaf*, Nayouf's information agrees with that of former Iraqi General Georges Sada, which reveals that Saddam's weapons were transferred out of Iraq into Syria prior to the war. Nayouf said there were three locations where the weapons were stored. The first was in an underground tunnel under the town of al-Baida in northern Syria, which was part of an underground factory built by North Korea and initially planned for building missiles for Syria. The second location was in the village of Tal Snan, near a Syrian military base that was used for the Syrian Air Force. The third hiding place was in Sjinsjar, on the border with Lebanon.[9]

In a report containing satellite imagery, even our own government revealed that two months before the war began, a long convoy of Iraqi trucks were lined up at the border between Iraq and Syria.[10] When discussing the issue of Saddam moving his weapons—including certain chemical and biological agents—to Syria, several Israeli military persons have told me, "There is no doubt about it. All of our information says they were removed." In fact, prior to the war, the Israeli intelligence had located more than 160 places where component parts, weapons, and other items banned under UN sanctions were being stored. After the U.S. invasion, these factories, buildings, and places were found empty of the expected munitions.

Even Iraqi military documents discovered by the Iraqi Survey Group weapons search team were translated, revealing Saddam's plans to hide his weapons of mass destruction prior to the U.S. invasion. Some of the documents reported by *The Weekly Standard* are listed as:

- Chemical agent purchase orders (December 2001)
- Formulas and information about Iraqi's chemical weapons agents
- Locations of weapons/ammunition storage (with map)
- Denial and deception of WMD and killing of POWs
- Ricin research and improvement
- Chemical gear for Fedayeen Saddam
- Memo of Iraqi Intelligence Service to hide information from a UN inspection team (1997)[11]

One of the criticisms against former President Bush was the belief that there were never any weapons of mass destruction in Iraq. Some felt that the war was Bush's own personal revenge on Saddam. The very politicians who made this claim barked a different story prior to the war in Iraq:

> It is incontestable that on the day I left office, there were unaccounted for stocks of biological and chemical weapons.[12]
>
> —BILL CLINTON

> Saddam Hussein has been engaged in the development of weapons of mass destruction technology which is a threat to the countries in the region and he has made a mockery of the weapons inspection process.[13]
>
> —NANCY PELOSI

> He will use those weapons of mass destruction again, as he has ten times since 1983.[14]
>
> —SANDY BERGER (CLINTON SECURITY ADVISOR)

Another criticism against Bush was that there was no evidence that Saddam was linked to al Qaeda and the Taliban. Thus, the innuendo was that Bush's motive was personal, and the possible link to outside terror groups was not there. Again, the documents discovered disprove this political theory. Other documents included:

- Secret meeting with Taliban group members and Iraqi government (November 2000)
- Document from Uday Hussein (Saddam's son) regarding Taliban activity
- Possible al Qaeda members in Iraq
- Iraqi Intelligence Services report on Taliban-Iraq connections claims
- Money transfers from Iraq to Afghanistan[15]

The most shocking, undeniable evidence of Saddam's link to chemical weapons involves a plot foiled by Jordanian security services in April and May of 2004. A group of al Qaeda agents had a truck containing twenty tons of chemicals in their possession and were planning on filling three cars with deadly chemicals and exploding them, sending a deadly chemical cloud throughout the city of Amman. The targets were said to be the prime minister's office, the Jordanian Intelligence Services, and the U.S. embassy. Along with the deadly chemicals were large quantities of hydrogen peroxide, which would have been mixed with "ground black cumin" to create "an explosion stronger than TNT." Twelve defendants stood trial in Jordan for their terror plots. Abu-Musab Al-Zarqawi, who was later killed in Iraq by U.S. forces, prepared the original plan. Had this chemical attack been successful, thousands would have died, been blinded, or become ill. There were seventy-one lethal chemicals, including VX nerve gas and Sarin, in the mix.[16]

Saddam Knew Before 9/11

According to a former Iraqi general, since these chemicals originate out of Syria and were a part of Saddam's arsenal that was sent into the country prior to the war, he believes that not only did Saddam have a link with key terror leaders, but he was also aware of the 9/11 plot before it occurred.

In June of 2001, three months before 9/11, I received a call to go online at a particular Web site. This Web site (which has long been removed) had a photo of Osama bin Laden and Saddam Hussein, with a prediction that in or around July 4 of that year, America would be attacked. The attack never occurred. However, the state-run Iraqi newspaper published an article titled, "America, an Obsession Called Osama bin Laden," written by Naeem Abd Muhalhal, a member of Saddam's Baath Party. Muhalhal stated that bin Laden would attack the United States "with the seriousness of the Bedouin of the desert about the way he will try to bomb the Pentagon after he destroys the White House." In another statement, the paper predicted that bin Laden "will strike America on the arm that is already hurting," and the United States will "curse the memory of Frank Sinatra every time he hears his songs," perhaps a reference to Sinatra's famous song "New York, New York."[17]

As if this was not enough evidence that Saddam had the weapons and chemicals but moved them prior to the war, another report that was released in 2008 revealed that 550 metric tons of yellowcake were purchased by Canada and transported out of Iraq to Canada in July of 2008.[18] Yellowcake, or uranium oxide, could be used to construct a nuclear weapon. Several tons would need to be refined using very sophisticated technology to build a single bomb.

President Bush came under severe criticism for stating that the Iraqis were shopping for yellowcake in Africa. Later the information was rejected as being based on forged documents. However, according to another report about the 550 metric tons of yellowcake sent to Canada, the yellowcake had been stored at an Iraqi nuclear complex located about twelve miles from Baghdad.

According to retired Major General Jerry Curry, who wrote about this totally underreported story: "He [President Bush] made a very brave stand, a resolute stand…in which he decided that he wasn't going to blab everything to the press….And in the meantime, while he kept it quiet, he was buying time from the terrorists to get all that stuff out of the country."[19] Knowing the material had been in Iraq, and that he could have announced to the country that this weapon, which could be used to create nuclear weapons, had been discovered, the president instead chose to remain silent, taking the continual blasting from the media for lying about alleged dangerous weapons or materials in Iraq. As the blogger states: "President Bush's actions took courage, and all Americans should be thankful to have such a brave president who puts the welfare of the American people above personal considerations."[20]

Secrets in the Mosque

In retrospect, I believe that certain Muslims throughout the world knew some form of attack was being planned against America. One story was related to me of a Jewish family in New York who had become friends with a Muslim family who lived across the street. One day prior to September 11, 2001, the Muslim businessman warned the Jewish friend not to be in downtown New York anytime on September 11. He told him he could not give any details, but to please not go into New York. On the morning of September 11, the Jewish man noticed that his neighbor's house was empty. Apparently the family had moved out in the middle of the night and has not been heard from since.[21]

Behind the doors of some Islamic mosques, Muslims with Middle Eastern and Asian connections heard whispers from fellow worshipers about an attack that was being planned against the United States. They may not have known the details, but some knew it was coming.

Months before the attack, a Jewish friend named Israel was residing in Florida and, on one occasion, was at the same flight school where one of the future hijackers was being trained to fly planes (unknown to the school). Israel actually met one of the men and knew there was something very suspicious about him. When he saw the pictures on television of the nineteen hijackers, Israel reported his information to intelligence agencies in Washington DC.[22] Mounting evidence indicates that several agencies received vague warning signs prior to the attack, but the written memos were lost in a pile of papers. I believe that the *red-tape bureaucracy of the beltway obscured the handwriting on the wall.* One example of such ignorance of the facts can be seen in the report of a U.S. government agency that released visas for two of the hijackers months after they had already enacted their plot and had died on the very planes they seized for their mission.[23]

What the Russians Knew

In July 2001, Dr. Tatyana Koryagina made a prediction that America would experience a "financial attack." Dr. Koryagina is a senior research fellow at the Institute of Macroeconomic Researches. Her article published in the Russian paper *Pravda* was titled, "Will the Dollar and America Fall Down on August 19?" She was quoted as saying:

> The U.S. has been chosen as the object of financial attack because the financial center of the planet is located there. The effect will be maximal. The strike waves of economic crisis will spread over the planet instantly and will remind us of the blast of a huge nuclear bomb.[24]

According to Koryagina, the individuals behind the attacks were not the nineteen terrorists but were sponsored by a large group of men seeking to reshape the world. She claims this is an extremely powerful group of private individuals, with total assets of about $300 trillion, who are behind the idea of legalizing their power and forming a new world government. Dr. Koryagina has predicted that the terrorists will again "strike America in the back" and will bring it down. The purpose is to destroy America as the world's number one economy and make room for a group of elite wealthy persons to eventually control the world through their personal wealth and power.[25]

Before you write off her predictions, remember that Scripture predicts the formation of a seventh and eighth world empire. The seventh empire will rule for a "short time," followed by the eighth empire, which will trample the nations through the domination of the Antichrist (Rev. 17:10–12). In the time of the end, ten kings (countries) will give their kingdoms over to the Antichrist!

At some point, the ten kings and the final empires of prophecy must form. Biblical scholars note that prophetic writers speak of the East, South, and North, but the West appears to be missing. Many of the End Time prophecies will be fulfilled around the Middle East, Europe, and in Asia. The West could be missing because we have come under a devastating attack or because we are consumed with our own internal difficulties. At some point the globalists will succeed, and an Islamic leader will stand in the shadows until it is time to make his move. In light of this prophetic revelation, Koryagina's information has credibility.

The question is: How would someone in Russia predict such economic attacks and compare them to the "blast of a huge nuclear bomb" two months before the events? Was the doctor previously informed, or was it coincidence? She is said to be in Putin's inner circle.

Intelligence reports indicate that the Russian Mafia for some time had been selling supplies, including components for chemical, biological, and nuclear weapons, to Osama bin Laden and his al Qaeda network.[26] In the past, Russia has been a backer of some of the world's worst terrorist nations, including Iran, Iraq, Libya, Syria, and North Korea.

The sale of weapons and components was part of the al Qaeda operation in Afghanistan. The Taliban grew poppy plants, which are used to produce heroin. The seeds could be sold to the Russian Mafia on the black market in return for weapons, weapons building information, and raw materials needed to successfully wage a terrorist campaign. The dangerous aspects of such an alignment are the possibilities of chemical and biological agents being unleashed upon a major American city. Knowing this threat, the U.S. federal government is preparing vaccines and suggesting that cities have contingency plans in the event of an emergency.

What Does the Future Hold?

In those twenty-four hours beginning with the attacks on the twin towers of the World Trade Center, New York City and America were changed forever. Since New York is considered the economic capital of the world, then New York would be a prime target to rip the economic structure of the nation into shreds. Benjamin Netanyahu, currently the prime minister of Israel, said: "America received a wake-up call from hell!"[27] He and others have pointed out that New York is home to the largest Jewish population of any single city in the world. He, along with others, believe that in a matter of time, New York will again be assaulted and could eventually become the site of one of America's first nuclear attacks.

The sad picture of a gaping pit in New York will be a visual reminder of what happened on that fateful September morning. But let us be thankful for what did not happen. The findings of the commission that investigated the 9/11 events concluded that: "The plot originally called for hijacking 10 planes and attacking targets on the eastern and western coasts of the United States." According to the commission: "Khalid Shaikh Mohammed, the mastermind of the plot, planned to have nine of the planes crash into the FBI and CIA headquarters, the Pentagon and the White House, as well as nuclear plants and the tallest buildings in California and Washington state."[28]

There are no doubts that the two top cities being targeted for a future strike are New York and Washington DC. New York is the economic center, the headquarters for the United Nations, and the home of a huge population of Jews. Washington DC is the nation's capital, and it also contains the historic symbolism and government buildings that keep the nation on course.

In October of 2000, I received a phone call from a retired military colonel. Our weekly television program aired a series of specials from Israel, including one in front of a tank in the Golan Heights and a second teaching series in front of the Eastern Gate in Jerusalem. The information released on our program had created quite a stir among both Israelis and Muslims. I was informed that a group of Muslims had viewed the programs on satellite and were making copies of the teaching, distributing them in several Islamic nations. It appears I had shared information about Israel's military, and certain Muslims were very interested in these facts. Several noted individuals had asked this man to contact me with a rebuke.

Eventually the conversation turned from the television programs to Islamic terrorists. I was expressing my opinion that America would be struck by Islamic radicals in the future. The colonel not only agreed but also added this observation: based upon his personal knowledge and evidence from intelligence sources, he was convinced that terrorists would strike with a biological or chemical attack in a major city or at a major event where a large number of people were gathered. He said it was "not a matter of *if*, but a matter of *when*." The colonel believed it was possible for literally hundreds of thousands of people to be killed at one time, with countless numbers severely injured.

The possibilities of a massive terrorist attack are now so great that some Americans are living with an apprehension of the future. This may be what Jesus alluded to when He predicted: "...men's hearts failing them from fear and the expectation of those things which are coming on the earth, for the powers of the heavens will be shaken" (Luke 21:26). A rise in heart failure would be a result of what *will be* coming to pass and not what *has previously* occurred. *Smallpox, anthrax, Ebola, mustard gas, nuclear weapons...* these are words that create mental images of violent suffering and sudden death— and each of those things can presently be made into weapons used to strike the nation.

When God allowed the ungodly masses to be punished in Noah's day, He unleashed a huge volume of water, a universal flood. When He permitted the destruction of Sodom and Gomorrah, fire and brimstone from an underground explosion near the Dead Sea became the *weapon*. Both times Jerusalem fell into the hands of her enemies, and the city was consumed in fire.

The question is not: *Will America be hit again?* The question is: *What will we do the next time?* According to a Barna Poll taken in November 2001: "It appears that [church] attendance, which nationwide increased by perhaps 25% immediately after the attack, is back at normal levels. The November survey found 48% of adults attending on a typical weekend."[29] Today Barna Research indicates an average 43 percent of Americans say "they typically attend weekly worship services."[30]

Perhaps Americans were confused immediately following 9/11. The nation became patriotic but did not repent of the sins of murder, abortion, addictions, and unbelief. The rise in patriotism caused a "feel-good goose bump" sensation to warm the hearts of Americans.

We may have missed the point. When will we learn that without God in our nation, we will be at the mercy of our enemies? Our hope may lie in this ancient biblical promise:

> If My people who are called by My name will humble themselves, and pray and seek My face, and turn from their wicked ways, then I will hear from heaven, and will forgive their sin and heal their land.
>
> —2 Chronicles 7:14

The Nation of Israel—and the Nation of America

The blessings God promised to the Jews through Abraham and the nation of Israel are the same blessings we have experienced in America since our Founding Fathers established a nation where people could live in freedom. But, as we can see through biblical history, God also released curses upon Israel for their sins. Today we are seeing many of the same sin problems found in biblical Israel in our nation, and we are susceptible to the same judgments and curses for our sinning as was Israel.

This is because both nations, Israel and America, were founded and built upon a spiritual covenant with God, and the Bible is the source of their moral laws and the foundation of both nations' spiritual constitutions. Israel's blessings were contingent upon their full obedience to the Word of God. If they lived free from sin and walked in the commandments of God, then blessings would follow their nation and impact their families:

> Now it shall come to pass, if you diligently obey the voice of the LORD your God, to observe carefully all His commandments which I command you today, that the LORD your God will set you high above all nations of the earth. And all these blessings shall come upon you and overtake you, because you obey the voice of the LORD your

God: Blessed shall you be in the city, and blessed shall you be in the country. Blessed shall be the fruit of your body, the produce of your ground and the increase of your herds, the increase of your cattle and the offspring of your flocks. Blessed shall be your basket and your kneading bowl. Blessed shall you be when you come in, and blessed shall you be when you go out.

—DEUTERONOMY 28:1–6

If the Hebrew nation failed to follow the righteous laws of God and began to sin against the covenant by worshiping idols, committing adultery, and mistreating their fellow man, then God would lift the favor and the blessing and allow great trouble and distress to strike the nation in order to bring them to humility and repentance.

And I will bring a sword against you that will execute the vengeance of the covenant; when you are gathered together within your cities I will send pestilence among you; and you shall be delivered into the hand of the enemy.

—LEVITICUS 26:25

God instructed Israel that one of the first manifestations of His judgment upon the nation would be that they would experience "terror."

I will even appoint terror over you.

—LEVITICUS 26:16

The sword shall destroy outside; there shall be terror within for the young man and virgin, the nursing child with the man of gray hairs.

—DEUTERONOMY 32:25

America has fought several wars on our own soil, including the Revolutionary War and the Civil War. Never in our young history have we fought a war with such a small group of people (nineteen hijackers) whose actions impacted the economy and bred the fear factor so quickly. It was as though the Almighty allowed a protective hedge to be lifted for a brief period of time to say to America, "Here is what can happen if I am not protecting you."

After Israel inherited the Promised Land, the people became complacent in their spiritual walks with God. The very pattern of decline that followed the Hebrew nation is being repeated in an eerily similar manner in the United States.

When the first generation of Hebrews entered the Promised Land, they were fresh from the wilderness and thrilled to possess their own land. They dislodged the many tribes living in the land and began building, planting, and possessing their Promised Land. As time passed, their prosperity created laziness, and God allowed internal wars to break out with surrounding nations and coastal tribes (the Philistines). Eventually the hedge of protection was removed, and God permitted surrounding enemies to take the people into captivity for a season. Only when they repented did the Lord reverse their captivity and bring them back into their land.

Israel's spiritual and moral decline is so parallel to the spiritual lukewarmness and moral muck that America is sinking into.

- Israel allowed the foreign nations to keep their idol gods and build their false temples.
- Israel allowed sexual immorality (fornication and adultery) to creep into the nation.
- Israel allowed homosexuality to become prominent. One entire tribe, Benjamin, turned gay.
- Israel followed the heathen pattern and offered its own children up to the idol god Molech.
- Israel allowed religion to become a ritual, and drunkenness and immorality entered the temple.
- Israel refused to keep the Sabbath, and this led to the captivity in Babylon.

Now consider the progressive road of secularism that America is following and the generations of young minds that are being educated in America's universities, which have little or no biblical or Christian values inbred in them.

- We continually hear about being tolerant. We have now accepted actual idol gods as a part of the new American culture. False temples and religious buildings are being constructed beside Christian churches.
- Sexual immorality was promoted during the sexual revolution of the sixties.
- The gay lifestyle is now considered in the mainstream of society, as men are marrying men, women marrying women, and adopting children.

- In 1973 we passed legislation legalizing "Molech worship." Just as innocent infants were passed through the fires of the idol Molech and thrown into the burning iron belly of this Canaanite idol, doctors can legally enter the protective womb of a woman and pull the infant from the womb and actually get paid for the process.

- The full gospel churches (older Pentecostal groups) were once considered a backwoods cult for their stand against sin and worldliness. Eventually they grew and prospered, attracting a more prosperous crowd that provided more tithes and offering to move from the other side of the tracks to the more upscale sections of town. Often individuals without strong Christian backgrounds pulled the others into a lifestyle of drinking alcohol, partying, and drunkenness.

- While Christians debate the true Sabbath (Saturday or Sunday), I recall as a child that no local businesses were opened on Sunday, the "Lord's Day." The entire day was for worship and spending time with the family. Today, Christian parents have their children in softball, soccer, and other sports that practice and play their games on Sunday. The malls and restaurants are open and booming with business. Only one major fast-food chain, Chick-fil-A, closes on Sunday. This is because the owner is a strong Christian and provides the workers with a day of rest and worship with their families!

World Empires—Past, Present, and Future

In the remaining chapters of this book, I will compare some of the amazing prophetic parallels between the ancient nation of Israel and the founding of America. I will also discuss the parallels to be found between our nation and some of the past major world empires. There are six distinct things that constitute a world empire.

1. The world's strongest military

Each empire from Egypt to Assyria, Babylon, Persia, Greece, and Rome became world empires because of their military prowess and strength. At the peak of their influence and power, no other nations could conquer them. With the rupture of the Soviet Union and the lack of technology in China (except for what they steal from other nations), America came to the forefront when directing the first and second wars in Iraq.

2. The world's strongest economy

For the past one hundred years, the world's stock markets and economies have revolved around the success and failure of U.S. stocks and banking markets. For many years, every nation, including rogue nations directed by dictators and self-acclaimed American haters, has conducted business in American dollars. Today, Iran's dictator and Hezbollah call America *the Great Satan*. However, after the 2006 war with Israel, Hezbollah handed out millions of U.S. dollars—$12,000 to each family whose home had been destroyed by the rockets.[31] They hate the American *devil* but love the devil's money.

3. The main influencer in commerce and trade

Roman ships once sailed the Mediterranean carrying soldiers, food, and goods from nation to nation. If blood was the lifeline, then the ships were the veins carrying the life of the empire from nation to nation. The economies of the world are linked to America's trade and commerce. The majority of China's wealth has come from trade agreements with America. The same is true with Canada, Mexico, and the third-world nations in Africa and Latin America.

4. The world's economy impacted by the empire's success or failure

In 1929, America went into a great depression that continued for about fifteen years before the country finally recovered. For years Americans learned to live with less. Once again today the negative economic climate in America is impacting the nations of the world.

5. The world's leading lender of money

Past empires of biblical prophecy were all lenders of money in their day. The Babylonians lent to the Persians, and when the Persian Empire flourished, it lent to the Greeks so they could build their navy. Eventually the Greeks invaded the Persians and seized Babylon, canceling their debts and inheriting the wealth of the Persians. As Rome expanded, it eventually took control of the Greeks, and the Roman Empire formulated one of the earliest banking systems. History is clear: those who control the money control the world.

6. The main language among the nations

In the time of Christ, three languages were common around the Mediterranean: Latin, Greek, and Hebrew. The Jews used Hebrew, the Romans spoke Latin, and many others throughout the empire spoke Greek. The Greek language became prominent through the reign of the Grecian Empire. Latin became the main language for centuries through the influence of the Roman Catholic Church, which was felt throughout Europe.

As England became the prominent force in the sixteenth and seventeenth centuries, the English language spread throughout the nations, including America. The English translation of the Bible was printed and presented to the nations. Today, in every nation of the world, there are people who can speak the English language. It has been one of the premier languages that people desire to learn.

America has had all six marks of an empire!

Both secular and Christian historians and sociologists note that America may be on the same path to decline as the ancient Roman Empire. Edward Gibbon wrote his six-volume book *History of the Decline and Fall of the Roman Empire* in the late 1700s. He summed up five reasons why great civilizations eventually faded away and died.

1. The undermining of the dignity and sanctity of the home as the foundation for human society

2. Higher and higher taxes and public (government) spending

3. The craze for pleasure, sports, and the increase of violence and brutality in sports

4. The building of great armaments when the real enemy was within: the decay of individual responsibility

5. The decay of religion: faith fading into mere form, losing touch with life, religion losing its power to guide the people[32]

The average age of the world's greatest civilizations is about two hundred years. It has been reported in recent years that empires appear to go through a series of eight cycles:

1. From bondage to spiritual faith

2. From spiritual faith to great courage

3. From courage to liberty

4. From liberty to abundance

5. From abundance to complacency

6. From complacency to apathy

7. From apathy to dependency

8. From dependency back to bondage[33]

America began under the spiritual bondage of the English, then found its way to spiritual faith in the new continent of America. Our founders had great determination and courage and fought for their rights to freedom and liberty. After the Revolutionary War, we formed our own navy, built ships for trade, and began commerce. This led to the boom cycles of industry and trade. Great abundance came to America after World War II. As technology gave way to television, phones, and cars, America became the land of milk and money! However, as with ancient Israel, the abundance leads to complacency and eventually apathy. Moral values no longer matter. We are numb to complete immorality and sin.

We were energized out of our apathy after the attacks of 9/11, when the nation united and more than 90 percent of Americans demanded the war against terrorists. Now we are ready to pull out of Iraq, move from Afghanistan, release the detainees from Gitmo prison, stop listening in on terrorist conversations, and keep the borders open for business. We have short memories! Because there have been no terrorist attacks in America from 9/11 to 2008, we are apathetic and could care less.

Eventually the apathy leads to dependency. Just as it was in Rome, today multitudes are turning to the government to bail them out of economic and material distress. This dependence will lead us back to bondage.

As a minister and an American citizen, this is my observation of America's pattern.

1. Purpose: Our purpose was religious freedom and freedom from government oppression.

2. Passion: Our passion was to settle the new land and form colonies to grow a nation.

3. Perseverance: Our goal was to win wars against our enemies and keep the land undivided.

4. Prosperity: We were seeking the American Dream, including a nice home, car, good job, and family.

5. Pleasure: We took pleasure in sports and luxury, forgetting God and engaging in sports and pleasure on the Lord's Day.

6. Perversion: We have accepted same-sex relations, abortion, and, in some areas, legalized prostitution.

7. Passing: Eventually America will pass out of prominence, leading to our decline in economy, power, and influence as a nation.

What Is Happening Prophetically?

The prophetic agenda for America is fascinating and reveals the providential reason America may climax as the leading Gentile superpower and leading Christian nation.

From a prophetic perspective, biblical prophets and John in the Apocalypse picture the condition of the nations prior to the return of the Messiah. There will be wars and rumors of wars, and a shaking among the nations. Weapons of mass destruction will be unleashed in certain areas, destroying entire cities. This will create the need for a merging of nations into coalitions, thus removing the present sovereignty of major democratic nations. In apocalyptic literature, one main nation no longer is the leading superpower controlling other nations. There are coalitions of kings and leaders.

We are informed that there will be ten kings who will submit their kingdoms to a final dictator called the *Antichrist*. This is only one coalition. Another group will arise, a group called the *kings of the East*. Although they are not specifically identified in Scripture, scholars believe they are Asian nations uniting as one unit. This would include China, Japan, Vietnam, Korea, and so forth. Presently we see the area of the old Roman Empire reforming into one unit identified as the European Union (EU). Oddly, the future ten kings will rule in and around the Mediterranean area. The EU controls much of Europe, and the kings of the East are just that—kings from the East. In the prophecies we can identify nations that will stick together like glue, forming coalitions, perhaps according to religion (examples: Buddhists from Asia, Muslims, the ten kings around the Mediterranean, and Roman Christians in Europe) or according to the need to survive economically, uniting as ethnic groups, such as Europeans, Arabs, and Asians.

Oddly, in prophetic Scriptures there is little if anything said about a coalition from the West. It has been speculated that the reason for this is:

1. Christ will have already returned for the church, and the gathering together has emptied out large sections of the West, thus leaving the government weak and ineffective.

2. There will have been a major war paralyzing the Western powers, especially America.

3. America, like ancient Rome, will have experienced an economic collapse, thus the need for other nations to form their own coalitions.

Before counting out the third possibility, remember that all previous empires of biblical prophecy from Egypt to Rome went from being the economic center of the world to being replaced by another more superior empire or organized group of people. In many cases, it was huge debt and economic woes that brought on the death of one empire and the reformation and resurrection of another part of the world.

We will explore biblical prophecy as it relates to America in great detail in this book. In the first section of the book, beginning next with chapter 3, we will take a closer look at America's amazing history, starting with Christopher Columbus and his Hebrew connection.

••• Section 1 •••
AMERICA'S AMAZING HISTORY

••• Chapter 3 •••
COLUMBUS AND HIS HEBREW CONNECTION

For the execution of the journey to the Indies, I did not make use of intelligence, mathematics, or maps. It is simply the fulfillment of what Isaiah had prophesied. All this is what I desire to write down for you in this book.

—CHRISTOPHER COLUMBUS

To understand America's prophetic history, one must examine the events surrounding the discovery of the New World, which is credited to a man believed to be an Italian Jew named Christopher Columbus. The details of Columbus's journey expose an interesting *Hebrew link* between America and the ancient nation of Israel.

Christopher Columbus—the Christ Bearer

If one reads the diaries of Christopher Columbus, it is evident that, more than finding a trade route to the East, more than finding gold, he was being compelled to sail west by, in his words, "inspiration from the Holy Spirit." Columbus wrote, "It was the Lord who put into my mind (I could feel his hand upon me) the fact that it would be possible to sail from here to the Indies."[1]

Opinions about Columbus are varied. Some say he was a hero; others say he was a villain responsible for genocide. Many events from Columbus's life portray him in an unflattering way. However, our objective is to investigate the purpose he played in God's plan for America and the fascinating Hebraic connection.

Although Christopher Columbus was born in Genoa, Italy, some clues suggest that his lineage was of Spanish-Jewish origin. (His name in Italian was *Cristoforo Colombo*, which is translated into English as *Christopher Columbus*, into Spanish as *Cristóbal Colón*, and into Portuguese as *Christovão Colom*.)[2] His decision to use the Spanish form of his name, his diaries and letters, and certain oddities associated with his voyages to the New World lend credence to the idea that he was Jewish. *Colón* was considered a Spanish-Jewish name, and this fact supports the argument that Columbus was Jewish. Research of

61

the name *Colombo* reveals that it is synonymous with the name *Jonah*, which means "dove." It is interesting to compare Jonah's story in the Bible to the events surrounding Columbus. (See the Book of Jonah in the Bible.)

The book *The Light and the Glory* says that on the return journey home from the New World, Columbus, having been deceived by the lust for gold, found his fleet being tossed at sea by a violent storm.[3] The storm was so strong that Columbus recommended they appease God with a sacrificial vow that one of them would make a pilgrimage to a particular monastery. The men agreed, so Columbus took thirty-nine beans and marked a cross on one of them. They put the beans in a hat, drew lots, and the first time the beans were drawn, Columbus drew the marked bean. They drew lots three more times, with the marked bean being drawn by Columbus twice more. The odds of this happening are rare. It seems that Columbus was living up to the heritage of his namesake, and God was trying to get his attention!

Jonah was the first Hebrew prophet sent to a Gentile nation. His mission was to go to Nineveh and be a light unto them. When Jonah strayed from this, God intervened with a storm. Likewise, Columbus's mission was to open the curtain on the New World. This New World would create a nation that would further the mission of bringing Christ to the nations, and God would not allow greed to undermine His plan.

It is believed that Columbus's paternal grandfather was a *converso* (convert) and had changed his name from Colon to Colombo. Conversos were Jews who had, by choice or necessity, converted to Christianity. Apparently, in the midst of the Spanish Inquisition, Columbus was raised to accept Christianity, possibly to save his life from the hands of Jewish persecutors.

Hebrew Clues Indicating Columbus's Hebrew Heritage

In letters to his son Diego, Columbus put a mark in the upper-left corner of the paper that resembles the Hebrew letters *bet* and *hei*. These letters denote the Hebrew blessing *b'ezrat haShem*, meaning, "with the help of God." The use of *bet hei* is a blessing that Jews often place in the upper-left corner of a letter to a loved one. In Columbus's papers, this mark only appears in letters to Diego. In one letter that also was to be read by the king and queen, the mark is missing. This implies that Columbus did not want the monarchs to see this potentially incriminating evidence of his Jewish roots.

During the last years of his life, Columbus made efforts to put his affairs in order. Unusual symbols began to appear in his writings, which suggested that he might have been familiar with Jewish mysticism. For example, he began to sign his name in a triangular fashion, asking that his descendants continue to use this signature.[4] This strange signature is believed to be a cryptic substitute for the Kaddish, the mourner's prayer. If Columbus was Jewish, the Spanish Inquisition would not allow his sons to say Kaddish for their father. Thus he supplied them with a signature that would serve that purpose.

> Listen, O coastlands, to Me,
> And take heed, you peoples from afar!
> The LORD has called Me from the womb;
> From the matrix of My mother He has made mention of My name....
> And now the LORD says,
> Who formed Me from the womb to be His Servant,
> To bring Jacob back to Him,
> So that Israel is gathered to Him
> (For I shall be glorious in the eyes of the LORD,
> And My God shall be My strength),
> Indeed He says,
> "It is too small a thing that You should be My Servant
> To raise up the tribes of Jacob,
> And to restore the preserved ones of Israel;
> I will also give You as a light to the Gentiles,
> That You should be My salvation to the ends of the earth."
> —ISAIAH 49:1, 5–6

Columbus's idea of traveling west seems to have solidified in 1484 when, at age thirty-three, he was working as a cartographer. This is the year in a man's life that the Italians call *anno de Christo*, "the year of Christ," which, according to tradition, is reserved for revelation. The name *Christopher* means "Christ bearer." Columbus felt as if this was a sign to him that he had been selected for a specific purpose. Apparently, at least in his mind, Columbus did receive revelation from the Lord about sailing west. He felt that he was given the task of bearing Christ to the ends of the earth, fulfilling what the prophet Isaiah predicted. Interestingly, the context of the verse deals with a light to the Gentiles, coupled with Israel's restoration. Later in his diaries, Columbus would liken himself to Moses, the man who led the Jews to the Promised Land.[5] Is it possible that Columbus felt that part of his mission was to aid in the restoration of the Jews to their ancient homeland?

After moving to Spain, Columbus reverted to his old family name Colon, according to his son and biographer Don Ferdinand Colon. This may have been an attempt to signal the conversos in Ferdinand and Isabella's court.

There were many conversos in the royal court, including one Don Isaac Abravanel, who traced his ancestry directly to King David. Colon, the old family name, was the name with which Columbus was presented to Ferdinand and Isabella. Columbus gained the support of the conversos, which made it possible for his expedition to get under way.

The Expedition and the Ninth of Av on the Hebrew Calendar

When Columbus was given an audience with the monarchs of Spain, a trade route to the Indies and riches may not have been the only thing on his mind. Near the end of his life, Columbus wrote: "Gold is most excellent, a valuable thing, and whoever possesses it does whatever he wants with it in the world.... Jerusalem and Mount Zion will be rebuilt by a Christian."[6] It is possible that Columbus wanted to find a trade route to finance an expedition to the Holy Land and expel the Muslims. It is also possible that he saw the need for gold in order to finance the reconstruction of the city and possibly the temple itself. At one point in his life, "Columbus had converted the year 1481 to the Jewish calendar and came up with the year 5241," which was the date according to the Hebrew calendar.[7]

Columbus wrote: "From the destruction of the Second Temple according to the Jews to the present day...are 1413 years."[8] This would fix Columbus's date for the destruction of the temple at A.D. 68, a date often cited by Jews, as opposed to A.D. 70, the date used by Christians. Columbus apparently saw some significance in the destruction of Jerusalem and the temple and felt that he would play a part in the restoration of the Holy City.

On March 30, 1492, King Ferdinand and Queen Isabella signed a decree to expel the Jews from Spain.[9] Until that time, Spain had been one of the few safe havens for Jews. As mentioned earlier, many Jewish converts were in the royal court, including Luis de Santangel, Ferdinand's budget minister. Now there seemed to be no place for the Jews to go. Oddly, this date coincides with some key events in Israel's history, including the crowning, according to tradition, of Cyrus, the king of Persia. His crowning made it possible for the Jewish exiles to return to Israel and rebuild the city of Jerusalem for the holy temple. Exactly one year later, Ezra left Babylon with the intention of aiding in that rebuilding. Was it coincidence that the Jews found themselves wandering once more, longing for a homeland where they would not be tormented? If Columbus was Jewish, it most certainly would have crossed his mind. We can only imagine that the *coincidence* crossed the mind of God.

On April 30, 1492, one month after the edict of expulsion was signed, it was read publicly. On this same day, Columbus received the order to ready his expedition. Initially, Columbus's request to sail west had been declined. Had it not been for the persuasiveness and money of Santangel and Abravanel, Columbus's voyage would not have been commissioned by Spain. Ironically, the expedition these Jews helped make possible became a reality the same day they were ordered to leave the country they had served.

The year 1491–1492 corresponds to the Hebrew year 5252, written as הרנב. This also spells the phrase *har nov*, meaning, "mount of fruit." According to Strong's Concordance, *har* is a shortened form of *harar*, which is from an unused root meaning "to loom up." *Nov* (fruit) is from *noov*, which is, "to germinate, flourish, to bring forth" (Matt. 21:43). It seems that the year bears the message to "rise up and bring forth fruit." America, the nation that would "bring forth fruit," was about to be established!

On August 2, 1492, thousands of Jews gathered at different Spanish seaports to depart from the only home many of them had ever known. One of those ports of departure was Palos, Spain, the same port from which Columbus had intended to sail. Furthermore, the date Columbus had originally designated to set sail was August 2, 1492. Faced with throngs of despairing, heartbroken people at the port on that day, Columbus decided to delay his voyage by one day. Were the Jewish refugees the only reason Columbus decided to wait?

Jews gathered at the ports, clutching whatever possessions they had been allowed to keep, as well as dirt from the earth, on the day that commemorated the destruction of both temples—the ninth of Av. For centuries, this day had been observed as a day of mourning. On August 2, 1492, the ninth of Av took on a whole new meaning. According to Jewish tradition, to undertake any enterprise on the ninth of Av is considered bad luck. Consider some of the following negative events transpiring in Hebrew history on the ninth of Av.

- The twelve scouts sent out by Moses returned with a bad report.
- The Exodus generation was condemned to die.
- Nebuchadnezzar set fire to the first temple.
- Romans destroyed the second temple.
- Romans plowed up the Temple Mount to convert it to a Roman colony.
- The last independent outpost of the *Bar Kokhba* rebellion fell to the Romans.
- King Edward of England expelled all Jews in 1290.

- The last group of Jews left Vienna in 1670 after expulsion from Austria.

- The Turkish government banned immigration of Russian and Romanian Jews into Palestine, 1882.

- World War I broke out. This was precipitated by the assassination of Archduke Francis Ferdinand.

- A decree to expel Jews from parts of Hungary was issued in 1941.[10]

It seems this day was a sign of how Jews were unwelcome in the world. As Christopher Columbus gazed upon his despairing countrymen, is it possible that he harbored in his heart a secret desire to find a safe haven for them? What better way to have the discoverer of the New World witness such injustice than on the day he had planned to leave for a land that would one day give safe haven. For whatever reason, Columbus decided to wait until the next day.

The Voyage and the Hebrew Feast

On August 3, 1492, Columbus received Communion and set sail. He was aboard his flagship, the *Santa Maria*, followed by the ships *Niña* and *Pinta*, which were commanded by brothers Vincente and Martin Pinzon respectively, with a third brother, Francisco, piloting the *Pinta*. Columbus opened his diary with: "In the name of our Lord Jesus Christ..."[11] Later in the diary, he made a note of the fact that his departure had coincided with the expulsion of the Jews. The date of his departure was the tenth of Av on the Hebrew calendar. Historically, on this date, fires were set to both temples.

Columbus had planned very carefully for his voyage, even to include some distinct personnel, of whom many were Jews. The most famous of these was Luis de Torres. Columbus had hired him as an interpreter due to his expectation of finding a remnant of the lost tribes of Israel.[12] Torres was there so he could speak to them in Hebrew. The surgeon, the physician, the mapmaker, and the officer in charge of nautical instruments were also of Jewish descent.

> Save now this nation, once firm as a rampart, and clear as the sun; she is exiled, a wandering one.
> —Jewish prayer for the intermediate days of Sukkoth

Troubles plagued the journey throughout, and many of the crew were ready to turn back. Columbus came face-to-face with the possibility of failure.

On Tuesday, October 9, the Pinzon brothers met with Columbus to discuss turning around before a mutiny occurred. Columbus agreed that if in three days land was not sighted, they would turn around.[13] This date on the Hebrew calendar was 18 Tishri 5253. The critical meeting took place in the middle of the Jewish Feast of Tabernacles, or Sukkoth. This feast commemorates Israel's wandering through the wilderness with no place to call home. God instructed Israel to dwell in booths during this feast, to remember the nights that they slept under the stars. Even as Israel wandered through the wilderness toward their destiny, Columbus and his men wandered the sea under the night stars toward their destiny.

> As thou didst save together God and nation, the people singled out for God's salvation—so save thou us.
>
> They passed between the deep divided sea and with them for their guide, the light from thee—so save thou us!
>
> Establish us as thy chosen vineyard and make us as a tree planted by the streams of water...plant us we pray upon a faithful sod.
>
> —Portions of the prayers recited on Hoshanah Rabbah

Around 2:00 a.m., on Friday morning, October 12, as the three days were coming to an end, Rodrigo de Triana, possibly a Jew, sighted land. What happened at that point is very interesting. In the book *Christopher Columbus' Jewish Roots*, it has been suggested that when de Triana spotted land, he spoke to another Jew in Hebrew: "*I, I* [island, island]." The other Jewish sailor replied, "*V'annah?* [And where?]" De Triana, pointing, replied, "*Hineh* [there]."[14]

On Hoshanah Rabbah

This day was the beginning of the seventy-first day of the voyage. The Bible implies that seventy represents restoration. (Israel was in Babylon seventy years and returned to the Holy Land in the beginning of the seventy-first year.) It was also 21 Tishri on the Hebrew calendar. This day is the Hoshanah Rabbah. *Hoshanah* is a Hebrew phrase that means "Please save now." *Rabbah* means "many." The liturgy for this day is composed of many prayers that plead with God to save us. In temple days, as well as in synagogues today, worshipers would take the four species (three types of branches and one type of fruit, which are held together and waved) and march around the court of the temple seven times while reciting Psalm 118, "Please save us—*hoshanah*." On this day the divine judgment of man, which began on Rosh Hashanah and climaxed on

Yom Kippur, is concluded. Thus, Hoshanah Rabbah is a minor Yom Kippur.

In 1492 when he reached land, Columbus went ashore, wearing a scarlet doublet, with several others of his expedition. As he stepped onto the shore, he kneeled on the sand and began to pray:

> O Lord, Almighty and everlasting God, by Thy holy Word Thou hast created the heaven, and the earth, and the sea; blessed and glorified be Thy Name, and praised be Thy Majesty, which hath designed to use us, Thy humble servants, that Thy holy Name may be proclaimed in this second part of the earth.[15]

The prayer concluded, Columbus christened the island *San Salvador*, which means "Holy Savior."[16]

The Thread of *Shemini Atzeret*

The day following the discovery of the New World would have been *Shemini Atzeret*, or the eighth day of Convocation (22 Tishri). Traditionally, this day is accepted as the day that Solomon dismissed the people from the temple dedication celebration, which is recorded in 1 Kings 8:66. Coincidence or not, the discovery of the New World corresponds to a significant event in Jewish history. Was a new temple being dedicated?

In Israel, this day is also called *Simchat Torah*, or rejoicing in the Torah. On this day there is much celebration as the Torah scroll is rolled back to the beginning of Genesis. In the beginning, God created the heavens and the earth. Is it possible that Columbus could have had this day in mind when he prayed on the shores of San Salvador?

The timing of the discovery was incredible. God was beginning to create a new world. As a point of interest, the very first letter in the Book of Genesis is the Hebrew letter *beit*. The symbol for this letter is a house. The word *beit* (house) is often used to refer to the Jewish temple. Is it possible that God, on this important Jewish date, was beginning construction on a new house, a new temple, a new dwelling among a new chosen people? The above-mentioned Hoshanah Rabbah liturgy certainly seems to support this possibility that the prayer is for God to "plant us on a fruitful sod...establish us as Thy chosen vineyard."

There is a tradition on Hoshanah Rabbah (21 Tishri) of baking bread with a hand on top of it. The hand is to symbolize that God has sealed His decision made for that time. The hand is also said to represent the document or the verdict of that decision. "It shall come to pass in that day that the LORD shall set His hand again the second time to recover the remnant of His people who are left, from...the islands of the sea. He will set up a banner for the nations, and will assemble the outcasts of Israel, and gather together the dispersed of Judah from the four corners of the earth" (Isa. 11:11–12). It would seem that on Hoshanah Rabbah 1492, God indeed made a decision and set His hand to recover His people.

Part of that decision included a Jewish man from Italy sailing west into the unknown to discover a new land. This new land would, in the End Times, become the world's economic, military, and political superpower. More importantly, it would become a nation that would carry the Word of God to the nations of the world and offer a safe haven for the Jews.

As you will see, America's connection to Israel and the Jewish people is not merely political or economic—there is a strange link of prophetic symbolism...an umbilical cord connecting America to the Hebrew people and the land of Israel.

God's People Needed a Safe Haven

In 1492, at the time of Columbus, the Jewish people were being persecuted in Spain and throughout Europe. The journey of Columbus would lead others to the discovery of a new continent that would become a refuge to the Hebrew people. God knew that approximately 450 years later, the greatest assault on the Jewish people in their long history would occur in Europe, as the Nazi legions marched millions of Jews into death camps.

During World War II, America was the safest place on Earth for the Jewish people. God ensured that the natural seed of Abraham would not experience annihilation, and a strong nation, namely America, would fight off the demonic hordes of Nazi troops, restraining them from world domination.

But the parallels between America and the Jewish nation do not stop there. America holds prophetic importance for the Jews for another reason: it was America that assisted in the reforming and the recognition of Israel's rebirth in 1948.

Often nations surrounding Israel feel animosity against America for her stand with Israel. They consider our connection to be a political link and do not understand that Christianity has its roots in the same Scriptures used by the Jews. They do not comprehend that our thread to Israel is a spiritual umbilical cord and not a political tightrope.

••• Chapter 4 •••

BIBLICAL PARALLELS IN EARLY AMERICAN HISTORY

We have no government armed with power capable of contending with human passions unbridled by morality and religion. Avarice, ambition, revenge, or gallantry, would break the strongest cords of our Constitution as a whale goes through a net. Our Constitution was made only for a moral and religious people. It is wholly inadequate to the government of any other.[1]

—*John Adams, October 11, 1798*

A s we begin to travel through the door of early American history, we will continue to unlock amazing prophetic parallels and patterns between America and the biblical history of God's chosen people, the Hebrews. Many of the significant events that determined the destiny of America fell on the same date as certain biblical Hebrew feast days, creating an amazing prophetic cycle.

Perhaps the most impressive parallel is one that is found when comparing Isaiah's prophetic words with those of Matthew. By using the analogy of a vineyard, we discover God's plan to take His chosen vineyard (Israel) and transplant it into another people or another nation. The prophet Isaiah revealed this plan more than twenty-six hundred years ago.

Now let me sing to my Well-beloved
A song of my Beloved regarding His vineyard:

My Well-beloved has a vineyard
On a very fruitful hill.
He dug it up and cleared out its stones,
And planted it with the choicest vine.
He built a tower in its midst,
And also made a winepress in it;
So He expected it to bring forth good grapes,
But it brought forth wild grapes.

"And now, O inhabitants of Jerusalem and men of Judah,
Judge, please, between Me and My vineyard.
What more could have been done to My vineyard
That I have not done in it?
Why then, when I expected it to bring forth good grapes,
Did it bring forth wild grapes?
And now, please let Me tell you what I will do to My vineyard:
I will take away its hedge, and it shall be burned;
And break down its wall, and it shall be trampled down.
I will lay it waste;
It shall not be pruned or dug,
But there shall come up briers and thorns.
I will also command the clouds
That they rain no rain on it."
For the vineyard of the LORD of hosts is the house of Israel,
And the men of Judah are His pleasant plant.
He looked for justice, but behold, oppression;
For righteousness, but behold, a cry for help.

—ISAIAH 5:1–7

Hundreds of years later, Jesus took the parable of the vineyard written in Isaiah chapter 5 and revealed additional information concerning a new vineyard that God would raise up, thereby alluding to future events.

"Hear another parable: There was a certain landowner who planted a vineyard and set a hedge around it, dug a winepress in it and built a tower. And he leased it to vinedressers and went into a far country. Now when vintage-time drew near, he sent his servants to the vinedressers, that they might receive its fruit. And the vinedressers took his servants, beat one, killed one, and stoned another. Again he sent other servants, more than the first, and they did likewise to them. Then last of all he sent his son to them, saying, 'They will respect my son.' But when the vinedressers saw the son, they said among themselves, 'This is the heir. Come, let us kill him and seize his inheritance.' So they took him and cast him out of the vineyard and killed him. Therefore, when the owner of the vineyard comes, what will he do to those vinedressers?" They said to Him, "He will destroy those wicked men miserably, and lease his vineyard to other vinedressers who will render to him the fruits in their seasons." Jesus said to them, "Have you never read in the Scriptures:

'The stone which the builders rejected
Has become the chief cornerstone.
This was the LORD's doing,
And it is marvelous in our eyes'?

"Therefore I say to you, the kingdom of God will be taken from you and given to a nation bearing the fruits of it. And whoever falls on this stone will be broken; but on whomever it falls, it will grind him to powder."

—MATTHEW 21:33–44

Israel was the true vineyard of the Almighty. Years of disobedience to God's Word brought judgment from the Almighty. The Hebrew prophets saw a time when God would remove the hedge and allow the vineyard to be trampled down. This happened twice: once in 606 B.C. with the invasion of the Babylonians, and once in A.D. 70 with the invasion of the Roman Tenth Legion. The difference between the two is that after Babylon, the Jews returned and repossessed the land. After 70, the Jews were dispersed for more than nineteen centuries. Thus the prophetic words of Psalm 80:15 rang loud and clear:

And the vineyard which Your right hand has planted,
And the branch that You made strong for Yourself.
It is burned with fire, it is cut down;
They perish at the rebuke of Your countenance.

Some of the Old Testament Hebrew prophets were rejected, and some were slain by their own people because the tone of their rebuke was so negative against the national sins. While on Earth, Christ warned His generation that: "On you may come all the righteous blood shed on the earth, from the blood of righteous Abel to the blood of Zechariah...whom you murdered between the temple and the altar" (Matt. 23:35). The parable in Matthew 21 reiterates how God sent prophets to the "vineyard of Israel," but the people of Israel slew the prophets. Jesus announced that God would transfer His vineyard and give it to a nation "bringing forth the fruits thereof" (Matt. 21:43, KJV).

Most scholars believe this nation was the same nation that Moses, Hosea, and the prophets foresaw: a nation and a people "which be not as though they were" (Rom. 4:17, KJV), which God would one day raise up for His name. This nation is the same "holy nation" the apostle Peter spoke of when he wrote,

"But you are a chosen generation, a royal priesthood, a holy nation" (1 Pet. 2:9). This new nation is the church, the body of Christ! When the workers in the vineyard killed the son, then the vineyard was given over to another.

After Christ's rejection in Jerusalem, God raised up Gentiles who eventually carried the gospel of Christ to the nations of the earth. Since America has been the premier nation representing Christ to the world, could America be a part of the *transplanted vineyard*? Let's explore the prophetic history of America and see if the vineyard theme can be found.

Transplanting the Vineyard—the Early Beginnings of America

Most Americans believe Columbus discovered America. You will learn this is not totally accurate. The native Indians were here long before Columbus arrived, and the Vikings were some of the first groups to actually come to America centuries before the Pilgrims made their historic journey to our shores.

The Vikings were a collective band of Nordic people—Danes, Swedes, and Norwegians—who traversed abroad from about 800 to 1100. Called the *Viking Age*, this period has long been associated with piracy, pillaging, and barbarism. This, however, is now being recognized as a gross oversimplification. It would seem the Vikings were more interested in *trading* than in *raiding*. As commerce developed, Vikings assimilated into local populations. A century and a half after settling Normandy, their Franco-Viking descendants were responsible for conquering England (in 1066)—the country that would one day be America's birth mother.

The Vikings brought with them various languages. They introduced new forms of administration and justice, such as the jury system. Even the word *law* is from an old Norse word. English law originated in the customs of the Anglo-Saxons and of the Normans (Franco-Vikings), who conquered England in 1066. These kings established a strong centralized system for the administration of justice, and the courts developed a complex system of rules based on custom. These traditions would later lay the foundation for the U.S. Constitution.

His Beloved Son Discovers the Vineyard

About 986, a Viking explorer en route to Greenland, Bjarni Herjolfsson, was driven off course by a storm. He is believed to be the first European to see North America.[2] The land was not explored and named until several years later when it was visited by the Norse explorer Leif Ericson, who sailed south along the coasts of Labrador and Newfoundland. He called this area *Vinland*, or *Wineland*, because of the number of grapes growing there (the vineyard).

The name *Leif* means "beloved," and *Eric* means "the ever powerful." So his full name means "the beloved son of the ever powerful."

Ericson is believed to have been one of the first Europeans to set foot on North American soil. Shortly before 1000, Leif, a sailor like his father, Eric the Red, sailed from Greenland to Norway, the homeland of his family. There, according to tradition, he converted to Christianity and was sent back to Greenland to convert its Viking settlers over to the Christian faith. Traveling westward, Leif lost his way and came upon the North American shore. He returned to Greenland and carried out his commission to bring Christianity to the settlers.[3]

Tradition says that Leif later purchased Bjarni's ship and, based on his description, retraced Bjarni's voyage. While sailing, he encountered several islands before reaching Vinland on October 9, 1000. The exact location of Vinland remains controversial. Some scholars say it is Newfoundland in Canada, while others say Nova Scotia or even New England. Leif later lent his ship to his brother for further exploration of Vinland. Natives killed his brother there during the winter of 1004.

It appears that about one thousand years after Christ's birth, God was already preparing to raise up a new nation.

Thorfinn Karlsefni was an Icelandic trader who led the first known pre-Columbian attempt by Europeans to settle in North America. On a trip to Greenland in the first years of the eleventh century, he met and married the widowed sister of Ericson. Soon afterward, he led a large group of colonists to Vinland with the intent to establish a permanent colony. However, the local Indians drove the settlers out after three years. Because of this, the Vikings were unable to settle this new vineyard.[4]

Although the Vikings failed to settle America, we believe that the history of their visit to this continent underscores the fact that God was preparing a vineyard for His End Time purposes to fulfill what Jesus said so long ago, that He would lend His "vineyard out to another nation." As we shall see, America's amazing Hebrew patterns and history may indicate that the United States has been God's End Time spiritual Israel until the "times of the Gentiles" are fulfilled. Then the Almighty will turn His attention back to natural Israel to graft back in the natural house of Israel into the olive tree.

It must be remembered that long before America was finally settled, the nation of Israel no longer existed. The area the Romans called *Palestine* was being fought over by the Christians and the Muslims. These battles were going back and forth as the land of Bible prophecy experienced wars and desolations. The city of Jerusalem fell into the hands of the Byzantines, the Muslims, the

Mamelukes, the Crusaders, the Ottoman Turks, the British, and finally back to the hands of the Hebrews.

Prophetically, God's plan for Israel will be completely fulfilled in the time known as "Jacob's trouble" or the "Great Tribulation." Before this could transpire, Israel had to be rebirthed as a nation. Since America would play a role in the reestablishing and preservation of national Israel, God would need America in place as a superpower long before Israel would be rebirthed in 1948. Amazingly, God would use Jewish people to assist in the discovery and establishment of this new vineyard. The first would be an Italian Jew named Christopher Columbus.

Christopher Columbus

Christopher Columbus, an apparent Italian Jew, died before he realized he had discovered a continent that would become the most powerful Gentile nation on the earth. He would never realize the many Hebrew parallels that would be associated with America's early history.

By 1503, Columbus was out of the picture as far as exploration of the New World was concerned. He still thought that he had discovered remote parts of Japan and China. It would seem that Columbus's portion of God's plan was finished. Ironically, the man Columbus had chosen to liken himself to, Moses, was not allowed to enter the land to which he led the people of Israel.

What did Columbus's voyages accomplish? They paved the way for colonization of North and South America, partly in an effort to spread the gospel to the natives. Although many natives were forcibly converted, there were some honest, caring men who truly wanted to help the natives. These men founded missions and schools such as San Antonio, San Diego, and San Francisco. In these missions, they taught the natives about the one true God. Many of these men met their deaths at the hands of the natives they were sent to convert. Fifteen hundred years earlier, Jesus had said, "Most assuredly, I say to you, unless a grain of wheat falls into the ground and dies, it remains alone; but if it dies, it produces much grain" (John 12:24).

We believe these men and others who followed in their footsteps were the "grains of wheat" that God used to seed His new vineyard. Where Columbus had discovered the site for this new house, these martyred missionaries had built the foundation. Many would follow and build the house itself. They would open the door for literally millions to come in and find freedom and safety.

The Naming of America

For several years after Columbus's initial discovery, no one realized that a new continent had been discovered. Columbus sailed along the South American shore, never realizing the vastness of his find. In 1499, Amerigo Vespucci, an Italian who helped outfit Columbus's voyages, began making journeys across the Atlantic. It is believed that Vespucci made a total of three journeys. The first of these was along the coast of what is now Venezuela. The second and third voyages took him to the coastline of Brazil. It was on one of those journeys that Vespucci wrote a pamphlet named *Mundus Novus* (New World), which included these words: "On a former occasion I wrote to you concerning my return from those new regions which we found and explored with the fleet.... These we may rightly call a new world. Because our ancestors had no knowledge of them...I have found a continent more densely peopled and abounding in animals than our Europe or Asia or Africa."[5] Even though he never commanded an expedition, and most likely never discovered anything, Vespucci was credited as being the first to recognize that Columbus's discovery was actually another land, previously unknown.

It just so happened that a German mapmaker named Martin Waldseemüller was about to publish a new map of the world. Having read Vespucci's letters, he decided that: "But now these parts have been more extensively explored and another fourth part has been discovered by Americus Vespucius (as will appear in what follows): wherefore I do not see what is rightly to hinder us from calling it Amerige, or America—i.e., the land of Americus, after its discoverer, Americus, a man of sagacious mind, since both Europe and Asia have got their names from women."[6] The name *Amerigo* in Italian means "rich in wheat." In 1507, the name America appeared on a map for the first time. Soon after, the idea of calling the New World "America" spread.

English Colonization

While the Spanish concentrated on converting the Indians of Central and South America, not to mention taking their gold and enslaving their people, the English began, timidly at first, exploring North America. In 1497, an Italian named John Cabot sailed from Bristol, England, aboard the *Matthew*. Cabot had been commissioned by the English king Henry VII, and on June 24, 1497, he landed on Newfoundland, claiming it for the English. Thus began Britain's first efforts at colonizing the New World. Humble as it was, it would forever impact the world in a manner that was unimagined. However, it would be 110 years before a permanent English colony would be established.

Britain's Hebrew Heritage

It was a group of Viking people who had assimilated into Franco communities, thus creating a mixed breed known as the Normans, who conquered England in 1066. There is another strange affiliation that the British may have had that reveals Britain's link with the Jews.

For centuries, people have pondered what became of the lost tribes of Israel. So that you understand the historical and biblical record about the ten northern tribes of the Israelites, this overview will provide some helpful information:

> The concept of lost tribes dates back to the exile of the Israelite kingdom in 722 BCE. The kingdom of Israel, which had separated from Judea following Solomon's death, could hardly survive the onslaught of the clashing empires of the ancient Middle East, while it struggled on with its own internal crisis, idolaters against monotheists, Elijah against the decadent Jezebel. Taken away to a definitive exile in Babylon by Assyrian armies, these tribes were eventually dispersed throughout the Middle East and we know virtually nothing of their fate. Whereas the progeny of the tribes of Judea, Judah and Benjamin, were eventually permitted to return to their lands under Cyrus the Great of Persia, a fact duly recorded in the Bible, there are, curiously, no biblical records regarding the whereabouts of the ten northern tribes.[7]

Countless legends and theories have arisen, but still no one but God is sure of what became of them. I do not want to imply that any legend or theory is a fact, and I do not want to validate the theory that Anglo-Saxon people are members of the lost ten tribes. I do want to mention several interesting topics as they relate to the lost tribes.

First, let me ask the question: Why did God select Britain as the nation that would give birth to the United States? The first possible reference in the Bible to Great Britain is the name Tarshish. (See Genesis 10:1–4.) Tarshish was a great-grandson of Noah whose descendants migrated into Western Europe, Spain, and the British Isles. There was a city in southern Spain called Tartessus, which was often visited by Phoenician merchants. One theory points to this town as the ancient city of Tarshish. This mysterious city was associated with the trade of tin (Ezek. 27:12). It is known that there were tin deposits in Spain and Great Britain. In fact, Great Britain was originally called *Britannia*, due to the tin mines located in Cornwall, which had been in existence for thousands of years.

Ezekiel 38:13 refers to "Sheba, Dedan, the merchants of Tarshish, and all their young lions..." This terminology infers that the mother lion is Tarshish. Since Britain's emblem is the lion, this further strengthens the claim that Tarshish is Britain.

In Judges 5:17 we discover that the tribe of Dan had ships. Due to their proximity to the Mediterranean, the Danites were likely expert mariners. Dan's tribal inheritance included the famous port city of Joppa. The Danites were later forced to migrate north, where they occupied another district called Bashan, or the Golan Heights as we know it today. Moses prophesied: "Dan is a lion's whelp; he shall leap from Bashan" (Deut. 33:22). The word *leap* can mean, "to gush out."

In Irish history, there is a group of people who were known as the *Tuatha de Danann*. *Tuatha* means "people of God." *Dunn* in the Irish language means "judge." Coincidentally, this also is the meaning of the name Dan. Some have speculated that during the Assyrian invasion of the northern kingdom, a small group of people from the tribe of Dan fled in boats (leapt from Bashan) and eventually ended up in Britain. If Britain was the biblical Tarshish, then the Danites would have known that the journey was possible. If this did happen, then Britain became a safe haven for some of God's people. Could this account for God selecting Britain to be the New World power and the mother of the greatest nation the world has seen? We are not saying that this alleged migration of Danites is undeniably true, only that in the light of our research, it becomes an interesting point.

A Hebrew Name?

Israel is known as *the covenant people*. The Hebrew word for *covenant* is *brit*. The Hebrew word for *man* is *ish*. If the word *British* were translated into Hebrew, it would mean, "covenant man." This may be more than mere coincidence. There are many in Britain, especially in the area of England, who believe that their nation was the location where some of the lost tribes settled. This may not be too far-fetched.

According to early Jewish American history, after the decision to evict the Jews from Spain was made on March 31, 1492, many Jews fled to the east and north of Spain. In 1502, a Jewish man, Juan Sanchez de Saragossa, was awarded a royal trading license to promote trade and settlement in the New World.[8] Modern research indicates that some of those who followed Cortez to Mexico were converted Jews seeking freedom in the New World. Some fled to what is today Texas and New Mexico. Jews settled in parts of what would later be America more than one hundred years before the landing at New Amsterdam in 1654.[9]

As an interesting note, there would have been no Jews in the English colonies because a four-hundred-year-old law forbade Jews from settling in English lands. A rabbi, Menasseh ben Israel of Amsterdam, Holland, addressed Oliver Cromwell, Lord Protector of England, with this fervent messianic argument: "Before all [prophecies] be fulfilled the people of God must first be dispersed into all places and countries of the world." The ban on Jews was lifted and Jews were free to settle in the new colonies.[10]

Elizabeth and Raleigh—More Strange Parallels

> But the angel said to him, "Do not be afraid, Zacharias, for your prayer is heard; and your wife Elizabeth will bear you a son, and you shall call his name John. And you will have joy and gladness, and many will rejoice at his birth. For he will be great in the sight of the Lord, and shall drink neither wine nor strong drink. He will also be filled with the Holy Spirit, even from his mother's womb. And he will turn many of the children of Israel to the Lord their God. He will also go before Him in the spirit and power of Elijah, 'to turn the hearts of the fathers to the children,' and the disobedient to the wisdom of the just, to make ready a people prepared for the Lord."
>
> —Luke 1:13–17

An interesting fact gained from this story is the meaning of the names of John's parents—Zacharias and Elizabeth. Zacharias means "God remembers," and Elizabeth means "God's oath." What was His oath? God had promised as far back as the Garden of Eden that He would send a deliverer who would reconcile God and man so that God could once again commune with man (Gen. 3:15). The fruit of Zacharias and Elizabeth's union, John the Baptist, was the forerunner of Jesus the Messiah, who was born of a young virgin named Mary. Jesus accomplished the reconciliation on the cross but has not yet physically established His kingdom whereby we might see Him face-to-face. Therefore, a part of God's oath is yet to be completely fulfilled. We are awaiting the arrival of the Messianic kingdom.

It would seem that America fits into God's plan for the advent of this kingdom by allowing us to propagate the gospel and support His special people, Israel. Should we be surprised to learn that there may be a parallel in American history with the story of Elizabeth and Zacharias?

In the mid to late 1500s, there reigned a queen known as the virgin queen,

Elizabeth I. Until this time, England had been very hesitant to follow up on Cabot's initiative to explore the New World. At the time, England was intimidated by the Spanish and did little to explore the New World. That changed when Elizabeth I came to power and England started a policy of spiritual and material expansionism. Vessels flying Elizabeth's ensign traveled as far away as present-day San Francisco and several points in between. However, colonization efforts always fell short. (Note: Elizabeth's cousin was Mary, Queen of Scots, mother of King James I. James is the English version of Jacob/Israel.)

In 1578, Sir Walter Raleigh, Elizabeth's favorite courtier, sailed with his half brother Sir Humphrey Gilbert to America. It was this voyage that probably stimulated Raleigh's plan to found an English empire there. Oddly enough, on the Hebrew calendar this year means "to stretch out, to extend." It seems that this is what Raleigh was planning to do. It can also mean, "to initiate or launch something," as well as, "to send a plague." Raleigh's motives seem to have been riches, a motive that would plague many English expeditions.

In 1585, Raleigh, commissioned by Elizabeth I, sent out a colonizing expedition of one hundred men to settle on Roanoke Island in present-day North Carolina. The colony included a Bohemian Jew named Joachim Ganz, who was sent to prospect for minerals. This expedition was short-lived. In 1587, Raleigh sent out a fresh expedition consisting of more than one hundred men, women, and children. This colony might have been permanent if England had supported it from home, but as fate would have it, the Spanish were preparing an armada to invade England. This great naval battle, which the English won, delayed any supply efforts for more than two years. When Raleigh finally arranged for some ships to sail to Roanoke Island, they found nothing but the word "CROATOAN" carved on a nearby tree. To this day, nobody knows what became of the Lost Colony.[11] There are claims by the Lumbee Indians of North Carolina that the blood of Raleigh's colonists runs through their veins, but no one can be sure. Coincidentally, 1587 on the Hebrew calendar means "the desolation, the ruin."

Although the colony was lost, England learned a valuable lesson about colonization in the New World. It would try to do a better job of resupplying the outposts until they could get on their feet. Though she never saw an English colony survive in the New World, Elizabeth I was responsible for igniting English colonization efforts. She and her courageous explorers were preparing the way for other English monarchs and private citizens to expand English influence, including its unique freedoms, to the Western Hemisphere. It is my belief that through the efforts of Elizabeth I and Sir Walter Raleigh, God was remembering His oath to plant a vineyard that would yield spiritual fruit one day.

Jamestown—or Jacobstown

We, greatly commending, and graciously accepting of, their Desires for the Furtherance of so noble a Work, which may, by the Providence of Almighty God, hereafter tend to the Glory of his Divine Majesty, in propagating of Christian Religion to such People, as yet live in Darkness and miserable Ignorance of the true Knowledge and Worship of God, and may in time bring the Infidels and Savages, living in those parts, to human Civility, and to a settled and quiet Government.[12]

This preamble indicates that the Virginia Company had noble goals in mind when they decided in 1606 to plant a permanent colony in Virginia. They had promised the settlers that they would enjoy "all Liberties...to all Intents and Purposes, as if they had been abiding and born, within this our Realm of England."[13] This principle held true for most people. In fact, Americans today owe a huge debt of gratitude to those early principles of freedom and liberty. Their stated motive for this new settlement was to propagate the gospel of Christ to the natives, but their true motives became apparent almost from the day they landed on the banks of the James River.

In December 1606, three ships left England for the New World carrying 144 men, only one of them a minister—Robert Hunt. In May 1607, this expedition sailed up the Chesapeake Bay and continued up the James River for about forty miles. Finally, on May 14, 1607, they made landfall on the spot they would name Jamestown. I find it fascinating that the first English colony in America was founded on the very same day—May 14—that the modern nation of Israel would be founded 341 years later on May 14, 1948.

King James or King Jacob?

The settlement was named Jamestown after His Majesty, King James I. This was the same King James who had commissioned the translation of the Bible into English, hence the 1611 King James Bible. The name *James* is the English version of the name *Jacob*, or in Hebrew *Ya'akov*. Jacob, the son of Isaac, was the father of the twelve tribes of Israel. Jacob's life story is checkered with accounts of plotting and deceit. We feel it is fair to say that Jacob schemed and deceived people for most of his early life, thus the meaning of his name, "supplanter." Yet God promised Jacob that the covenant made with his fathers, Abraham and Isaac, would be fulfilled through him. God even changed his name to Israel, which means "prince of God" or "ruling with God."

In 1626, Captain John Smith wrote a history of Virginia and New England. On the book's cover page are sketches of the three English monarchs who had commissioned the English exploration. They were Queen Elizabeth I, King James I, and King Charles I. Instead of using their English names, however, their names were written in Latin. James was referred to as "Jacobus," and this clearly identifies James I as a namesake of Jacob, or as he was later called, Israel. Because of this relation in names, we could claim that the first English colony in the New World was named after Israel, the father of the twelve tribes of Israel. Just as the twelve tribes issued forth from Israel, the other twelve of the thirteen original colonies came from the Old Dominion, Virginia. History records that, at one point, all of the Eastern shore of North America was referred to as *Virginia*. The Hebrew thread is seen weaving a pattern in the New World.

Jamestown—the Supplanter

Just as Jacob of the Bible deceived and manipulated those around him, the people of Jamestown did no less to their neighbors, the Indians. Threats, robberies, and even a kidnapping stain the legacy of those early settlers. Starvation, cannibalism, and death are a part of their beginnings.[14] On several occasions, the people of Jamestown faced starvation. Instead of asking their Indian neighbors for help, they demanded it and, in some cases, stole it.[15]

The Indian chief Powhatan was apparently a very patient man. God had allowed this English group to settle in an area where the natives would have taught the colonists how to plant, fish, and be self-sufficient, but the attitudes of the Englishmen were to let someone else do the work so that they could turn their attention to more pressing matters—looking for gold. Ironically, this is the same serpent that bit Columbus. The only time the Englishmen became concerned about the lack of food was when it was too late to do anything about it. No doubt God wanted to use these men to further His purpose, but their unwillingness to conform to God's principles would not allow for that. Matters degenerated quickly to the point that men and women were forced to eat the corpses of their comrades who succumbed to starvation.[16]

At one point, the colonists became so desperate for food that they kidnapped the chief's favorite daughter, Pocahontas. They held her for ransom and demanded that Powhatan give them food. This was their method of survival. Instead of working to provide for themselves, they took what belonged to another. When they should have been planting and preparing for the winter, their attitude was, according to John Smith, "No work, but dig gold, wash gold, refine gold, load gold."[17] The irony is that there was no gold!

At one point, the death rate in Jamestown was 90 percent. In May 1610, a decision was made to abandon the settlement and return to England. This could have aborted God's plan for America. This would have happened had it not been for the timely arrival of the new governor, Lord De la Warr. He made everyone return to the settlement. Eventually, discipline, a work ethic, and church services were instituted.[18] This and other issues helped Jamestown on the road to recovery. It would be another twenty years before the colony became self-sufficient. During that time, the tobacco industry grew and became profitable. Once again, the Englishmen decided it would be more profitable if someone else did the work for them, so in 1619, Jamestown received its first African slaves and put them to work in the tobacco fields.[19] The issue of slavery and the Englishmen's cavalier attitude would explode about two hundred fifty years later, as brother fought against brother.

In the Bible, God allowed Jacob to endure some difficult times in his life, possibly due to his deceitfulness. Later, Jacob would fall victim to the deceit he had sown. His brothers sold Joseph, his favorite son, into slavery. Jacob was deceived into believing he was dead and, for many years, mourned the loss of his son, never knowing he had been deceived. Joseph told his brothers years later, "But as for you, you meant evil against me; but God meant it for good, in order to bring it about as it is this day, to save many people alive" (Gen. 50:20). Virginia did survive and develop into a wealthy colony, but at a great price. Today, monuments are all that is left of Jamestown—the town itself is a memory. The lessons learned at Jamestown would prove beneficial as America grew.

An Interesting Look at Dates

> And it shall come to pass in that day, that the Lord shall set his hand again the second time to recover the remnant of his people, which shall be left, from…the islands of the sea. And he shall set up an ensign for the nations, and shall assemble the outcasts of Israel, and gather together the dispersed of Judah from the four corners of the earth.
>
> —Isaiah 11:11–12, KJV

The Hebrew word for *ensign* is *nec*. This word can also be interpreted as the sail of a ship. This word *nec* comes from the word *nacac*, which means "to gleam from afar or to be conspicuous, like a signal." It carries the idea of a flag fluttering in the breeze, to raise a beacon, a standard bearer. When translating the Hebrew letters back to their number value, the Hebrew numerical value is 110. One hundred ten years after Columbus's discovery of the New World, a lesser-known event occurred. We think this event proves to be interesting in light of what we are about to discuss.

Exactly 110 years after Columbus landed at San Salvador, Bartholomew

Gosnold, an English explorer, discovered the Cape Cod peninsula, which is now Massachusetts. The date was May 15, 1602.[20] May 15 was also the date that Israel officially became a nation. Through these dates, we are reminded of the America-Israel connection. Could it be that Gosnold's discovery alludes to the raised "ensign" mentioned in Isaiah 11? Compared to the rest of the world, the United States does stand out as a beacon for the gospel and freedom. Where did we inherit this love of the gospel and of freedom? It was from our English forefathers.

On this voyage, Gosnold sailed along the North American coast from Maine to Narragansett Bay in what is now Rhode Island. He named not only Cape Cod but also some of the islands in Nantucket Sound, including Martha's Vineyard and the Elizabeth Islands. When he returned to England, Gosnold promoted the establishment of colonies in the areas he had explored and supported the merchants who obtained a charter from King James I to colonize Virginia. Gosnold was appointed to command the *Godspeed*, one of three ships that left England in 1606 for Jamestown. Exactly five years after his discovery of Cape Cod, Gosnold was standing on the banks of the James River aiding in the construction of the first permanent English colony in America—Jamestown. The English were beginning to assemble on the shores of the New World in a place named after James I.[21] (Remember, James was the English form of Jacob, and the Jacob of the Bible became Israel.)

The Pilgrims and the Hebrew Letter *Beit*

The Hebrew letter Beit is composed of three lines resembling a square, yet open on the left side. From the perspective of Torah, the top line of the square faces east, the right side faces south and the bottom side faces west. The open side faces north.[22]

The Hebrew letter *b* (בּ), pronounced *beit*, is the first letter used in the Hebrew Bible, in Genesis 1:1. The first word is *b'reshit*. Rabbis have wondered why God began creation with the *b*, which is the second letter of the Hebrew alphabet, instead of the *a* (א) (pronounced *alef*), which is the first letter. Rabbis say one reason might be because *beit* represents a house. Throughout the Bible, God's interaction with man has been in an effort to establish and maintain a relationship whereby God might dwell among men. "And let them make Me a sanctuary, that I may dwell among them" (Exod. 25:8). The word *sanctuary* is מקדש (*miqdash*). The temple in Jerusalem came to be known as the בית־מקדש (*bet miqdash*), the house of sanctuary, where God would dwell among the children of Israel. If we are correct in our interpretation of the "Nation Parable" (Luke 13:6–9) that the United States will serve as God's vineyard, then God must have a dwelling place, a house.

God chose a specific place in Israel to place His home, as we read in Deuteronomy 12:5: "But you shall seek the place where the LORD your God chooses, out of all your tribes, to put His name for His dwelling place; and there you shall go." The place of His habitation was in Jerusalem upon the Temple Mount. Looking at an aerial photograph of the Old City, you will discover that the three valleys in Jerusalem's proximity form the Hebrew letter שׁ (*shin*). According to rabbinic Judaism, this letter represents the name of God. God literally placed His name in the landscape where He would dwell among His people. Can we expect the same phenomena to show up in America?

Cape Cod and the Letter *Beit*

If you look at a map of Cape Cod starting at the tip of Provincetown where the Pilgrims first landed, and follow it around to Plymouth, you will find that the peninsula forms the letter *beit*, or a house. Notice that the open side of this geographical *beit* is on the north side. We mentioned earlier that Gosnold explored a small island just off the coast of the peninsula. This particular island was discovered with vines, so he named it *Martha's Vineyard* after his daughter. It is separated from Cape Cod by Vineyard Sound. It seems that God chose this particular geographic area, a vineyard, to start building His house. Once again we see the aspect of the prophetic vineyard coming into play:

> Unless the LORD builds the house,
> They labor in vain who build it;
> Unless the LORD guards the city,
> The watchman stays awake in vain.

> —PSALM 127:1

Building the House

Eighteen years after Gosnold's discovery, and thirteen years after the founding of Jamestown, the Pilgrims (who had intended to settle at the mouth of the Hudson River) were blown off course. On November 9, 1620, they found themselves about one hundred miles north at a place one of the sailors recognized as Cape Cod. After much debate and prayer, they decided that perhaps God had led them to this spot and did not want them to proceed to the Hudson. So, on November 11, 1620, they dropped anchor in the waters of the Cape.[23]

Settling there, however, presented a small problem. This area was outside of the jurisdiction of the Virginia Company, and they would have nobody to answer to. Due to the fact that there were people on the *Mayflower* who would be unwilling to conform with strict adherence to biblical law, as did the Pilgrims, a quick solution was needed. The result was the *Mayflower Compact*. This document provided for equality and government by the consent of the governed and was a precursor of our U.S. Constitution. The Compact was signed on November 11, 1620.[24]

William Bradford, who later became governor of the colony, wrote of their landing at Provincetown: "Being thus arrived in a good harbor and brought safe to land, they fell upon their knees and blessed the God of heaven, who had brought them over the vast and furious ocean, and delivered them from all perils and miseries thereof, again to set their feet on the firm and stable earth, their proper element. And no marvel if they were thus joyful."[25] This is remarkable in light of all the hardships they had endured. One hundred two people had been stuffed between decks. The conditions were miserable, at best. They had to endure sickness and taunts from the crew. After they had already arrived at Provincetown, Bradford's wife fell overboard and drowned. Although there were hardships, there were miracles as well.

While they were in the middle of the Atlantic, a fierce storm arose and snapped the crossbeam that supported the main mast. The situation was grave. The Pilgrims did the only thing they knew to do—they prayed! At this time, William Brewster, one of the elders, remembered that a large iron screw from his printing press was on board. A search ensued to find the screw. Once found, it was used to support the sagging crossbeam in its proper position. Everyone praised God for deliverance from a sure death.[26]

On December 21, 1620, after scouting for the best place to settle, a group of ten men stepped onto Plymouth Rock and made history. One might wonder if, as they stepped onto the rock, they thought of the scripture: "Upon this rock I will build my church" (Matt. 16:18, KJV). As they looked around, they saw an area that was perfect for habitation. There were four sources of water nearby, the harbor was deep enough to receive large ships, and the land was already cleared and seemed to have been used for planting corn. It was as if someone had cleared it, used it, and then left. Coincidentally, this day was the second day of Chanukah, the Jewish celebration of the rededication of God's house in Jerusalem. God's vineyard was growing, and His house was about to take shape.

The Miracles of the Plymouth Plantation

The reality of the harsh New England winter set in quickly upon the Pilgrims. By the time the *Mayflower* left for England in April 1621, only half of the

102 Pilgrims who made the voyage were still alive, yet not one person boarded the ship to return. Instead, everyone pitched in and constructed a blockhouse, which also served as the meetinghouse. This was a pattern that would be repeated many times in Puritan New England. At the founding of each new community, one of the first structures built was a meetinghouse. They believed that their covenant with God and with their fellow man was the basis of their colony. Apparently, this is exactly what God wanted from them, because miracle after miracle attested to God's favor.

One of the strangest events regarding this new settlement involved their acquaintance with the Indians. One day as the men were meeting in the blockhouse, one Indian approached the compound. To their amazement, he spoke English. His name was Samoset, and he was a chieftain among the Algonquin tribe who lived in Maine. He had learned English from men on fishing expeditions off the coast of Maine. When asked about the local Indians, Samoset told a story that shocked the Pilgrims. According to Samoset, the territory the Pilgrims were occupying had belonged to a hostile, murderous tribe known as the Patuxets. They had cleared the land. About four years before the Pilgrims had arrived, a mysterious sickness had swept through and killed all of the tribe. The neighboring tribe, fearing some supernatural reason for this devastation, would not venture near the area. So the land the Pilgrims were occupying did not belong to anyone. Furthermore, it seems that God had dispossessed the previous owners in favor of the Pilgrim believers.[27]

The Lord had done the same thing for Israel so many years ago. The Book of Joshua says that the Lord, through Joshua, told Israel: "I sent the hornet before you which drove them out from before you, also the two kings of the Amorites, but not with your sword or with your bow. I have given you a land for which you did not labor, and cities which you did not build, and you dwell in them; you eat of the vineyards and olive groves which you did not plant. Now therefore, fear the LORD, serve Him in sincerity and in truth, and put away the gods which your fathers served on the other side of the River and in Egypt. Serve the LORD!" (Josh. 24:12–14).

The Pilgrims discovered that the nearest tribe was the Wampanoags, who were some distance away. Their chief was Massasoit, who was probably the only chief along the Northeastern seaboard who would befriend the white men. The hand of God was evident as He provided the ideal place for the wandering Pilgrims to live.

As it turned out, there was one Patuxet named Squanto who had been in England while his tribe fell victim to the mysterious illness. He has spent many years in England and had returned to his native land with, of all people,

Captain John Smith. However, after Smith left, another ship's captain returned and captured many Indians, including Squanto, with the intention of selling them as slaves. Squanto was rescued by a friar who introduced him to the Christian faith. After several years of instruction, Squanto was returned to his native land. It was then that he discovered his tribe had been wiped out. Sad as this may have been, Squanto had seemingly been chosen by God to aid the Pilgrims in their first years as newcomers to the land. Bradford wrote that Squanto was a "special instrument sent of God for their good beyond their expectation."[28] It is recorded that Squanto taught them how to fish, plant maize, hunt deer, refine maple syrup, and select the proper herbs for medicines. It was this kind of friendly relationship that led to the first Thanksgiving. What a remarkable contrast to the colony at Jamestown!

The Puritans and the "Land of the Covenant"

The first person on record (other than an Indian) to use the word *American* when referring to a European colonist was Cotton Mather, a Puritan minister. The Puritans, distinct from the Pilgrims, began to immigrate to the New World in 1628. What started as a trading company developed into a theocracy. Regarding their strict adherence to the Bible, the Puritans have been given a bad rap. The Puritans, probably more than any other group that settled in America, defined what God was looking for in a people and a nation. They also provided the blueprint for the American system of government. Is it coincidence that the American Revolution began in the area where the Puritans had settled? They felt they had been given a divine opportunity to construct a colony that existed and thrived on biblical principles. Their philosophy of living the Christian life in the New World was based on covenant—covenant with God and man.

This same feeling existed in 1776, when America declared its independence. The closing statement of the Declaration of Independence says: "And for the support of this declaration, with a firm reliance on the protection of Divine Providence, we mutually pledge to each other our lives, our fortunes, and our sacred honor."[29] Many of the men who signed the Declaration of Independence were descendants of the Puritan fathers. Ironically, the Hebrew name for the United States of America is ארצות־הברית (*ertzot ha brit*)—Lands of the Covenant.

The City of Salem

John Endicott, born in Cornwall, England (the area of the tin mines), joined with six other men to obtain a parcel of land in the new Massachusetts Bay Colony. In 1628, Endicott and a group of about one hundred settled at a place they called Salem.[30] When Abraham met Melchizedek at the time God established His covenant with Abraham, the name of the place where they met was Salem (Gen. 14:18). This city, Salem, was the city that later become the city of Jerusalem, the capital of Israel. The events surrounding the formation of America would center in the area of Massachusetts in the same manner that Jerusalem would become the nerve center for the nation of Israel.

The founders of Salem considered themselves to be the spiritual heirs of the Old Testament—the new Israelites. Understanding this, it was only suitable that they should name their first settlement after the Holy City of God, Jerusalem.[31] They likened their leaving England and crossing the Atlantic to Israel leaving Egypt and crossing the Red Sea. This persuasion continued into at least the next century. At the dawn of the American Revolution, a State Assembly referred to the American people as "God's American Israel."[32]

The American Nehemiah

John Endicott served as governor until the appointed governor, John Winthrop, arrived in 1630. Winthrop and about nine hundred colonists settled first at Salem. From Salem, they moved on to settle Charlestown. During the American Revolution, the battle of Bunker Hill would be fought at Charlestown. The colonists continued moving and finally settled at the mouth of the Charles River, where Boston was established. This is the city that would one day represent the cause of the American Revolution and freedom from tyranny.

Cotton Mather, the famous Puritan minister, referred to Winthrop as "Nehemias Americanus"—the American Nehemiah.[33] In the Bible, Nehemiah was the man who led Israel back from captivity to the Promised Land and began rebuilding the walls of Jerusalem and the temple. Winthrop saw New England as a religious and political refuge. In his letters, he referred to it as a city on a hill (Matt. 5:14) and the New Jerusalem. Winthrop became God's man to assist in building up the new vineyard of the Lord, America.[34]

For the Love of Hebrew

This Hebraic theme seems to form the foundation of the Bay Colony. Many of the Puritan ministers were well versed in the Hebrew language. Cotton Mather is recorded as having said, "I promise that those who spend as much time morning and evening in Hebrew studies as they do in smoking tobacco would quickly make excellent progress in the language."[35] William Bradford, a Pilgrim, echoed this interest in the Hebrew language. Bradford intimated that he studied Hebrew intensely so that when he died he would be able to speak the "most ancient language, and holy tongue…in which God, and angels, spake."[36]

It's a unique feature to consider that the original Jewish language is the Hebrew, and the early founders of America even considered accepting Hebrew as the official language of America. Hebrew seems to have played an important role in early New England development. The language is found on the insignias of seals of schools such as Columbia and Dartmouth. Harvard University, founded by the Puritans in 1636, viewed Hebrew as an important component of higher learning. From the school's foundation, Hebrew was taught by several of the presidents. Harry Dunster, the first president of Harvard, was considered "the best Hebraist of his time."[37]

John Endicott wanted to make the Mosaic Law the basis of law in Massachusetts. Settlers who moved from Massachusetts to settle in Connecticut adopted a government based on Mosaic Law.[38] The main reason that the Salem Witch Trials of 1692 occurred was because of the Puritan's attempt to enforce the Mosaic Law. The Law of Moses said that you must not "suffer a witch to live" (Exod. 22:18, KJV). It is safe to say that the Hebrew Scriptures were at the heart of Puritan society. Just as the language of Israel was Hebrew, the Hebrew language was emphasized in the new vineyard, America.

The Puritan's intention in the New World was to found a New Israel, a city set on a hill. As they sought to do this, they constantly taught that unless the Lord builds the house, those who build it labor in vain. Their colony developed to such an extent that in 1691 they were given a new charter, which incorporated an area from Plymouth all the way to Maine. Out of this great society came forth elements that would influence not only the Declaration of Independence but also the U.S. Constitution, as both documents have their roots in the Bible.

A Second Exodus

The Puritans had tried to purify the Church of England from within but were met with obstinate resistance. For years, Puritan ministers had pleaded with church officials to fix corrupt practices within the church. Oddly, from autumn of 1628 to 1629 was the Hebrew year 5389. Translating these letters back to the Hebrew alphabet, it spells the Hebrew word *hishaphet*, which means "to judge or plead." It was during this time that the Great (Puritan) Migration began.

You will recall that the Jewish exodus from Egypt was born out of God's judgment upon Egypt and its tyrant, Pharaoh. The pressure from Pharaoh caused the Hebrews to want to leave. In 1628, William Laud was appointed as the Church of England's bishop. Laud began immediately to aid King Charles I in suppressing the Puritans. This settled the issue of whether or not the Puritans should remain in England. It was this repression that caused the Puritans to want to leave. Just as oppression in Egypt drove the Hebrews to the Promised Land, oppression in the Church of England drove the Puritans to their new promised land.

The timing of this and other events seemed to have predestined the great number of Puritans who left for America in the Great Migration. The book *The Light and the Glory* says: "Today we can see what lay ahead of them...and sense just how extraordinary was the timing of the Puritan exodus. If Laud had not come to power and abetted King Charles in his drive to bring the Puritans to heel...there might not have been a Puritan exodus of sufficient numbers to seed America with spiritual liberty."[39] Persecution brought forth a new people in a new nation.

Charles I consented to let the Puritans initiate a colony. Soon after, he was confronted with discontented subjects who pleaded with him to curtail his power. Charles reluctantly consented. However, in 1629, he dissolved Parliament and ran the country himself. Over the course of several years, the issue continued to fester until civil war resulted. The end result for Charles I was death by execution. We wonder if the Hebrew year 5389, meaning in Hebrew, "to judge or to plead," had predicted this.

The Pruning of the Vineyard

The law of God requires that every vineyard be pruned (Lev. 25:3). If the Plymouth and Massachusetts Bay Colonies were the fruitful vines of the new vineyard, then God requires every vineyard to be pruned. In 1636, Roger Williams and Thomas Hooker, members of the Massachusetts Bay Colony, founded the colonies of Rhode Island and Connecticut. Both colonies reinforced the religious freedom and codes instituted in Massachusetts. The theme of the vineyard continued with these new "branches," especially with Connecticut, whose state motto is: "He who transplanted still sustains." This phrase alludes to a vineyard, for on the state seal there are three grapevines representing a vineyard!

Often in ancient Israel, God's people eventually strayed away from His laws and commandments, bringing war and captivity to themselves with the people in the land. Just so, eventually the Puritans strayed from the biblical principles that had been guiding them, and trouble erupted. In 1675–1676, the Indians, who had lived in harmony with the settlers, began turning on them. *King Philip's War*, as it was called, began, led by Metacom, the Wampanoag chief. Metacom, or Philip, as he was referred to, was the second son of Massasoit, the same Indian chief who befriended the settlers fifty years earlier. The war was bloody, but it accomplished two things: it caused the churches to be filled with people who were praying and repenting, and it taught the settlers how to fight in a war.[40]

During the times of the judges with ancient Israel, the various Canaanite tribes inhabiting Israel would rise against the Hebrews and fight. The Hebrews would then cry out to God for help. In reality, the Lord allowed these tribes to remain in the land to "teach the people about war." In like manner, the settlers, through fighting Indian tribes, learned from the Indians the secrets of successful warfare; they would later use the same methods against the British.

A Strange Tale About Concord

There is a strange story to tell about King Philip's War and the town of Concord. It is said the town was named *Concord* to reflect the peaceful way in which the settlers acquired new land from the Indians for the settlement. During the war, many New England towns were attacked and burned, but Concord was spared and Sudbury attacked instead. One reason why Sudbury was attacked instead of Concord is that the Indians feared the influence Concord's minister Edward Bulkeley had with the "Great Spirit." In his book *History of Middlesex County, Massachusetts*, Samuel Adams Drake records an Indian as saying, "We no prosper, if we burn Concord. The Great Spirit love that people. He tell us not to go there. They have a great man there. He great pray." [41] Because of this man of God, Concord escaped the war. Exactly one hundred years later Concord would be the place where the "shot heard around the world" would be fired. The shot happened near the home of another great man of God, William Emerson, the great-grandson of Edward Bulkeley.

A Rebellion Was Building

While New England fought the war with King Philip, another problem developed in Virginia. Due to the Navigational Acts of 1651 and 1660, the farmers were forced to trade only with English businesses at prices established by England. The outrageous prices levied by officials were only a part of the problem. The governor, Sir William Berkeley, had a monopoly on the fur trade.[42] One hundred years later these same Navigational Acts would resurface at the start of the American Revolution.

Toward the end of 1675, the Indians began raiding plantations in Virginia. While Berkeley made a half-hearted attempt to stop the attacks, the colonists formed an army, making Nathaniel Bacon their leader. Bacon defeated the Indians twice and occupied Jamestown, the capital of the colony. Governor Berkeley felt Bacon rebelled against the English Crown and marched against him. Bacon burned Jamestown in 1676. The following month he made a stand near Yorktown in order to meet the force sent against him by the governor. One month later Bacon died of malaria, thus ending the rebellion.[43] One hundred years later, another rebellion would change the destiny of America.

The Prophetic Significance of the Indian Wars

Some historians interpret Bacon's Rebellion as the forerunner of the American Revolution. This war and King Philip's War are interesting for several reasons. First of all, there is a hundred-year cycle. One war started in 1675 and lasted into 1676. One hundred years later, the American Revolution began in 1775 and American independence was declared in 1776.

Second, both wars taught the settlers how to fight as the Indians did. The British wore heavy clothing and stood in formation in an open field. The Indians wore light clothes and hid to ambush the enemy. It was these tactics that would help the Americans win the Revolutionary War.

Third, King Philip's War was fought in Puritan New England. It was there that the American Revolution began. Bacon's Rebellion was fought in Virginia and actually ended in Yorktown. One hundred years later, the American Revolution would end in this same spot. These cycles and patterns are more than just a coincidence. A close study of the American Revolution in the next chapter will continue to reveal the Israel-America connection, along with more unique Hebraic patterns and parallels.

••• Chapter 5 •••
THE AMERICAN REVOLUTION AND THE CHILDREN OF ISRAEL

The American Revolution was not a common event. Its effects and consequences have already been awful over a great part of the globe. And when and where are they to cease?[1]

—JOHN ADAMS,
LETTER TO H. NILES, FEBRUARY 13, 1818

THE CHILDREN OF Israel journeyed into Egypt a free people. They had the favor of Pharaoh and the protection of Joseph, himself a Hebrew. (See Genesis 47.) As years passed, the Hebrew population grew larger and became a threat to the Egyptians. The only solution was for Pharaoh to make slaves out of the Hebrews (Exod. 1:7–12). The only solution for the Hebrews was to cry out to God for help and deliverance (Exod. 2:23–25).

In comparison, by the year 1775, the colonists were crying out to God and to one another for freedom from the lion of Britain. It was Patrick Henry who cried out, "Give me liberty or give me death."[2] The desire for freedom was brewing in the hearts of Americans.

In Egypt, the focus of the conflict was oppression from Pharaoh. In America, the focus of the conflict was oppression through taxation. The British imposed the Navigation Acts, the Stamp Acts, the Townshend Acts, and the Intolerable Acts. The idea was to make the independent-minded colonists submit. George III had written to Lord North, prime minister of Great Britain: "The dye [*sic*] is now cast, the colonies must either submit or triumph."[3]

In Egypt, God sent Moses to tell Pharaoh, "Let My people go" (Exod. 5:1). During the time the British were pressuring the colonists, it was the Puritan ministers who began preaching liberty and freedom from Britain. Citizens were told not to give up their right of self-rule. The British dispatched troops to Boston, the seat of American patriotism, in order to suppress the rebels in the colonies. The king would not permit any form of self-rule among the people.

In Egypt, when Moses said, "Let My people go," Pharaoh sent more task-masters to add extra burdens on the Hebrews. He felt he could suppress their spirits and cause them to forget their idea about separating from Egypt. In similar fashion, the British felt that their troops would bring the colonists into subjection. In both Egypt and America, the enemy was wrong.

In March of 1770, the Boston Massacre occurred. In December 1773, Boston citizens, dressed like Indians, raided British ships and dumped the expensive tea into the harbor. This Boston Tea Party became a triggering point for the war. New England had led the way in establishing spiritual standards based upon the Bible. The colonists felt God had brought them into their promised land, and now a new pharaoh named King George III was equal to the tyrant the Hebrews faced so long ago. Moses and Aaron faced the strongest nation on earth, Egypt, and with God's help saw a great deliverance. One of our founders drew a seal for the nation with Israel crossing the Red Sea and Pharaoh being drowned in the waters. Another strange prophetic parallel is this: just as Israel was delivered from Egypt during Passover, America would see the beginning of its liberation during the same Jewish feast of Passover.

America and the Passover Connection

And thus you shall eat it: with a belt on your waist, your sandals on your feet, and your staff in your hand. So you shall eat it in haste. It is the LORD's Passover.

—EXODUS 12:11

As you have read and will continue to observe in this book, many important events in U.S. history have coincided with Jewish festivals and special days in Hebrew history. One such parallel involves the birthing of the minutemen. As tension built between the British and the colonists, British General Thomas Gage sent soldiers to seize the munitions stockpiled in Summerville, Massachusetts. Caught off guard, the colonists then met in Worcester, Massachusetts, on September 21, 1774, and urged town meetings to organize companies of minutemen, who could ride and warn of any approaching British force.[4] September 21 was the sixteenth of Tishri and corresponds to the Feast of Tabernacles, the feast commemorating Israel's wanderings in the wilderness. The next Hebrew feast in order would be the feast of Passover. It would be in the spring of the following year, on another Jewish feast day, that America would be ready to *separate from Great Britain*.

According to Scripture, on the fourteenth day of the Hebrew month Nisan, the Hebrews prepared the Passover meal in Egypt. Late that night, as they sat eating in their homes, the destroyer went through the land of Egypt killing the firstborn males and animals.

April 14, 1775, corresponds to the Hebrew date Nisan 14, 5535, the day when Jews were preparing for Passover. On April 14, 1775, orders arrived for Thomas Gage, the British commander in Boston, to move against the rebels and arrest their leaders. Captain Oliver De Lancey carried the orders to Gage from England. The captain was assigned to the 17th Light Dragoons, a cavalry unit. The insignia of the 17th regiment, displayed upon their helmets, was a huge smirking death's head and crossbones. This insignia made an appropriate symbol for the dreadful news that was delivered by his messenger of war. Thousands of years before as the Hebrews prepared for Passover, the destroyer (death angel) would make his way across the land. Is it just a coincidence that De Lancey's arrival fell on the eve of Passover, or is this another amazing connection to Hebrew history?[5]

On Saturday, April 15, the first day of Passover, the Provincial Congress left Concord after being warned by Paul Revere that the British were coming. On Easter Sunday, Revere rode to Lexington to warn John Adams, John Hancock, and others of the danger. On April 18, British patrols were scouring the countryside to find any colonials who might be attempting to warn the countryside of what was coming. A farmer from Lincoln, Massachusetts, met one of these patrols. The colonial farmer heard them coming and, mistaking them for countrymen, said, "Have you heard anything about when the regulars are coming?" Upon hearing this one of the British soldiers swung his sword and slashed the man across his head and took him prisoner. Finally the poor man was released and told not to tell anyone or his house would be burned and he taken prisoner. This was the first American blood drawn at the beginning of the fighting. The man's name was Josiah Nelson.[6]

The Josiah Connection

> And behold, a man of God went from Judah to Bethel by the word of the LORD, and Jeroboam stood by the altar to burn incense. Then he cried out against the altar by the word of the LORD, and said, "O altar, altar! Thus says the LORD: 'Behold, a child, Josiah by name, shall be born to the house of David; and on you he shall sacrifice the priests of the high places who burn incense on you, and men's bones shall be burned on you.'"
>
> —1 KINGS 13:1–2

The Holy Scriptures give us another repeat of history in the story of King Josiah. According to the Bible, Jeroboam was inspired to institute false worship due to his fear of losing his kingdom to the true worship taking place in Jerusalem. Jeroboam initiated false worship in Bethel and Dan so that his subjects would not have to travel to Jerusalem. There were three times in a year that a Jewish male was required to go to Jerusalem and worship. These three festivals were Passover, Pentecost, and the Feast of Tabernacles. No doubt, one of these three festivals was approaching when Jeroboam started considering his predicament, but which one? The Bible tells us in 1 Kings 12:33 that Jeroboam "made offerings on the altar which he had made at Bethel on the fifteenth day of the eighth month, in the month which he had devised in his own heart. And he ordained a feast for the children of Israel."

To identify this eighth Hebrew month, we must understand that in Judaism there are two calendars. The civil calendar begins with the month Tishri; thus, the eighth month would be Iyar, the month following the Passover season. However, in Exodus 12:2, God told Moses, "This month shall be your beginning of months; it shall be the first month of the year to you." The month referred to is the month Nisan. Nisan is the first month of the religious or holiday calendar. So, starting with Nisan, the eighth month would be Cheshvan, the month that follows the Feast of Tabernacles season. So, it was either the approach of Passover or Tabernacles that incited Jeroboam to establish his own religious holiday. Josephus identifies the Feast of Tabernacles as the holiday that Jeroboam sought to keep his subjects away from.[7] So, it was at this time of year that the prophet came and delivered his ominous tidings.

According to *Wilmington's Guide to the Bible*, this prophecy took place around the year 931 B.C. Josephus reveals the identity of the unnamed prophet as Jadon.[8] In Hebrew, the name *Jadon* means "thankful." The name comes from the word that means "hand" or "to stretch out the hand." If Josephus is correct, this has some significant implications. The object of the prophecy, Josiah, whose name means "founded by God," was born approximately in the year 649 B.C.—a difference of 282 years!

Josiah, the boy king, was born to King Amon and his wife, Jedidah. The name *Amon* means "a multitude." It comes from either a root meaning "a tumult," or a root that means "faith, belief, or training." This particular root is also where we get the word *amen*. It is interesting to note that the name Amon is synonymous with the name of the Egyptian sun god. Amon, the Bible says, was a wicked leader who "forsook the LORD God of his fathers." Some of his servants conspired against him and slew the king in his own house (2 Kings 21:22–23).

Due to a revolution, Josiah (founded by God) came to power when he was only eight years old. Josiah broke a long series of rule by absolutely wicked rulers. Before and after him there existed immorality and darkness. The Bible says that when Josiah was sixteen, he began to seek after God. At twenty years, he began purging Jerusalem and Judah of idolatry. At age twenty-six, he began restoring the temple. In the restoration process, a copy of the Law of Moses was found. After hearing the words of the Law, Josiah reinstituted the Law of Moses as the law of the land, basing the government on the Torah's statutes.

Not long after this, Josiah destroyed the altar and burned the high place at Bethel, which Jeroboam had made, fulfilling the prophecy. The Bible goes on to say:

> As Josiah turned, he saw the tombs that were there on the mountain. And he sent and took the bones out of the tombs and burned them on the altar, and defiled it according to the word of the LORD which the man of God proclaimed, who proclaimed these words. Then he said, "What gravestone is this that I see?" So the men of the city told him, "It is the tomb of the man of God who came from Judah and proclaimed these things which you have done against the altar of Bethel." And he said, "Let him alone; let no one move his bones." So they let his bones alone, with the bones of the prophet who came from Samaria. Now Josiah also took away all the shrines of the high places that were in the cities of Samaria, which the kings of Israel had made to provoke the LORD to anger; and he did to them according to all the deeds he had done in Bethel. He executed all the priests of the high places who were there, on the altars, and burned men's bones on them; and he returned to Jerusalem. Then the king commanded all the people, saying, "Keep the Passover to the LORD your God, as it is written in this Book of the Covenant." Such a Passover surely had never been held since the days of the judges who judged Israel, nor in all the days of the kings of Israel and the kings of Judah.
>
> —2 KINGS 23:16–22

Notice that Josiah completely fulfills the prophecy and, in doing so, discovers the sepulcher of the man who had prophesied of him. Instead of desecrating his tomb, Josiah honors him by allowing it to remain. Furthermore, the Bible gives us the general time frame of this event, for as soon as Josiah returns to

Jerusalem, he instructs the people to "keep the Passover." Therefore, the fulfillment of this prophecy came around the time of Passover.

The Prophetic Implications

At about 2:00 a.m. on a Wednesday, the nineteenth of April 1775, Josiah Nelson became the first man to shed his blood for the American Revolution. Let us look at him as representing the Revolution itself. Doing this, we now compare the story of Josiah the king with the American Revolution personified by Josiah Nelson of Lincoln, Massachusetts.

First of all, the name *Amon* (Josiah's father) means "faith, training," or it can mean "multitude." It is also associated with Amon, the Egyptian sun god. Originally, Amon was the Theban god of reproduction, thus the association with the meaning "multitude." Later it was associated with *Ra*, god of the sun, and became known as *Amon-Ra*. Amon-Ra was the most revered of the Egyptian gods.

Apparently, the Hebrew king Amon forsook the "faith" and "training" of his ancestors and lived a life similar to those who worshiped Amon-Ra. King Amon became so evil that his own subjects killed him in his house—you might say they revolted! Only then was Josiah allowed to ascend the throne.

As we have related, the American Revolution is comparable to the Israeli exodus from Egypt, whose chief deity was Amon, the sun god. As Americans, we owe our love of liberty, law, and the gospel to our English forefathers. Their faith and training are what shaped our nation in its infancy. However, there arose a pharaoh who knew not Joseph, and his name was King George III. British subjects revolted against a tyrant king and became their own rulers, just as Amon was overthrown in his own house. It was at this point that the sun began to slowly set on the British Empire. The Americans, personified by Josiah, began the ascent to the throne. Josiah means "founded by God." We believe God founded this nation and that the Revolution was the construction project that would erect His house in the midst of His End Time vineyard.

As stated, the prophecy concerning Josiah was made 282 years before he was born. If America is personified by Josiah, at what point would we have been prophesied about, and by whom?

> I said that some of the prophecies remained yet to be fulfilled. These are great and wonderful things for the earth and the signs are that the Lord is hastening the end. The fact that the gospel must still be preached to so many lands in such a short time—this is what convinces me.
> —CHRISTOPHER COLUMBUS, *BOOK OF PROPHECIES*

> Establish us as thy chosen vineyard and make us as a tree planted by
> the streams of water... plant us, we pray, upon a fruitful sod.
> —PORTIONS OF PRAYERS RECITED ON HOSHANAH RABBAH

You will recall that Columbus saw himself as fulfilling prophecy. He considered that his expedition had accomplished God's will and that he had been God's instrument for furthering the gospel and for the liberation of Jerusalem. Consider also that the day he stepped foot in the New World was Hoshanah Rabbah. On this day the holiday prayers called for God to, "Establish us as His chosen vineyard.... Plant us... on a fruitful sod."

Remember that Columbus saw his discovery as a last-day fulfillment of God's plan to preach the gospel to the nations. All these facts point to Columbus as the personification of the prophet who spoke to Jeroboam. Two hundred eighty-two years after the prophet spoke to King Jeroboam, Josiah (founded of God) was born. According to Josephus, a man named Jadon delivered this prophecy at the end of the Feast of Tabernacles. Jadon comes from a word meaning "to extend a hand."

Hoshanah Rabbah, the day of Columbus's discovery, falls on the first day after the conclusion of the Feast of Tabernacles. The holiday is considered a minor Yom Kippur due to God's decision to seal His decisions from the High Holy Days season. So to illustrate God's seal, a hand is baked upon the holiday bread. The theme of God setting His hand is linked to the prophecies concerning the return of the Jews to the land of Israel in Isaiah 11:11–12 (which was quoted on page 83). Thus, the timing of Columbus's discovery and the motif of God's extended hand (the meaning of Jadon) match perfectly with the prophecy of 1 Kings 13.

October 12, 1492, corresponds with the Hebrew date 21 Tishri, 5253. If we add 282 years to this year, it brings us to the Hebrew year 5535. On the Gregorian calendar, this year would correspond to the fall of 1774 until the fall of 1775. This means that April 19, 1775, the first day of the Revolution, would have been during this Hebrew year. Furthermore, the Bible says that Josiah fulfilled the ancient prophecy at about the time of Passover. The first shots of the Revolution were fired during the seven days of unleavened bread known as Passover.

After Jadon delivered the prophecy, he began his return to Jerusalem by a different route, obeying the word of the Lord saying: "'You shall not eat bread, nor drink water, nor return by the same way you came.' So he went another way and did not return by the way he came to Bethel" (1 Kings 13:9–10). However, the prophet, being coaxed by another "prophet," fell into disobedience and was killed, though not consumed, by a lion.

Likewise, Columbus, being coaxed by greed, fell into disobedience. The nation he represented, Spain, followed suit and killed, persecuted, and sold into slavery those they were supposed to convert—all in the name of Christianity. For a century, Spain dominated the exploration of the New World. Yet that all changed in 1588, when the Spanish Armada was defeated by Great Britain—the lion. This defeat, though not totally destroying the Spanish, helped bring about their subsequent demise. After this battle, the Spanish coffers, previously filled by gold from the New World, were depleted. This famous naval battle also established Britain as the chief naval power of the Old World and, consequently, the dominant power in the New World.

Although the United States was born in April 1775, it would not officially realize that freedom until September 3, 1783, when Great Britain recognized the United States as free and independent states under the Treaty of Paris. So, only after eight years of struggle would America assume her role in the destiny of nations. In like manner, Josiah became king, not at his birth, but when he was eight years old. The Bible relates that Josiah reigned for thirty-one years. This means that he died at the young age of thirty-nine. Thirty-nine years after the Revolution began, America, having survived another war with Britain, signed the Treaty of Ghent. This treaty would forever end America's conflict with Britain.

Josiah's reign was seen as a bright spot in the darkness of the preceding and succeeding Jewish monarchs. At just sixteen years of age, Josiah began seeking the God of his ancestors. During his reign, Josiah reinstituted the Law of Moses as the law of the land. He was responsible for restoring the temple to its previous glory and, of course, ridding the land of the false gods, false prophets, and places of idol worship.

In the same manner, America has been a bright spot in a dark world. We have led the fight for freedom, human rights, and the spread of the gospel. In 1791, sixteen years after the Revolution began, we ratified a revolutionary document called the United States Constitution. This Constitution would insure the liberties of our society and would also serve as a model for other societies in the future. Remarkably, there were originally ten amendments known as the Bill of Rights, corresponding to the Ten Commandments, which outlined God's Law. Our constitutional form of government is based on biblical principles. Certainly, we can see Josiah's story being illustrated throughout our country's history.

Another interesting event happened in 1791. It was in this year that plans were started to build a capital city. It was decided that the city would be along the banks of the Potomac River. George Washington personally selected the site at the head of the navigable Potomac where it meets the Anacostia. Virginia and Maryland donated land to the site, which was called *Columbia* to honor the discoverer of the Americas, Christopher Columbus. Remember that Josiah would not allow the bones of the prophet to be disturbed. To the contrary, the king honored the prophet's memory. In like manner, to this day the memory of Columbus is honored in the capital district of our nation.

One of Josiah's greatest accomplishments was the restoration of the disregarded house of God. We believe the American Josiah continued to restore God's house as well. In its infancy, America based law and order upon the statues from the Bible. The Pilgrim and Puritan fathers had so influenced the Americans that one hundred years later, their descendants were relying on the only credible form of government and self-rule they had ever known. In effect, they were building on the foundation their forefathers had laid. The temple in Jerusalem had long since been destroyed, and Jews were scattered throughout the world. Therefore, it seems God began constructing Himself a "house" in the Americas. In 1838, an American writer named John O'Sullivan wrote: "The far-reaching, the boundless future will be the era of American greatness.... [T]he nation of many nations is destined to manifest to mankind the excellence of divine principles; to establish on earth the noblest temple ever dedicated to the worship of the Most High."[9] As you will see later in this book, Mr. O'Sullivan was more precise in his editorial than even he could have imagined.

Other Prophetic Utterances

In September 1768, the *Boston Gazette* wrote: "If an army should be sent to reduce us to slavery, we will put our lives in our hands and cry to the Judge of all the earth.... Behold how they come to cast us out of this possession which Thou hast given us to inherit. Help us, Lord, our God for we rest on Thee, and in Thy name we go against this multitude."[10] This gives us some insight into what the residents of Boston may have thought about the prospect of war with Britain. Apparently, they felt God was on their side and would fight for them.

Earlier in March and April 1768, the *New York Gazette* had reported the words of William Livingston, Christian statesman and governor of New Jersey:

> Courage, Americans... the finger of God points out a mighty empire to your sons. The savages of the wilderness were never expelled to make room for idolaters and slaves. The land we possess is a gift of Heaven to our fathers. Divine Providence seems to have decreed it to our latest posterity. The day dawns in which the foundation of

this mighty empire is to be laid by the establishment of a regular American Constitution…before seven years roll over our heads, the first stone must be laid.[11]

This is an amazing statement, for exactly seven years later, in April of 1775, the first shots were fired at Lexington-Concord.

The Shot Heard Around the World

By the rude bridge that arched the flood,
Their flag to April's breeze unfurled,
Here once the embattled farmers stood,
And fired the shot heard round the world.

—RALPH WALDO EMERSON,
PORTION OF THE CONCORD HYMN

That first stone, mentioned by the *New York Gazette*, would prove to be a stumbling stone for England (see Matthew 21:42–44), but on the night of April 18, 1775, no one was sure what the next day would bring. Around 10:30 p.m. that evening, a British detachment of about seven hundred men boarded boats, knowing that the secrecy of their expedition had been compromised. Earlier that evening, a British officer had overheard a man say, "The British troops have marched, but they will miss their aim."

"What aim?" the officer asked.

"Why, the cannon at Concord," the man replied.[12]

At about the same time that the British left their barracks, Paul Revere and William Dawes were summoned by Dr. Joseph Warren. Apprised of the British movements, he dispatched these two men to convey the news to the outlying areas. Dawes took the overland route, while Revere was assigned to cross the river to Charlestown. Before fetching his boat, Revere charged Captain John Pulling to have someone hang two lanterns in the steeple of the Old North Church. He then hurried to the north shore where two friends were waiting to ferry him across the river.

Years later, Revere wrote: "It was then young flood, the ship was winding, and the moon was rising."[13] Having nearly a full moon in the sky, it would seem that Revere's boat would have been easy to spot. Even more foreboding was the presence of the great British ship, HMS *Somerset*. It must have seemed hopeless to pass the ship without detection. However, as it turned out, it was the moon that allowed Revere to elude discovery.

Under normal circumstances, Revere's boat would have been seen in the moon's reflection upon the water as the vessel passed near the *Somerset*. However, this night the moon did not rise to the east as it normally did. Instead, it moved to the south and hung very low on the horizon. This caused Revere's boat to be miraculously obscured in a moon shadow that was even darker because of the light around it. Thus, Paul Revere made good his flight from the completely encompassed city of Boston. Although he was eventually caught, Revere, along with Dawes, was successful in alarming the countryside to the British advance.[14]

Sometime after midnight, the town of Lexington was made aware of the British invasion. Shortly after 2:00 a.m., Concord was alarmed by the ringing of the town house bell. With gun in hand, the Reverend William Emerson was the first to answer the call. Reverend Emerson was the great-grandson of Edward Bulkeley. Bulkeley was the man the Indians credited with their unwillingness to raid Concord during King Philip's War one hundred years earlier. They believed that the Great Spirit would punish them if they attacked Concord due to this man's relationship with the Great Spirit. Now, one hundred years later, his descendant rushed to defend his community from the British.

On April 19, 1775, dawn revealed seventy-seven men assembled on the triangular green in Lexington waiting to oppose the British. It was here that Captain Parker, commander of the Lexington militia, uttered the famous words, "Stand your ground! Don't fire unless fired upon! But if they mean to have a war, let it begin here!"[15] At 5:00 a.m. Wednesday morning, it did. Nobody knows exactly who fired the first shot, but when the smoke cleared, eight Americans lay dead, and ten other wounded soldiers were fleeing with their comrades. Jonas Parker had fired once and stood his ground even after being wounded by a bullet. Sinking to his knees, he tried to reload, with bullets, wadding, and flints tossed into his hat upon the ground. Before he could finish reloading, a British bayonet cut him down. Jonathan Harrington, mortally wounded, dragged himself to the door of his house, opposite the northwest corner of the Green, where he died at his wife's feet. Thus, the village of Lexington provided the blood of the first American fatalities of the Revolution.[16]

Even today, as one stands on the Green, he can sense what happened there. Buckman Tavern, from which Paul Revere retrieved a trunk belonging to John Hancock (even as the British were marching up the road), can still be seen. The Hancock-Clarke House, which gave refuge to John Hancock and Samuel Adams, still stands as well. Across the way is the Jonathan Harrington house. One's imagination can almost picture the home's owner sprawled upon its steps, bleeding and dying. It is there that he takes his last breath. Harrington and the other patriots lie underneath a large marker on the southwest corner of the Green. This small parcel of land and its surroundings bear silent witness to the sacrifice made by those first American martyrs.

As one takes all this in, he cannot help but reflect upon what brought them out that Wednesday morning. Was it bravado? Was it an unwillingness to submit to authority? Or was it something more? Many years later, Captain Levi Preston of Danvers, Massachusetts, was asked why he went to battle. Preston denied any knowledge of the Stamp Act and stated that he never drank tea. Captain Preston said he never read a book about the principles of liberty. "In fact," Preston said, "the only books we had were the Bible, the catechism, Watts Psalms and Hymns, and the almanacs." His interviewer then asked, "Well then, what was the matter?" Preston replied, "Young man, what we meant in going for those redcoats was this: we always had governed ourselves and we always meant to. They didn't mean we should."[17]

These people were descendants of the Puritans. Their forefathers were a strong-willed people who loved and trusted God and lived in a committed covenant with the Almighty. They had recognized that it was God who had provided for them since they first inhabited the American shore. It was God who had given them this land for a purpose, and now someone was trying to deny them the right to live free in their God-given inheritance. Paul Revere and his countrymen believed themselves to be heirs of John Winthrop's city on a hill. The godly example of their ancestors inspired them to pursue the destiny God had ordained for them. It is my belief that this covenant relationship was the true motivation for those men at Lexington and the men who were simultaneously assembling at Concord.

The North Bridge

Aside from Reverend Emerson and other Concord civilians, the first militias to arrive at Concord were two companies of the Lincoln militia. Other companies soon joined these men from near and far. As the British advanced, the Americans withdrew across the Concord River to Punkatasset Hill. Just as the Americans were completing their muster, a small British force showed up at the bridge that spanned the river, known as the North Bridge. The rest of the British force remained in the town and began to set fires to several buildings. Upon seeing the smoke, the minutemen and militia, which numbered about four hundred men, began to advance toward the British. At approximately 9:30 a.m., the two sides squared off, separated only by the North Bridge. Just a short distance away was the Old Manse, home of Reverend Emerson. The Puritan minister, who had been instrumental in inspiring the citizen-soldiers, watched from there. Suddenly, there was a burst of gunfire. The British had fired and killed two militiamen. In obedience to orders, the Americans had not fired first. But now Major John Buttrick barked the command, "Fire, fellow soldiers, for God's sake, fire!"[18] Immediately, there was an explosion of musket fire that dropped three redcoats and wounded many others. The veteran British soon broke ranks and ran back to town. They would be running all day—all the way back to Boston!

The Historical Significance of Nisan 19

The fight at Concord lasted only two or three minutes. Yet the result of what was "physically so little, spiritually so significant" was that the way lay open for all that America has since done. Americans were beginning their long journey to complete freedom and self-government. As the Americans pursued the retreating British forces, they were, in a spiritual sense, personifying the waters of the Red Sea overcoming the armies of Pharaoh who had gone to pursue and harass the children of Israel. In fact, it was only by a small miracle that the entire British force was not destroyed or taken prisoner. According to the Hebrew calendar, April 19, 1775, was Nisan 19. Oddly, the Jewish commentator Rashi records that this is the date in Jewish history when Pharaoh set out in pursuit of Israel. So, here at the North Bridge was the birth of the American exodus.

Another striking peculiarity in Jewish history occurred on April 26, 1655. This day was also Nisan 19. On that day, the Dutch West India Company refused to grant permission to Governor Peter Stuyvesant to exclude Jews from New Amsterdam (present-day New York). Therefore, Nisan 19 is a red-letter day in the history of the Jews, and especially the American Jews. This refusal effectively ended official efforts to bar Jews from North America. Furthermore, this guaranteed Jewish economic development and progress, which led to growth of the Jewish population in the New World. To this day, more Jews live in the United States than in the nation of Israel. Is it coincidence that on this same day, Nisan 19, the nation destined to be the greatest nation in the world revolted against its pharaoh?

This nation, throughout its history, has been a haven for Jews. As a nation, we have helped bring about the birth of modern Israel. This rebirth occurred only after the destruction of the greatest threat to modern-day Jewish existence. America was instrumental in ensuring the defeat of Adolf Hitler, who was born on April 20, 1889. In the year 1889, April 20 corresponds to the Hebrew date Nisan 19!

The Stone of Stumbling

Escaped from the house of bondage, Israel of old did not follow after the ways of the Egyptians. To her was given an express dispensation; to her were given new things under the sun. And we Americans are the peculiar, the chosen people—the Israel of our time; we bear the ark of the liberties of the world....God has predestinated, mankind expects, great things from our race; and great things we feel in our souls....We are the pioneers of the world; the advance-guard, sent on through the wilderness of untried things, to break a new path in the New World that is ours.[19]

—Herman Melville

Jesus said to them, "Have you never read in the Scriptures: 'The stone which the builders rejected has become the chief cornerstone. This was the Lord's doing, and it is marvelous in our eyes'?

"Therefore I say to you, the kingdom of God will be taken from you and given to a nation bearing the fruits of it. And whoever falls on this stone will be broken; but on whomever it falls, it will grind him to powder."

—Matthew 21:42–44

Our theory that America is God's End Time vineyard is founded upon these combined scriptures. We believe the nation that would "bring forth fruit" is not only the Christian church but is also the leading Gentile nation, America! Notice also that Jesus identifies the stone the builders rejected as the same stone that causes some to fall and be broken. This is the same stone Peter refers to in his epistle.

Therefore, to you who believe, He is precious; but to those who are disobedient, "The stone which the builders rejected has become the chief cornerstone," and "A stone of stumbling and a rock of offense." They stumble, being disobedient to the word, to which they also were appointed.

But you are a chosen generation, a royal priesthood, a holy nation, His own special people, that you may proclaim the praises of Him who called you out of darkness into His marvelous light; who once were not a people but are now the people of God, who had not obtained mercy but now have obtained mercy.

—1 Peter 2:7–10

Peter calls those who believe in the stone of stumbling a "chosen generation," a holy nation...who once were not a people but are now the people of God." If this can apply to an individual believer, is it possible that it can apply to an entire nation that puts its trust in Jesus, the stone of stumbling? Actually, Peter is quoting Exodus 19:5–6. These same words were spoken by God to Israel at Mount Sinai forty-seven days after they left Egypt. So, originally, this office was given to an entire nation. Israel was to provide a light to the rest of the world and teach the nations of the one true God. After the destruction of the temple, the kingdom of God was taken from them and given to a nation to become temporarily the "chosen generation," a peculiar people and a holy nation.

As I have shown, America, just like her counterpart Israel, was birthed during Passover. I also want to point out the connection that is made with the parable of Matthew 21 and the stone of stumbling mentioned in 1 Peter 2:8. This unites the nation that will render fruit with the stone of stumbling. When the first shots of the American Revolution were fired, the Hebrew year was 5535, written as התקלה. The Hebrew word formed by these letters is *ha takalah*, which according to the Shiloh Hebrew-English Dictionary means "the stumbling block."

Jesus predicted He would become the "stumbling stone," and certainly this has happened. Presently among the Jewish community, if a Jew becomes a believer in Christ as the Messiah and Savior, he or she is often excommunicated not only from the synagogue but also from their family. Some Jews believe a Jew cannot be a Christian and be a Jew at the same time. Therefore conversion to Christianity is considered the ultimate offense. I have a Jewish friend (in Israel) who began stating his faith in Christ, and he was removed from the family will and told never to come into the house again. Christ has become a "stumbling stone." America forever coupled herself with the "stone of stumbling" in order to become a "holy nation." This is our prophetic heritage. To deny America was founded a Christian nation and built upon biblical principles from both the Old and New Testaments is to be willfully ignorant and spiritually blind at the same time.

Summary of the Hebrew Thread

From Columbus through the American Revolution, below is a list of the Hebrew threads that wove together the garment of the American Republic.

1. The Hebrew language: The second governor of the Plymouth Colony, Sir William Bradford, said in his book *History of the Plymouth Colony* that the Hebrew language was the language in which "God, and the angels, spoke to the holy patriarchs of old time." Bradford used the Hebrew language at the beginning of his books. The Founding Fathers discussed making the Hebrew language the official language of the colonies. The early Ivy League universities often taught Hebrew.

2. Israel and America's national documents (the Torah and the Constitution) are both based upon the Scriptures.

3. In England the Pilgrims were called "separatists." The earliest Jews from Abraham's time were called *Ivrim* (Hebrews), which translates as "separatists."

4. Both Abraham and the Pilgrims came into a land that was already inhabited by other people. Both had to possess the land and attempt to teach the native people about God.

5. Both nations were divided between the North and the South.

6. When the Hebrews built Jerusalem as their capital, it belonged to no tribe and was the center of the nation for all thirteen tribes. When the Founding Fathers began to build Washington DC, it was considered a separate city with all colonies claiming it as their capital.

7. The city of Jerusalem was actually built up when the second king, David, took control of the kingdom. David built his house on the mountains of Zion. The White House was completed in time for America's second president, John Adams, to live in it (1800).

8. Israel was founded with thirteen tribes, and America was founded with thirteen colonies.

9. Saul, the first king of Israel, and George Washington, America's first president, were both a head taller than the average man. Oddly, neither King Saul nor George Washington actually wanted to be the leader.

10. When George Washington ran for president, the only man it was suggested to run against him was a man named Israel!

••• Chapter 6 •••

BIBLICAL PATTERNS IN THE NATION'S CAPITAL

I happen temporarily to occupy this big White House. I am living witness that any one of your children may look to come here as my father's child has.[1]

—ABRAHAM LINCOLN

As if these various patterns of American history falling on Hebrew dates are not enough, there is amazing visual evidence of the spiritual connection of our nation to ancient Israel concerning the layout of America and the Mall in Washington DC. This will give us a visible overview of the divine design of our nation.

> Whatever is has been long ago; and whatever is going to be has been before; God brings to pass again what was in the distant past and disappeared.
>
> —ECCLESIASTES 3:15, TLB

In my book *Living in the Final Chapter*, I wrote these words: "There exists a principle in the Bible that teaches: significant events of today almost always have a historical precedent. Moreover, it is God Himself who establishes the pattern in the beginning and who causes it to be repeated in the future."

The greatest examples of this truth are found in the seven feasts of Israel. The crucifixion of Jesus fits the pattern of the Feast of Passover, as we see below:

THE OLD TESTAMENT PASSOVER	THE CRUCIFIXION OF JESUS ON PASSOVER
Lamb was taken into the house on tenth of Aviv.	Jesus entered the temple on the tenth of Aviv.
Lamb was a young male without blemish.	Pilate "found no fault" in Christ.
Lamb was examined for four days.	Jesus was tested by leaders for four days.
Lamb was slaughtered on the fourteenth of Aviv.	Jesus was crucified on the fourteenth of Aviv.

THE OLD TESTAMENT PASSOVER	THE CRUCIFIXION OF JESUS ON PASSOVER
Lamb was killed at 3:00 p.m.	Jesus died at 3:00 p.m.
Lamb was tied to a wooden pole.	Jesus was crucified on a wooden cross.

Another pattern relates to the Feast of Pentecost. The Christian church was birthed on the Day of Pentecost (Acts 2:1–4). The first Pentecost occurred in the wilderness with Moses and Israel. Exodus 19 gives the details of how God came down on the mountain and spoke to Moses, giving him the law of God. Below are a few comparisons to the first Pentecost and the Day of Pentecost when the church was born.

PENTECOST IN MOSES'S TIME (EXODUS 19)	PENTECOST IN PETER'S TIME (ACTS 2)
God spoke in seventy languages so all could hear.	They spoke in the tongues of sixteen nations.
God's voice issued forth as a flame of fire.	Tongues of fire descended upon them.
The mountain shook and quaked.	A sound came like a rushing mighty wind.
Three thousand men were slain.	Three thousand men were converted.

These are two of many biblical examples where one can compare a major prophetic event in the past that is repeated thousands of years later. In America, we can see various prophetic designs and patterns in the nation and in the nation's capital.

As I have illustrated, a Hebrew thread runs throughout America's early history, beginning with Columbus and continuing with the spiritual ideas and writings of the early founders. This thread becomes amazingly clear when comparing the patterns of the tabernacle of Moses in the wilderness with a map of modern America. It is also visible when viewing the four major federal buildings in Washington DC with the symbols of the tribes of Israel that camped in the wilderness. America's heritage is based more on spiritual and religious freedom than just on social justice. The first Pilgrims were seeking religious freedom and a stop to social injustices. This again becomes clearer when seeing the patterns we will share in this chapter.

In Bible prophecy, symbolism is used to represent something that is literal. For example, a lamb can represent Christ (Rev. 5:5–7). A serpent is a common biblical symbol for Satan or the devil (Rev. 12:9). A horn on a beast can represent a king or a kingdom (Rev. 17:12). In prophetic symbolism, the Bible will interpret itself. One of the great symbols of God dwelling among His people is found in the tabernacle of Moses that was constructed in the wilderness and in the magnificent temple in Jerusalem that King Solomon built hundreds of years later.

Both the tabernacle and the temple consisted of a "three-room house," or three sections. There was the outer court, the inner court, and the holy of holies. In 1 Corinthians 3:16, Paul writes: "Do you not know that you are the temple of God...?" Every human is a tripartite creation consisting of a body, soul, and spirit (1 Thess. 5:23). When comparing the earthly temple with our body, we discover the outer court represents the body, the inner court represents the soul, and the holy of holies can represent the human spirit.

Each of the three areas of the tabernacle and temple contained pieces of sacred furniture:

1. The outer court contained two pieces: the brass altar and the laver of water.

2. The inner court contained three pieces: the menorah, the table of showbread, and the golden altar.

3. The holy of holies contained one piece of furniture: the ark of the covenant.

The Old Testament is full of symbolism, and so are the prophetic Books of Daniel and Revelation, both of which deal with the time of the end and contain many prophecies to be fulfilled in the time before Christ's return. The tabernacle in the wilderness was a portable tent in which God's presence dwelt while the Hebrews were receiving the law of God (Torah) and preparing to organize their nation, Israel. While it is not important to detail the tabernacle itself, the position of the sacred furniture is important to understanding the prophetic significance of the United States.

The Position of the Sacred Furniture

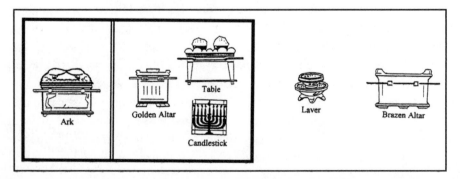

In Moses's tabernacle, the only entrance was situated on the east, where the tribe of Judah camped. Traveling east to west, the sacred furniture in the tabernacle was placed in the following manner.

There were two pieces of furniture in the outer court. The first was the brass altar where the animal sacrifices were offered. (See Exodus 27:1–8.) Fire continually burned upon this altar. In fact, three fires were burning; two were used as backup in case the main fire went out.

The second piece of furniture you would encounter traveling east to west would be the brass laver. (See Exodus 30:17–21.) This was a large round bowl made of brass that in Solomon's day held more than thirty thousand gallons of water. The priest used the brass laver to cleanse his hands and feet before entering the inner court.

Three pieces of furniture were located in the inner court area. To the south was a seven-branched candlestick called a *menorah*. (See Exodus 25:31–40.) Its main function was to provide light for the inner court. Olive oil was placed in the shafts of the menorah, and it was used to light the inner court. Directly across from the menorah to the north was a table of showbread. (See Exodus 25:23–30.) On this table were placed twelve pieces of bread, prepared for the priest from the grains that were harvested from the land.

Continuing westward one would come to the golden altar. (See Exodus 30:1–10.) The golden altar was situated just before the large veil between the inner court and the holy of holies. On this golden altar were placed hot coals of fire and special incense made by the priest. This altar represented the prayers of the saints going up before God to heaven.

Traveling past the golden altar, traveling in a straight line east to west, one would need to pass through a giant veil. This veil was a dividing point between the inner court and the holy of holies. Entering through the veil, one would be in the holy of holies, the most important room in the tabernacle (and the temple). It contained the most important piece of furniture—the ark of the covenant. (See Exodus 25:10–22.) It was to the holy of holies that God came down to visit with the high priest once a year on the Day of Atonement, known as *Yom Kippur*. This entire tabernacle was a dwelling place for the Lord.

Each of these six pieces of furniture had a unique purpose, and each was crafted from a substance that set it apart from the other pieces. For example:

THE FURNITURE	SUBSTANCE USED
The brazen altar	Fire
The brass laver	Water
The candlestick (*menorah*)	Oil
The table of showbread	Wheat and grains

The Furniture	Substance Used
The golden altar	Coals and spices
The ark of the covenant	Gold

This tabernacle in the wilderness was a visible representation of the heavenly temple, where the Almighty is worshiped. This earthly tabernacle was the place where the Lord would visit His people and speak directly to Moses and Aaron. Each piece of furniture had a specific spiritual function. Just as this man-made tabernacle prepared a dwelling place for the Lord, likewise America was a new *spiritual tabernacle* that welcomed the Holy Scriptures and the presence of the Lord. Here the Almighty would have freedom to perform His will through His new vineyard!

The Tabernacle in America

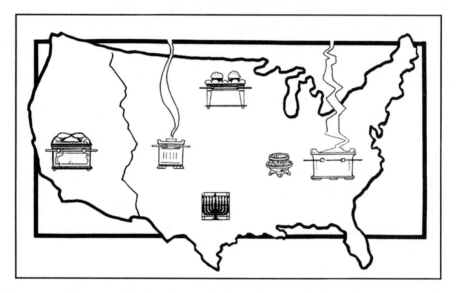

An astonishing pattern develops when we overlay the furniture of the tabernacle on a map of the United States. The shape of Moses's tabernacle was in the form of a large rectangle, with the furniture positioned at exact predesignated locations. If we place a rectangle over a map of America and position the furniture of the tabernacle in this rectangle in the exact positions as in the tabernacle, we discover God's predesigned prophetic parallel in America.

The only entrance to the tabernacle was from the east. America's founders came across the sea and landed on the East Coast. They began building the nation from the east toward the west, in the same manner as one would walk through the wilderness tabernacle. An amazing pattern occurs in America by placing the furniture on a map of America. The furniture positions perfectly on America, but the geographical placement of each piece of furniture from the tabernacle would not fit on any other nation of the earth. Each piece of tabernacle furniture, as well as the main substance or purpose of that furniture, reveals something about that specific area of America. For example:

Coming from the east toward the west, the brass altar would fit in the area of Tennessee, on the edge of Kentucky and Virginia. Fire was the central feature on the brass altar. This area of America is where some of the most dynamic revivals occurred before and after the Civil War, which impacted the entire East Coast. Great revivals burned in Kentucky throughout the 1800s. Many people do not realize that the first major outpouring of the Holy Spirit, one that birthed a major denomination, happened just outside of Cleveland, Tennessee. In 1896, near Murphy, North Carolina, a group of Baptists were baptized in the Holy Spirit. From their experience, the Christian Union was formed, which developed into the Church of God, now headquartered in Cleveland, Tennessee. In fact, the oldest continuing Pentecostal church in the United States is a thriving congregation with thousands of members located in Cleveland, Tennessee. Those revival fires burned in this area where the brass altar is positioned on the map of America.

Traveling in a straight line westward, the next piece of furniture would be the brass laver filled with water, and it would be positioned in the area where the Mississippi River flows. The mighty Mississippi is recognized as the *waterway* of America. It is the source for shipping materials by barge, and it also provides irrigation for thousands of farms in mid-America. I have been fishing several times at the mouth of the Mississippi River, located just south of New Orleans, Louisiana. The main substance in the tabernacle laver was water, and the mighty Mississippi River—the waterway of America—is where the laver would be located on our map of America.

The next piece of furniture in the tabernacle is the golden candlestick, called the *menorah*, whose main substance is oil. Not surprising, the tabernacle menorah would fit on the map of America in Texas and Oklahoma—the two major oil-producing states! The oil in the menorah was used to light the seven-branched candlestick. The oil from Texas and Oklahoma is used to produce energy of every type for much of America. In early America, lanterns containing oil were used to light colonial homes in the evening and early morning hours.

Following the pattern of the tabernacle, by looking to the north we discover that the table of showbread would be placed in the states of Nebraska, Kansas, and the Dakotas. These farming states are recognized as the *breadbasket* of the nation. Many other states also grow corn and wheat, but these states are central to the survival of the nation. In ancient Israel, grains were used to make the bread on the table of showbread, and it rests on the breadbasket of the nation on our map.

The next piece of tabernacle furniture, the golden altar, would be positioned in the region of Colorado. The main substances on the golden altar were hot coals of fire and incense. This incense used in Moses's time was red in color and contained eleven different types of spices. It is believed that some of the incense from the ancient temple was discovered in Qumran, Israel, several years ago, in one of the caves where the Dead Sea scrolls were found. The substance discovered had a deep red color and contained ten of the eleven spices of the temple incense.[2] The state of Colorado was named after the Colorado River, which was named *Rio Colorado*, or "Red River" by Spanish explorers. It means "reddish colored." Red-hot coals were used in the altar in the tabernacle to burn the incense. Colorado has been one of America's highest producers of coal since mining began; today the average coal production is 8.52 tons per miner-hour, one of the most efficient rates in the nation.[3]

After passing the golden altar, the next main feature in the tabernacle was a large veil—a huge curtain dividing the inner court from the holy of holies. On a map of America, the "veil" fits perfectly where the Continental Divide is situated! The Continental Divide is an imaginary line that marks the highest regions in the country. It is clearly seen on any map of America and from any satellite picture.

After passing the veil in the tabernacle, the priest would enter the holy of holies. This was the most important area of the tabernacle. The ark of the covenant, made of purest gold, was the central piece of furniture. On our map of America, this ark would be positioned at the most extreme western area of America. It should come as no surprise that it fits in the area of Nevada and California—two states (especially California) noted for the discovery of gold. In fact, the state of California was founded in the late 1800s because of the *Gold Rush*.

The Almighty designed a dwelling place in the wilderness and designed the size and exact location of each piece of furniture. This moving tent was God's dwelling place among His chosen people. Here they brought offerings, worshiped the Almighty, and heard God's Word spoken through Moses and Aaron.

How sovereign that America is the only nation on earth where the locations of the tabernacle furniture fit perfectly in states that have the same substances as each particular piece of furniture! America is a nation whose finances have brought the gospel to the world, whose worship has reached the heavens, and whose population each week can freely hear the gospel from men and women of God.

Throughout the Scriptures, the Almighty uses biblical symbolism to reveal His mysteries and His greatness. The overlay of the tabernacle is only one indication of America's prophetic design and Hebraic connection. Could this be another visible indication of America being God's new vineyard?

Emblems of the Hebrew Tribes in Washington DC

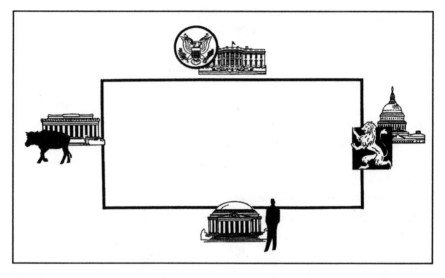

Another interesting visual can be seen when comparing the emblems of the tribes of Israel and several major buildings built around the National Mall. The unique Hebrew patterns continue in America as we examine the governmental heart of the nation, Washington DC. After Israel broke the chains of Egyptian bondage, they crossed the sea toward the Promised Land, just as our founders crossed the sea to the new land of America. The tribes traveled in an orderly fashion, and after the tabernacle was built, they were organized in groups of three tribes to the north, three tribes to the south, three tribes to the east, and three tribes to the west

In each of the four directions there was a main tribe. For example, Judah was on the east, Dan to the north, Reuben to the south, and Manasseh to the west. Judah's entire camp had 186,400 men, making them the largest group (Num. 2:9). The camp to the south, with Reuben at the center, had 151,450 men (v. 16). The second largest camp was Dan to the north with 157,600 men (v. 31). To the west were Ephraim and Manasseh (along with Benjamin) consisting of a total of 108,100 men (v. 24). By including the tribe of Levi, which camped in the middle of camp near the tabernacle, all thirteen tribes were properly positioned.

Each tribe had a special emblem that would become their seal of national identity. The emblem of Judah was a lion, the emblem of Dan was an eagle, Reuben's emblem was a man, and Manasseh's emblem was an ox or a bull.

During the early stages of America there were thirteen colonies, as there were thirteen tribes in ancient Israel. In David's time, Jerusalem became the capital of Israel. Jerusalem is located in the center of the nation of Israel. On July 16, 1790, after seven years of argument over where the permanent seat of government for the young nation of America, President George Washington signed the bill establishing Washington DC as the permanent seat of government of the United States. It was purposely situated in the center of the young nation on the east.[4]

Ancient Jerusalem was built on a foundation of white *Jerusalem limestone*, and the stones on the outer wall were originally white in color. When plans to build the city of Washington were discussed, one man said: "I see white buildings glistening in the sun. I see wide avenues and tree-lined parks. In the exact center of the city, on Jenkins Heights, I see the Capitol. This will be the home of the Congress, the men who make the laws of our new nation." That man was Pierre L'Enfant, an engineer and the main designer of our capital city.[5]

In ancient Israel, at the temple dedication, animals were offered as a sacrifice and eaten as the people rejoiced! When the cornerstone of the first federal building, the Capitol, was placed in 1793, the residents of the village came to see George Washington lay the cornerstone. After the ceremony, a five-hundred-pound ox was killed and served to the guests.[6]

As we all know, over the years the National Mall has become the central feature of Washington DC. It is here, situated along the Mall, that some of the most recognizable buildings and monuments in America stand. These structures are the White House to the north, the Capitol to the east, the Jefferson Memorial to the south, and the Lincoln Memorial to the west, with the Washington Monument in the very heart of the Mall. Several years ago, Bill Cloud showed me something very interesting about the layout of the National Mall and the primary monuments situated on that Mall. By comparing the Mall to the wilderness camp of Israel, some very interesting patterns emerge.

The Emblems of the Camp

Situated at the north of the wilderness camp was the camp of Dan, whose emblem was the eagle. The corresponding "camp" on the National Mall is the White House. The man occupying the White House is the president, whose official seal is the eagle, the same emblem of ancient Dan.

Judah was the tribe on the east of the camp and is represented by a lion. On the eastern extremity of the National Mall sits the Capitol building. In front of the U.S. Capitol stands a statue of Ulysses S. Grant. Grant is memorialized riding upon a horse, overlooking a beautiful fountain. Surrounding this fountain are four stone lions. The lions represent the authority of the lawmakers. Just as Judah's tribal emblem was a lion, and they would be the "lawgiving tribe" (Gen. 49:10), so too the men in the Capitol would pass the laws and legislation for America. Judah was the tribe that led the nation and would produce the *lawgiver*. Congress leads the nation in passing the legislation needed to govern the nations.

To the south was Reuben, whose emblem was a man. It was Reuben who forgot God's laws and tried to act upon his decisions and strength. The Jefferson Memorial sits to the south of the National Mall. Jefferson was not a Christian in the traditional sense of the word but was more of a Deist and ultimately a Unitarian. He believed in a God who had retreated and left the affairs of men to themselves. Only the good nature of men and their reasoning could be trusted. Men like Jefferson were forerunners to what we recognize today as the secular humanism movement. The Jefferson Memorial sits south in the same position as Reuben in the ancient camp in the wilderness and is characterized by the statue of the man himself.

To the west of the National Mall is the Lincoln Memorial. Lincoln was the only president whose first name, Abraham, was the same name of the founder of the Israeli nation. During the time of Abraham, God told the patriarch: "I am your shield, your exceedingly great reward" (Gen. 15:1). God revealed that He would bless Abraham in times of conflict. God also promised Abraham that he would be a great nation. God would bring Abraham's seed out of Egyptian bondage. In order to confirm God's covenant, Abraham took animals and divided them down in the middle. Afterward, "a deep sleep fell upon Abram; and behold, horror and great darkness fell upon him" (v. 12).

In the time of another Abraham, Abraham Lincoln, God had to shield the nation from destruction as it split between the North and the South. A "horror of darkness" ensued, but as old Abraham survived his test, so Abraham Lincoln saw the end to the horrible Civil War.

The camp of Ephraim pitched their tents to the west in the wilderness camp. These two men were sons of Joseph, who was sold into slavery by his own brethren. In the time of Lincoln, slavery was the fuse that ignited the Civil War. Ephraim and Manasseh were born to Joseph in Egypt. As their camp was in the west, so the Lincoln Memorial sits to the west on the National

Mall. During the Civil War in Lincoln's time, two brothers, the North and South, were at war, even as the two brothers, Ephraim and Manasseh, would later divide in Israel. The emblem of Ephraim was a bull or ox. Ironically, the first battle of the Civil War was at Bull Run, in the area of Manassas, Virginia. In the English translation of the Bible, the tribe of Manasseh is called "Manasses" (Rev. 7:6, KJV).

In summary, the eagle is to the north (Dan—the White House), and the lions are to the east (Judah—the Capitol). The emblem of the man sits to the south (Reuben—the Jefferson Memorial), and the bull or ox on the west side (Manassas—the Lincoln Memorial).

The emblems represented by four major tribes surrounding the tabernacle are uniquely a part of the four main federal buildings on the National Mall. These four emblems—the eagle, lion, ox, and man—are the same emblems found on the living creatures that worship God in the throne room in heaven (Rev. 4:6–7). The wilderness camp reflected that setting in heaven. These emblems surrounded the tabernacle where God dwelt. Likewise, in Washington, these four emblems surround one of our most important national monuments, the Washington Monument, dedicated to the memory of the father of our nation. Interestingly, the original plans for that monument intended it to be a temple![7]

The Nation Is Divided

There is a recorded split in Israel's history that parallels the split in America history. David and Solomon ruled for forty years each, or a total of eighty years. Then the kingdom of Israel was divided between the North and the South. The American Civil War started in 1861. Eighty years prior, in 1781, George Washington and the Continental Army had the British commander, Cornwallis, surrounded at Yorktown, Virginia. Cornwallis had to surrender, and for all practical purposes that ended the American Revolution.[8] The new nation had been born. Cornwallis sent an envoy to surrender; Washington also sent one named Benjamin Lincoln. Benjamin Lincoln preserved the work after the Revolution, and Abraham Lincoln, eighty years later, kept the nation from total collapse.[9]

The Cross on the Mall

When the ancient camp of Israel pitched their tents in the wilderness, there were three tribes on four different sides of the camp. The tabernacle sat in the center of the camp, with the twelve tribes pitched around the tabernacle on the north, south, east, and west. If one viewed the camp of Israel in the wilderness from the air, it formed the shape of a cross. In Washington DC, the capital city of America, the Washington Monument sits in the center of the National Mall, and the Mall design itself forms a cross. It is difficult to determine if these designs in Washington were planned purposely or are a matter of chance. Since the Almighty is a God of design and pattern, it is not out of reason to believe there is a visible Hebraic design in America.

Strange Prophetic Numbers and Cycles

We continue to emphasize that God uses patterns, symbols, and cycles to reveal His mysteries. The designs are not just found on the American landscape or the emblems representing the federal buildings. There is another series of patterns with the use of biblical numbers that are important to the Hebrew people and that seem to have a parallel in America.

1. The thirteenth year

On the thirteenth year (plus one day) of a Jewish male child's life, he is inducted into manhood through a ceremony called a *bar mitzvah*. While some hotels refuse to have a thirteenth floor and many consider the number thirteen to be bad luck, this thirteenth year is an important time in the life of a Jewish male child. The only record of Christ's youth is when, as a twelve-year-old young man He debated the scribes and doctors in the temple (Luke 2:46). It was customary at that age for the young men to begin discussing the law and questioning their elders as they prepared for the change from a child to a young man.

In Israel's history there were a total of thirteen tribes. Jacob had twelve sons, and we often hear of the twelve tribes. Yet one of the sons, Levi, was not given a tribal inheritance since the Levites' position was at the tabernacle and the temple. Joseph had two sons, Ephraim and Manasseh, and both were counted with the twelve sons of Jacob, Therefore, there were thirteen tribes taking possession of the Promised Land.

America had thirteen colonies in its early beginning, in the same way Israel had thirteen tribes when it came from the wilderness to settle the Promised Land! The original thirteen colonies evolved over a period of 169 years. Originally there was one colony called Virginia—the *Old Dominion*, named after the virgin queen, Elizabeth I. Over time the others developed, including Massachusetts and the New England colonies, Pennsylvania and the mid-Atlantic colonies, the Carolinas, and finally Georgia.

There is an interesting story about the Carolinas. The Carolinas were divided between North and South Carolina. Joseph had two sons who shared borders in the Promised Land—Ephraim and Manasseh. Afterward, there was a division between the two brothers.

The number thirteen is visible throughout the symbolism of America.

- There were thirteen colonies.
- There are thirteen stripes on our flag.
- Notice the number thirteen in connection to the seal:
  ◊ There are thirteen steps on the pyramid.
  ◊ There are thirteen letters in the Latin above the pyramid.
  ◊ There are thirteen letters in "E Pluribus Unum."
  ◊ There are thirteen stars above the eagle.
  ◊ There are thirteen plumes of feathers on each span of the eagle's wings.
  ◊ There are thirteen bars on the shield.
  ◊ There are thirteen leaves on the olive branch.

2. The thirtieth year

At the age of thirty, a man could enter the priesthood (Num. 4:3). Jesus began His ministry at age thirty (Luke 3:23). The priests in Israel were men from the tribe of Levi who were chosen to lead the nation in spiritual matters and present the offerings and gifts to the Lord in the tabernacle and later at the temple. Thirty is a time of spirituality and spiritual maturity.

Thirty years after the signing of the Declaration of Independence, America experienced one of its greatest revivals since the founding of the new nation. From 1800 to 1810, the flames of revival spread throughout the East Coast and throughout the states. Just as the priest could enter God's presence at age thirty, so our nation began experiencing powerful soul-saving and life-changing revivals in the states and on the frontier at age thirty. Previously, the rather stiff English-style worship was prominent in the northeast. In the southeast, revival fires filled with emotion and conviction were sweeping the states. America was becoming acquainted with the tangible presence of God.

3. The number fifty

Fifty is an important number in the Bible and in Jewish belief. A priest could retire at age fifty (Num. 4:39). Fifty was also important because every fifty years Israel experienced a time of jubilee. The silver trumpets were blasted, and liberty was proclaimed throughout the land. It was a time of release from debts and from slavery. The people were not to oppress one another, and great increase was experienced as God blessed the land with additional fruit and food (Lev. 25:1–55).

During the jubilee year, God instructed that a "stranger" was not to be oppressed. The nation of America has opened its doors to the strangers and foreigners from its beginning. We are a melting pot of immigrants. It is not by chance that America has fifty states. Fifty is the number of rest for the priest and the number for the jubilee cycle. People from around the world come to America to find rest from oppression and to experience freedom.

In 1701, the founder of Pennsylvania, William Penn, signed a charter that was adopted for the entire colony. Fifty years after peace and prosperity reigned in Pennsylvania, a special commemorative bell was cast. Since 1751 when it was hung in the steeple tower to Independence Hall, that bell, known as the *Liberty Bell*, has served as one of America's most beloved symbols of freedom. Before the bell was cast, a speaker named Isaac Norris, a Quaker, selected a portion of scripture from Leviticus 25:10 to be inscribed on the bell. The verse read, "Proclaim liberty throughout all the land unto all the inhabitants thereof" (KJV). The Liberty Bell suffered several hairline cracks, and on George Washington's birthday in 1846, the crack grew larger, and the bell was never rung again. Fifty years after its birth, in 1873, the Liberty Bell was lowered to a spot directly under the tower.

America is marked as a land of freedom for all. In New York sits the Statue of Liberty, a visible symbol for all who come to our shores seeking freedom from oppression. Every fifty years a jubilee transpired in Israel. America grew from thirteen colonies to fifty states. These fifty states are united to encourage life, liberty, and the pursuit of happiness. Just as those who obeyed the Torah were given spiritual liberty and blessing, those who would obey and follow the American Constitution were given a guaranteed right to experience liberty!

This Hebrew thread is alluded to in the name of our country. "The United States of America" is, in Hebrew, literally, "the Covenant Lands of America." Just as ancient Israel was the land of the covenant, likewise America has become the land of the covenant. Consider this:

1. Both Israel and America are founded upon the Bible, the Word of God.

2. Both Israel and America were given responsibility to teach the Word to the nations.

3. Both Israel and America have many patterns and parallels not found in any other nations.

Even the election cycle of the president has a biblical foundation. In the Book of Numbers, the twelve tribes were being counted. The people "assembled all the congregation together on the first day of the second month, and they declared their pedigrees after their families, by the house of their fathers, according to the number of the names, from twenty years old and upward, by their polls" (Num. 1:18). This "polling" or "numbering" revealed how many men were in each tribe. Today, on the second Tuesday of November of every four years we go to the *polls* from every state to vote for our president. The numbers are counted, and the person with the highest electoral votes wins.

The Vikings, Columbus, the Revolutionary War, and the patterns of the tabernacle all reveal the Hebrew thread that wove the fabric of America. This thread is a biblical cord, as America is based upon Judeo-Christian beliefs. The biblical-Hebraic patterns in America continue into the time of the Civil War, as we will see in the next chapter.

Chapter 7

A NATION DIVIDED—THE SPLIT BETWEEN NORTH AND SOUTH

Every kingdom divided against itself is brought to desolation, and a house divided against a house falls.

—LUKE 11:17

A BIBLICAL-HISTORICAL PATTERN WRITTEN in the Old Testament is repeated in American history as we continue to examine the amazing Hebrew connection. Another interesting example is revealed when comparing the division of the nation of Israel and the division in America during the time known as the American Civil War.

When God brought the Hebrews out of Egyptian bondage, there were six hundred thousand men of war (Exod. 12:37). When counting the wives and the children, most scholars estimate the total Hebrew population leaving Egypt at three million. According to the book *Lee's Brief History of the United States*, printed in 1896, the population of America at the signing of the Constitution was about three million![1]

In her 1896 book, Mrs. Susan Lee writes that, "In 1763, slavery existed in all the colonies.... Slaves were much more numerous in the south."[2] Statistics tell the story: "In New England, there were fifty-two free persons to one slave...whereas in the South there were only five free persons to four slaves."[3] Interestingly, when the Hebrews headed toward the Promised Land, among their group was a "mixed multitude" (v. 38). While enslaved in Egypt for four hundred years, some of the Hebrews had married Egyptians. When the Hebrews left the slavery of Egypt, they did not leave the "mixed multitude" to die in the plagues of Egypt. They came out with them, and eventually they became a part of national Israel. White Europeans founded America, but by the time of our independence, we were a "mixed multitude," and our emphasis was upon freedom.

David was the second king of Israel and came from the tribe of Judah, the tribe of the "lawgiver" (Gen. 49:10). David ruled Israel for forty years, then his son Solomon followed for forty years. Their entire combined rule was eighty years. After Solomon's death, his son Rehoboam took control of the nation.

According to the account given in the Bible, it was Rehoboam who caused a split in Israel between the northern and southern kingdoms (1 Kings 12:1–27). This split began eighty years after David became king. As seen earlier, eighty years after God saved America from division, the Civil War dividing the North from the South began.

Splitting Over the "Yoke"

The reason for Israel dividing between the northern kingdom and the southern kingdom is prophetically similar to the reason why America divided between the North and the South. Rehoboam was King Solomon's son who took rule after Solomon's death. Rehoboam sought the advice of both younger and older men as to how he should direct the kingdom. The older men complained that Solomon had placed them under "a grievous yoke" (1 Kings 12:4, KJV). Solomon had forced many Hebrews into heavy labor in order to construct cities and towns and to build a name for himself. The people were tired of the yoke and the heavy taxes. In a strange turn of events, Rehoboam then received advice from the young men he grew up with. Instead of easing the people's burdens, the young counselors said: "Tell the people their yoke will be heavier, and you will chastise them with scorpions!" (See 1 Kings 12:10–11.) The king had been treating his own people as though they were slaves. In the Bible, a yoke is a heavy burden. Solomon had overworked his own people, and they were frustrated. Soon a social rift split the nation, and the kingdom was divided between the north and south. People were tired of being treated like *slaves*. A political rebellion began. "So Israel rebelled against the house of David unto this day" (1 Kings 12:19, KJV).

The split was not only a spiritual and political problem. Rehoboam took one hundred eighty thousand men from Judah and Benjamin to fight "against the house of Israel" (v. 21). Literally, brother was fighting brother. God was grieved with the king's action and warned, "You shall not go up nor fight against your brethren the children of Israel…for this thing is from Me" (v. 24). The split had already been prophesied and predicted to happen; therefore fighting against one another would only cause innocent blood to be shed. The king refused God's instruction and armed the cities of Benjamin and Judah with shields and weapons (2 Chron. 11:12).

Two Capitals and Two Kings

Ten tribes seceded from Israel. Before the Civil War, eleven states seceded from the United States. In Israel, two kings were appointed, one over the northern and one over the southern kingdom. It was Rehoboam who served as "king of the south" and Jeroboam who was appointed as the king of the northern group that seceded.

On February 8, 1861, seven states formed the Confederate States of America and adopted a provisional constitution. The following day, Jefferson Davis was chosen as their president, while Lincoln remained the president of the Union. For a time in America, both the North and the South had two different *kings*.

During the split in ancient Israel, there were two capitals. The established capital was Jerusalem, where Rehoboam ruled. The new capital of the northern kingdom was Dan, where Jeroboam ruled. Notice the strange parallel. As with ancient Israel, America was divided between the North and South. There were two separate presidents and two capitals: Washington DC, the capital of the North, and Montgomery, Alabama (later it was Richmond, Virginia), the capital of the South.

During most of the time Lincoln was president, there was fighting between the North and South. The Bible tells us that in ancient Israel the fighting between the northern and southern kings continued. "And there were wars between Rehoboam and Jeroboam continually" (2 Chron. 12:15, kjv).

The Two Southern Generals

For those who have never studied the Civil War, the South had two famous generals who were effectively defeating the North on almost every front. One was General Robert E. Lee, and the other was Thomas Jonathan "Stonewall" Jackson. Lee was asked to serve as the general of the North by Lincoln, but he declined. When asked about slavery, he replied, "If I owned the four millions of slaves in the South, I would sacrifice them all to the Union—but how can I draw my sword upon Virginia, my native state!"[4] Lee also said, "The future is in the hands of Providence, but, if the slaves of the South were mine, I would surrender them all without a struggle, to avert the war."[5] Many do not realize that Generals Lee and Jackson were both strong praying men and prayed for God to bring revival among their soldiers.[6]

General Lee personally insured that Jewish troops in his command were excused for Sabbath worship, and he issued orders calling for periods of prayer and fasting in his army. He said, "I am nothing but a poor sinner, trusting in Christ alone for salvation."[7] Jackson and his army won victory after victory against the Union armies. When asked how he managed to be so calm in battle he replied, "Captain, my religious belief teaches me to feel as safe in battle as in bed."[8] He prayed often and gave God glory for the smallest successes. He even tried to avoid marching or fighting on the Sabbath day.

According to historians, Jackson prayed that "God would baptize the whole army with His Holy Spirit."[9] His personal letters indicate he ordered religious services to be conducted. During the winter of 1862 and 1863, while the Confederate army camped near the Rappahannock, a great revival broke out. It is estimated that more than one hundred fifty thousand Confederate troops were converted to Christ during the war.[10]

Lincoln's Prayer That Changed the War

In the story of Rehoboam, the nation of Egypt was preparing an invasion of Judah and Jerusalem, the capital city. Scripture says: "So the leaders of Israel and the king humbled themselves; and they said, 'The LORD is righteous.' Now when the LORD saw that they humbled themselves, the word of the LORD came to Shemaiah, saying, 'They have humbled themselves; therefore I will not destroy them, but I will grant them some deliverance. My wrath shall not be poured out on Jerusalem'" (2 Chron. 12:6–7).

According to history, there was great confusion among several of the Union military leaders Lincoln had selected to serve the North. In various places the North was losing battles, and they lost an important battle in Fredericksburg, not far from Washington. Lincoln began to question why the South was so successful in battle. Apparently he realized that prayer, fasting, and faith in God were a key to victory. On July 2, 1864, Congress adopted a resolution that sounded like a lamentation from the Old Testament prophets. It requested citizens to "confess and repent of their manifold sins, implore the compassion and forgiveness of the Almighty, and beseech him as Supreme Ruler of the world not to destroy us a people."[11] It was similar to the prayer that was prayed by the leaders in a divided Israel.

Finally, in the summer of 1864, General Sherman, Admiral Farragut, and General Grant were making inroads in the South and winning major victories. These summer victories caused Lincoln to be elected for another term as president.

It seems that the real turning point in the war favoring the North came after a major decree made by President Abraham Lincoln. The president was concerned why the North was losing so many battles. He concluded it was the nation's chief sins of slavery and pride. Lincoln called for a national Day of Humiliation, Fasting, and Prayer throughout the North. On April 30, 1863, Lincoln stated:

> Whereas it is the duty of nations as well as of men, to own their dependence upon the overruling power of God, to confess their sins

and transgressions, in humble sorrow, yet with assured hope that genuine repentance will lead to mercy and pardon...

He concluded by saying:

> It behooves us then, to humble ourselves before the offended Power, to confess our national sins, and to pray for clemency and forgiveness.[12]

After this decree was made and acted upon by the people in the North, the events of the Civil War began almost immediately to change in their favor. Two days after the decree, in an accidental shooting, General Stonewall Jackson was killed by one of his own men. Soon the battle at Gettysburg came, but without Jackson and Divine Providence, the South would never succeed in the war.

Lincoln later revealed his personal prayer concerning the battle at Gettysburg. If Gettysburg were lost, then the Union would be dissolved. Lincoln confessed:

> In the stress and pinch of the campaign there I went to my room and got down on my knees and prayed Almighty God for victory at Gettysburg. I told Him that this is His country and that the war is His war, but that we really couldn't stand another Fredericksburg or Chancellorsville. And then and there I made a solemn vow with my Maker that if He would stand by the boys at Gettysburg I would stand by Him. And He did, and I will![13]

It is written in 2 Chronicles 12:7, that when God saw the princes and the king of Israel humbling himself, He declared: "They have humbled themselves; therefore I will not destroy them, but I will grant them some deliverance. My wrath shall not be poured out on Jerusalem." Abraham Lincoln was one of America's most humble presidents. Had other leaders been in power, the nation could have been harmed permanently, and the capital, Washington, taken and razed to the ground.

As with ancient Israel, the nation was divided over the *yoke*. Israel's yoke was King Rehoboam making the Hebrews work harder under a heavy tax burden. America's yoke was working people (without pay) as slaves. God promised Israel that one day He would rejoin the divided nation together as one (Ezek. 37:16–19). Divine Providence saved our republic, and America was eventually joined back together as one nation through the prayers and leadership of humble, praying men. The most amazing element of this war was the simple fact that this weary, war-torn nation did not divide permanently. After four years of fighting, Lincoln said he had no hatred in his heart for the people in the South. He would say, "Judge not that ye be not judged. They are just what we would be if in their position."

On March 4, 1865, on the occasion of his second inauguration, Lincoln delivered a speech that some say was the greatest of his life. Stepping forward and kissing a Bible that was open to the fifth chapter of Isaiah, he began his speech. We quote Lincoln's closing remarks:

> Fondly do we hope, fervently do we pray, that this mighty scourge of war may speedily pass away. Yet, if God wills that it continue until all the wealth piled by the bondsman's two hundred and fifty years of unrequited toil shall be sunk, and until every drop of blood drawn with the lash shall be paid by another drawn with the sword, as was said three thousand years ago, so still it must be said "the judgments of the Lord are true and righteous alltogether."
>
> With malice toward none, with charity for all, with firmness in the right as God gives us to see the right, let us strive on to finish the work we are in, to bind up the nation's wounds, to care for him who shall have borne the battle and for his widow and his orphan, to do all which may achieve and cherish a just and lasting peace among ourselves and with all nations.[14]

Little did anyone know that this humble man, who suffered much misfortune and hurt, would go down in history as being one of America's greatest presidents. Also, few suspected that the bullet of a radical young actor named John Wilkes Booth would suddenly cut him down.

During the speech given by Lincoln, he quoted from Isaiah chapter 5, which is the parable of the vineyard. Isaiah 5 is the same Scripture reference we have used as our foundation, showing how God transplanted His spiritual vineyard and raised up America for His purposes! Apparently, Lincoln believed that the prophecy in Isaiah chapter 5 dealt with America and the Civil War. Two months later, to the day, this speech was read at Lincoln's funeral in Springfield, Illinois. The vineyard had survived. It was not the first time nor would it be the last time that America would encounter war. Neither would it be the final time that the nation would grieve over the premature death of its beloved leaders. One hundred years after the death of Lincoln, another famous president would die by the hand of an assassin.

••• Section 2 •••

THE PERILS OF AMERICA'S PRESENT

Chapter 8

THE DESTRUCTION OF AMERICA'S FAMILIES

He shall be a wild man;
His hand shall be against every man,
And every man's hand against him.
And he shall dwell in the presence of all his brethren.

—*GENESIS 16:12*

IF THE DETERIORATION of America's families continues, one hundred years from now a portrait of the American family could be the central feature in a history museum. The God-ordained family unit was the Almighty's method of passing blessings on from one generation to another. The breakup of the home creates stress, financial burdens, anger, and a generation of youth who often turn against the faith of the grandparents and parents. America has a major shortage—a *daddy shortage*. Too many men have gone AWOL on their own children, born in their image and likeness, and it is the children who suffer.

- Fifty percent of first marriages, 67 percent of second, and 74 percent of third marriages end in divorce.[1]
- In 2007, 23 percent of children under the age of eighteen lived with only their mothers, 3 percent of children under eighteen lived with only their fathers, and 4 percent lived with neither parent.[2]
- In 2006, 38 percent of all births were to unmarried women.[3]
- In 2006, 1.8 million households consisted of gay or lesbian couples.[4]

In the 1970s and 1980s, many people argued that the traditional two-parent family consisting of a married biological father and mother and their children was outdated. Today, after three decades of experimenting with the fatherless family, one researcher has come to this conclusion:

> For the best part of thirty years we have been conducting a vast experiment with the family, and now the results are in: the decline of the two-parent, married-couple family has resulted in poverty, ill-health, educational failure, unhappiness, anti-social behaviour, isolation and social exclusion for thousands of women, men and children.[5]

Still today, more and more fathers are leaving their families to live a lifestyle of fornication and promiscuity. When children have no father figure, they will seek something or someone to fill the void.

During World War I, millions of young men lost their lives in battle. Children throughout Europe were fatherless and without brothers and cousins. The rise of Communism sought to fill the gap as Stalin became the father for the masses.

World War II followed as millions again fought throughout Europe. The loss of men created a second-wave void in the homes of mothers and wives. Suddenly, Germany became the mother and Hitler the father of a new German race that the dictator dreamed of forming. The youth of Germany pledged their soul, bodies, and hearts to their new father.

In Islam, a Muslim man can have up to four wives at one time and as many children as he desires. For example, many media reports have stated that Osama bin Laden has more than fifty siblings. Although Muslim children have biological fathers, the religion of Islam actually becomes the father of the family. In nations such as Sudan, millions of men have been murdered, leaving behind their wives, daughters, and children.

Ishmael—the Wounded Teenager

We are beginning to recognize the problems created for children living in fatherless homes. A recent statistical report about children living in fatherless homes states:

CHILDREN FROM FATHERLESS HOMES ARE:
• 4.6 times more likely to commit suicide
• 6.6 times to become teenage mothers (if they are girls, of course)
• 24.3 times more likely to run away
• 15.3 times more likely to have behavioral disorders
• 6.3 times more likely to be in a state-operated institution
• 10.8 times more likely to commit rape
• 6.6 times more likely to drop out of school
• 15.3 times more likely to end up in prison while a teenager[6]

Ishmael is a biblical example of what type of person a child becomes when he is separated from his father. Ishmael was the son of Abraham (Gen. 16:15). His mother was an Egyptian handmaiden who served Abraham's wife, Sarah. For thirteen years Ishmael was Abraham's only son. He had the full attention and affection of Abraham. After Sarah had her own son, Isaac, she demanded that Hagar and Ishmael be expelled from the house (Gen. 21:14). I can only imagine the grief and pain the mother and son experienced. The separation from his biological father birthed a bitter feeling in the young lad. That bitterness is evident today between the sons of Isaac (Israel) and the sons of Ishmael (the Arabs).

Armed with the clothes on their back and a bottle of water, Ishmael and his mother, Hagar, both became stranded in a desert, suffering from heat exhaustion.

> And the water in the skin was used up, and she placed the boy under one of the shrubs. Then she went and sat down across from him at a distance of about a bowshot; for she said to herself, "Let me not see the death of the boy." So she sat opposite him, and lifted her voice and wept.
>
> —Genesis 21:15–16

As Hagar cried out, God provided a well of water to sustain the single mom and her son. Ishmael survived, living in the desert as an archer. Years earlier, before Ishmael was born, God had spoken these words over the young man:

> He shall be a wild man;
> His hand shall be against every man,
> And every man's hand against him.
> And he shall dwell in the presence of all his brethren.
>
> —Genesis 16:12

The word *wild* in Hebrew means to "run wild." It is used for a wild donkey. God was saying that Ishmael would have no stability. He will be like a wild donkey that no one can control. He will be a man of contention and conflict with others, because his "hand shall be against every man." Without fatherly instruction in his teen years, Ishmael became uncontrollable and had no respect for others.

The same wild spirit can be observed in many of our major cities. Gangs of youths roam the alleys and streets, robbing, fighting, maiming, and killing. Their hands are against every person who is not with their group. No one can control them, and fear rules. So many young men in this Ishmael generation end up on drugs and, eventually, in prison.

Dad and God

Most Christian psychologists believe a child compares the nature and love of God with that of their father. If Dad is always angry, then God is mad all the time. If Dad is continually punishing the child, God is always seeking revenge. If Dad is never home, then God is never there when you need Him. Should Dad be lazy, the reflection is that God doesn't really care. If Dad, however, is a caring, affectionate, and loving father, then his nature becomes a reflection of the nature of God in the mind of the child.

Without the male in the life of the child, something or someone else will fill in the gap. Too often the lack of male attention tends to cause a young girl to seek attention from a young man, who all too often is immature and self-serving. She enters a serious relationship, becomes physically involved, and is dumped in a few weeks, only to suffer pain again.

I believe one reason there is much homosexuality in the nation is the fact that many fathers are AWOL from the family.

Why have homosexuality and lesbianism become so widespread in our time? I believe something is seriously lacking in the church, society, and home, which has brought about the increase. Often a young woman who was wounded by men (dad, husband, or relative) connects with another woman, and soon an unhealthy emotional bond is forged. In the case of young men, many young men who tend toward the gay lifestyle have effeminate actions and are mocked as weak and "sissy." At times they are seeking strong male affirmation and are not receiving it through the normal family channels. This causes them many times to seek attention from the wrong crowd.

The Curse of Benjamin

In Israel's early history, one tribe, Benjamin, almost lost its entire heritage. The men of this tribe became completely engrossed in same-sex relationships. (See Judges 19–21.) The other eleven tribes fought the men of Benjamin until it appeared no men would be left. A word came that the other tribes should allow the men to marry women so that their seed would be carried on and their tribe would not be destroyed (Judges 21).

During recent months, there have been many discussions, some aired in interviews on national television, debating the homosexual issue. Some people are saying that there is no place in the Bible where the word *homosexual* is used and no direct reference that forbids a same-sex relationship. While it is true that the word *homosexual* is not in the King James translation of the Bible, sexual activity between the same sex is forbidden:

> You shall not lie with a male as with a woman. It is an abomination.
> —Leviticus 18:22

Sexual immorality, including adultery, fornication, incest, rape, bestiality, and homosexuality, is strongly forbidden in both the Old and New Testaments. Many heathen nations participated in terrible idolatry and sexual sins and were judged by God (Lev. 18:24–25). God warned the Hebrews they too would encounter His wrath if they followed the same path of the ungodly (vv. 26–30). Under the Old Covenant, the Almighty was swift to bring judgment on any form of abomination.

> If a man lies with a male as he lies with a woman, both of them have committed an abomination.
> —Leviticus 20:13

Some may say these warnings were in the Old Testament, and today we are under the New Testament Covenant. Let's view the warnings given in the New Testament. Paul wrote:

> Do you not know that the unrighteous will not inherit the kingdom of God? Do not be deceived. Neither fornicators, nor idolaters, nor adulterers, nor homosexuals, nor sodomites, nor thieves, nor covetous, nor drunkards, nor revilers, nor extortioners will inherit the kingdom of God.
> —1 Corinthians 6:9–10

The King James Version uses the word *effeminate* in place of *homosexuals*. The word *effeminate* in Greek is *malakos*, which means, "a male who submits his body for unnatural lewdness."[7] In the King James Version the phrase "nor abusers of themselves with mankind" is used in place of "sodomites" in the New King James version. In Greek, the term "abusers of themselves with mankind" is *arsenokoitou*, which means "one who lies with a male as a female."[8] This clearly speaks of sexual immorality in the form of homosexuality. Not inheriting the kingdom alludes to not spending eternity with God in His eternal kingdom.

Paul also wrote these words:

> And such were some of you. But you were washed, but you were sanctified, but you were justified in the name of the Lord Jesus and by the Spirit of our God.
>
> —1 CORINTHIANS 6:11

There is hope and deliverance through Jesus Christ for someone bound in a sinful lifestyle!

Paul also wrote to the Christians in Rome, a city controlled by Nero, a persecutor of the Christian faith:

> For the wrath of God is revealed from heaven against all ungodliness and unrighteousness of men, who suppress the truth in unrighteousness...because, although they knew God, they did not glorify Him as God, nor were thankful, but became futile in their thoughts, and their foolish hearts were darkened. Professing to be wise, they became fools, and changed the glory of the incorruptible God into an image made like corruptible man—and birds and four-footed animals and creeping things. Therefore God also gave them up to uncleanness, in the lusts of their hearts, to dishonor their bodies among themselves, who exchanged the truth of God for the lie, and worshiped and served the creature rather than the Creator, who is blessed forever.
>
> For this reason God gave them up to vile passions. For even their women exchanged the natural use for what is against nature. Likewise also the men, leaving the natural use of the woman, burned in their lust for one another, men with men committing what is shameful, and receiving in themselves the penalty of their error which was due. And even as they did not like to retain God in their knowledge, God gave them over to a debased mind, to do those things which are not fitting.
>
> —ROMANS 1:18, 21–28

Three times Paul said, "God gave them over [or up]," because they became vain in their imaginations.

The Early Fathers

Were same-sex relationships permitted in the early church? How did the early fathers of Christianity view the occurrence of men with men and women with women? According to statements from the early fathers, this sexual problem was also prevalent in their time, even among some in the church. The fathers wrote their views as follows.

For the unbelievers and for the contemptuous, and for those who do not submit to the truth but assent to iniquity, when they have been involved in adulteries and fornications and homosexualities and avarice and in lawless idolatries, there will be wrath and indignation, tribulation and anguish; and in the end, such men as these will be detained in everlasting fire.[9]

—St. Theophilus of Antioch, *To Autolycus*, 1, 14

All the other frenzies of passions—impious both toward both [human] bodies and toward the sexes—beyond the laws of nature, we banish not only from the threshold, but from all shelter of the Church, because they are not sins, but monstrosities.[10]

—Tertullian, *On Modesty*

He who is guilty of unseemliness with males will be under discipline for the same time as adulterers.[11]

—St. Basil of Caesarea, "To Amphiilochius, the Canons," Letter 217, 62

If you (O, monk) are young in either body or mind, shun the companionship of other young men and avoid them as you would a flame. For through them the enemy has kindled desires of many and then handed them over to eternal fire, hurling them into the vile pit of the five cities under the pretense of spiritual love...[12]

—St. Basil, *The Renunciation of the World*

[Certain men in the church] come in gazing about at the beauty of women; others curious about the blooming youth of boys. After this, do you not marvel, how bolts are not launched [from heaven], and all these things are not plucked up from their foundations? For worthy both of thunderbolts and hell are the things that are done; but God, who is long-suffering, and of great mercy, forbears awhile His wrath, calling you to repentance and amendment.[13]

—St. John Chrysostom, "Homily 73 on Matthew"

All of these affections then were vile, but chiefly the mad lust after males; for the soul is more the sufferer in sins, and more dishonored, than the body in diseases.... The men have done an insult to nature itself.[14]

—St. John Chrysostom, "Homily 4 on Romans 1:26, 27"

Those shameful acts against nature, such as were committed in Sodom, ought everywhere and always to be detested and punished. If all nations were to do such things, they would be held guilty of the same crime by the law of God which has not made men so that they should use one another in this way.[15]

—ST. AUGUSTINE, *CONFESSIONS* 3:8:15

The Ghost of Sodom Is Rising Again

If history repeats itself, then history will repeat both the good and the bad. The ancient cities of the Middle East became filled with idolatry, fornication, bestiality, and homosexuality. Although these biblical cities are buried beneath tons of dirt, the spirit of those cities is reviving in our nation. The ghost of Sodom is rising again.

Liberal theology and secular "Christians" are offended when a minister preaches on the danger of following the sins of ancient empires. Often they contend: "That's just some story from the Old Testament, and we are in a different time." Perhaps the following warnings penned by Jude and Peter make the case as continual reminders for the super seeker-sensitive believers in North America.

As Sodom and Gomorrah, and the cities around them in a similar manner to these, having given themselves over to sexual immorality and gone after strange flesh, are set forth as an example, suffering the vengeance of eternal fire.

—JUDE 7

And turning the cities of Sodom and Gomorrah into ashes, condemned them to destruction, making them an example to those who afterward would live ungodly.

—2 PETER 2:6

The destruction of the city of Sodom stands as an example to all future generations. If any nation follows the example of the men of Sodom, God makes it clear that nation can, and eventually will, receive the same punishment for their sins. The twenty-first century has witnessed a revival of immorality and an emphasis on special rights, including the right for gay men and women to marry and adopt children. The question is often asked, "Where did this type of sin originate?" The answer appears to be, "After the flood of Noah."

The Curse of Canaan

Years following the universal flood, Noah planted a vineyard and became drunk with the wine. The Bible tells us he was uncovered (naked) lying in his tent (Gen. 9:21). Noah's son Ham (the father of Canaan) entered the tent and saw his father's nude body. He immediately told his two brothers, who entered the tent backward to cover their father (v. 23).

When Noah awoke, Scripture says that he "knew what his younger son had done to him" (v. 24). He then said, "Cursed be Canaan; a servant of servants he shall be to his brethren" (v. 25). For years Christians taught that Ham was cursed, but no place in the Bible does it teach this. Also, Ham was not the younger son of Noah; he was the second son according to the listing in Genesis 5:32; 7:13; and 10:1. So who was the "younger son"? I believe that Noah was speaking of the youngest son of his son Ham, which was Canaan. Noah never cursed Ham, but he did curse Canaan, who is listed as the youngest son of Ham (Gen. 10:6).

Why did Noah curse Canaan? The Bible is not specific in naming the reason, and biblical scholars have differing ideas about the reason. Some believe that, "He pronounces a curse on Canaan the son of Ham (v. 25), in whom Ham is himself cursed, either because this son of his was now more guilty than the rest, or because the posterity of this son was afterwards to be rooted out of their land, to make room for Israel."[16]

Others say: "The real reason must either lie in the fact that Canaan was already walking in the steps of his father's impiety and sin, or else be sought in the name Canaan, in which Noah discerned, through the gift of prophecy, a significant omen; a supposition decidedly favoured by the analogy of the blessing pronounced upon Japhet, which is also founded upon the name."[17]

Still others say that it appears that Canaan went into the tent of his grand-father and performed a homosexual act upon him while he was drunk. After awaking, Noah realized what had happened and placed a curse on Canaan.[18]

According to the Word of God, Canaan and his sons eventually settled in a land known as Canaan land. This region of the country was filled with several descendants of Canaan who had formed large tribes and were identified as the *Canaanites*. A list is found in Genesis 10:15–19.

- The Jebusites
- The Amorites
- The Hivites
- The Arkites

- The Sinites
- The Arvadites
- The Zemarites
- The Hamathites
- The Girgasites

Further insight from Jewish religious literature, the Book of Jasher, reveals more detail about the children of Canaan. Some of his descendants built cities in the land. Several of these cities are mentioned in the Bible.

> And the children of Canaan also built themselves cities, and they called their cities after their names, eleven cities and others without number. And four men from the family of Ham went to the land of the plain; these are the names of the four men, Sodom, Gomorrah, Admah and Zeboyim. And these men built four cities in the land of the plain, and they called the names of their cities after their own names.[19]
>
> —JASHER 10:24–26

The four cities—Sodom, Gomorrah, Admah, and Zeboyim—are named in the Bible as cities of the plain, an area in ancient Israel located near the southern part of the Dead Sea (Gen. 14:2). It was Canaan's descendants who built these cities, and it appears that many in his family lineage were affected with the same *generational curse* as their ancestor. Sodom was a city filled with homosexual activity to the point that Lot was grieved every day with the filthiness of the wicked. What he saw and heard vexed his soul (2 Pet. 2:7).

The writings in Jasher add more insight into the wickedness of Sodom. The laws passed by the four judges opened the door to all forms of sexual perversion.

> And the cities of Sodom had four judges to four cities, and these were their names, Serak in the city of Sodom, Sharkad in Gomorrah, Zabnac in Admah, and Menon in Zeboyim....And by desire of their four judges the people of Sodom and Gomorrah had beds erected in the streets of the cities, and if a man came to these places they laid hold of him and brought him to one of their beds, and by force made him to lie in them.[20]
>
> —JASHER 19:1, 3

Not only was the sin of Canaan transferred through his family seed living in Canaan land, but the judges also passed laws where men could lie in beds in the streets and have relations with another man. No wonder the Bible records: "And the LORD said, 'Because the outcry against Sodom and Gomorrah is great, and because their sin is very grave'" (Gen. 18:20). When it came time for Lot to be evacuated from the city of Sodom, he requested to flee up the mountain to a small city called Zoar. Permission was given, and when the four vile cities were destroyed, Zoar was spared (Gen. 19:19–22). The Book of Jasher does not mention Zoar having a judge. The same laws were not passed in the smaller city, but they were popular and accepted among the larger, more "liberal-minded and tolerant" citizens of the four larger cities.

The Return to Sodom

As I said earlier, it appears that the ghost of Sodom is rising again. When the city existed, both the young and old men were involved in sexual immorality (Gen. 19:5). These lust-filled individuals would come out in the night searching the streets for male strangers they could molest or rape (Gen. 19:4–5). Their wickedness and bondage were so intense that the rioters attempted to tear down the door of Lot's house to gain access to the two male strangers who were spending the night (v. 6).

In a somewhat shocking offer, Lot told the mob he had two daughters who were virgins. He offered his daughters to the rioters to do whatever they wished with them, but he begged them to leave the strangers alone. This passage troubled me for years until I realized that Lot knew the men were so vile they were not interested in women. Their craving was for men only. Had it not been for the supernatural intervention by two angels, Lot himself would have become a victim of the predators.

> And they said, "Stand back!" Then they said, "This one came in to stay here, and he keeps acting as a judge; now we will deal worse with you than with them." So they pressed hard against the man Lot, and came near to break down the door.
>
> —Genesis 19:9

There are places in our nation that host large marches and celebrations for those who practice the same-sex lifestyle. One such city is San Francisco, California. Years ago a fellow minister mailed out a video showing a major gay rally. I was grieved to see signs that read "God is Gay" and "Jesus says gay is cool." Others were dressed like nuns and Catholic priests, as they literally performed vulgar acts on the streets in public in broad daylight.

Two days before Hurricane Katrina struck the coast, there was an annual celebration hosted by the Southern Decadence group. For thirty-five years the group met in New Orleans on the Sunday before Labor Day. It was billed as a large celebration with tens of thousands of gay men dressed in drag. The literature for this group states: "... the whole drunken, rowdy group weaves its drunken way down the streets of the Quarter, one year cutting through St. Louis Basilica when a Mass was in progress."[21]

In 2005, the group was expecting 125,000 to attend this gay celebration and bring $100 million of income to the city. On the planned week of the march, the city was lying in ruins and in water. Prior to the event they boasted, "Not even the fire from the dragon's breath would keep participants and watchers from assembling in the 1200 block of Royal Street..."[22] It wasn't fire from a "dragon" but water from a flood that canceled the event for the first time in thirty-five years.

The New Testament has already warned that Sodom was destroyed as an example to those who would follow in the same sins. While Christians love all sinners and all who do not know Christ, we cannot tolerate the promotion and practice of vile iniquity, which we know will bring the disfavor of God to the nation.

The judges of Sodom were responsible for passing laws that led to the spiritual and moral deterioration of the citizens. During recent years, American judges have legislated from their benches and inserted their personal social opinions into the law instead of defending the law. From prayer and Bible reading being removed to the approval of same-sex marriage, the judges have failed the righteous people in the nation.

The Balaam Strategy Against America

If the righteous do not wake up, speak up, stand up, and pray up, we may find ourselves falling into the Balaam strategy—a plan designed to bring the disfavor of God on the nation. The strange story of Balaam's manipulation, found in Numbers 22–24 and 31, should serve as a warning to us.

Balaam had a unique gift. He was an Old Testament prophet and a seer—one who could see into the future and speak words that came to pass. He was hired by the king of Moab, Balak, to place a verbal curse on the Hebrews after they left Egypt. As Balaam stood to curse Israel, only words of blessing flowed out of his mouth. In frustration, the Moabite king wanted to know how he could curse the Hebrews. This is where Balaam compromised, to his own demise.

The prophet told the king to set up a strategy for bringing the beautiful women of Moab into the camp of Israel, and he instructed the women to seduce the men. (See Numbers 31:15–18.) This action would be a sin in the eyes of the Hebrew God, and He would bring a curse against them for their iniquity. The plan was effective as the Jewish men fell into fornication with the Moabite beauties. God became angry and sent a terrible plague, which spread throughout the camp. Because Balaam "set up" God's elect, his name is negative throughout the Bible.

> Look, these women caused the children of Israel, through the counsel of Balaam, to trespass against the LORD in the incident of Peor, and there was a plague among the congregation of the LORD.
>
> —NUMBERS 31:16

> But I have a few things against you, because you have there those who hold the doctrine of Balaam, who taught Balak to put a stumbling block before the children of Israel, to eat things sacrificed to idols, and to commit sexual immorality.
>
> —REVELATION 2:14

Balaam's strategy was a "stumbling block." This Greek word is *skandalon*, which means "a trap, or a snare set for a person."

As I studied this account, I came to an amazing realization. America is a great nation and has been blessed by the hand of Providence. The Creator planned our beginnings and placed in the hearts of our founders the spiritual desire to make a Christian nation. There are millions of true, God-fearing Christians scattered like lights in the darkness across the nation. Because of the number of righteous people, Satan is unable to curse this nation. I have said, "If God would have spared Sodom for ten righteous, America has far more than ten righteous."

I believe Satan's End Time plan is to cause a majority of the people in our nation to practice sin and live lives of iniquity. In this way, Satan can raise the anger of God, who will be forced to judge us in the same manner Sodom was judged.

The key to preventing Satan's plan from working rests with the righteous remnant. But take heed to this verse in 1 Peter: "And if the righteous scarcely be saved, where shall the ungodly and the sinner appear?" (1 Pet. 4:18, KJV).

• • • Chapter 9 • • •

THE TROUBLE ON AMERICA'S COASTLINES

The nations will rush like the rushing of many waters;
But God will rebuke them and they will flee far away,
And be chased like the chaff of the mountains before the wind,
Like a rolling thing before the whirlwind.
Then behold, at eventide, trouble!
And before the morning, he is no more.
This is the portion of those who plunder us,
And the lot of those who rob us.

—Isaiah 17:13–14

THE ATTACK ON the World Trade Center of 9/11 was called *the worst attack on American soil since Pearl Harbor* and the worst terrorist attack in America's history. That was before the storms that struck the coasts of Louisiana, Alabama, and Mississippi in 2005. Such destruction brings numerous theological questions: Why did God allow this storm? Why couldn't He stop it before it struck? Why did God allow so many churches and Christian's homes to be destroyed along with the casinos, strip clubs, and voodoo shops? Was this storm just another natural disaster, a storm cycle, or a chastisement from God?

These questions always cause a rift among ministers and pastors. In order to balance our positive faith with the understanding of God's judgment of sins, ministers often skirt the issue altogether or stand on opposite sides of the ring attacking those on the other side who hold an opposing view as to why God allowed such destruction.

All Men Suffer at Some Time

First, it must be clear that suffering is a part of living. Human suffering comes in different forms at different times. It may be separation caused by a death or a divorce. It may be loss caused by a job layoff or a violent hurricane. From the cradle to the grave, at some point, all humans will feel pain, and life will seem unfair. Job said, "Man is born to trouble, as the sparks fly upward" (Job 5:7).

146

Living in the End Times

Living in the End Times is exciting. However, we must understand that certain prophecies will be fulfilled in our time, and some of these predictions are not always pleasant. We love the precious promises, but we want to shun the painful prophecies. We must not ignore the warnings, but we must discern their meanings, such as in the prediction Jesus gave in Luke 21:

> And there shall be signs in the sun, and in the moon, and in the stars; and upon the earth distress of nations, with perplexity; the sea and the waves roaring; men's hearts failing them for fear, and for looking after those things which are coming on the earth: for the powers of heaven shall be shaken. And then shall they see the Son of man coming in a cloud with power and great glory.
>
> —Luke 21:25–27, kjv

Notice how four other Bible translations translate verse 25:

> And there will be signs in the sun and moon and stars; and upon the earth [there will be] distress (trouble and anguish) of nations in bewilderment and perplexity [without resources, left wanting, embarrassed, in doubt, not knowing which way to turn] at the roaring (the echo) of the tossing of the sea.
>
> —AMP

> There will be signs in sun and moon and stars, and on the earth dismay among nations, in perplexity at the roaring of the sea and the waves.
>
> —NAS

> There will be signs in the sun, moon and stars. On the earth, nations will be in anguish and perplexity at the roaring and tossing of the sea.
>
> —NIV

> Strange things will happen to the sun, moon, and stars. The nations on earth will be afraid of the roaring sea and tides, and they won't know what to do.
>
> —CEV

Each translation emphasizes that trouble will arise from the sea in the form of waves and billows. The phrase "sea and the waves roaring" (kjv) indicates a noise from the water. The word *roaring* in Greek is *echos*. During the 2004 tsunami that struck the Pacific Rim, eyewitnesses who survived stated they heard a "roaring sound coming from the sea." During a major hurricane there is a roaring sort of echo that can be heard as the winds claw their destructive grip from the sea to the coastlines. We could therefore say that what we have witnessed with the tsunami and the hurricanes fits the imagery given in Christ's warning.

In this same passage He indicated that nations would be in perplexity, not knowing a way out or not knowing what to do because of the agitation caused on the sea and the waves. This is certainly true. Americans have now witnessed how a major hurricane over a major city does more than destroy buildings. The aftermath produces shortages of water, food, and fuel and can birth disease and famine. In 2004, the state of Florida was hit by four major hurricanes, causing stress and great sorrow to many citizens who were stretched almost beyond their human limitations. No wonder Christ said that men's hearts would fail them "from fear and the expectation of those things which are coming" (Luke 21:26).

The Repeat of Noah's Days

A second observation concerns the correlation with the days of Noah. Christ said, "But as the days of Noah were, so also will the coming of the Son of Man be" (Matt. 24:37). Noah was the tenth generation from Adam. Jewish historian Josephus writes that Adam's son Seth, and his sons, recorded in brick and stone a warning concerning the destruction of the earth by water and fire:

> They [Seth's sons] also were the inventors of that peculiar sort of wisdom which is concerned with the heavenly bodies, and their order. And that their inventions might not be lost before they were sufficiently known, upon Adam's prediction that the world was to be destroyed at one time by the force of fire and at another time by the violence and quantity of water, they made two pillars, the one of brick, the other of stone: they inscribed their discoveries on them both, that in case the brick might be destroyed by the flood, the pillar of stone might remain, and exhibit these discoveries to mankind; and also inform them that there was another pillar of brick erected by them. Now this remains in the land of Siriad to this day.[1]

The prediction of water covering the earth was fulfilled in Noah's time when the floodwaters covered the planet. In the Genesis account, there were two major things that produced the floodwaters: "All the fountains of the great deep were broken up, and the windows of heaven were opened" (Gen. 7:11). Water was pouring out from two different places. The word *deep* is the Hebrew word *tehom*, which alludes to underground chambers under the earth that hold underground springs and rivers. At the moment of the Flood, the earth began to split, and the waters underground began gushing out on the earth. The windows of heaven allude to the rain coming from the sky.

This is a perfect picture of both the tsunami and the hurricanes. The tsunami was caused by a major earthquake, which occurred when the plates under the Pacific Rim shifted and a massive tidal wave was created, leaving a large underwater rift under the sea. The "fountains of the deep" were broken! Hurricanes are a result of the wind and rain coming from heaven.

We can look at both of these tragedies and say that they are signs of the "days of Noah" being repeated in our day and time.

Heeding the Warnings

The Scriptures reveal that God visits in mercy before He visits in judgment. Often, prior to His judgment, He warns His people, giving them an opportunity to escape the coming trouble. Such an example is found in Matthew 24. The disciples were bragging on the beauty of the temple in Jerusalem, when Jesus warned:

> Then Jesus went out and departed from the temple, and His disciples came up to show Him the buildings of the temple. And Jesus said to them, "Do you not see all these things? Assuredly, I say to you, not one stone shall be left here upon another, that shall not be thrown down."
> —Matthew 24:1–2

This was a shocking prediction, since the Babylonians had destroyed the temple six hundred years earlier. Later, Christ revealed that they would see a sign indicating the timing of the disaster. He told His followers what to do when they saw Jerusalem surrounded by armies:

> Then let those who are in Judea flee to the mountains. Let him who is on the housetop not go down to take anything out of his house. And let him who is in the field not go back to get his clothes. But woe to those who are pregnant and to those who are nursing babies in those days!
> —Matthew 24:16–19

Three important elements are contained in Christ's prediction. First, He said to get out of the city immediately and head to the mountains. Jerusalem is on a mountain twenty-five hundred feet in elevation. The mountains He referred to were mountains on the other side of the Jordan River, away from the city. Second, He warned that if they were on a housetop, not to come down, and if they were away from home, not to attempt returning to their home to retrieve personal possessions. Finally, He warned that it would be difficult if a woman had a nursing infant when she had to flee the city. Christ knew what was going to occur in the future.

He knew the Roman soldiers would slaughter everyone within the walls of the city. He knew that if a person returned to his or her house, hungry mobs would be robbing and stealing. History reveals a famine that was so bad that people were killing each other for small amounts of food and were boiling their leather boots, attempting to eat them. Jesus gave a warning that destruction was coming, and He revealed the timing—when armies surrounded Jerusalem. He also gave a plan of escape, to the mountains.

This warning was given about forty years prior to the destruction of Jerusalem and the temple in 70. About four years before the Roman troops seized the Holy Mountain, there were a series of signs indicating the soon destruction of the city. These were a combination of supernatural signs and verbal signs.

The Supernatural Signs of the Destruction

According to the Jewish historian Josephus, an eyewitness to the destruction of the city, there was a star resembling a sword that stood over the city. A comet was seen in the sky during an entire year. On the feast of Unleavened Bread, at the ninth hour of the night, a light appeared in the holy house and made it appear as bright as day.[2] There was a mixed reaction among those at the temple:

> This light seemed to be a good sign to the unskillful, but was so interpreted by the sacred scribes, as to portend those events that followed immediately upon it.

Josephus continues to tell how a heifer (female cow) was being led into the temple to be sacrificed, and it gave birth to a lamb. He then tells how the eastern gate of the inner court, which took twenty priests to close, suddenly opened and closed of its own accord. Once again, there was a split reaction among the people. Josephus recalls:

This appeared to the vulgar to be a very happy prodigy, as if God did thereby open them the gate of happiness. But the men of learning understood it, that the security of their holy house was dissolved of its own accord, and that the gate was opened for the advantage of their enemies.

One of the final signs occurred on the feast called Pentecost. While the priests were ministering, they heard a voice saying, "Let us remove hence."[3]

Verbal Warnings Given Before the Invasion

Verbal warnings were also given through a man named Jesus of Ananus, a husbandman. Several years before the destruction, this man went through the city pronouncing a woe of judgment against the city and the temple. At the time, the city was in peace and prosperity, and his predictions were considered out of line among the wealthy and the elite. At the feast of Pentecost he warned:

A voice from the east, a voice from the west, a voice from the four winds, a voice against Jerusalem and the holy house, a voice against the bridegrooms and the brides, and a voice against the whole people!

This stranger went day and night in the lanes of the city crying out and pronouncing warnings. The prominent within the city seized the fellow and had him beaten, hoping to silence his cries. He only continued his warnings. He was then taken by the Roman leaders, who had him scourged to the bone. As he was being whipped he said, "Woe, woe to Jerusalem!" For seven years and five months, at every Jewish festival, he yelled and never grew hoarse. When the Romans invaded the city, the man was standing on the wall still pronouncing his denunciation of the city. Finally, he yelled, "Woe, woe to myself also," and a stone from a Roman catapult struck him and he died.[4]

Two Opposite Predictions

Then, as today, there were two opposing groups. One group recognized the ancient prophecies, saw the sins of the city, and realized that Jerusalem's days were numbered. Others, some even within the temple, discovered a sacred oracle in the temple files that spoke of a leader being raised up. Their faith in this prediction brought a false sense of security and a belief that nothing bad would happen to the city. Josephus concludes his observations by saying:

But these men interpreted these signals according to their own pleasure, and some of them they utterly despised, until their madness
was demonstrated, both by the taking of their city and their own
destruction.[5]

These two groups are present in America. One group is a seeker-sensitive,
people-pleasing ministry that refuses to preach the cross, the blood of Christ,
or the baptism of the Holy Spirit. They do not believe, will not preach, and
mock the idea that God would ever judge America for its sins. The other group
discerns the times, knows the Scriptures that warn about breaking covenant
with God, and recognizes the danger of rejecting the truth. This group can
sense divine chastisement for a nation that has turned its back on God.

As the Roman Tenth Legion broke into the gates of Jerusalem, there were
three categories of people linked to the destruction.

The false prophets who encouraged Jews to remain within the walls of the
city saw the innocent people slaughtered by the swords of the invaders. They
had expected a last-minute divine intervention from God to spare *His city*, but
it never came, because judgment was already set.

A second group simply turned themselves over to the Romans with the
intent of being taken as slaves but having their lives spared. They would
be displaced from their homes, leaving behind their valuables and personal
possessions.

The third group consisted of Christians who heeded the warning of Jesus
to get out of the city and flee to the mountains. According to Philip Schaff
in his eight-volume history, *History of the Christian Church*, this group was
able to escape, apparently between 66–70.[6] For a brief period of time before
the destruction, people had access in and out of the city. Instead of staying
around and waiting to see if God would or would not intervene in the situation, some chose to *get out while the getting was good*. This group escaped to
Pella in the country of Jordan and received asylum. It was necessary for them
to leave behind their familiar surroundings, their homes, and their property
and relocate in order to save their lives from the judgment on the city. A large
Christian community developed from these believers.

Therefore, some heeded the warnings given and escaped destruction. But
others had a false sense of security that nothing would happen to the sacred city.

America's Coastlines

Behold, disaster shall go forth
From nation to nation,

And a great whirlwind shall be raised up
From the farthest parts of the earth.

—JEREMIAH 25:32

Hurricanes and storm surges are nothing new. History has shown that large destructive hurricanes seem to hit the same areas about every forty years.[7]

During the 2005 storm season, the most devastating storm to strike America came to the shores of Louisiana, Alabama, and Mississippi. The damage skyrocketed into billions of dollars, and the loss of life escalated into the thousands.[8] The storm itself did the normal damage of flooding, ripping buildings and homes apart, changing the landscape of the beaches, and tossing ships around like a child playing with plastic toys in the bathtub.

After the initial impact, a breach came in one of the levies protecting New Orleans. The city, which sits below sea level, was suddenly flooded, stranding thousands in their homes and apartments, including countless poor in the projects. As the days passed, the scene turned into something from a horror movie. We watched on television as Americans were called refugees for the first time.[9]

Having association with ministers in Louisiana, I was fully aware that New Orleans had a reputation of being *Sin City*. In fact, in some areas it was not just *Sin City*, but it had the nickname of *Sodom and Gomorrah*.

New Orleans

New Orleans was founded by Jean Baptiste Le Moyne as a port colony in 1718. According to the early history, Indians and slaves were among the thieves, cutthroats, prostitutes, and beggars who were the first settlers in the city.[10]

As of 1994, approximately 15 percent of the population of New Orleans practices voodoo.[11] This religion was introduced through the slave trade around 1510. Voodoo is an ancient African religion, which in New Orleans was mingled with Catholicism. When the slaves came to America, the slave traders attempted to separate the tribal and pagan beliefs from the slaves. However, the slaves simply replaced the names of the African gods with the names of Catholic saints in order to disguise their religion from the general public.

The island of Haiti has the highest concentration of voodoo worship in the Western Hemisphere, but New Orleans has the second highest level. It was, and still is, common to see the candles and altars in shops, homes, and bars across the city. The religion has been inbred there for so long until it was almost a part of the tradition of the city.[12]

One purpose of voodoo is to bring a curse to your enemies, but the main purpose is to open yourself up to evil spirits in order to use the power of the evil spirits to get what you want.

The Mardi Gras

Ancient Romans celebrated a carnival-like event called *Lupercalia* in mid-February every year. When Christianity was introduced to Rome, the early church fathers believed it would be easier for Romans to embrace Christianity if some of the rituals from Roman pagan practices were incorporated into their Christian faith. The carnival atmosphere of *Lupercalia* evolved into what we know today as Mardi Gras, which is celebrated in New Orleans each February.

I have never participated in or personally witnessed Mardi Gras, but I have friends who have attended to minister and witness to the many people present. They admit it was the most perverse *party* in the United States. The idea for most attendees is to abandon all restraint (including moral restraint) by drinking, partying, and having sex before Lent arrives, during which the person must repent. This event was celebrated in Paris and France in the Middle Ages and was brought to America by the French (remember the French Quarter in New Orleans). In French, *Mardi Gras* means "Fat Tuesday," which falls on the day before Ash Wednesday.[13]

In New Orleans, the pre-Christian roots of Mardi Gras have today become linked with the Creole traditions based in voodoo, and Mardi Gras has little, if any, Christian expressions of spiritual experience. The combination of the Mardi Gras festivities and voodoo practices earned New Orleans the title of "America's Most Haunted City" in 1999.[14]

Nations whose religion centers on idolatry and ancestral and spirit worship are nations ruined by poverty. Spirits operating through religions such as voodoo bring a curse of oppression on the people and their land. To illustrate this point, at one time the nation of Haiti was under French control. To provide labor for the rich plantations established on the island, the French imported African slaves. The slaves constantly fought back against their horrible conditions, and in 1804, Haiti became the world's first independent black republic.

During the years of their enslavement, many slave leaders also sought freedom to follow their voodoo practices. "On August 14, 1791, many slave leaders of Haiti held a secret meeting at which they dedicated their country to Satan. Every year since then, witch doctors have met to rededicate the country to Satan, and President Jean-Bertrand Aristide—a Roman Catholic priest—renewed the vow in 2004. When the Haitians won their independence from Napoleon's armies in 1804, they attributed their victory to voodoo."[15]

Today, the cities in Haiti are known as some of the poorest in the Western

Hemisphere. Superstition and poverty reign throughout the island, except in those areas where there is a strong Christian presence.

Hurricane Katrina

The conditions of Sodom prior to God's judgment are recorded in Ezekiel 16:

> Look, this was the iniquity of your sister Sodom: She and her daughter had *pride, fullness of food*, and *abundance of idleness*; neither did she strengthen the hand of the *poor and needy*. And they were *haughty* and *committed abomination* before Me; therefore I took them away as I saw fit.
> —EZEKIEL 16:49–50, EMPHASIS ADDED

The six sins listed by the prophet were:

- Pride
- Overabundance of food
- Prosperous ease (idleness)
- Did not help the poor
- Haughtiness (arrogance)
- Committed abomination (detestable sins; i.e., sexual perversion)

None who understand Scripture would doubt that the destruction of Sodom was some form of divine chastisement or judgment. What about, however, a major city in America? What about the sins of New Orleans? The following sins were prominent in New Orleans prior to the arrival of Hurricane Katrina:

- Prostitution
- Homosexuality and cross dressing
- Strip clubs
- Voodoo worship
- Illegal drugs
- Alcoholism and drunkenness
- Occultism

The most difficult question to answer is: "Was such a tragic event as Hurricane Katarina possibly a time of divine chastisement for the sins of the cities?"

The answer is controversial, due to the fact that so many good people suffered loss and pain. Before attempting to answer this question, we should look at the biblical definition of the word *judgment*. The Old Testament word for *judgment* is the Hebrew word *mishpat*, which means "to pass a verdict, whether favorable or unfavorable." It alludes to God passing a final sentence upon someone or something.

In the New Testament, there are several different words used for the word *judgment*. The first is the phrase *judgment hall* (John 18:28), where Jesus stood trial. There will be a heavenly judgment when the believers will stand before God and be judged for their actions on earth, called the *Bema Seat of Christ* (Rom. 14:10–14).

Paul uses the word *judgment* in Philippians 1:9 (KJV) when he alludes to correctly discerning a matter. Another Greek word is used by Paul for "judgment" in 1 Corinthians 7:25, meaning "an opinion based on information in a court." One word, *krima*, alludes to making a decision related to a crime.

One of the main words is the word *krisis*, from which we derive the word *crisis*. This word means "a separating and then a decision." It is used in a forensic sense, especially of divine judgment:

> [It] denotes a process of investigation, the act of distinguishing and separating—hence a judging, a passing judgment upon a person or a thing; it has a variety of meanings such as judicial authority, tribunal...[16]

In summary, when God sends judgment, it is actually a crisis in which a separation occurs and individuals make a decision to either repent and follow God or to continue to reject God. The Almighty permits severe trouble, or a crisis, after He has investigated the situation and believes the object therein needs to be judged.

How Does Judgment Happen?

Throughout the Scriptures there are four main items used to initiate judgment:

1. The sword—war
2. Fire—burning cities
3. Famine—drought and war and flood
4. Pestilence—plague and disease

The Biggest Question

Any believer could understand why God would permit a divine chastisement or judgment on a wicked city such as Sodom and Gomorrah, or a contemporary city whose sins have reached the heavens. It is difficult, however, for some to believe God would permit the homes and businesses of Christians to be lost along with the homes of voodoo worshipers, drug dealers, and porn kings.

God often gives a warning to provide a way of escape before a major incident occurs. This warning can come through His Word, a dream, a vision, a sign, or a prophetic alert. It can also be given through warnings in the news media. In the Scriptures, warnings are often given to escape to the mountains.

When the five kings of the plain fought against the kings of Shinar, some fell into the slime pits near the Dead Sea, and others escaped:

> Now the Valley of Siddim was full of asphalt pits; and the kings of Sodom and Gomorrah fled; some fell there, and the remainder fled to the mountains.
>
> —GENESIS 14:10

Later, angels warned Lot that the cities of the plain (all five) would be destroyed by God's wrath. There were five large cities and one small city nestled on a mountain overlooking the other four cities. Lot requested to flee to the Zoar, the small city on the mountain. The angels said:

> And when they had brought them forth, they said, Escape for your life! Do not look behind you or stop anywhere in the whole valley; escape to the mountains [of Moab], lest you be consumed.
>
> —GENESIS 19:17, AMP

Lot lost everything, but he was spared from death.

Jesus told His followers to leave Jerusalem and head for the mountains (Matt. 24:16). During the dreaded Tribulation, men will take to the mountains: "And the kings of the earth, the great men, the rich men, the commanders, the mighty men, every slave and every free man, hid themselves in the caves and in the rocks of the mountains" (Rev. 6:15).

The prophet Ezekiel speaks of judgment coming and how some escaped to the mountains:

> The sword is outside,
> And the pestilence and famine within.

Whoever is in the field
Will die by the sword;
And whoever is in the city,
Famine and pestilence will devour him.
Those who survive will escape and be on the mountains
Like doves of the valleys,
All of them mourning,
Each for his iniquity.

—Ezekiel 7:15–16

Going to the Mountains

Often, even though a verse may not make a direct statement, it does imply a truth hidden within the passage. In each of the references in the last section, the verses mention fleeing to the mountains for protection and fleeing from trouble. Jesus said that trouble would occur on the sea and the waves. If storms are going to increase in intensity and in number, then the coastal areas will be the strongest hit. Do these verses indicate that there will be more safety in the mountains than in other areas?

Clearly, the coastal areas of the world are experiencing a shaking on the sea. The Pacific Rim saw a deadly tsunami, killing thousands in eleven nations along the coastal areas. India experienced monsoons, and the Philippines were devastated with floods. In 2004, Florida experienced four large hurricanes, and three southern states saw entire communities wiped out.

A hurricane and a tornado take on the form of a whirlwind or a twister. The biblical prophet Jeremiah saw a vision of how whirlwinds would bring death and destruction throughout the earth:

Thus says the Lord of hosts:

"Behold, disaster shall go forth
From nation to nation,
And a great whirlwind shall be raised up
From the farthest parts of the earth.

"And at that day the slain of the Lord shall be from one end of the earth even to the other end of the earth. They shall not be lamented, or gathered, or buried; they shall become refuse on the ground."

—Jeremiah 25:32–33

Behold, the whirlwind of the LORD
Goes forth with fury,
A continuing whirlwind;
It will fall violently on the head of the wicked.
The fierce anger of the LORD will not return until He has done it,
And until He has performed the intents of His heart.
In the latter days you will consider it.

—JEREMIAH 30:23–24

What About the Righteous?

Lot and his family moved into the city of Sodom, not knowing that the wickedness in the city was gaining the attention of God. Once the iniquity was full, God sent two angels to warn Lot, a righteous man, and to provide a way of escape. This is alluded to by the apostle Peter in 2 Peter 2:4–9:

> For if God did not spare the angels who sinned, but cast them down to hell and delivered them into chains of darkness, to be reserved for judgment; and did not spare the ancient world, but saved Noah, one of eight people, a preacher of righteousness, bringing in the flood on the world of the ungodly; and turning the cities of Sodom and Gomorrah into ashes, condemned them to destruction, making them an example to those who afterward would live ungodly; and delivered righteous Lot, who was oppressed by the filthy conduct of the wicked (for that righteous man, dwelling among them, tormented his righteous soul from day to day by seeing and hearing their lawless deeds)—then the Lord knows how to deliver the godly out of temptations and to reserve the unjust under punishment for the day of judgment.

Many scholars believe there were ten family members connected to Lot living in Sodom, including several married daughters and sons-in-laws (Gen. 19:14).[17] However, only Lot, his wife, and two unmarried daughters escaped. Lot left behind his home, all his furniture, his clothes, food, and personal possessions. He escaped with the clothes on his back and even lived in a cave for a period of time.

Peter called Lot a "righteous man," and yet he lost everything—except his life and two daughters. He and his daughters eventually moved out of the cave and had to rebuild. Often those who survive a disaster will say that what they lost can be replaced, but their family is the most important gift they have. Thankfully, Lot heeded the warning.

Several years ago the Holy Spirit impressed upon me that we would soon enter a time of *selective blessing* and *selective judgment*. The coming moves of the Holy Spirit would not sweep the entire nation as a blanket, but they would fall on selective areas where saints have been in prayer and deep intercession for revival. Likewise, judgment (divine chastisement) would come in selective areas. We see an example in the story of Lot and Zoar. This small community was a part of the five cities marked for destruction. However, Zoar was spared because Lot needed a place of protection and security.

The Separation

In these final days there will be a spiritual separation of the wheat from the tares, the sheep from the goats, and the righteous from the unrighteous. The separation principle is clear in the Book of Exodus where God sends judgment to the Egyptians. The Hebrews lived in the same geographical region where the plagues were striking the Egyptians, yet God made a division between the two. The Almighty said:

> I will make a difference between My people and your people. Tomorrow this sign shall be.
>
> —Exodus 8:23

When the judgment of the flies arrived, the Egyptians were beating them away, but the Hebrews saw none.

> And in that day I will set apart the land of Goshen, in which My people dwell, that no swarms of flies shall be there, in order that you may know that I am the LORD in the midst of the land.
>
> —Exodus 8:22

The plague of darkness should have affected both the Hebrews and Egyptians. God, however, had provided light for His people:

> They did not see one another; nor did anyone rise from his place for three days. But all the children of Israel had light in their dwellings.
>
> —Exodus 10:23

Moses warned that a plague of deadly hail was coming to the area. He instructed the Hebrews to place all their cattle in their homes for protection from the hailstorm. Some in Egypt ignored the warning. Guess whose cows survived when *hail* broke out?

> But he who did not regard the word of the LORD left his servants and his livestock in the field.
>
> —EXODUS 9:21

The mercy of God upon His chosen people was so great that no hail fell in the land of Goshen, a place marked for the Jewish people:

> Only in the land of Goshen, where the children of Israel were, there was no hail.
>
> —EXODUS 9:26

We must remember that in some cities, it has been the sins of the people that brought income into the region, including income from drugs, alcohol, pornography, prostitution, large block parties with profane and vulgar interaction, as well as Gay Day parades and other fleshly sins.

If a city is built on honest business and the integrity of honest leadership, it will be blessed in many ways. Sin cities may prosper for a season; however, that season will be short-lived when God performs His personal investigation.

The Final Sins of the Fathers

Prophetic Scripture indicates that the gay lifestyle will be one of the prominent sins during the time of the end. Jesus compared the seasons of His return to the days of Lot. This righteous man was living in a large city where young and old men alike were involved in homosexual activity (Gen. 19:4–5). This same sin will infest the major cities on Earth prior to Christ's coming. The city of Jerusalem will be referred to spiritually as *Egypt* and *Sodom* during its final days (Rev. 11:8). Even the future Antichrist will be a person who will have no desire for women (Dan. 11:37).

As I mentioned in the previous chapter, while many Americans no longer consider same-sex relations as wrong, the Bible gives this warning, using the example of the destruction of Sodom:

> And turning the cities of Sodom and Gomorrah into ashes, condemned them to destruction, making them an example to those who afterward would live ungodly.
>
> —2 PETER 2:6

> As Sodom and Gomorrah, and the cities around them in a similar manner to these, having given themselves over to sexual immorality

and gone after strange flesh, are set forth as an example, suffering the vengeance of eternal fire.

—JUDE 7

The New Testament writers warn future generations not to follow the same sins of Sodom, since the fiery judgment against the city is an example of the same type of judgment that will follow the practice of the same types of sins today.

• • • Chapter 10 • • •
CHAOS IN AMERICAN CITIES

Give me your tired, your poor,
Your huddled masses yearning to breathe free,
The wretched refuse of your teeming shore.
Send these, the homeless, tempest-tossed, to me:
I lift my lamp beside the golden door.
—INSCRIPTION ON THE STATUE OF LIBERTY

WHEN AMERICA WAS established, thousands of people thronged to our shores and settled in our cities because of the hope of freedom and liberty they had been unable to find in their homelands. Yet today, thousands flee American cities each year because of the violence and danger that face them daily in the danger-filled streets of those cities.

If every nation on Earth has a leading national bondage, what is the spirit of bondage over America? The vision of John recorded in chapters 4 through 22 in the Book of Revelation is a vision concerning things "to come" (Rev. 1:8). The apocalyptic book reveals numerous truths about the time of the end, including the major sins that will be infecting the nations during the time of the Great Tribulation.

> But the rest of mankind, who were not killed by these plagues, did not repent of the works of their hands, that they should not worship demons, and idols of gold, silver, brass, stone, and wood, which can neither see nor hear nor walk. And they did not repent of their murders or their sorceries or their sexual immorality or their thefts.
>
> —REVELATION 9:20–21

The five End Time sins are:

- Idol worship
- Sexual immorality

- Stealing
- Killing other people
- Sorceries

The nation of India and many Asian countries are steeped in idol worship. Sexual immorality is considered a normal human desire and function in all Gentile nations. Murder, including abortion, is an acceptable form of birth control.

But just what does the word *sorceries* mean, and what controls this sin?

The Prince Spirits

There are both angels and strong evil prince spirits that have been given authority over the nations on the earth. The archangel Michael is called the chief prince for the nation of Israel (Dan. 10:13, 21; 12:1). The Hebrew word *chief* is *ri'shown* and alludes to an angel first in time, place, or rank. The word *prince* is *sar* in Hebrew and means a captain or a general. Michael was one of the first chief angels of God's creation. Michael's involvement with Israel is so important that he personally wrestled with Satan concerning the physical body of Moses (Jude 9). Michael also has a host of angels under his command, and they will remove Satan and his angels from the second heaven and cast them to the earth at the middle point of the seven-year tribulation (Rev. 12:7–9).

Satan also has an entourage of evil, identified with the title *principalities* (Eph. 6:12). These strong spirits are demonic generals under the direct control of Satan and are involved in the affairs of nations, especially nations linked to prophetic seasons. These spirits are mentioned in Daniel 10. In that chapter, Daniel had been fasting for twenty-one days in order to receive the understanding of a vision he had received. An angel of God appeared after three weeks and informed the prophet that a prince of the kingdom of Persia had hindered his message. This Persian spirit restrained the messenger of God in the second heaven, leaving Daniel alone to intercede his way into a breakthrough.

At the time of this heavenly battle, the Jews had returned to Jerusalem and were rebuilding the temple. However, they were being greatly hindered by Satan himself (Zech. 3:1–3). Evil prince spirits had been assigned to hinder and delay the prophetic progress of the Jews and the destiny of God's chosen.

In the New Testament, the word *principalities* is also used of earthly magistrates and governmental leaders. Principalities work through personalities. No evil spirits can work in a community, city, or a nation without a willing vessel who submits to the darts and evil thoughts being shot into his or her mind from these agents of evil.

Both angels of God and spirits in Satan's kingdom have been active in the heavens and on the earth since the fall of man in the Garden of Eden. As men moved throughout the earth, setting up cities and empires, both angels and prince spirits took their domain in and around these important centers of human activity.

Selecting the Strongholds

How does a particular prince spirit of Satan determine what region of the earth to seize? I believe the sins of the early founders often became a spiritual magnet to attract spirits that were attracted to a particular sin. There are lying spirits (2 Chron. 18:21), seducing spirits (1 Tim. 4:1, KJV), unclean spirits (Matt. 12:43), foul spirits (Mark 9:25, KJV), deaf and dumb spirits (Mark 9:25), spirits of infirmity (Luke 13:12), spirits of divination (Acts 16:16), spirits of slumber (Rom. 11:8, KJV), and spirits that hinder (2 Cor. 12:7), to list a few. Each spirit has a particular feature that attracts it to a particular sickness, problem, circumstance, and so forth.

After the fall of Adam, there were men who were righteous who called on the name of the Lord (Gen. 4:26). Enoch was so close to God that he was translated into heaven, and Noah found enough grace in God's eyes to be protected from the Flood (Gen. 5:24; 6:8).

However, there were also many wicked men whose imaginations were continually evil and who promoted violence (Gen. 6:13). Between the days of Adam and Noah, which is 1,658 years, a strange race of giants was conceived on Earth, the offspring of fallen angels and the daughters of men.[1] According to Jewish belief, after the flood of Noah, the spirits of the giants became evil spirits, roaming the earth and attacking men.

After the Flood, the three sons of Noah—Shem, Ham, and Japheth—settled with their families into three regions around the Mediterranean. As the population grew, so did the iniquity. Soon the spirits of evil were roaming the earth, seeking those whom they could control. Thus, idolatry, witchcraft, sorcery, and other evils began to spread throughout the earth. Eventually, strong spirits marked their territory for long-term dominion.

Spirits Are Territorial

In Mark 5, Christ was ministering in the land of the Gadarenes, a region of mountains on the eastern side of the Sea of Galilee. A madman met him who was possessed by thousands of evil spirits. The main demon was named *Legion*, a Latin word referring to six thousand Roman soldiers. The spirits asked

Christ not to send them out of the country (Mark 5:10). Christ commanded the demons to depart out of the man, and the spirits exited the madman and entered two thousand swine that were feeding on the hillside.

These particular spirits desired to remain in the region of the country with which they were familiar. This was perhaps due to the large temple that had been constructed for the Greek idol Zeus that towered over the lake. The priest of Zeus offered pigs on the altar! These spirits entered the pigs that were being raised for the altar of Zeus. Jesus not only delivered the maniac, but He also ruined Zeus's offerings![2]

This incident reveals that spirits seek to remain in the land where they have organized and settled. The prince of Persia controlled the land of Persia, just as the prince of Greece had his grip on Greece (Dan. 10:20).

How Spirits Take Dominion of an Area

Every major city has a *personality*. Some have an oppressive atmosphere, and others have a seducing attraction. I have spent the night in hotels where I had difficulty sleeping because I could sense strong spiritual opposition and activity in the heavens. I believe the spirits influencing the leaders in any city are spirits that came to that area as the land was being settled.

Before the Pilgrims founded our first colonies, there were numerous Indian tribes scattered throughout our continent. These included the Cherokee, Choctaw, Cheyenne, Navaho, Creek, Seminole, and Chickasaw, to name a few. Most Indian tribes had a medicine man. This person was not a medical doctor but a spiritual, religious leader.

In such states as New Mexico there are shamans, powerful men who are controlled by evil spirits and are able to perform frightening supernatural feats that frighten and impress their followers. Included in their occult arsenal are objects called *dream catchers* and *kachina dolls*. Missionaries have informed me that the dolls are actually cursed by the shamans and sold to the white men in order to curse them for oppressing the Indians. There are also skin walkers who can levitate and have power to curse people with sickness and accidents. The skin walkers are feared and revered by the other Indians. These occult leaders use various drugs to enhance their spiritual perception.

One of the tragedies among Native American Indian tribes is alcoholism. Much of this can be traced back to the white men who brought the hard liquor to the ancestors of the Indians when they were trading, buying, and selling.

In the early days of the colonies, there were strange manifestations in areas like Massachusetts. In the Salem area there were numerous accusations that some people were possessed with demons. These individuals were accused of being witches and were burned at the stake. Several centuries have passed, and today, Salem, Massachusetts, is a stronghold for literal witchcraft and the practice of the occult.

Another example of territorial evil spirits is the state of California. This large western state became famous when gold was found at Sutter's Mill (near San Francisco) in 1849. This discovery initiated a massive exodus from the East to the West, as miners and common men sought wealth through mining gold. Many men took this rough journey, often leaving women and children behind hundreds of miles away to keep the home fires. On Saturday nights, men would often dress as women, and the other miners would dance with them, since the "real" women were not in the mining camps. At times this led to other activities such as same-sex relations.[3]

Today, the state seal of California depicts *Minerva*, a Roman goddess (woman) dressed in a Roman soldier's military outfit, overlooking the San Francisco Bay![4] For years the city of San Francisco has been recognized as the gay capital of America, especially the West Coast, and as one of American's most liberal cities. How strange that this women who is dressed like a man overlooks the bay.

Some of America's cities were founded by leaders who were heavily involved in secret orders and lodges.[5] In each instance, this secrecy eventually led to a spirit that hid the many sins and iniquities of its leaders and opened the door to corruption.

America's Prince Spirit

Individual cities have their own personalities, and all fifty states have their own chief spirits working within the borders of that state. America is a nation with fifty states and one capital, Washington DC. Is there one main principality hovering over our nation, and if so, what is its name and assignment?

I believe America's chief evil spirit is linked to the main sin sweeping our nation—the sin of sorcery.

> And they did not repent of their murders or their *sorceries* or their sexual immorality or their thefts.
>
> —REVELATION 9:21, EMPHASIS ADDED

The English word *sorcery* paints a mental picture of a sorcerer or witch casting spells on its victims. The Greek word, however, carries a broader meaning. The word *sorceries* in Revelation 9:21 is *pharmakeus*. We derive the words *pharmacy* and *pharmaceutical* from a form of this word. The Greek dictionary gives this definition for the word *pharmakos* (another version of *pharmakeus*): "An adjective signifying 'devoted to magical arts,' is used as a noun, 'a sorcerer,' especially one who uses drugs, portions, spells, enchantments."[6]

The word can signify the use of drugs. May I say…the root cause for most crimes in America is the use of illegal drugs. The vast majority of men and women incarcerated in American prisons are there because of selling or buying hard-core drugs. The majority of crimes committed, such as robberies, break-ins, and even murder, are the result of stealing money or stealing something to sell for money in order to support a drug habit and drug addiction. America is an addicted society.

In the early church, the Christians encountered the spirit of sorcery in different forms. During the revival at Ephesus, many occult books valued at thousands of dollars were burned (Acts 19). In Samaria, Simon the sorcerer bewitched the people and was rebuked by Peter during the great Samaritan revival (Acts 8). In Paphos, Elymas the sorcerer was a main leader (Acts 13). In Philippi, Paul had to confront a woman with a spirit of divination (Acts 16). The word *divination* is the word *puthon*, or in English, *python*. A large temple had been built to house a snake, and people would go into the temple to receive information about their futures from the snake. Once this evil spirit was cast out of this female fortune-teller, the men of the city became angry with Paul because the superstitious citizens refused to buy their idols any longer.

During the 1990s, the television was filled with infomercials of so-called *psychics* who claimed to tell your future for only $5.95 a minute. Ignorant Americans ran up their phone bills to hear an alleged psychic tell them things they already knew! One woman admitted to spending $30,000 during the course of a few months because she was addicted to talking to the psychic. She would not even go out of the house without consulting the so-called fortune-teller.

Many of these moneymaking psychics failed to discern their debts, and a majority of them went off the air, unable to pay the high cost of television airtime. However, our current economic crisis has once again caused many to begin seeking the advice of psychics. CBS station WCBS-TV in New York City recently reported: "With a lot of people cutting back in this tough economy, more and more people are looking to psychics for answers."[7]

I do not believe that these fakers are the real spirits in the nation. The real spirits are killing and destroying the minds of millions of Americans through drug addiction. The *pharmakeus* spirit of sorcery is the chief spirit controlling the United States. Millions have experimented with and are addicted to many kinds of drugs, including:

- Marijuana (pot)
- LSD
- Heroin
- Cocaine
- Crack cocaine
- Meth
- Ecstasy
- Prescription painkillers
- Antidepressants
- Steroids

One of the most addictive drugs is cocaine. For years I thought cocaine was a modern invention. I was shocked to discover how long this drug has been in our culture.

Andean Indians have long chewed leaves of the coca plant to decrease hunger and increase their stamina for work. In 1863, Europe introduced Vin Mariani, or coca wine, which quickly became the world's most popular prescription. "Writers loved it. Anatole France, Henrik Ibsen, Émile Zola, Jules Verne, Alexander Dumas, Robert Louis Stephenson, Sir Arthur Conan Doyle, and other literary luminaries all indulged freely. Composers such as Massenet, Gounod, and Fauré gratefully honoured the Corsican druggist in their music. Vin Mariani was celebrated by royalty as well: by Queen Victoria; King George 1 of Greece; King Alphonse XIII of Spain; the Shah of Persia; and by William McKinley, President of the United States."[8] By the 1880s in the United States, physicians were freely prescribing the cocaine extracted from the coca plants for exhaustion, depression, and morphine addiction. It was also available in many patent medicines. After users and physicians began to realize its dangers and various regulations were enacted, its use decreased, and by the 1920s the epidemic had abated.

A new epidemic began in the United States in the 1970s and peaked in the mid-1980s as a crack cocaine epidemic. Violence erupted in crack-infested neighborhoods, and young people, lured by the power and money of being crack dealers, began carrying guns and murdering each other in the drug gang wars that followed.[9]

Perhaps the most interesting early link was with a drink concoction developed by John Stith Pemberton. The pharmacist wanted to invent a "pick-me-up" drink, so he prepared a special syrup that he mixed with soda fountain water. One of the key ingredients in the early drink was cocaine. The new drink would be called Coca Cola! Coke became a smash hit, even though the cocaine was removed in 1903 after a presidential commission revealed the danger and addictive power of cocaine.[10]

The Addiction Demon

Millions of Americans are addicted to something. For some it is illegal drugs, and for others, pornography. Some cannot break the desire to gamble, and some are bound by alcohol.

The statistics on alcohol in America are staggering:

- Americans spend over $90 billion total on alcohol each year.[11]
- Over 15 million Americans are dependent on alcohol, with five hundred thousand being between the ages of nine and twelve.[12]
- Up to 40 percent of all industrial fatalities and 47 percent of industrial injuries can be linked to alcohol consumption and alcoholism.[13]
- Forty-three percent of Americans have been exposed to alcoholism in their families.[14]
- Alcohol is involved in 50 percent of all driving fatalities.[15]
- Each year students spend $5.5 billion on alcohol, more than they spend on soft drinks, tea, milk, juice, coffee, or books combined.[16]

Although alcohol is America's number one drug problem, there are alarming statistics available to show the severity of America's drug problem.

- Among teens age twelve to seventeen, the average age of first trying marijuana was fourteen years old.[17]
- According to the Minnesota Institute for Public Health and drug prevention resource center, in 1985, each day five thousand adults in the United States tried cocaine for the first time.[18]
- Today it is estimated that 22 to 25 million people have tried cocaine at least once. Conservative estimates indicate that there are over 2 million cocaine addicts in the United States today.[19]
- Heroin is a highly addictive drug, and its use is a serious problem in America. Current estimates suggest that nearly six

hundred thousand people need treatment for heroin addiction. Recent studies suggest a shift from injecting heroin to snorting or smoking because of increased purity and the misconception that these forms of use will not lead to addiction.[20]

Cursed Cities

The spirit of drug addiction has brought a terrible curse on our cities. This spirit breeds off a spirit of poverty. The largest drug strongholds are among the poor in the inner cities. The feeling of hopelessness hovering over the projects induces the desire to escape the pain, suffering, loneliness, and rejection of life. Drugs become addicts' best friend, taking them to high highs and low lows, promising them a trip of escape that ends in a pit of more despair.[21]

Poor young men join gangs for acceptance and survival, and they begin selling drugs to their own friends for a small piece of the pie. Soon the children are seeing Junior riding in a new car with gold chains hanging halfway down his chest. Sadly, they don't see Junior in the morgue twelve months later or attend his trial for selling the illegal powder.

A former big-time drug dealer told me that the little man means nothing to the big bosses. They are expendable and are knocked off on a continual basis. He also said the reason that America cannot get a grip on illegal drugs is because too many men in high places are paid to turn their heads the other way. This includes certain members of the border police, U.S. Customs, and local police. He also said that the payoffs go as high as men in Washington. He said, "Often when you see a drug bust, it is a bad batch that is permitted to get seized for the news so it appears the war on drugs is being won. All the time the real good stuff is coming from another direction." He added, "The war on drugs will never be won because too many men have their hands in the pockets of the drug kingpins."[22] Drug money from Afghanistan helps provide funds for terrorists, and drug money from Lebanon is also used to provide weapons for terror groups.[23]

Yes, America has been hypnotized by greed and addiction, and this addiction is passed down from generation to generation, which is the very reason for this spirit to work. The attack is always about the *future seed*. Every sin in our generation is an assignment against children. Abortion stops the life of a human soul. Same-sex couples cannot reproduce a child. Drugs can make a man impotent, and alcohol destroys the family unit. The AIDS virus destroys the future of an entire generation. The attack is on the *seed*. As proof, we are seeing more child abuse, more molestation, and a greater rise in the numbers of pedophiles than ever before.[24]

What Can We Do?

It is not wise for a believer to challenge head-on the ruling spirits over a nation or a country. There is evidence that those who have attempted this have often found themselves fighting life-and-death personal battles that overwhelmed their souls. In the Bible, God sent His highest-ranking angels to directly engage in spiritual conflict with the prince spirits. In Daniel 10, Michael the archangel had to come to the rescue of Gabriel (the angel of God's presence), who was hindered by the prince of Persia for twenty-one days.

However, we have been given spiritual authority though prayer! As an example, Colombia is noted as the drug capital of the world. Years ago I was the speaker for a telethon to raise money to help place a stronger television tower in Cali, Colombia, so the gospel could reach more in the city. That night we raised almost a hundred thousand dollars. The telethon leader called one of the pastors of the area and woke him to tell him the money was raised for the tower.

On the phone, over live television, this pastor began to tell us that he and his associate pastor had received death threats from the drug lords in Colombia. The pastor had started a prayer meeting asking God to bring down the drug kingpins in the nation. At first people were afraid to attend the meeting, since the drug cartel was known to kill people they disagreed with. Soon the crowds swelled to more than thirty thousand. As prayer went up, the drugs lords went down. One at a time they were either captured or killed. In fact, nine of the ten were removed by the power of prayer.[25]

Just as Michael the archangel restrained the prince of Persia, we need to ask God to send His strongest heavenly warring angels to engage in the heavens over America. We need the spirit of *pharmakeus* restrained and his authority broken so this generation coming up will have no interest in drugs, alcohol, and the bondages that come with addictions. If it can happen in Colombia, it can happen in America. God is just looking for the intercessors.

> So I sought for a man among them who would make a wall, and stand in the gap before Me on behalf of the land, that I should not destroy it; but I found no one.
>
> —EZEKIEL 22:30

Chapter 11

AMERICA'S IDENTITY CRISIS

One of the great strengths of the United States is—although ... we have a very large Christian population, we do not consider ourselves a Christian nation or a Jewish nation or a Muslim nation; we consider ourselves a nation of citizens who are bound by ideals and a set of values.[1]

—PRESIDENT BARACK OBAMA

SINCE THE FOUNDING of America, our nation has been on a slow downward spiral in our acceptance of the fact that America was founded on Christian principles and established as a Christian nation. Today, the hatred and bias against Christianity carry over into the writings of those who write the content for our public schools' curricula.

One of the remarkable stories that was once found in most American history books is never told in today's public school classrooms. You may have never heard about the miracle of George Washington's protection in time of war, but the story is too important not to be told, so here it is.

George Washington was a man of destiny. A strange historical account reveals that even bullets could not kill him! In a letter to his mother, he acknowledged God's providence and protection. In April of 1755, British General Braddock invited Washington to assist in the French and Indian War. When Washington accepted the invitation, his mother was concerned for his safety. Washington wrote her:

> The God to whom you commended me, madam, when I set out upon a more perilous errand, defended me from all harm, and I trust He will do so now. Do not you?[2]

Soon thereafter, on July 9, 1755, Washington served as an aide to British General Braddock. A terrible battle ensued near the Monongahela River. In the heat of the battle, hundreds of American and British soldiers were slain.

Washington rode through the gunfire and gave orders to soldiers. When the battle ended, sixty-three of the eighty-six British and American officers lay dead. Washington was the only officer on horseback who was not wounded. In a letter to his brother, Washington told a remarkable story, proving Washington's destiny had been sealed by the hand of God.

> By the all-powerful dispensations of Providence, I have been protected beyond all human probability or expectations; for I had four bullets through my coat, and two horses shot under me, yet escaped unhurt, although death was leveling my companions on every side of me.[3]

According to an early historical account, an Indian who was present at the time was reported saying, "Washington was never born to be killed by a bullet! For I had seventeen fair fires at him with my rifle, and after all could not bring him to the ground."[4]

In the biography of Mary Draper Ingalls, she reported that while being held by the Indians, she overheard a conversation between French soldiers and her captors. They said that an Indian chief named Red Hawk personally told them that he shot Washington eleven times without killing him. Finally he ceased firing and was convinced that the Great Spirit was protecting him.[5]

David Barton wrote:

> Eighty years after the battle, Washington's gold seal and his initials on it were found on the battleground. It was a belt buckle that had been shot off him in the battle. The relic is in the possession of the family. True to the Indian's prophecy, Washington was never wounded in battle.[6]

Why would revisionists of history want to erase any reference to this amazing story of our first president from American history textbooks?

It's sad, but true, that while no secular humanist, liberal journalist, or college sociologist considers America a *Christian nation*, every nation outside of America does consider us a Christian nation, especially Christians in persecuted countries who seek refuge from dictators and safety from persecution.

Jesus Embarrasses Many Americans

When Franklin Graham, the son of the evangelist Billy Graham, offered a prayer at the 2001 inauguration of President George W. Bush, he concluded his prayer with the words: "We pray this in the name of the Father, and of the Son, the Lord Jesus Christ, and of the Holy Spirit. Amen."[7] As a Bible-believing Christian, this is the way a Christian is commanded to pray (John 15:16). We are to approach God through the name of Jesus Christ. This name so offended some that a lawsuit was brought against Reverend Graham.

On April 28, 2004, James E. "Jim" King, president of the Florida Senate, apologized to members of the legislative body after Florida Baptist pastor Clayton Cloer invoked the name of Jesus in his prayer in the Senate chamber as guest chaplain of the day. Another minister who works with legislators has said that "the opposition to the use of Jesus' name in the Senate" has caused him to decline invitations to pray in the Florida legislature.[8]

At the recent inauguration of President Barack Obama, prayers were offered by two ministers. The first, by Gene Robison, the first openly gay Episcopal bishop, did not mention the name of Jesus.[9] The second prayer, by Pastor Rick Warren, attempted to avoid controversy by including several names of Jesus used by different religions, including Islam: "I humbly ask this in the name of the one who changed my life—Yeshua, Isa, Jesus, Jesus..."[10]

A leading bishop of one of the largest Pentecostal denominations in the world was invited to an ecumenical meeting and asked to offer a "Christian prayer." The only stipulation was he could not say the name of Jesus. The bishop declined the invitation. How could he not pray in the very name of the person who had brought him redemption and changed his life? He was reminded of the warning given in Scripture about denying Christ in public (Matt. 10:33).[11]

Why Have We Changed?

If we compare the America in the 1950s to the America of today, there is startling evidence of the decline of our Judeo-Christian foundation. Why have we changed? I believe the following are some of the reasons for this change.

1. The removal of prayer from public school

My public school education began in the small Appalachian town of Big Stone Gap, Virginia. The beautiful community, nestled in the southwestern Virginia mountains, was a close-knit community whose people were both stubborn in spirit and strong in their personal convictions. Everyone—whether Baptist, Methodist, or Pentecostal—took their faith seriously and raised their children to respect God and country.

At age three, my family moved to this rural community. My father assumed a pastorate, and I begin my public education at age five at a school located within walking distance from our house. Each morning I grabbed my little leather pack with books and walked across the concrete bridge to school.

As a child in public school, I can recall the teacher standing before the class, opening a Bible, and reading a story. Often she would ask the class questions from the biblical narrative and offer a brief prayer. At times a student in the class would offer a simple thank-you to God. I can remember the feeling of security and safety when I heard the prayer. Being a momma's boy, I missed home. The prayer reminded me of my dad and mom. It brought me comfort. I don't ever recall one child, from the first to the third grade, ever mocking, resisting, or complaining about the Bible reading or the prayer.

After moving to Northern Virginia in the late 1960s, I noticed there was no prayer or Bible reading in the public schools. I later understood that the Supreme Court in Washington DC had voted to remove these two traditional religious acts from the public school.[12]

According to Scripture, the power of God's Word has the supernatural ability to restrain the free run of evil. Relating a biblical story or repeating a prayer can be a simple routine, but the Holy Scripture is a living thing. The Word of God is compared to a seed, which, when planted, can produce fruit or living results in the character or the heart of the believer (Mark 4:3–20).

The Bible is more than a religious book of Judeo-Christian theology. The Word of God contains the life of God in word form. By removing the Word of God from the minds and hearts of America's children, we have raised an entire generation of people who are now parents whose faith is weak and whose spiritual grade would be an F on a report card. Their moral values are the equivalent of a strip club owner, and their motto is, "If it feels good, do it."

The door was shut on moral and spiritual absolutes when the Supreme Court of the United States voted God out of the public schools.

2. Changing the draft

Previous generations remember when the draft was mandatory. When a young man turned eighteen years of age, he was required to attend military boot camp where he trained in a branch of the United States Armed Services. Federal law mandated that young men serve their country for a period of four years.

The mandatory draft ended in 1977. Many felt it was an important change in government policy, but unseen seeds may have been planted that are beginning to be harvested in our lifetime.

Three important character traits were developed in anyone who has ever served in the military:

- Mental and physical discipline
- A respect for authority and the chain of command
- The skills to obey orders and follow through

In previous times, by the time most young men were twenty-two years of age they had matured physically, emotionally, and, in many cases, spiritually into an upstanding American citizen with a solid work ethic.

Now, after many years, we see a generation of young Americans who often appear spiritually dumb, physically numb, and emotionally a bum. Respect for teachers, ministers, or parents has flown out the window. Unless these young Americans are self-motivated, their skills are limited, and they often have a low work ethic, working only for a paycheck to pay a few bills and party with the change they have left over.

Before you think this observation is a stretch from the truth, let the statistics speak for themselves by reviewing the findings of a 2006 Barna Poll on the differences between those in their twenties and those in their forties and older.

- Busters (those in their twenties and thirties) were twice as likely to have viewed sexually explicit movies or videos, two and a half times more likely to report having had a sexual encounter outside of marriage, and three times more likely to have viewed sexually graphic content online.

- Fifty-nine percent of Busters believe that cohabitation is morally acceptable.

- Busters were twice as likely as their parents' generation to use profanity in public, to say mean things about others behind their back, to tell something to another person that was not true, to do something to get back at someone who hurt or offended them, to take something that didn't belong to them, and to physically fight or abuse someone.[13]

3. Social programs

While I am certainly thankful for the government programs that assist the poor and lower-income families, there is an important observation to be made. In Scripture, God instructed the children to set aside the funds needed to care for their mothers and fathers when they became too old to work. This was God's form of *family social security*. Before President Roosevelt initiated the Social Security system, it was common to see Grandma and Grandpa living with their kids in a spare bedroom. They were not considered a *weight* but a joy as they shared their wisdom, humor, and love with the kids.

Social Security allowed parents to work and upon retirement have more freedom to be independent from other members of the family. This was good financially, but it was not always the best situation socially.

According to the Scriptures, those who had farms, fields of grain, or fruit trees were to set aside a portion of their harvests for the poor and needy. God also established a tithe in Israel that provided a percent of support for the poor and strangers living among the Hebrews. Again, this was God's way of providing for those less fortunate than others. The local synagogue became the place where these funds and goods could be distributed. In ancient times, the temple in Jerusalem contained rooms called *storehouses*, where food supplies could be brought and the needy could receive provision. The priests were required to distribute the goods according to the needs.

After the birth of the Christian church, leaders developed a plan to assist the poor among the people. When believers met together, special offerings were collected and distributed to relieve the needs of the poor and needy.

Therefore, for hundreds of years the plan of God was that His covenant people would take a portion of their finances and plant it as seeds into the lives of the widows, orphans, and poor among them.

Somewhere there has been a massive breakdown of the spiritual principles established by the Lord.

4. Government social programs

In the 1960s, many government-assisted programs were initiated. These programs were paid for by the funds collected from taxpaying Americans. I am certain God has blessed America because we have been willing to help those in need. Yet, as the government stepped forward to initiate programs to help needy people, the church became anemic in fulfilling its God-called mission. Millions of Christians have assumed it is the role and responsibility of federal governmental agencies to provide food stamps, shelter, and medical assistance to those in the inner cities. As a result, the people in the inner cities received *gifts without the gospel*. The food and financial assistance were notable and much needed, but it was not the responsibility of the government to be the provider—it was the responsibility of the church.

Because the church failed for many years in its assignment, the inner cities became turf-controlled by gangs and street corners owned by the drug lords. Government food provision may have filled an empty stomach, but it never impacted the empty soul.

During the 1980s and 1990s, there was a sudden surge by churches to take the gospel into the inner cities.

One such ministry, Metro Ministries, began in 1980 and is dedicated to serving inner-city children throughout the five boroughs of New York City and in various urban centers around the world. Metro Ministries reaches more than forty-two thousand children today through Sunday school services, child sponsorships, special programs, and personal home visits on a weekly basis. Due to the success of Metro's programs, President George H. W. Bush appointed the organization's founder, Pastor Bill Wilson, to serve on the National Commission of America's Urban Families in 1991. Metro's influence was also identified as a factor in the noticeable reduction of crime in the Bushwick community, and the organization has been featured on national media.[14]

Today, many churches are catching the vision of clothing, feeding, and bringing the gospel to those who need it rather than allowing the government to carry the burden. Exciting programs sponsored by local churches are dramatically changing many inner cities.

5. America's electronic babysitter

From the turn of the twentieth century to the 1970s, most breadwinners were the fathers in homes. As the cost of living rose and the desire to own more nice gadgets and expensive toys increased, it became necessary for the moms to work. Raising the children became a second priority, as the need for income increased. The invention and development of the television became what I call *America's electronic babysitter*. You don't have to work around its schedule, you don't have to feed it, and you don't have to pay it five dollars an hour to watch your children. In fact, it can actually keep your child's attention better that a flesh-and-blood person, if you know how to use it.

In the days of *I Love Lucy, The Beverly Hillbillies*, and good old Andy Griffith, there was little concern from Mom and Dad that the one-eyed electronic picture machine would ever cause mental or emotional instability in their children. Now, America's favorite babysitter, Mrs. Cable Network or Mrs. Satellite Television, can keep your children spellbound for hours. They can also contain some of the most graphic and verbal filth, innuendos, and anti-Christian propaganda your child can receive, all piped right into the comfort of your living room.

By the removal of prayer from the schools, a generation was produced that has no moral absolutes. By changing the mandatory draft, a generation was never taught discipline, how to respect authority, and a strong work ethic. By allowing the government to be the only source of supply for the inner-city poor, the gospel remained in the suburbs and among the middle to upper middle class, while the cities suffered. And, because of the ever-increasing erosion of Christian values depicted daily through America's electronic babysitter, the television, our downward spiral as a Christian nation is taking place not only in our institutions and public venues but also in our very homes.

The Day We Banned God From America

When David Barton wrote the book *America: To Pray or Not to Pray,* he compiled a series of charts indicating the drastic, downward spiral America took after rejecting prayer and Bible reading in the public schools in 1963. Divorce rates went up, SAT scores plummeted, and the spread of sexually transmitted diseases moved from adults to teens. More than public education was affected. A generation was infected with a spiritual cancer of unbelief.[15]

I remember the moment when it all began. Before I entered fifth grade, we moved to a large city in Northern Virginia. We rented a house in Arlington. Not only was it cultural shock, but also I noticed something very different in fifth grade. No teacher offered to read the Bible or pray. I finally asked why, and the teacher said, "We can no longer do this in a public school." My simple mind couldn't believe it! Perhaps the teachers in the small rural town of Big Stone Gap were doing it despite this new law. Being a kid I hadn't watched the news or paid attention to adult conversations that may have related to the situation. In the large city area, things were different. I remember hearing the name of the atheist who proudly boasted of removing prayer and Bible reading from school: Madalyn Murray O'Hair.

According to Madalyn's son, William Murray, "My mother was not just Madalyn Murray O'Hair, the atheist leader. She was an evil person who led many to hell. That is hard for me to say about my own mother, but it is true."[16]

According to Murray, when he was a child, his mother would spend the day in X-rated theaters. Their house was filled with statues of mating animals, which she worshiped. She was filled with constant rage and violence. She could not hold down a job and accepted the Communist doctrine, conducting Socialist group meetings in the basement of their home.[17]

William, who is now a Christian minister, was a young boy attending public school when his mother, in 1959, set out to remove prayer and Bible reading from the public schools. She had worked on the case for four years when finally the Supreme Court heard arguments on *Murray v. Curlett* on February 27, 1963. Four months later, on June 17, 1963, the Court ruled in O'Hair's favor, and reverential Bible reading and prayer recitation were removed from the nation's public schools.

In my later years I thought, "How could one woman accomplish this?" I wondered why there wasn't more of an outcry from Christians who believed in Bible reading and prayer. After all, Christians were the majority—or were they? The Christian reaction was weak, if not anemic. Christians complained and criticized the decision, but few Christians attempted to protest or challenge it. Since 1963 when this law was passed, morale, along with the moral fiber of our nation, has slid slowly downward. From 1963 onward, something unexplainable happened in America.

Five months after removing God from the public schools, President, John F. Kennedy was assassinated in Dallas, Texas. Then our nation—invincible in every previous war—was suddenly humiliated by the Vietnam War, eventually pulling out our troops. Hippies marched on Washington, screaming antiwar slogans and demanding peace as dope and blaring rock music dragged their minds into the twilight zone. Racial fighting continued in the South, and the nation was divided over the issue. Civil rights leader Martin Luther King Jr. was suddenly assassinated, thus creating more strife in the nation.

The downward spiral continued with the oil embargo and the events leading up to Richard Nixon stepping down as president. Years later, an Islamic nation, Iran, captured and held Americans hostage at our embassy in Tehran for 444 days. One former agent in Israeli intelligence told me that Israel had informed President Carter that they would send a special team into Iran and help release the hostages. President Carter replied that his plan was to conduct a secret mission before the presidential election, free the hostages, and possibly win reelection. The mission failed, and Carter lost the election.[18] The high-flying eagle was now slightly wounded.

The Evidence Is In

> Take heed to yourselves, lest you forget the covenant of the LORD your God.
>
> —DEUTERONOMY 4:23

I believe that Washington, Adams, and most signers of our founding documents would have kicked their way out of their tombs to object to the removal of Bible reading and prayer from the public schools. It was Washington who said in his farewell address in 1796: "Reason and experience both forbid us to expect that national morality can prevail to the exclusion of religious principle. . . . Let us with caution indulge the supposition that morality can be maintained without religion."[19]

A new spirit has taken root in American homes and in the hearts of America's people. This is a critical change, one we need to investigate closely. A spirit that attempted to influence the leaders and government dominated each of the great empires that existed in the past—and there are many parallels that can be discovered in what is happening in America today.

I personally believe that the response to O'Hair in 1963 was the beginning of our national leadership saying to God, "We are rejecting the covenant our fathers had with You." When ancient Israel rejected the covenant, God allowed the hedge of protection to be removed and great trouble to impact the land and people. This was the only way the Almighty could get Israel's attention and turn its people's hearts back to Him.

Research indicates a connection between the removal of prayer and Bible reading and the moral decline in the nation. From drugs to inner-city gang violence, lower grades in school, rape, and verbal and physical abuse, something changed in the hearts of the people and in the atmosphere of the country. But it is not just the moral environment that has changed. The youth from the sixties are the parents of today. Those from the sixties' generation are now the decision makers in our cities, states, and government. Is it any wonder that the odor of spiritual unbelief is filling the nation like the stench of a rotten cancer? Many national leaders were youth when the Supreme Court said, "No more God in school." Look at the end results of such faithlessness-based education.

1. By removing Bible reading out of school you remove the absolutes.

The moral guidelines in the Bible are summed up in the Ten Commandments: the five dos and the five do nots. Reading the Bible in school planted positive seeds into the minds of previous generations. Without the Bible, there is no right or wrong. Imagine if we removed every law in our land that had its foundation in Scripture. Anarchy would dominate! Laws are enforced tools to restrain evil. Likewise, the laws of God's Word act as a restraint against unbridled lust, pride, and deception. A child without rule will become as wild as an unbridled donkey. Without the Bible, who or what determines what is right and wrong?

2. By removing prayer from the public school, personal faith in God was crushed.

In order to pray you must believe in something. Prayer involves addressing a being higher than you. The only god students are permitted to believe in is the "god in you," and the only faith taught is "have faith in yourself."

3. By removing Bible reading and prayer, telling the Bible's story of Creation was forbidden, and evolution was espoused.

Public school officials often ask, "Why do the youth today have such low self-esteem?" It is difficult to have high self-esteem when you are taught that your ancestors were apes climbing in trees swinging from their tails and that you are truly a *monkey's uncle*. My grandfather John Bava put this poem in a book he wrote that mocks the utter nonsense of evolution:

Three monkeys sat in a coconut tree,
Discussing things that are said to be.
Said one to the other, "Now listen, you two;
There's a certain rumor that can't be true.

"That man descended from our noble race,
This very idea is a big disgrace.
No monkey ever deserted his wife,
Starved her babies and ruined her life.

"And you've never known a mother monk,
To leave her babies with others to bunk,
Or pass them on from one to another,
Till they scarcely know who is their mother.

"And another thing you will never see:
A monk build a fence 'round a coconut tree,
And let the coconuts go to waste,
Forbidding the other monks to taste.

"Why, if I put a fence around a tree,
Starvation would force you to steal from me.
Here's another thing a monk won't do:
Go out at night and get a stew.

"Or use a club, a gun, or knife
To take another monkey's life.
We're fully convinced without any fuss,
Man has descended, but not from us."[20]

When youth become violent and uncontrollable, don't blame them; blame their ancestor, Uncle Ape. Certainly their uncontrollable temper is only a monkey gene that has suddenly kicked in. Perhaps we need to build a rain forest in the schoolyard so the kids can swing from branches, releasing and venting their ancestral jungle frustration! Since creationism is a biblical teaching, it is banned because liberals refuse to allow any form of religion in school, even though in many communities large numbers of youth attend a local church occasionally or are active in church youth groups.

4. Then there is the issue of sex education in our public schools.

Modern educators are convinced that a condom is the twenty-first-century cure for all sexually transmitted diseases. Stretching condoms over a cucumber in a sex education class illustrates to the youth how to conquer the many sexually transmitted diseases. There is little or no teaching on abstinence; therefore, showing them how to have "safe sex" is the cure since they are going to *do it anyway*. A cucumber wearing a condom never got a teenage girl pregnant, but a young boy's uncontrolled hormones certainly have. Hormones have no conscience, and lust has no fear. The transmittable diseases are still being transmitted; teens are still becoming pregnant—so much for sex education class.

In July 2008, the President's Emergency Plan for AIDS Relief (PEPFAR) made a commitment of $48 billion (USD) spending on HIV/AIDS initiatives around the world.[21] However, in spite of billions of dollars of spending to prevent the disease, an estimated 1.9 million of Americans are living with HIV, and 81,000 people were newly infected with HIV in 2007.[22]

This forty-eight-billion-dollar problem has a solution that can be found in any forty-dollar Bible in your local Christian bookstore! Teach the Bible, and save the tax money! It is not "politically correct" to teach youth in a public school setting that they should abstain from sex before marriage. This borders too much on the "D" word—*discipline*! Since the Bible teaches discipline, the public school cannot repress the youth with such moral controls.

5. Youth are taught that any pregnancy can be terminated at any time by choosing abortion.

When our nation wonders why kids are killing kids, it may be because they are taught no respect for life in the womb. Partial-birth abortion kills newborns and uses the "fetal tissue" for research. It reminds me of Hitler and the Jews. Since Hitler's henchmen considered Jews as lower class, innocent Hebrews were cut up for medical research—some while they were still living! Thousands of Jews became human guinea pigs in order to advance the Third Reich's research. Fetal tissue for medical research...sound familiar? America's holocaust is not being played out behind a locked door at a Nazi concentration camp. It is being hidden behind the closed doors of abortion clinics. The loss of respect for life is frightening. If an infant is nothing more than fetal tissue, then in the future our older citizens will simply be wrinkled tissue, and euthanasia will become appealing.

Ronald Reagan once said, "We cannot diminish the value of one category of human life—the unborn—without diminishing the value of all human life."[23] Perhaps this is why some violent teens find it easy to murder their schoolmates. If respect for an unborn infant is null, then respect for the grown will be dull.

Some nations use abortion population control. Others allow euthanasia, meaning that a weak, sick, mentally retarded, or older person who is not fit for the *state* can be eliminated in a *humane manner*, such as by an injection. I believe the only restraint keeping some left-wing politicians progressing from partial-birth abortion to euthanasia is that infants can't vote but older people can. If godless liberalism continues to spread, we can expect change with our elderly. I can see the debate now. "We can save hundreds of millions in Social Security and Medicare by removing millions of nonproductive people from the nation through humane termination. The saved money can be used to invest in the education of our youth." Impossible? Not to those who have no moral and spiritual convictions.

As we have explored America's Hebrew connection in this book, it has become more clear that God raised up this nation and that our Founding Fathers made a spiritual covenant in our early national documents. If God judged Israel in the Old Testament for breaking His covenant, then where do we stand? God's full judgment is never released before He visits in mercy. The Bible teaches that the cup of iniquity must become full before God swiftly unleashes the wrath from His mighty hand: "...for the iniquity of the Amorites is not yet full and complete" (Gen. 15:16, AMP). The Ten Commandments were not ten recommendations. Obedience to them would keep people focused and spare the nation from divorce, greed, murder, stealing, lying, and such sins. Ancient Israel eventually broke all Ten Commandments after they possessed the Promised Land. At that moment, God prepared a plan for them to enter into captivity into Babylon.

America's captivity is of a different nature. We are not plagued by foreign troops pointing guns in our backs or forcing Americans into slavery in Siberia. Our captivity is both inward and outward—the inward spiritual void is manifested outwardly. Our mental prison is spiritual ignorance, which leads to spiritual bondage. Today, if Christians sing, speak, or read the gospel in the wrong place or at the wrong time, they are threatened with legal action. Gangs, like uncaged animals, roam the cities as the elderly tremble in fear locked at home behind windows with bars. Fear stalks the inner cities after sunset. Our captivity is an entire generation addicted to crack cocaine, unable to get free.

America's captivity is a generation so addicted to lust that premarital sex is considered normal before a girl turns thirteen. Some men think they are trapped in a female body, and some women believe they are actually men. Sexual liberation ends with sexual addiction and bondage. We have already lost a previous generation. The only hope to reach this End Time generation of young people is with the message of hope and freedom through an experience with Christ.

God has a way of avenging His spiritual opposition. Madalyn O'Hair used her young son, William, to remove prayer from the public school. Years later, this same young man was converted to Christ, was filled with the Spirit, and today is preaching the gospel! Certainly God had the final say-so! In August 1995, O'Hair and her other son and her granddaughter were taken hostage by David Waters, a former office manager who sought $600,000 for their release. According to FBI information, Madalyn and her granddaughter were held captive for about thirty days until her son, under the kidnapper's direction, obtained the ransom money. Afterward all three were killed. Almost five and a half years later, in January 2001, their dismembered and burned bodies were discovered on a farm in Texas. David Waters was never tried for the crime and died of cancer in prison in 2003.

This eerie story of O'Hair reminds us of the story of a very wicked woman in the Old Testament. Jezebel, this queen of evil, set herself up as a goddess and surrounded herself with four hundred false prophets. She threatened to kill Elijah and had undeniable control over her husband, King Ahab. In time she met her death when she was thrown from the wall of the palace. The chariot driver, Jehu, ran over her body. Soon thereafter, dogs came and began to devour her remains. The only parts the dogs would not touch were her skull, feet, and hands. I believe her thoughts (head), deeds (hands), and actions (feet) were so wicked that even the lowest animals were repulsed by her (2 Kings 9).

I believe it is possible that by removing prayer and Bible reading from the public schools, America entered a spiritual warfare zone aimed at separating our nation from its founders' covenant with God. God can remove a protective hedge and allow the enemy to attack (Job 1:10–12).

Perhaps as evidence of God's removal of His protective hedge, five months after prayer and Bible reading were banned by the Supreme Court in 1963, the president of the United States was shot in Dallas, Texas—the same state where O'Hair set up her atheist organization and where she later met her death. How unusual that Kennedy was shot from a schoolbook depository building! Some years later, in 1968, the untimely and tragic death of Martin Luther King Jr. struck the nation. In 1973 we witnessed the resignation of the vice president, Spiro Agnew, followed by the near impeachment and resignation of President Richard Nixon on August 8, 1974. Just six short years later, sixty-six Americans were held hostage for 444 days in Iran as inflation was destroying the economy.

In the election of 1980, evangelical Christians prayed, fasted, and voted. As a result, Ronald Reagan was elected and was used to change the atmosphere of the nation from pessimism to hope. At his inauguration, Reagan placed his hand on a Bible that had belonged to his mother. It was noted that a special scripture was marked in the Bible, which reads:

> If My people who are called by My name will humble themselves, and pray and seek My face, and turn from their wicked ways, then I will hear from heaven, and will forgive their sin and heal their land.
>
> —2 Chronicles 7:14

The year 1963, God was no longer welcomed in the public schools. Since that time, thousands of court battles have occurred with various groups attempting to erase every object, phrase, and symbol of Christianity from America.

The Spirits of the Past Empires

Just as a new spirit has invaded America and set it on a downward spiral, in every major world empire of biblical prophecy there is evidence of a domination spirit that attempted to influence the leaders and government. In Daniel 10, two of these spirits are identified as the "prince of Persia" and the "prince of Greece" (Dan. 10:13, 20). "Prince" in these passages does not allude to an earthly ruler but to a strong principality spirit. In another verse in this chapter, Michael the archangel, whom we have identified as the guardian of the nation of Israel, is identified as "Michael your prince" (v. 21).

We learn in Revelation 13:2 that the Antichrist will be given power and authority from Satan to reform the ancient empires under his domain. The spirits that have controlled previous regions of the world will again be permitted to rise again and control the minds of future world leaders. These spirits are now bound, but they will be released in the future:

> And I heard a voice from the four horns of the golden altar which is before God, saying to the sixth angel who had the trumpet, "Release the four angels who are bound at the great river Euphrates." So the four angels, who had been prepared for the hour and day and month and year, were released to kill a third of mankind.
>
> —Revelation 9:13–15

It is clear that global armies that are under the influence of evil spirits will conduct the prophetic wars of the future:

> And I saw three unclean spirits like frogs coming out of the mouth of the dragon, out of the mouth of the beast, and out of the mouth

of the false prophet. For they are spirits of demons, performing signs, which go out to the kings of the earth and of the whole world, to gather them to the battle of that great day of God Almighty.

—REVELATION 16:13–14

When examining the spirits that dominated the major empires of prophecy, one can see their influence in the United States.

The spirit of Babylon

The Babylonian empire was noted for large numbers of astrologers, star-gazers, and occult activity. Daniel and his Hebrew companions were captives in Babylon and were asked to compromise their spiritual convictions. They refused, and the Hebrew God protected them from the mouths of lions and a furnace of fire. (See Daniel 3 and 6.)

During recent years, America has experienced a revival of occultism. It began with innocent television programs showing witches. Eventually it developed into popular programs where men and women claimed to be able to contact the dead (which is forbidden in Scripture). Television infomercials promoted self-acclaimed psychics, who cash in on the ignorance of people concerned about their future. Fifty years ago Americans would have rejected the idea that astrology and occult activity influenced their daily lives. Today, this activity is not only accepted but also popular. It is an indication that the spirit of Babylon is on the rise.

Consider the pervasive influence of the occult. Students are involved with role-playing fantasy games that introduce them to occult concepts. Universities offer courses in paranormal and occult science. Occultist themes provide popular material for television shows and movies. Police departments are beginning to realize that many of the crimes they investigate have occult origins. Everywhere we go, it seems that the occult is present.[24] According to a 2003 Harris Poll, 31 percent of people polled believed astrology is accurate. For young people ages twenty-five to twenty-nine, 43 percent believed astrology is accurate.[25]

The spirit of Media-Persia

The Medes and Persians overthrew the Babylonians. The Medes and Persians were known for passing laws. Once the law was set, it could not be reversed (Dan. 6:15). Once in Babylon, a group of Persian lawyers plotted to destroy Daniel. The Hebrew prophet was praying three times a day while facing Jerusalem. Through deception, the king signed a decree that no person could pray to any God, but instead must petition the king himself. Daniel rejected the petition and continued praying to God. The governmental leaders stood before the king and commanded Daniel to be punished.

The influence of the Medes and Persians is evident when laws are passed that are contrary to the statutes and commandments of God's Word. In America, the Supreme Court has made three major decisions that have influenced America in a negative manner:

- In 1963 they removed prayer and Bible reading from the public schools.[26]
- In 1973 they legalized abortion on demand.[27]
- In 2003 they began to permit more freedom to the homosexual community.[28]

In Daniel's time, Daniel felt the law of God was superior to the law of the Medes and Persians. When Daniel followed the commandments of the Lord, he was sent to the lions' den. Today, some believers have been maligned, arrested, and even jailed for their spiritual stand when they attempted to read a Bible in a public school or offer prayer, protest against abortion, or speak out against the sins of homosexuality. At the time of this writing, political activist, author, and former diplomat and presidential candidate Alan Keyes was arrested on the campus of Notre Dame for his involvement in an anti-abortion protest. In a statement released days before his arrest, Keyes said: "I will step foot on the Notre Dame campus to lift up the standard that protects the life of the innocent children of this and every generation. I will do it all day and every day from now until the Master comes if need be…"[29]

The spirit of Greece

The Greeks sought after wisdom. In the process they began to listen to every form of teaching and philosophy. This included the beliefs of the many religions in the world. During the time of the Grecian empire, the Greeks worshiped Zeus. This mythological god was popular in the Greek culture, along with numerous other gods. These gods included Eros, Aphrodite, Hercules, Dionysus, Apollo, and numerous others. When Paul preached in Athens on Mars Hill, he observed countless gods and philosophers who were promoting their beliefs. He noted one monument dedicated to the Unknown God (Acts 17:23).

The Greek culture was noted for their tolerance. The idea of tolerance has become the politically correct word for America. We are to be tolerant of every religion, every belief, and every alternative lifestyle. Author Martha Nussbaum recently addressed the topics of religious tolerance and equality in America on

Bill Moyers Journal by saying: "The University of Virginia said that student activity fees could be used to fund every student group: the Young Democrats, the lesbian and gay students group, the gardening club, the choir. But the one thing they couldn't use the money to fund was the Young Christians. Now, there really is an issue of fairness. I mean, why should it be just because you're a religious group that you don't get what everyone else gets to pursue their own conscientious commitment?"[30]

It is true that America is a melting pot and a diversity of ethnic groups, religious beliefs, and philosophies (just as in ancient Greece). However, the spiritual destinies of men and women are at stake, and the gospel of Christ is the only truth that promises eternal life to a person who will receive Christ.

The spirit of Rome

The United States has many parallels to the Roman Empire. For example:

- Rome had a Senate, and America has a Senate.
- Rome had a hill, *Capitolina*, and America has Capitol Hill.
- Rome had one man as the head (Caesar), and America has one head (a president).
- Rome had Roman-Greek architecture, and Washington has Roman-Greek buildings.
- Rome's emblem was an eagle, and America's emblem is an eagle.
- Rome had the world's greatest military, and so does America.
- Rome occupied the Middle East, and so does America.
- Rome dealt with Palestine, and America deals with Israel.
- Rome loved the chariot races, and America loves the NASCAR races.
- Rome loved stadium sports, and America's main sports are in stadiums.
- Rome fell from immorality, and America is being corrupted by immorality.[31]

The Babylonian Empire was extremely rich with gold. Because of their wealth, the Babylonians were able to make loans to their Persian neighbors at a rate of 33½ percent interest. The Persians were required to repay double interest every three years. Eventually, the Persians were unable to repay their debts to the Babylonians. Commerce halted, and they were unable to pay creditors and had no gold for taxes. As indicated in the Book of Daniel, the Persians planned a secret invasion of the city of Babylon. While King Belshazzar hosted a huge party with thousands of his lords and leaders in the Babylonian banquet hall, the Persian army was moving underground, and late in the night the Persians overtook the Babylonians, crashing the party! Cyrus, the king of Persia, now sat on the throne of Babylon, initiating the Media-Persia Empire. At that moment the debts of the Persians were canceled.

The Persians began building and expanding their empire with their new wealth. According to the Book of Daniel, the Persians controlled 120 provinces. By canceling their government loans, it freed up huge amounts of gold to both build and to offer credit to surrounding nations, such as Greece. In 421 B.C., Sparta borrowed five thousand talents from the Persians to build warships. In 405 B.C., Lysander of Sparta used these ships to destroy the whole Athenian fleet. This event made Sparta number one in Greece.[32]

The debt mounted in Greece. The five thousand talents Greece borrowed from the Persians amounted to a debt of $37,457.51 over the seven-year period. Years later when the mighty military general Alexander the Great inspected the treasury, he discovered $120,000, yet he owed $1.5 million. In Alexander's mind it became necessary to invade Babylon and defeat and take possession of the Media-Persia territory. Not only did Alexander's highly trained and motivated army smash the Medes and Persians, but also upon seizing the headquarters city, Babylon, Alexander immediately took possession of $440 million in gold! The invasion and the overthrow of the Persians brought an immediate cancellation to the money the Greeks owed the Persians.[33]

The Greek Empire expanded their influence and power using their newfound wealth. The Greeks began to build cities in each area of the world they conquered. In each major city a temple was built. The temple actually served as the "bank" where a person could make a loan with interest.

The Greeks began building cities in northern and southern Italy. The Roman Federation was headquartered in the center of Italy. The wealth and influence of the Greeks became evident as they began to trade with the Romans. The Greeks were willing to make loans to the Romans for goods purchased, and they required that the loans be repaid at high interest rates. As the Romans borrowed the gold at high interest, it became clear they would be unable to pay their loans back. Rome had expanded and built a large army. It was only a matter of time until it became *necessary* for the Romans to take control of the land controlled by the Greeks. Thus the Roman Empire began to form and flourish in the very areas where the Greek–Hellenistic government and culture had blossomed. As the Romans invaded these cities, two things happened. The Romans were able to cancel their debts, and they could seize the wealth in the temples. In that time, the money of the empires was in the form of gold, silver, and brass coins.

The growing burden of debt incurred by the Roman government eventually created stress on the government and the people of the Roman Empire. The Romans placed great emphasis on their military. The Romans were the best-trained and most-equipped military force in history. They were highly trained, well protected, and extremely loyal to the empire. The Romans had armies occupying areas, especially any region where they believed a resistance to their authority could occur.

Such a resistance began to heat up in Palestine (Israel). In A.D. 66, the Roman armies marched their legions into Israel to squelch the Jewish rebels who were weary of the taxation and heavy financial burden being carried by the common people.

The Jewish revolt failed, and in 70 the Roman Tenth Legion, using battering rams, collapsed the large walls surrounding Jerusalem and entered the sacred temple compound where the Jewish temple, whose holy chambers were covered with gold, was set to flames. As the famous arch of Titus in Rome indicates, the golden and silver treasures of the Hebrews were captured in the invasion and carried away by the Roman army. The wealth of Israel was stored in the temple chambers, and the Romans, desperate for gold and silver to continue financing their army, found a cache of wealth locked in the sacred rooms of the house of God.[34]

Ancient history reveals the danger to powerful empires when their debt becomes uncontrollable and leads to invasions. Wars are initiated, money shifts hands, and new empires are forged who control the credit or money supply. America's massive debt and financial bailouts are similar to the debt of the Roman Empire. Just as Rome moved from a producing empire to a purchasing empire, so America is traveling the same path.

••• Chapter 12 •••
AMERICA—FROM PRODUCER TO PURCHASER

He causes all, both small and great, rich and poor, free and slave, to receive a mark on their right hand or on their fore-heads, and that no one may buy or sell except one who has the mark or the name of the beast, or the number of his name.
—*REVELATION 13:16–17*

SCHOLARS AND STUDENTS of biblical prophecy have noted for hundreds of years that at an appointed time, identified as the *end of the age*, there would be a major transition among the nations that would result in a global system of purchasing and selling. This system emerges during a time when ten major kingdoms are united as one unit and submit their leadership under the control of one man, often identified in the apocalyptic Scriptures as the "beast" and his kingdom. The term *beast*, used by the Hebrew prophets Daniel and John in the Book of Revelation, does not refer to an animal, but it is the Greek word *therion*, denoting a wild beast that devours its prey.[1]

This future economic system is designed to control the masses by limiting their ability to purchase or sell by the method of a mark, name, and specific number. Presently, we are all identified by numbers: Social Security, credit cards, personal identification numbers (PINs), phone numbers, license plate numbers, and security numbers for the Internet. There remains a mystery as to the meaning of the "mark" and the "name." This will probably be revealed in the future, although cards with chips are already developed, as well as small chips that will be implanted in the hand or just under the hairline; plans are being made to make them operational.

Notice that the purchasing power is *not* with gold, silver, or cash. Among the ancient empires, from Egypt to Rome, silver and gold were powerful standards of exchange and barter. When dark clouds of economic depression hang over the world, there is a run for the precious commodities of gold and silver, as throughout history these two metals have been the safer haven from economic crisis and collapse. Yet, in the future, the system makes mentions of numbers being used, not gold or silver.

For this method of financial control to work effectively, there must be a joining of the banking systems, or the default of all banks and the rise of one international global bank monopoly. This is not inconceivable, for whenever a major recession and depression strike a nation, the population will easily give up freedoms and even present currency to ensure the prevention of total disasters.

Throughout history, any national financial disaster and collapse of governments have not been a coincidence, but they are well-orchestrated and manipulated events linked to bankers.

The New Thieves

On a snowy winter day, February 11, 1933, my father, Fred Stone, was born in a log cabin in the coal-mining community of Bartley, West Virginia. Eventually, each coal camp had an individual doctor who would assist injured miners and their families. They also assisted in childbirth. Those who could not afford a doctor used a midwife, a woman who (without medical training) would assist in the delivery of a child. Dad speculated that as many as half of the infants born in the rural mountains in the thirties were delivered with the assistance of the midwife. Seldom did the midwife charge for her services.

Now, fast-forward to the year 2010. When a woman becomes pregnant and follows through with the routine checkups, eventually giving birth in a good hospital, the cost may be as high as $10,000. Once this child is carried home in his or her mother's arms, the cost of living begins, and the invisible hand of the government slips a hand in the pocket of the parents and will later place the other hand in the pocket of the child. From the cradle to the grave, this living being will pay a steep price to enjoy living in America.

As this infant matures, he or she finishes college, seeks out a small business opportunity, and pursues the America Dream. The new business grows, workers are hired, offices are constructed, and income increases. This blueprint is called *success*. Today the motivation for working hard to create generational wealth is being crushed by *tax-and-spend legislators* who are robbing from Peter to pay Paul, apparently believing they are modern Robin Hoods seizing the money of those mean rich people to hand out to those who don't have it.

The Bible has 774,746 total words when combining the Old and New Testaments. How long would it take you to read through the Bible? Many believers take one year to read several chapters a day in order to complete a reading of the entire book. Now, how many words are in the United States tax code?

As it currently stands, according to the U.S. Government Printing Office,

Title 26 of the U.S. Code of Federal Regulations (the part written by the IRS) is a total of 13,458 pages. The complete set of Title 26 of the U.S. Code of Federal Regulations has twenty volumes and can be ordered from the Government Printing Office for $974.[2] The full text of Title 26 of the U.S. Code, which includes material written by Congress, is 3,387 printed pages, bringing the adjusted total page count to 16,845. If you add the various IRS rulings appending the tax codes, in 2003 the total page count for all pertinent tax code information was a staggering total of 54,846 pages. In addition to that, there are hundreds of individual IRS tax forms used by taxpayers.[3]

My average study Bible has 1,500 pages. Thus, the twenty-volume set of Federal regulations is about nine times larger than an average Bible! If you combine all the codes and forms, they are a whopping thirty-six times larger than an average Bible! Perhaps this is why everyone in Washington is a lawyer, since it would take a lawyer to interpret this mishmash of bogged-down legislation. During tax seasons, many Americans get frustrated when IRS agents are asked a question, and three different agents give three different answers. Don't blame them. If it takes one year to read the Bible, a few chapters at a time, it would take a person nine to thirty-six years to read all the pages of the Federal regulations a few paragraphs at a time!

Americans pay local, state, and federal taxes. In Colonial times, taxes were levied, not so much from individuals, but from excise taxes, tariffs, and customs duties. The states needed revenue, and they raised it in the South through taxing imports and exports. The middle colonies also imposed a property tax and a "head" tax on each adult male, and the New England colonies raised taxes through real estate taxes and excise and occupations taxes.[4]

The American Revolutionary War began because of *taxation without representation*. The English Parliament had levied two taxes on the colonies: one was the Stamp Act, and the other was a tax on English tea purchased by the colonies. The anger over taxation was addressed in the 1781 Articles of Confederation, which gave more power to the individual states to levy taxes than to the federal government, which was small and in the infant stages at the time. The founders clearly saw the danger of a central government and left much of the responsibility of tax revenue to the individual states. In 1789, the Constitution granted the federal government the rights to: "...lay and collect taxes, duties, imposts, and excises, pay the Debts and provide for the common Defense and general Welfare of the United States."[5]

In early America, it seemed that the federal government would levy taxes during times of war. The first tax on individuals was called a *direct tax*, initiated by the federal government in the late 1790s during America's confrontation with France. These taxes were abolished in 1802 under Thomas Jefferson, who only permitted excise taxes, which were the only internal revenue for the federal government for the next ten years.[6]

Congress initiated the second wave of taxes in 1812 to assist in raising money for the War of 1812. During this season, Treasury notes were issued. However in 1817, the taxes were repealed, and for the following forty-four years there was no collection of taxes from individuals. Once again, taxes were collected by the government through custom duty charges and sale of land.[7]

The war that initiated a major tax increase was the Civil War. In 1861, Congress legislated the Revenue Act of 1861, which also imposed a tax on individual incomes, amounting to a 3 percent tax on all incomes higher than $800 a year. During the war, the government debt was growing by $2 million a day. Suddenly the Congress passed a new tax that seemed to tax everything—including feathers, gunpowder, playing cards, medicine, telegrams, and practically anything that had to be purchased. All forms of licenses and legal documents were taxed. The government's war debt opened the way for a new form of tax that levied taxes on higher incomes in a two-tiered tax structure. Any person with an income up to $10,000 paid a 3 percent tax, and higher incomes were charged a 5 percent tax rate.[8]

As war debts were paid, most taxes were repealed, and in the late 1860s, tax income was derived from the normal taxation on tobacco and liquor, two popular items that were sold throughout the colonies. It may come as a surprise to learn that there was no federal income tax from 1868 to 1913, or a period of about forty-five years. The federal government operated on the excise taxes still in effect.[9]

The Sixteenth Amendment

The Constitution has been amended twenty-seven times, first on December 15, 1791, and the most recent, May 7, 1992. Congress passed and ratified the Sixteenth Amendment and adopted it into law on February 25, 1913.[10] It reads:

> The Congress shall have power to lay and collect taxes on incomes, from whatever source derived, without apportionment among the several States, and without regard to any census or enumeration.[11]

After this legislation was attached to the Constitution, Congress then set a new tax rate beginning at 1 percent and increasing to 7 percent for individuals with incomes over $500,000 a year. Once again it was war (World War I) that created the need to increase taxes to pay for war efforts. In 1916, the lowest rate was raised from 1 percent to 2 percent, and the high rate was raised to 15 percent on those with incomes of over $1.5 million. Taxes were collected on a person's estate and any excess business profits, and exemption benefits were removed to provide higher collections. One year later, in 1917, more changes came as anyone making as low as $40,000 was forced to pay 15 percent of their income in taxes. Those making $1.5 million were shocked to discover that in just twelve months their tax rates had jumped from 15 percent to 67 percent! Like a runaway train, the war debts piled up, and Congress raised taxes the following year. In 1918, the lowest rate was 6 percent and the highest rate was 77 percent![12]

As the economy began to grow in the 1920s, the tax rates were changed five times, and eventually rates were dropped to a lowest rate of 1 percent and a top rate of 25 percent. With the stock market crash of 1929 and the birth of the Great Depression, more than 25 percent of the nation's people were out of work, and wages were lowered. Thus, the government's receipts dropped from $6.6 billion in 1920 to only $1.9 billion in 1932! To increase the government's receipts, the Congress foolishly raised taxes three times between 1932 and 1936, to where the lowest rate topped 4 percent and the top rate was up to 79 percent. This meant that a *rich person* was giving the government an average of eighty cents out of every dollar! This act caused more damage to an already lifeless economy.[13]

The state of the economy during the Depression led to the creation of Social Security, which included unemployment compensation and public aid, financed by an additional 2 percent tax and shared equally with employees and employers.

As the Depression continued, America was again thrust into war, and the only way to add needed billions of dollars was to alter the tax laws again. At this time the highest tax rates ever were levied on individual Americans and corporations. Any person earning only $500 had to pay 23 percent in taxes, and anyone with a $1 million income was burdened with a top rate of 94 percent! To ensure that the government secured more tax for their coffers, numerous deductions were eliminated from the tax code. The top tax rate continued until the time of President Ronald Reagan, who on October 22, 1986, signed into law the Tax Reform Act, which lowered the top rates from 50 percent to 28 percent.[14]

A Look at Your Taxes

You may have never considered the number of taxes you actually pay. You pay:

- State sales tax for everything you purchase except food, clothes, and daily living supplies (seven states have no state sales taxes)

- Property tax
- Taxes on your home
- Taxes for each gallon of gas
- Taxes on public utilities
- Taxes taken from your paycheck (payroll tax)
- Taxes on the purchase of a car
- Taxes on any capital gains
- Taxes on your profit from savings and investments
- Taxes on your outside additional income
- Taxes on your inheritance
- Taxes on your estate
- Taxes called "death tax"
- Taxes collected on toll roads
- Taxes (VAT) from purchases overseas
- Taxes on cell phones, Internet, cable, etc.

The Redistribution of Income

It is clear that wars cost money and that money is collected in wartime by raising taxes. However, as the government expands its spending, there is an old strategy that dates back to the Roman Empire, which strategizes to grow the government by collecting more revenues from rich citizens. This is often called *the redistribution of income*. It is the concept that made national news when Senator Barack Obama met Joe Wurzelbacher outside his home in Toledo, Ohio. Joe is better known by his nickname "Joe the Plumber." In his comments to Obama, Joe made this comment: "I'm getting taxed more and more while fulfilling the American Dream."

In reply to him, Obama said: "I've got a tax cut. The only thing that changes, is I'm going to cut taxes a little bit more for the folks who are most in need, and for the 5 percent of the folks who are doing very well, even though they've been working hard—and I understand that; I appreciate that—I just want to make sure they're paying a little bit more in order to pay for those other tax cuts."[15]

This statement was picked up and aired on the more conservative news networks as an indicator that, if elected, Obama would tax the rich to give to the less fortunate. Prior to the election, a radio interview with then Senator Obama, broadcast on WBEZ radio in 2001, discussed the Supreme Court and the possibility of redistribution of wealth.

But the Supreme Court never ventured into the issues of redistribution of wealth, and of more basic issues of political and economic justice in society. To that extent, as radical as I think people try to characterize the Warren Court, it wasn't that radical. It didn't break free from the essential constraints that were placed by the Founding Fathers in the Constitution, at least as its been interpreted and Warren Court interpreted in the same way.... One of the, I think, tragedies of the civil rights movement was, um, because the civil rights movement became so court focused I think there was a tendency to lose track of the political and community organizing and activities on the ground that are able to put together the actual coalition of powers through which you bring about redistributive change.[16]

Part of the American mystique is the belief that a person from any nation can immigrate to America, become a citizen, and dream big dreams without any limitations, including beginning a small business that becomes a world corporation, or creating and patenting an invention that sells millions and brings in millions of dollars in income. Today, however, the new swing toward Socialism and wealth distribution is killing the people doing the dreaming.

Today, if a person has worked hard to gain wealth, that person is heavily taxed—not merely to support the programs of their local and state governments, but to support thousands of *pork barrel projects* and *government waste*.

Thomas Jefferson warned America about this present goal of "redistributing the wealth":

To take from one, because it is thought his own industry and that of his father has acquired too much, in order to spare to others who (or whose fathers) have not exercised equal industry and skill, is to violate arbitrarily the first principle of association, "to guarantee to everyone a free exercise of his industry and the fruits acquired by it."[17]

The Changes

A slick politician can say, "I am not raising taxes on the average American." However, when that same silver-tongued pickpocket begins to eliminate the number of deductions that you can count, you then have more taxable income.

Starting in 2011, the following are the projected tax changes over the next ten years, according to an ABC News blog reported by Jake Tapper. Obama's budget has proposed $989 billion in new taxes. The tax revenues are shown as follows:[18]

Proposed New Taxes—2011 through 2021

PEOPLE MAKING MORE THAN $250,000	
$338 billion	Bush tax cuts expire
$179 billion	Eliminate itemized deductions
$118 billion	Capital gains tax hike
Total: $636 billion in ten years	
TAX CHANGES ON BUSINESSES	
$17 billion	Reinstate Superfund taxes
$24 billion	Tax carried–interest as income
$5 billion	Codify "economic substance doctrine"
$61 billion	Repeal LIFO
$210 billion	International enforcement, reform deferral, other tax reform
$4 billion	Information reporting for rental payments
$5.3 billion	Excise tax on Gulf of Mexico oil and gas
$3.4 billion	Repeal expensing of tangible drilling costs
$62 million	Repeal deductions for tertiary injections
$49 million	Repeal passive loans exception for working interest in oil and natural gas properties
$13 billion	Repeal manufacturing tax deduction for oil and natural gas companies
$882 million	Eliminate advanced earned income tax credit
$1 billion	Increase to seven years geological and geophysical amortization period for independent producers
Total: $335 billion in ten years	

What I Am Hearing

Let me give you two examples of the reactions from people who would be affected by these tax increases. These are comments given to me in personal conversations from individuals who are remaining unnamed in this book.

I know one successful businessman who works with hospitals and has offices in several states. His business has been so successful that he has hired men who were laid off by other companies. When he and his friends discovered that they were no longer going to be working for the American Dream, but that most of their increased income would simply be allocated into the government's coffers, he said, "I am willing to cut out several of my offices and take a pay cut to avoid these taxes. Why should I work seventy to eighty hours a week on projects, just to hand the money over to bureaucrats who are wasting most of what we are giving them now!"

I had dinner with one pastor from a large southern city who is involved in the business community. One of the most successful businesspersons in his area said to him, "If they are going to up my taxes by 20 to 25 percent, then limit my charitable deductions and omit other deductions. I will personally lay off the number of people that equal the amount the government gets and go ahead and allow the government to care for them."

Several businesses with large offices in America are already making plans to move their corporate offices to places such as Switzerland where the tax rates are much lower. It is my observation that in the past, hardworking Americans simply rolled with the punches and felt there was nothing they could do about the changes in high places, so why not just shut up and go to work. Not any more. The citizens of this land have seen the hypocrisy, the waste, and the corruption in the hands of too many professional politicians, and they are now in a silent revolt that will eventually affect the future of the nation. Without this peaceful uprising, we will most definitely speed our nation down the same road of ancient Rome.

Rome's Slow Death—America's Tax Burden

There are numerous reasons given as to why the western half of the Roman Empire declined while the eastern (Byzantine) prospered. One reason that continually appears in history books and discussions is that when Roman government grew, the income of the farmers dropped, and the tax burden eventually sunk the people.

By the third century, the burden of taxation had become so heavy that it had begun to consume the capital resources of the taxpayer. This was due to the increasing costs of the imperial administration without any corresponding increase in production on the part of the population of the empire.[19]

The increases in taxation coincided with a falling off in production and in manpower. The result was bound to be a heavier weight of taxation for the survivors and their gradual impoverishment, which, in turn, would cause a decrease in the public revenues.[20]

Rome began experiencing a declining birth rate, which was noticed by 235. America has grown with immigrants but has aborted nearly fifty million children since 1973.[21]

The attempt to enforce the economic and social reforms and to extract as large a revenue as possible from the civilian population led to increased departmentalization of the bureaucracy and also to an increase in the number of the civil service employees; this increased the cost of government. This, in turn, made the burden of the taxpayers still heavier and, under the declining economic conditions, led to further impoverishment.[22]

The crushing load of taxation and obligatory government services proved too great for the producing classes to support. They did not have the where-withal to raise and support families large enough to maintain, much less increase, their numbers from one generation to the next. Their lives were so burdensome that each of the obligatory occupation groups sought to escape from its status.[23]

In the fifth century, the decline in the Western Empire with its capital in Rome was complete. At that time, the aristocrats who were the wealthy from the Senate class of citizens were the only wealthy people remaining in the empire. The farmers had either handed over their lands or sold their properties to the government to keep from facing the high taxes. As Arthur Boak points out, "These few grew relatively richer as the middle classes were reduced to beggary and almost disappeared, and the poorer sank to even lower levels of wretchedness."[24]

America: Purchasers Instead of Producers

I once asked a wealthy Jewish businessman in Israel how he felt about the economic transitions occurring in America. He had substantial money invested in the U.S. stock market at the time and had lost some investment income. He stated, "The real problem America is experiencing and will experience in the future is that in the past, America was a producing nation, but now it's a purchasing nation. Lack of production and manufacturing leads to loss of jobs, and without jobs the tax revenues slow down, and eventually purchasing will decline."[25]

Consider how manufacturing has changed. North Carolina was the hub of major furniture manufacturing for many years. Dalton, Georgia, was known as the carpet capital of the world. Clothes were once made in the United States, along with the world's best automobiles. Over time, government regulations, high union fees, continual demands for pay raises, and the rise of another empire called *China* began to impact U.S. production. Recently, a group from Dubai visited one of the largest carpet factories in Dalton, Georgia, with the *intent* of giving the carpet mill millions of dollars in business for providing the best carpet in their new hotels being constructed in Dubai. They took video and pictures. The end result was that the Chinese used the video and picture information and built their personal carpet factory for use in Dubai. Many of the fine furniture factories in cities like Hickory and Statesville, North Carolina, have either shut down or moved their facilities overseas.

Today, Vietnam and Indonesia produce clothes sold in America. A personal missionary friend met a businesswoman from Indonesia who employs twenty-seven thousand workers in a clothing factory. The same factory produces three of the top American brand names, basically using the same fabric with different designs and sewing on the world-recognized emblems of each brand.

The three American carmakers—GMC, Ford, and Chrysler—were once labeled as "industrial giants" and held a monopoly on automobile sales in

America. The decline has been faster than anyone realized, and, "The Big Three's market share dropped from 74 percent in 1997 to 57 percent just 10 years later" in 2007.[26] Today, Japanese automakers now have a strong stake, reaching as high as 40 percent of all cars sold in America. The three former champions of the American automobile industry are losing the struggle to keep their factories and workers working.

Purchasers—Not Producers

America once led in manufacturing. China, Vietnam, and Indonesia replaced America's lead through low-wage jobs and lack of benefits, along with no lawsuits. We once led the auto industry, but we have been replaced by Japan. We once led in technology, but now China has soared ahead. We have become *purchasers* instead of *producers*. Producers provide job creation, and income creates tax revenues. Purchasers eventually run low on expendable income, resulting in jobs that are lost and eventually leading to their replacement by other nations that are producers.

The Houdini effect

Harry Houdini was an early American master of illusion. One of his greatest illusions, called the "Manacled Bridge Jump," involved men encircling his body in chains with locks; then he would jump into the water, sinking toward the bottom. No one caught the actual *secret* of his escape. His wife would suddenly act as if this might be the last time she would see her husband alive, so she ran and kissed him...inserting the key to the locks in his mouth. Minutes later, he emerged from the murky water to the shock of the crowds.[27]

Houdini was a master illusionist. He would love to see how the Federal Reserve, Treasury Department, and Congress in America are creating money *out of thin air*. Our nation's debt is not in the millions or billions, *but it is in the trillions*. And it is all backed by money created out of thin air. In fact, it is nothing but *hot air* and numbers on paper or on a computer's hard drive. Just how much *money* do we actually have? How much is in print? What would happen if everyone in America chose to withdraw their money from the banks?

According to the Federal Reserve, "As of December 2007, currency in circulation—that is, U.S. coins and paper currency in the hands of the public—totaled about $829 billion."[28] The Reserve has other types of money exchanges that it counts, including traveler's checks, demand deposits, and other checkable deposits, totaling about $1.5 billion. There is additional money in savings accounts and money market funds, which total about $8.3 billion.[29]

This sounds like a lot of money until you consider the national debt in America, which is more than *$10 trillion*, and the TARP (Troubled Asset Relief Program) bailouts and other promises, which have added another additional *$3 trillion*.

The Big Three

When a government begins to manipulate its currency, or creates national debt, there are three dangers: *deflation*, *inflation*, and *hyperinflation*, defined as:

- *Deflation*: A decrease in the prices of goods and services, linked to the contraction of money in circulation.

- *Inflation*: An increase in the prices of goods and services, usually tied to an increase of money in circulation.

- *Hyperinflation*: Extreme inflation, where in excess of four-digit annual percent change, the currency becomes worthless.

Hyperinflations occurred in Germany in the Weimer Republic in the early 1920s. Harvard University law professor Friedrich Kessler, an eyewitness of the German hyperinflation, said in a 1993 interview:

It was horrible. Horrible! Like lightning it struck. No one was prepared. The shelves in the grocery stores were empty. You could buy nothing with your paper money.[30]

Most Americans would suggest that we simply print more money and flood the banks and markets with the green stuff—and presto, you have money for your debts. That concept is an illusion. When there is a shortage of money or a lack of spending, prices drop across the board, and consumers often gain the benefit in their purchases. When excessive money is printed and the markets are flooded with cash, two negative things occur. First, prices begin to rise on products, and this produces inflation and a decline in the value of the money. Prior to the Great Depression, the Federal Reserve flooded the markets with cash. Later, in an attempt to *cool the markets*, they began withdrawing cash out of the system. Rumor had it that the banks were short of money, and so thousands of Americans *ran on the banks* to withdraw their cash, thus creating a major banking crash.

If free government money in a yellow envelope was handed over to each American, some would save it, and some would spend it. Massive spending creates a shortage of items and higher prices because of demand. The higher prices would erase the benefits of the additional money you received.

The other real danger is called *hyperinflation*. Should a major banking collapse occur, and the world lose complete faith in the American dollar and begin to cash in their Treasury bonds, then the demand for a new currency or a shift to another currency could occur, especially in nations that were buying bad debt. When German hyperinflation struck the German mark, it took more German marks to purchase goods.

After World War I, the Allies—Britain, France, and America—demanded reparations from Germany. Germany had signed the Treaty of Versailles in 1919. Part of the terms included Germany paying reparations for all civilian damages caused by the war. Limitations were placed on German armaments and military strength. In order to punish Germany, their money began to be devalued. In 1919, the German money, called the *mark*, was traded at 8.9 German marks to 1 American dollar. By 1922, that figure had risen to 4,500 marks to the dollar, and in 1923 reached 4.2 *trillion* marks to the dollar![31] Through the Allies, the banking system had effectively collapsed the German economy.

I once met a woman from Germany who was five years of age when Hitler rose to power. I asked her how he could convince the multitudes that the Jews were such enemies of the German people. She recalled hearing over and over that the Jews controlled the banks in America, France, and throughout Europe, and they could have prevented the economic collapse of Germany—but did not in order to take advantage of the economic crisis and punish Germany. Hitler was able to place the blame on the Jews (and Communists—who, he reminded the German people, originated from a Jew, Karl Marx). In his book *Mein Kampf*, Hitler blamed basically all of the world's ills on the Jews. The economic abyss gave room for a dictator to rise from the smoke of the pit. Thus, arresting Jews and confiscating their homes, property, and possessions were considered paybacks for the trouble the German Empire had experienced.

Economic crisis creates revolts, revolts lead to revolutions, and the end result is often the rise of a dictator. Three examples of this are the 1917 Russian Revolution, in which the tsarist autocracy was destroyed and replaced with the Bolshevik Communist government, the German crisis that brought Hitler to power, and the trouble in Italy that gave rise to Mussolini.

As an added note, when Hitler came to power, a new currency was printed. Hitler reminded the German people that the banks in Europe were either owned or controlled by wealthy Jews. He felt the Jews had a role in the destruction of the German economy. When Hitler began to arrest Jews, seize their property, and send Jews to camps, there was little outcry among many of the German people.

The destruction of the German economy formed a void of leadership, which was filled by Hitler and his Third Reich. The destruction of any nation's economy creates a void. In the future, this void will be filled by the Antichrist, who will control all buying and selling through his own economic system, known as the mark of the beast (Rev. 13:16–18).

So, where is America at this time? I believe we are repeating the same patterns of the ancient Roman Empire. As Rome went, so America is going.

• • • Section 3 • • •
AMERICA—THE FINAL PROPHECIES

••• Chapter 13 •••

AMERICA—THE NEW ROMAN EMPIRE

Does the eagle mount up at your command, and make its nest on high?

—*JOB 39:27*

THE REMARKABLE LINK between ancient Israel and America cannot be denied. This spiritual vine is interwoven by God's providence. The fig tree of Israel has the wild branches of the Gentiles grafted in it (Rom. 11). But America is more than a spiritual nation. It is a federal form of government that has its branches linked to another empire, namely the ancient Roman Empire.

The Republic of Rome—and America

The prophet Daniel predicted there would be four major world empires from his time until the return of the Messiah. In retrospect, these empires were Babylon, Media-Persia, Greece, with the fourth being Rome. This was the empire ruling during Christ's time and when the Roman Tenth Legion under the leadership of Titus destroyed Jerusalem and the holy temple in 70.

The Roman Empire is identified in the dream of King Nebuchadnezzar as the two iron legs on the metallic image (Dan. 2:31–35). The iron legs on the image represent the division of the Roman Empire between the East and the West. The Eastern headquarters was Constantinople (Istanbul), Turkey, and the Western headquarters was Rome, Italy. This division occurred in 330, during the time of the emperor Constantine. Centuries later, in 1054, another division occurred as the Roman Catholic church split; the Roman bishops controlled the Western branch, and the Byzantine Empire controlled the Eastern branch, with its center in Constantinople, Turkey.

At the end of days, prior to the return of Christ, there will be ten kings who will form a united coalition. These are the same ten kings identified as the ten toes on the image in Daniel 2:44–45. They are also seen as the ten horns on a beast and the ten horns on the dragon in Revelation 12 and 13:1–3.

The Roman Empire declined and ceased by the fifth century, and the Holy

Roman Empire filled in the gap as religion and politics mixed to form a system where the Roman Church gained political authority in matters of government. As we came into the late 1800s, there was a decline in the control of the Roman Church in Europe and a rise of the political authority of the United States and Great Britain. It appears that the United States has filled in the gap and taken on the same patterns of the ancient Roman Empire.

Rome was founded around April 21, 753 B.C.[1] Originally, Rome was ruled by seven kings, but eventually it moved from the control of kings to a democracy. The people gained independence from the Etruscan kings through a revolt. Eventually they established a constitution and became known as a republic, from the Latin word *republica*, meaning, "public affairs." Two traditional political parties eventually formed, one called the *populares*, meaning "people's party," and the other the *optimates*, meaning "senatorial party." One claimed to represent the poor people, and the other was accused of supporting the rich. The *populares* were considered *liberal*, and the *optimates* were classified as more *conservative*. There were surface clashes about ideology between these two parties, but in reality, neither party acted on behalf of the poor, only seeking the votes of the poor during elections.

Now consider the parallels with the formation of America. In our beginning, we were ruled and controlled by the kings of Europe, but we broke off that control as a result of the Revolutionary War. Our independence was sealed with the formation of the United States' Constitution, and our nation was called a republic by the Founding Fathers. A two-party system eventually emerged—the Democrats and the Republicans. During the twentieth century, the Democrats claimed to speak for the poorer class and accused the Republicans of being controlled and favored by the rich. The Democrats have become morally more liberal, and the Republicans are considered more morally conservative. While some politicians claim to speak for the poorer class, the sad fact is that it is an ideology presented for the purpose of gaining a voting bloc among the poor during an election year.

The Roman-American link can also been seen in the following correlations:

- **Superpowers:** Rome was the sole superpower during the peak of the empire. In the past, Russia and America were considered dueling superpowers. With the collapse of Communism, however, America has emerged as the single world power, especially in the realm of economics.

- **Military powers:** Rome was recognized as the mightiest military force in the world. Their soldiers were well trained with the best equipment of their day. Nations feared the Roman legions, and no country could stand against the Roman soldiers when they gathered en masse against their enemies. Today America is recognized globally as the best military in the world. America's technology is unsurpassed, and our military are the best trained, best organized, and best equipped in the world. Both nations occupied the Middle East. The Roman military occupied Roman nations in the Middle East. America is presently occupying the nations of Afghanistan and Iraq and has built military bases in Israel. In the period of Rome, the Romans called Israel *Palestine*. Rome controlled the land in the time of Christ.

- **Dealing directly with Israel and the Jewish people:** The Roman Empire had direct dealings with Israel, just as American administrations have direct contact and dealings with Israel.

- **Capitol Hill:** There was a large hill in the city of Rome called, in Latin, *Capitolina*. From this hill the Roman Senate met to forge laws and pass legislation impacting the Roman citizens. Washington DC is the U.S. capital, from which Congress initiates legislation that impacts the lives of the citizens of America. The capital is known as *Capitol Hill*!

- **A senate:** The Roman Empire had a senate. The United States has the Senate.

- **A main leader:** The Romans called the highest official ruling the empire from Rome *Caesar*. During the time of Paul's ministry, the Caesar was named Nero. He was one of the great persecutors of Christians. Every leader appointed over Rome was called Caesar. America appoints one main leader, called a *president*. Every leader elected to the highest office in the nation receives the title "president of the United States."

- **The eagle as its emblem:** One amazing link is the national emblem. The Roman Empire selected the eagle as their national emblem. The eagle sat atop the military standards of the Roman solders. The United States also selected the eagle as our nation's emblem. The eagle appears on the presidential seal and on all military seals.

- **Slave wars:** Slavery was common throughout the world in the time of the Roman Empire. Eventually there were several revolts among slaves, which led to several slave wars. America once allowed the purchasing and owning of slaves until the time of a revolt called the *Civil War*.

- **Killing of infants:** At the time of Christ's birth, King Herod instructed the Roman soldiers to enter an area called *Ramah* and Bethlehem, and carry out a door-to-door holocaust where all male children under age two were killed. The heathen king heard that a king of the Jews had been born. America has taken the same spirit of Rome by allowing infants in the wombs of their mothers to be aborted. Neither Rome nor America showed any respect for the lives of unborn infants. Most Americans could not comprehend the idea that a government would permit children from two years of age and under to be slaughtered alive with the swords of Roman soldiers, yet a large percentage of the population permits and supports abortion on demand. Roman tax money was paying the soldiers who slew the children in and around Bethlehem, just as American tax dollars are paying for the abortion of infants in America.

- **Freedom to homosexuals:** Rome was considered tolerant toward all forms of sexual activities, including same-sex relationships. During the time of the apostle Paul, the sin of homosexuality was very strong, especially in the ranks of the Roman Empire. History reveals that Nero was a homosexual and that homosexuality was accepted as a normal lifestyle among many of the Roman citizens. In America, the gay lifestyle is called *an alternative lifestyle*. This lifestyle is not only acceptable by most Western standards, but it is also growing at a rapid rate. Major cities host parties and parades where men flaunt their "sexual preference" publicly while Americans turn their heads and go on with life.

- **Stadiums for sports events:** The Greek and Roman citizens were captivated by sports events. This included running, wrestling, and chariot races. These events were often conducted in large stadiums, built to accommodate thousands of spectators. Sunday became just another day to work and to fill the stadiums for the many sporting events. America is also a nation filled with stadiums where thousands gather to watch their favorite teams compete. The wrestling industry has become a popular form of violent entertainment in America, and the car races have replaced the once popular chariot races of the parallel empire of Rome. Years ago in America, most stores were closed on Sunday to give employees opportunity to attend worship services and to provide a much-needed day of rest. Today, Sunday is no longer the Lord's day, but it is just another day for Americans to golf, go to the malls, and fill stadiums for games.

- **Sports becoming more violent and bloody:** Roman athletics moved from the Greek form of the games to more violent and bloody sports, including gladiator fighting in the stadiums. Eventually, hatred for Christians led to the blood sport of feeding the Christians to wild animals in the Roman coliseum. Crowds were worked into a frenzied mob as the arena was rocked by multitudes jeering and shouting. America was once content with the basic three sports of baseball, football, and basketball. Today, however, many in America are turning to more violent and bloody sports, some of which is classified as "entertainment."

- **A national anthem:** Rome had a national anthem, and America has a national anthem. In Rome, the anthem was sung in the stadiums and coliseums. Today it is common for the national anthem to be sung in major sporting events prior to the opening of the games.

- **Pledging allegiance to the flag:** In another strange twist, Rome had a special flag that represented the nation, and those faithful to the empire would stand and pledge their allegiance to the national flag. During certain national events, including special military events, it is a tradition for Americans to pledge allegiance to the flag.

- **Tolerant of every god from every nation—except Christianity:** Rome eventually turned to Eastern cults and religions. Foreign religions were easily established in the empire. The people of Rome filled in their spiritual gap by turning to Eastern cults. Rome had a mixture of spiritual ideas but did not consider religion as a spiritual experience. Today, Americans are filling their spiritual voids by turning to Eastern mysticism, Kabala, Hinduism, and Buddhism—all Eastern religions. Rome welcomed all religions (except Christianity). Roman leaders clashed with Christians who refused to call the Roman emperor "God." Christians would not participate in Rome's pagan holidays and set aside a day to worship Jesus, requiring them to be off work, which caused a conflict. As a result, Christians were targeted for persecution and were hated by the Roman political system. Although America is founded as a Christian nation, the Christian population is beginning to experience much opposition from organizations such as the American Civil Liberties Union (ACLU), who are removing freedom to practice the Christian faith from all public places. Those who are firm Christians and who will not deny the faith and the cross are called *right-wing religious fanatics* who are intolerant of others. This is a repeat of the Roman Empire.

- **Obsessed with luxuries:** The citizens living in Rome became obsessed with Roman glass, jewelry, and expensive luxuries. It was fashionable to attempt to outdo your neighbor with fancy clothes and "stuff." The same is true with Americans. Parents will pay twice as much just to be seen in brand-name shoes, clothes, and "stuff."

- **Conducting a census:** Rome conducted a census every five years, and every man had to report the number and names of his family and his slaves. The United States conducts a national census every ten years in which information is recorded concerning family members. Both Rome and America had a place known as the *suburbs*, where families lived on the outskirts of the city.

As pointed out earlier, the national emblem of the Roman Empire was the eagle. Cast-iron eagles were erected upon the military standards of the Roman soldiers and carved upon certain buildings. The correlations continue when comparing certain monuments and goddesses once prominent in the Roman Empire and the parallel to the United States.

The Statue of Liberty

In New York Harbor stands a large, light green metal monument named the Statue of Liberty. Most Americans believe it is simply a woman holding a torch welcoming strangers and visitors to America. This same woman also sits on several capitol buildings throughout America, including the U.S. Capitol in Washington DC.

The Statue of Liberty was actually designed by two Frenchmen who were Freemasons. The Romans borrowed the image of this woman from the Greeks, and several Roman coins were minted with this same woman on the coins. She is actually the "goddess of liberty," which was worshiped in Rome around 3 B.C. The ancient Romans placed a statue of this goddess on Aventine Hill in the city of Rome.

This is the same goddess of liberty known as *Lady Liberty*, which was minted on U.S. coins by the U.S. Treasury Department. Lady Liberty is not the only monument linking Rome with America.

This link between Rome and America continues with the design of the U.S. Capitol building in Washington DC. At the time designs were being drawn for the nation's capitol building, Thomas Jefferson suggested that the building be built in the form of the Roman Pantheon, which was a building dedicated to all the gods of Rome. Eventually the builders settled for a large dome to be mounted in top of the center of the building. In Rome, domes were used to symbolize the unity of the empire. The Roman named for such a structure is *Capitolium*. The name of our federal building is the Capitol, taken from the Roman name *Capitolium*. One early document even calls the Capitol the Temple of Liberty.

Many of the major federal governmental buildings constructed in Washington are built from marble and stone using the same architecture from the Roman and Greek periods. Huge Roman-designed columns tower above the porches in the same manner as the buildings constructed in Rome and Greece.

Rome's Decline and the Decline of America

Centuries ago, the mighty Roman Empire controlled military powers, economic authority, and trade routes among the nations in and around the Mediterranean Sea region. For several hundred years, it seemed Rome would dominate forever. This, however, did not happen. The empire fell into a moral abyss, which led to its eventual disappearance from history and replacement by other empires and nations.

It is important to note that the decline of the Roman Empire parallels the moral and spiritual decline now occurring in the United States.

The Roman Military and the Pax Romana

The Roman Empire was noted for its strong, dominating military. The empire had established the *Pax Romana*, or Roman peace. The purpose of the Pax Romana was to keep peace throughout the empire. Roman soldiers were stationed to protect the borders of nations, squelch civil uprisings, and defeat rebellions that would arise and form revolts against Roman troops, who were considered by some, including many Jews in Israel, as *occupiers*.

Roman soldiers spent countless weeks in physical and mental training to ensure that they worked together as a well-oiled fighting machine. The army gave a number and rank to each soldier in their legions. The training of Roman soldiers was paid for, and men were rewarded for their victories. Special necklaces and armbands were given, and embossed disks were worn on their uniforms. There was even an army of engineers to service roads and bridges! Needless to say, the occupation of lands, putting out uprisings among rebels, and guarding the borders cost huge amounts of money. As a result, the government of Rome incurred mounting debt.

In order to increase revenue for the government, taxes on the general public were increased. The higher the debt, the more taxes were raised. Evidence of global taxation is recorded in the Bible at the time of Christ's birth. Luke says: "And it came to pass in those days, that there went out a decree from Caesar Augustus that all the world should be taxed" (Luke 2:1, kjv). This taxation began to dip into the personal salaries of the common workers. The government was taxing income more frequently, and the "take-home pay" for workers was becoming less.

Eventually, once prosperous farmers could not repay their bills and loans, so they threw up their hands and quit. So many Roman farmers were unwilling or unable to work that the government developed a welfare system using doles.[2]

A bankrupt farmer had one of three choices:

1. Join the Roman army. In this manner a man would receive a steady salary and food.

2. Go to colonize new lands where the population was low and build from start.

3. Go on the welfare rolls and depend upon government doles (subsidies).

As the taxes went up, more Romans left their jobs, unable to survive. The welfare system began as a good initiative, but it eventually became a heavy load and burden upon the government as the masses became dependent upon the government assistance. The burden to provide taxes fell upon the rich as the government demanded them to bear the blunt of taxes. Eventually the middle class of society was squeezed out of existence. The burden fell on the government. Today in America we hear the cry from Washington that the government needs more tax revenue and how the rich need to pay more taxes!

The Declining Birth Rate of the Empire

As taxes rose, births declined. Couples could no longer afford to have children. This impacted the leaders of the Senate. Under Nero, four hundred senators lost their family lineage and heritage because they had no children to carry on their names.[3] As the estates and farms were placed on the public market, the rich began to purchase them for their estates. By A.D. 100, there were only two thousand landowners in all of Italy.[4] It may be that the Romans invaded Jerusalem, destroying the temple to seize the gold and silver vessels and bring them to Rome, thus increasing their need for wealth.

The temple in Jerusalem was the one place where the treasuries were filled with gold, silver, and precious things. In the year 70, General Titus broke through the strong walls of Jerusalem, giving instructions to his soldiers not to destroy the sacred temple. A soldier, however, threw a torch into the window, and eventually the inner sanctuary was on fire. The fire was so great that the gold within the holy temple melted and ran down the stone walls.

When the dust settled and the fires ceased, the soldiers toppled the stones in order to peel off the gold that had dripped down the stones. The holy treasures, such as the silver trumpets and the golden menorah, and other precious things were brought in a triumphant procession into the city of Rome and paraded before the cheering crowds.

However, the invasion of Jerusalem was not significant enough to undergird the economic crisis that enveloped the government. As time passed, the military began to decline as soldiers became slothful and unconcerned with their assignments. Careless living, the love for luxuries, and complacency eventually cost the empire its global control.

The Roman Empire eventually deteriorated into moral decay. Will this be the eventual ruin of the American Empire? Or will the rise of the European Union with its borderless travel, single passport system, and new currency take the lead in a new, revived Roman Empire? If the power shifts from the West to the East, then the EU could emerge as the seventh empire of Bible prophecy, which will continue for a short time before the final kingdom of the Antichrist (Rev. 17:10–11).

Rome Fell From Within—Not Without

From the time of Babylon to Rome, three of the four major empires of biblical prophecy fell because of war. One empire simply overthrew the previous empire. The Medes and Persians overtook the Babylonians, and the Greeks overthrew the Medes and Persians. The Romans eventually defeated the Greeks.

However, no army invaded Rome. No dictator rose to power and used military force to defeat the mighty Roman Empire. The famous empire that ruled the world in the time of the New Testament simply rotted from within. Morally, spiritually, politically, and socially, the vast empire went into a decline and could not recover from its internal disorder. In short, the love of pleasure created laziness. The love of power created division. The love of blood sports created persecution of the Christians. The love of sexual pleasure created immorality.

Like a flower cut from a growing bush that withers and fades without the life-giving source of the vine, the Roman Empire died from within. The spiritual and moral decline in ancient Rome is parallel to the same moral and spiritual decline in America.

Will America Fall Just Like Rome?

Rome loved all forms of sports, including chariot races, wrestling, and gladiator sports. Eventually the athletes were treated as gods and could do no wrong. In like manner today, when a professional athlete is caught in a criminal activity, that person seldom serves time, but highly paid lawyers get that person off the hook so fans will continue to enjoy seeing personal *idols* perform for their pleasure!

The spirits of the empire always precede the formation of the empire. Hitler was deeply involved in the occult. When Hitler viewed a relic called *The Spear of Destiny* on display in the Hapsburg's treasury at the Hofmuseum in Vienna, he "witnessed extraordinary visions of his own destiny unfolding before him."[5] Mark Harris, in his Internet article "Hitler and the Spear of Destiny," states: "The relic was said to have phenomenal talismanic power having once been used at the Crucifixion to wound the side of Christ. According to legend, possession of the Spear would bring its owner the power to conquer the world, but losing it would bring immediate death."[6] I believe this is evidence that an evil spirit preceded Hitler's decision to annihilate the Jewish race from Europe.

Those who believe that the answer to America's woes is to be *politically correct* may wish to skip the rest of this chapter. The information in this section is for those who can discern strong spiritual truth and understand the unseen battle raging for the soul and spirit of our nation, whose foundations are being eroded away.

America has been called the *melting pot*. This phrase alludes to the fact that America is a land of immigrants, coming from every nation under heaven to enjoy the freedoms offered by our Constitution. For most of us, the roots of our family tree are planted in Europe, Africa, or a nation outside of the United States. My great-grandfather came from Italy, and the relatives on Dad's side of the family are Cherokee Indian and Irish.

At the turn of the twentieth century, when early immigrants came to the shores of New York or Los Angeles, all people welcomed them. Their children were placed in public schools that taught accurate American history, and each morning a Bible story and a devotional prayer were offered by the teachers in all public schools. The early immigrants were often Catholic, Protestant, or Jewish in their faith. Yet there was no question that they were coming to a Christian nation that believed in the Bible. Although a melting pot for all, America was "one nation under God." Even the average "sinner" had a respect for the local preacher in the community and would bow his head in reverence whenever a prayer was offered in a public place. There were no threats being made against anyone who concluded a benediction by saying, "In Jesus's name I pray."

After the 1963 Supreme Court decision to remove prayer and Bible reading from public schools, there was a shifting in the attitudes of those who immigrated to America. Soon, individuals from Islamic nations, India, and other Asian countries began pouring into America to receive a college education or find work. Each person brought his or her own religious belief and his or her own *gods*, including statues and images that they used during their times of prayer.

A parallel of this is found in ancient history. When Alexander the Great and his armies conquered the known world, the Greek Empire brought the Hellenistic age to the known civilized world. This created a change in the political and spiritual landscape throughout nations that surrounded the Mediterranean Sea. Among the Greeks, numerous gods and goddesses were accepted and worshiped. Huge temples were erected throughout the empire to Zeus, Artemis, Apollo, Athena, Aphrodite, Dionysus, and a host of lesser-known gods such as Asclepius, Demeter, Persephone, and Poseidon, revered for their power and wisdom. By the time Christianity began making inroads into Europe, cities like Corinth and Ephesus were completely controlled by city officials who were making huge profits from pilgrims and local citizens who paid tribute and gave offerings in the temples of the gods. By the time Paul traveled through Asia, the superstition of the common people was at a peak. When miracles began to happen among the people, they declared that the "gods had come down" (Acts 14:11–12).

Wars Always Shift the Nations

Early Americans consisted of believers from the Church of England, Puritans, Quakers, Presbyterians, Methodists, Baptists, and Pentecostals, to name a few. These denominations flourished from the 1600s into the Revolutionary War period. The Methodists were noted for their large outdoor camp meetings. At the turn of the twentieth century, the Pentecostals, or *Spirit-filled groups*, began to rise in number, and today they are one of the fastest-growing groups both inside and outside of America.

Two world wars began to change the ethnic and religious groups in America. Following World War I and World War II, there were huge numbers of immigrants who flocked to America. The shaking among the nations of Europe caused many people to become refugees, seeking freedom from dictators and evil regimes.

Many immigrants were educated in faithless, prayerless public schools. After entering America's universities, they encountered spiritually dumb and ethically numb professors whose agenda was designed to remove all Christian faith from any student who would dare believe that Christ was the only true way to heaven. If you were "foolish enough to believe in God," then the liberal puppets of unbelief would rush the idea that all roads and all religions lead to God. This New Age concept of religion caused every belief to be accepted as truth, and any opposing voices were classified as those of prehistoric, close-minded Christian fundamentalists.

What harm could there be in other religions practicing their religion in America? After all, we ensure *freedom of speech* and *freedom of religion* in our nation. This is true, but in this chapter we are not concerned with political concepts as much as the spiritual impact.

Aren't Idols Harmless?

What impact can praying in front of a statue, image, or a painting actually do? After all, the image cannot hear, speak, or think. Many religions that use images and statues not only literally believe the inanimate object can hear the prayers of the petitioner, but they also believe that a *spirit* is connected to the idol. Food is often left out before the image, and many report that in a short period of time the food disappears.

From a biblical perspective, these images can attract familiar spirits, or demons, that can manifest various types of *miracles*, thus deceiving worshipers into believing the image is actually a god who is hearing their prayer.

Perhaps the most bizarre stories of such *miracles* come from the nation of India. A majority of Indians are Hindus. There are literally hundreds of thousands of gods that are worshiped among the Hindus. I have three personal friends who are missionaries to India. They have videotapes of people worshiping rats, trees, and, in one instance, a broomstick! Missionaries and Christians in India note that the level of demonic possession is so high that in almost every Christian worship service or outdoor evangelistic meeting numerous individuals who worship idols begin to manifest demonic influence, some actually having various voices speak through them, levitating into the air, or violently jerking. Once people are delivered from the grips of demonic control, they immediately destroy the idols in the home, thus freeing themselves from the evil influences.

The truth is, while the idol is an inanimate, man-made object, idols attract evil spirits. While this book is not a theological discourse to prove the existence of Satan or his demonic hosts, any person who reads the Scriptures knows that the existence of principalities, powers, rulers of the darkness of the world, and wicked spirits in high places is proven throughout the Bible (Eph. 6:12).

How can spirits connected to idols influence our nation? In ancient Israel, when the Hebrews crossed the Jordan River to inherit the Promised Land, God instructed the people not to make a league with the inhabitants of the land, but to take the territory and to destroy their idols. God warned that if they failed to follow these instructions, the idols would be a snare to them. History records that Israel failed to follow the divine instructions. Eventually, the Hebrews were throwing their children into the fiery belly of the idol god Molech. In the high mountains, trees were carved out for use in the worship of Baal. As time progressed, the patience of God wore thin. He allowed the nation of Israel to be taken captive by its enemies. God then mocked His own people by saying, "Now pray to your idol and see if he can help you." (See 1 Kings 18.)

The Spirit Behind the Idols

As new immigrants have entered America, many have brought their own religion with them. This has created a political and social *snare*, especially among those of us who teach that the Bible is God's inspired Word and that receiving Jesus Christ is the only guarantee to entering the kingdom of heaven. With millions of Muslims bowing to Allah yet denying the deity of Christ...Buddhists bowing to a large idol of Buddha...Hindus worshiping a smorgasbord of gods...and New Agers rubbing rocks and squeezing trees, any mention that non-Christian religious beliefs may not contain the truth brings accusations of being a narrow-minded, right-wing Christian fundamentalist.

This is not to say that America should not welcome people from other religions or nations. Certainly we should. At one time when they arrived on the shores of America, they understood who we were and what we stood for. They knew that the Bible and Christian faith were established by our founders as the pivotal truths of our religion. Today, no one knows what we believe. America is a confused nation that has lost its spiritual identity. When our faith in God is shattered, it will be replaced by an idol.

The Real American Idol

An idol does not need be a hand-carved, man-made object. An idol is anything that replaces God in your life. With the decline in spiritual values in our nation, America has chosen her own idols. Parallels to these idols can be found in the history of past empires.

The ancient Egyptians were a people steeped in idol worship. There was a god that controlled almost everything. At the time of the Exodus, when God sent the ten plagues against the Egyptians, it was actually an assault against ten of the main gods of Egypt. For example, the Egyptian sun god was named *Ra*. This god controlled the movement of the sun. When the almighty God sent darkness to Egypt, the old idol Ra could do nothing to stop the plague.

One of the main deities among the Egyptians was Apis, the bull god. When the Hebrews departed from Egypt, Moses spent forty days on Mount Sinai receiving the commandments of God. Without their spiritual leader, the Israelites took the earrings from the ears of their sons and molded a golden calf. They were *out of Egypt*, but *Egypt wasn't out of them*. When Moses returned from the mount, his anger was kindled, and he threw the commandments to the ground, breaking them into pieces. The sin of worshiping the golden calf caused three thousand people to die, and Moses destroyed the calf. The Hebrew people actually believed the golden cow was responsible for bringing them from Egypt.

In the nineties, enormous money was made in the stock market. This was a wonderful opportunity to invest and make money, which the Bible encourages us to do. The news continually boasted that the *bull market* was running, and there was no end in sight to the money that could be made. The only problem was that corruption and greed got in the way.

Presently, large corporations are being investigated for fraud, for lying to investors, and for padding the books. The CEOs ran off with the money, leaving investors holding an empty bag.

It is interesting to note that at the entrance of the New York Stock Exchange is situated a large brass bull. When I saw this bull, the thought came to my mind that if God would not allow His chosen people Israel to worship a golden calf, then neither will He permit America to place their trust in a *bull market*. The key word here is *trust*. The stock market is a wonderful tool if properly used with discretion, yet the Bible teaches, "Command those who are rich in this present age not to be haughty, nor to trust in uncertain riches but in the living God, who gives us richly all things to enjoy" (1 Tim. 6:17).

In ancient Israel, the cult of Molech flourished, especially among the Canaanite tribes in the Promised Land. The idol Molech was a huge iron god with the appearance of a bull from the waist up and a man from the waist down. The priests of Molech would build a fire in the belly of the iron god. At appointed times, they would offer a baby to Molech by "passing it through the fire." Some scholars believe this indicates that while the baby was held by its feet, it was waved between the burning hands of the hot iron beast. Musicians would beat drums to drown out the tormenting screams of the child. This act called "passing your sons and daughters through the fire" was totally forbidden by God and brought judgment upon the nation of Israel. (See 2 Kings 17:17.)

As repulsive as the thought of waving a baby through burning iron is, America is both numb and ignorant that the same spirit of Molech is the spirit of abortion. God created the womb of a woman to be a warm, safe place for a child. The sac of water forms a protective wall. Yet, nearly fifty million infants have been laid on the altar of Molech in America since 1973.[7]

When Elijah challenged the false prophets of Baal on Mount Carmel, he was dealing with 850 men who had aligned themselves with King Ahab and his wife Jezebel. Many Christian leaders believe that the spirit of Baal, which is a "ruling spirit," may be the principal demonic spirit affecting America today. In a recent communication, Dutch Sheets made this comment: "The Hebrew word *baal* actually means, 'husband' or 'marriage.' This spirit always attempted to cause Israel to 'divorce' or break covenant with God and 'marry' or align with him. Consistent with this, in so many ways America has broken covenant with God and married Baal. This is, I believe, the strongman behind most covenant breaking."[8]

The fourth spirit was the spirit of Ashtoreth. Statues of Ashtoreth are often unearthed in excavations throughout the Middle East. She was considered to be the goddess of sexual fertility. With the emergence of "free love" in the hippie days of the 1960s, an alarming sexual revolution began to take place in America. One leader states: "The sexual revolution was a national identity crisis, based upon discarded belief in God and a distorted view of human life and sexuality."[9]

● ● ● ● ● ●

The images of yesterday, molded in the furnaces of ancient Israel, are now relics in museums. Yet, behind these man-made idols are ancient spirits (Eph. 6:12) that are presently influencing the nations. These spiritual prince spirits and powers will be released unrestrained in the future to influence a final kingdom predicted by the prophet Daniel and the apostle John. These amazing prophecies reveal the future of major empires. What do they imply or teach about the West? Let's explore the predictions.

••• Chapter 14 •••

THE FUTURE OF THE WEST—TOLD 2,500 YEARS AGO

The nations of prophecy are aligning in position for the great battles of prophecy. Now let's get ready for the opening scene in the last-day drama. The curtain is about to rise. The action is about to start, and the actors are taking their position on stage. It is about to become interesting.[1]

—PERRY STONE

IT IS HUMAN nature to discover the future. If we believed everything that lies ahead is positive, good, and exciting, we would simply live each day without any fear or concern. Many Americans desire to know the future for two reasons: first, to prevent being caught off guard without plans for the bad times; and second, to discern the bad in hopes of changing the outcome. Secular Americans ignorantly seek advice from horoscopes, palm readers, and psychics. If psychics were as accurate as they advertise, why has no self-appointed fortune-teller revealed the location of Osama bin Laden and claimed the $25 million bounty on the terrorist mastermind's head? To know the future, you should examine the predictions of visionaries who have a reputation for 100 percent accuracy. Only one group fits this level of competence and accuracy: the biblical prophets.

These men, ethnically from the Hebrew nation of Israel, were inspired by a divine force identified as the *Ruach HaKodesh*, or the Holy Spirit (2 Pet. 1:21). These visionaries and spiritual dreamers are identified with names like Moses, David, Isaiah, Jeremiah, Ezekiel, Daniel, and John. The Scriptures consist of sixty-six individual books, and nearly one-third, or 30 percent, of the Bible's material is prophetic. The prophets made vast predictions of events that would transpire from their time to the time of the end, when the anticipated Messiah will return and set up a visible kingdom in Jerusalem.

For example, in the year 70, the Roman Tenth Legion was responsible for burning down the Jewish temple, destroying Jerusalem, and taking thousands of Jews captive as slaves. In that year Israel, as a Jewish nation, ceased to exist.

In 71, the Romans plowed the city under, spreading salt throughout the area to prevent the Jews from rebuilding or planting in the area. Christ had predicted this destruction in Matthew 24:1–2, about forty years before it occurred.

Throughout the centuries, few Gentile nations ever considered it possible for the Jews to return to Palestine, rebirth a nation called Israel, and make Jerusalem the capital. Yet, numerous Hebrew prophets not only predicted this would occur but also revealed details that today are considered miraculous signs of biblical inspiration. For example, the prophets predicted:

- *Israel* would be the name of the Jewish nation at the time of the end (Ezek. 39:1–4).
- Israel would be reborn in one day, and it was on May 14, 1948 (Isa. 66:8).
- Jerusalem would be the capital and would expand prior to the Messiah's return (Ps. 102:16).
- The Jews would survive a terrible destruction and return to form a great army (Ezek. 37:10).
- The Jews would return to Israel from the south, east, north, and west (Isa. 43:5–6).
- The desert lands in Israel would blossom and fill the world with fruit (Isa. 27:6; 35:1–7).
- Israel would be surrounded by enemies who would desire her destruction (Ezek. 38).
- The Jews would return and speak their original language (Zeph. 3:9).
- The gates would remain open in the city continually (Isa. 60:11).
- Little children would again be playing in the streets of Jerusalem (Zech. 8:5).

From 1948 to the present, all of the above predictions, many made more than twenty-six hundred years ago, have come to pass. With such accuracy, the question often arises, "Is America or the West mentioned in predictions concerning the time of the end?"

The Prophecies of the West

Some point out that in the time of both the Old and New Testaments, those living in the Middle East were unaware of America, Canada, and even South America, since the continent was not discovered until 1492 during Columbus's voyage. Thus, it is fruitless to engage in any search for an allusion to America in prophecy. While this basic theory is true, the West did exist in the concept of the ancients and was understood to be one of the four points of the compass, or called the "four winds" and "four corners of the earth" (Dan. 7:2; Isa. 11:12). It was also understood that such nations as Britain and Spain were considered the West, especially in the Roman period.

In Scripture, the four winds or four corners are identified as the North, South, East, and West. In the Old Testament, the North is mentioned 129 times, and the South is alluded to 134 times. The East is used 148 times, and the West, 62 times. In Scripture, the West is mainly used in connection with the western side of the tabernacle of Moses in the wilderness.

When comparing these four points of the compass with the nations of antiquity, and comparing the nations mentioned in the End Time ancient prophecies, we soon discover the nations and locations where major prophetic activity will be occurring:

End-Time Prophetic Nations		
GEOGRAPHICAL LOCATION	NATIONS INVOLVED	SCRIPTURE
NORTH: Northern Africa	Egypt, Libya, and Ethiopia	Daniel 11:43
WEST: Europe	Mystery Babylon	Revelation 17 and 18
SOUTH: Middle East	Edom, Moab, Israel	Daniel 11:41
EAST: Asia	Kings of the East	Revelation 16:12

Having researched the prophetic Scriptures for nearly thirty-five years, I can say with certainty that in the future, the North, South, and East will dominate the global scene. In both Daniel and Revelation, the Middle Eastern regions will be the hotbed of activity and wars. Daniel describes an empire that rises out of the "Great Sea," which scholars agree is today the Mediterranean Sea region. Oddly, there is little if any mention of the West in the final visions of the biblical prophets.

One main prophetic dream by Nebuchadnezzar, king of ancient Babylon, however, reveals that historical empires will be divided between the East and the West until the very time when the Messiah returns.

Empires of Prophecy from Daniel Chapter 2
The Vision of the Metallic Image

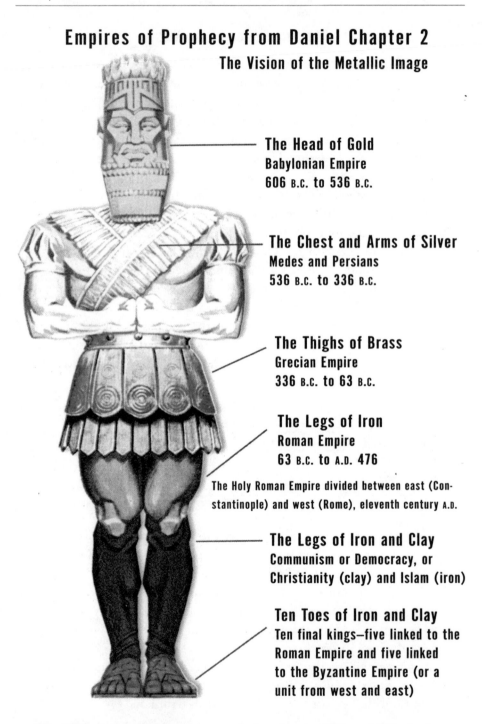

The Head of Gold
Babylonian Empire
606 B.C. to 536 B.C.

The Chest and Arms of Silver
Medes and Persians
536 B.C. to 336 B.C.

The Thighs of Brass
Grecian Empire
336 B.C. to 63 B.C.

The Legs of Iron
Roman Empire
63 B.C. to A.D. 476

The Holy Roman Empire divided between east (Constantinople) and west (Rome), eleventh century A.D.

The Legs of Iron and Clay
Communism or Democracy, or
Christianity (clay) and Islam (iron)

Ten Toes of Iron and Clay
Ten final kings—five linked to the
Roman Empire and five linked
to the Byzantine Empire (or a
unit from west and east)

The Bible itself interprets part of the dream. When Nebuchadnezzar consulted with the Hebrew prophet Daniel, Daniel told the king that the head of gold was the Babylonian Empire. It would be followed by a lesser kingdom (silver arms), then another lesser (brass), and finally would end in iron and clay.

History can now interpret the entire dream. The silver empire, the Mede and Persian kings, overtook the Babylonians and set up their headquarters in Babylon. Eventually, the brass kingdom of Greece followed the Persians and ruled throughout the area of the Great Sea and beyond. As time passed, a new empire rose, which was the Roman Empire. It was identified on the image as iron, and the Roman legions had weapons, chariots, and armor made with iron.

Two Legs of Iron

Eventually the Roman Empire split into two divisions—the East and the West. Imperial Rome ruled the western branch. However, the emperor, Constantine, took rule of Rome in 324 and constructed a *new Rome*, called *Constantinople*, in Asia (Turkey). Completed on May 11, 330, the new city was the Rome of the East and eventually headquartered the Byzantine Empire, which would last for almost a thousand years.

As Imperial Rome eventually fell into the control of ten major Germanic tribes, Rome became the center of the Roman Catholic Church, directed through the power of the pope. The eastern religious branch was headquartered in Constantinople. The Roman Church conducted services in the Latin language, and the Byzantines conducted their services in the Greek language. Thus, the two legs on the image were split between two cities, Rome and Constantinople, and two branches of religion, Roman and Greek Christianity.

It is noteworthy that in 800, Charlemagne formed a Holy Roman Empire that lasted from 800 to 1806, when the French leader Napoleon removed the pope's power out of France. Thus, the Holy Roman influence lasted nearly one thousand years. The eastern branch began in the fourth century and continued until the Muslims seized Constantinople in 1453, nearly a thousand years. The two distinct legs, both of iron, were split in two directions.

History reveals more interesting insight about the continual division of the two legs of iron—the East and West. In the year 1299, a new empire arose that would impact parts of Europe, Asia, the Middle East, and what is today the southern part of Russia. This new Islamic empire was the Ottoman Turkish Empire, whose influence spread in the same fashion as ancient Rome. In 1517, the year that the Ottoman Turkish Empire invaded and seized control of Pakistan, there was a new revolution in the Christian religion, directed by Martin Luther, called the *Reformation*. The Reformation introduced the Protestant religion to Western Europe, and its influence was felt in Germany,

Britain, England, and the western provinces. Thus, the split of East and West continued, this time between the Christians and the Muslims.

For about four hundred years, the Ottoman Turks controlled or directly influenced Northern Africa, Palestine, Lebanon, Syria, Iraq, Turkey, and five states in southern Russia. The Christian faith continued throughout the western half of the empire. Eventually, however, the Turks began slaughtering millions of Christians, and this caused the larger western nations to move against the Ottomans and make plans to run them out of the Middle East. The next transition would lead us to the events of 1917 and beyond.

The 1917 Transition

After World War I, there was another split between two social ideas that clashed with one another. After 1917, the United States, Britain, and France began to introduce *democracy* to the Middle East. Democracy was the clay in the feet of the image. In Europe there was even a move to unite all of Europe through the coal and steel industry; again, coal from the clay of the earth and steel.

In the East, a new ideology called *Communism* swept the Russian nation. The Communists introduced atheism to the nation and used military power to subdue all objectors. Russia began a vigorous campaign to organize a massive army with weapons of mass destruction. The secrecy of the ideological barriers the Soviet Union constructed was called the *iron curtain*. When the collapse of Communism came after seventy years, the Jews were permitted to return to Israel from the Soviet Union, beginning in 1987.

When the iron curtain began to melt, another iron began to form, which was Islamic fanaticism. These Islamic fascists make their political points through terrorism, death threats to the opposition, and by rejecting the social concepts of the West. The West is attempting to introduce the clay of democracy into the Middle East nations, including Iraq, Afghanistan, Pakistan, and among the Muslims living in the so-called *occupied territories* in Israel.

America has attempted to make a village of clay in a land of iron. America has confessed a desire to bring peace to a land of blood and war. But the iron and clay—democracy and Fascism—do not mix.

Daniel revealed to the king that the final empire at the time of the end would form in the days when the ten toes on the image, identified as the ten kings, would organize the final kingdom of prophecy. Daniel reveals that the merging of the iron and clay will not work.

> Whereas you saw the feet and toes, partly of potter's clay and partly of iron, the kingdom shall be divided; yet the strength of the iron shall

be in it, just as you saw the iron mixed with ceramic clay. And as the toes of the feet were partly of iron and partly of clay, so the kingdom shall be partly strong and partly fragile. As you saw iron mixed with ceramic clay, they will mingle with the seed of men; but they will not adhere to one another, just as iron does not mix with clay. And in the days of these kings the God of heaven will set up a kingdom which shall never be destroyed; and the kingdom shall not be left to other people; it shall break in pieces and consume all these kingdoms, and it shall stand forever.

—DANIEL 2:41–44

Why America Will Slowly Decline

At the present, it seems unlikely, and to many impossible, to imagine that the great American Empire has reached its peak of perfection and power and will eventually give up its sovereign control to merge with a more global form of rule. When exploring the numerous End Time prophecies revealed in the Scriptures, there are clues as to why the leading Gentile nation will move toward decline.

1. Economic unity—introducing the mark system

For many years, the dollar has been the leading and most desirable currency in the world market. Most of the world's commodities are priced in dollars. Other leading currencies include the Japanese yen, the British pound or sterling, the Mexican peso, and the European euro.

When the United States entered a full-blown recession in 2009, there was increased chatter that nations were interested in a global currency. Nobel prize–winner President Nursultan Nazarbayev announced his plan for a single world currency during an economic meeting at his new capital in Kazakhstan.[2]

The concept of one currency is spreading throughout the world. In a meeting with the financial chiefs of five of the six members, the Gulf Cooperation Council approved a proposal to form a monetary union. The five nations agreeing on the concept include Bahrain, Kuwait, Qatar, Saudi Arabia, and the United Arab Emirates. The idea is to form regional instead of national currencies.[3]

There is a belief in the Islamic world, handed down from the time of Muhammad, that in the last days there would be a failure of world currencies, and the only currency that would be used would be an Islamic currency consisting of silver and gold dinars. The concept of an Islamic currency based upon gold and silver originated in Malaysia and is based upon a prediction in the Islamic hadith. It is written:

> Abu Bakr ibn Abi Maryam reported that he heard the Messenger of Allah, may Allah bless him and grant him peace, say: "A time is certainly coming over mankind in which there will be nothing [left] which will be of use save a dinar and a dirham."[4]

In early Islamic history, a gold coin was minted called the *dinar*. After the collapse of the Ottoman Turkish Empire in 1924, there was a lapse in the Islamic currency, as most Muslim countries accepted the currency of Western nations, including the British pound and the American dollar. Several years ago an Islamic group in West Malaysia began minting the gold dinar. Meetings have been conducted in Egypt and in Arabia discussing the need for Muslims to accept the new coinage as the future official coin of the Islamic nations. In brief, many apocalyptic Muslims who hold to traditions concerning the last days believe there will be a worldwide economic crisis in which all paper money will be useless. The only money of value will be money consisting of gold and silver.

Some speculate this is one reason why gold and silver prices have risen from time to time by 40 or 50 percent in a short time. In 2001, the price of gold, which rarely reflected any change for nearly twenty years, was $250 per ounce. By early 2003, the price of gold and silver was rising, but after the invasion of Iraq, the price of gold increased dramatically, rising to more than $600 an ounce by 2006![5] There was no explanation for this, since the stock market was rising, the jobless rate decreasing, and the economy was again on the move. The explanation may be found when exploring who is hoarding the gold and silver.

Intelligence research indicates that Muslims are now telling fellow Muslim businessmen to purchase as much gold as possible and get an edge on the market.[6] Huge amounts of gold would provide enough material to produce large numbers of the thin gold dinars, and through an Islamic banking system these coins could then be sold to fellow Muslims.

Before you think this sounds too far-fetched, remember that in the 1980s, silver went to $50 an ounce, and gold spiked at more than $800 an ounce.[7] You may recall how one man attempted to get the market on the metals and was stopped by the government. History confirms that when a major economic crisis blankets the world, investors, businessmen, and private individuals seek after precious metals such as gold and silver.

Other nations, such as China and Britain, are now calling for a new order and the possibility of creating one stable currency.[8] Americans, by and large, would never exchange their dollars unless there came a major economic crash that would totally collapse the value of the dollar. At that point, Americans would readily accept a new monetary system that would ensure financial security.

Eventually, this currency will be replaced with a new system predicted in the Book of Revelation. We read:

> He causes all, both small and great, rich and poor, free and slave, to receive a mark on their right hand or on their foreheads, and that no one may buy or sell except one who has the mark or the name of the beast, or the number of his name.
>
> —Revelation 13:16–17

This prediction, written more than nineteen hundred years ago, is amazing for several reasons, chiefly because buying and selling will be linked to a "number" of a person's name. As I stated earlier, we are all recognized by numbers—Social Security, license plates and driver's licenses, the telephone, credit cards, and PINs. In the future, one man will merge ten nations together under a single government, and through his economic policy he will force a new order of buying and selling. The use of a number, a "mark," and the name of this specific world leader are significant in light of America's leadership in the world. There must be some form of decline in America's currency role in the world if it is to be replaced by this future system. Thus, the economic dominance of America must diminish to make room for this final system, which will emerge with its headquarters located in the Middle East and Europe.

2. From single nations to coalitions

The second reason that America will eventually slide down the mountain of world dominance is because the prophetic future reveals that a transition is coming in which sovereign nations will merge into regional coalitions.

For example, the Book of Revelation reveals a coalition called the "kings of the East" (Rev. 16:12). This unit, forged from the Asian region, could include China, Japan, Vietnam, and possibly Indonesia. A second unit, mentioned by Daniel and John, consists of ten kings headed by one man whom the Bible identifies as the "Antichrist." There are various opinions as to which ten kings and kingdoms these are, but most scholars agree they are a mix of nations in the Middle East and parts of Europe. Recent evidence points to nations that are under the influence of the Islamic religion, listing more than fifty countries.[9] Another coalition today is the European Union (EU), which consists of twenty-seven member states located throughout Europe.[10] The EU operates a single market common trade and monetary unit.

Presently, entire regions are forming coalition units:

- A union among the Gulf States
- A union among the African nations
- A union among the Asian nations
- A union among the Europeans
- A union of North America

It appears that these future units of cooperation are not formed just to organize the world into specific regions, but they seem to be in line with the ethnic and religious movements of the specific coalitions.

There have been rumors and discussions about a North American Union that unites Canada, America, and Mexico into one social, economic trade unit with a major road stretching from Mexico to Canada, paved in the middle of the United States—from Texas, through Oklahoma and the Midwest, ending in Canada. All trade between the nations would be transported on this NAFTA (North American Free Trade Agreement) road. This unit would also require a single currency, similar to how the euro is the single currency of the EU states.[11]

A suggestion was made for the development of a new currency called the *amero*, which would be introduced in America, Mexico, and Canada.[12] A coin designed by Daniel Carr has made its rounds on the Internet, but it is only a collector's coin and not actual amero currency as some have reported. The Internet is filled with coins and paper currency that are not in any form a new currency that is being produced but are hoaxes from conspiracy theorists.

However, the idea of a new currency and the possibility of a North America Union is not a hoax and has been promoted by several noted scholars and discussed on national television news. While campaigning for president, Barack Obama was asked about the North American Union and how Senator Ron Paul had spoken about it in public. When he was asked about the amero and the Union, he stated that he "saw no evidence of this taking place." He did admit of a highway being built in the center part of the United States, but said he saw no "evidence of this."[13]

However, Steve Previs with Jefferies International was interviewed on CNBC, and he mentioned the amero and the North American Union.[14] The facts are that if the entire world eventually moves to a global new world order, then the United States cannot, nor will it, stand alone but will join such a system for trade and economic survival.

Following World War I, the League of Nations was formed. After World War II, the United Nations was set up with its world headquarters in New York City. A future Middle East conflict mentioned in Ezekiel chapters 38 and

39 will create the need for another type of system to be set up, and it appears it will be a more global government, headed by regional coalitions.

3. Israel must stand alone and depend upon God.

There is a third reason why I believe that America will experience some form of demise in the future. The United States, Britain, and France, considered the Western powers of the twentieth century, were deeply involved in the reestablishment of the nation of Israel in 1948. President Harry Truman placed his approval on the partitioning of Palestine, giving the Jewish people a new homeland, following the Holocaust. The British forces had occupied Palestine since the defeat of the Turks in 1917. However, the British Mandate ended at midnight, May 15, 1948, and British forces began withdrawing from the territory marked as Israel.

Since Israel's rebirth in 1948, the young state has fought six wars:

- The war in 1948, called the War of Independence
- The war of 1956, directed by President Nassar of Egypt
- The war of 1967, which lasted six days
- The 1973 Yom Kippur War
- The 1981 war in Lebanon
- The 2005 war with Hezbollah

This does not include the struggle with Hamas, the Palestinian Liberation Organization (PLO) radicals, or the Gulf War in which Saddam Hussein attempted to pull Israel into the conflict, hoping to unite the Arab world against the Western coalitions. In each war, the Arab opponents and the internal enemies of the Jews have stated they believe Israel would have never survived without the military support of weapons, technology, satellite imagery, and money provided from the West to help defend Israel and defeat her enemies.

Thus, America is often given credit for Israel's ability to continually stand against her enemies. However, a time will come in which Israel's army will stand alone, and the God of Israel will receive all credit for defeating Israel's enemies. The war, called the *War of Gog and Magog*, will include a coalition of Islamic nations, including Persia (Iran), Ethiopia, Libya, and many northern enemies. During this war, the Almighty declares:

> So I will make My holy name known in the midst of My people Israel,
> and I will not let them profane My holy name anymore. Then the
> nations shall know that I am the LORD, the Holy One in Israel.... I

will set My glory among the nations; all the nations shall see My judgment which I have executed, and My hand which I have laid on them.
So the house of Israel shall know that I am the LORD their God from
that day forward.

—Ezekiel 39:7, 21–22

The Hebrew prophet reveals four methods the Lord will use to defeat
Israel's enemies on the very mountains of Israel. Ezekiel revealed that part
of the conflict would be in the "Bashan," which is today called the *Golan
Heights*—a large stretch of land from lower Galilee to the borders of Syria and
Lebanon. As the enemy hordes invade Israel, the following, revealed in Ezekiel
38:19–22 (KJV), will occur:

- An overflowing rain
- Great hailstones
- Fire and brimstone
- Shaking in the land

The Sea of Galilee is 695 feet below sea level, and the Golan Heights are
rolling hills and high mountains about 3,700 feet above sea level in the north.[15]
It is common during the rain season for the Bashan to experience large amounts
of rain, such as the "overflowing" or "a gushing rain" mentioned in Ezekiel. I
have witnessed these rains in the month of November while visiting Israel. On
one occasion, we saw numerous Israeli tanks stuck in mud due to the sudden
showers that had soaked the earth. Such a sudden rain would prevent the military equipment of the invading army from reaching certain areas.

The hailstones are literal. Again, I was in Israel in the early 1990s when a
hailstorm struck the area of Haifa. The icy stones, the size of softballs, show-
ered the entire city, knocking out windows in buses, cars, and businesses.
People walking outside were injured. Thus, hail can and does occur occasionally in Israel.

Hail is the last thing an army needs during a war. For example, in aircraft,
the sensitive equipment, including the electronics, are located in the nose of
the older planes. Large ice will not only knock out windshields, but it can also
cause a buildup on the wings and affect the engines of aircraft. Ezekiel said
that "great hailstones" would fall on the invaders.

The phrase "fire and brimstone" has often been viewed as some type of
weapon, such as a limited nuclear device. However, there is another *natural*
interpretation. The Bashan, or Golan Heights, has hundreds of millions of

acres of land covered with black basalt stones, the result of ancient volcanoes in the area. While there has not been a volcanic eruption in the region, the fact that the entire area is volcanic may give a clue to the "fire and brimstone" that will fall upon the invaders. Scripture reveals that Sodom and Gomorrah, two twin cities once located south of the Dead Sea, were destroyed in Abraham's time by "brimstone and fire…out of the heavens" (Gen. 19:24). There is geological evidence indicating that the area mentioned was also the site of a major volcanic plate, and perhaps these wicked cities were consumed during a sudden volcanic eruption.[16]

What could trigger a major eruption in the northern part of Israel? Consider the fourth statement by Ezekiel 38: "The shaking in the land…" (v. 19, KJV). Ezekiel writes:

> The fish of the sea, the birds of the heavens, the beasts of the field, all creeping things that creep on the earth, and all men who are on the face of the earth shall shake at My presence. The mountains shall be thrown down, the steep places shall fall, and every wall shall fall to the ground.
>
> —EZEKIEL 38:20

The fish of the sea would allude to the Sea of Galilee, the southernmost section of the Bashan and Golan Heights. The beasts of the field are the cattle and land animals. An earthquake could split the ground and cause volcanic smoke, fire, and hot lava to spew from the belly of the earth upon the enemies of Israel. The strange combination of a gushing rain, hailstones, a major earthquake, and fire and brimstone reveals that no human man or nation assists in the defeat of the Gog and Magog hordes coming like a storm cloud to take a spoil from Israel (Ezek. 38:13). In the insurance industry, an earthquake, flood, hail, and volcanic eruptions are classified as an *acts of God*. In this case, the entire battle is a setup to defeat 80 percent of Israel's adversaries, and the four methods used by the Creator are certainly *acts of God*!

America has been an ally of Israel from the beginning and a friend of the Jews since the inception of our nation. However, economic turmoil, internal conflicts, wars in other regions of the world, or perhaps a lack of interest or desire to intervene (or leadership who refuses to participate) could change that. For whatever the reason, America, or the West, seems strangely absent from defending and supporting Israel in this major conflict. The Hebrew text suggests, and many scholars agree, that the Islamic military units in this conflict will be under the direction and control of Russia and her allies. Thus,

America may wish to prevent a confrontation with Russia. All the reasons why the West is absent are speculation, and only time will interpret the reason why the "young lions" stand back and watch the war without ever becoming involved (Ezek. 38:13).

4. Judged for unrepentant sins

The fourth reason that the United States will prophetically experience a loss of control and influence in the world will be because of our national sins, which are never exposed and repented of. I personally believe that America has been given several opportunities as a nation to humble itself before God and repent or turn from our national sins. The Torah, the Psalms, and the four Gospels influenced our national documents. Our sins will be judged. In Leviticus 26, God said:

> If you despise My statutes, or if your soul abhors My judgments, so that you do not perform all My commandments, but break My covenant, I also will do this to you:
> I will even appoint terror over you...
> You shall sow your seed in vain, for your enemies shall eat it...
> Those who hate you shall reign over you...
> I will make your heavens like iron and your earth like bronze [no rain]...
> Your land shall not yield its produce, nor shall the trees of the land yield their fruit...
> I will...destroy your livestock...and your highways shall be desolate...
> When I have cut off your supply of bread...you shall eat and not be satisfied.
> —LEVITICUS 26:15–26

The Unseen Will Be the Breaking Point

American voters have selected forty-four presidents, from George Washington to Barack Obama. During every presidential campaign a candidate views the playing field and sees the visible difficulties, promising to make changes to better the situation. The roads will be paved, the potholes fixed, new jobs created, and "two chickens in every pot." Often, however, it is not what a newly elected president sees at the moment he is sworn in with his hand on the Bible but the unseen and unexpected that he will face that will test the metal in his spine, the grit in his determination, and the compassion of his heart.

The following presidents encountered a sudden, unplanned event that impacted the nations and formed public opinion about their leadership:

Sudden Events That Changed a Nation		
THE PRESIDENT	THE EVENT	THE RESULT
Abraham Lincoln	Civil War	Considered the greatest president
Franklin Roosevelt	Bombing of Pearl Harbor	Caused America to enter World War II
Harry Truman	Reestablishment of Israel	Credited with assisting the Jews
John F. Kennedy	Cuban Missile Crisis	Avoided a military confrontation with Russia
Ronald Reagan	Fall of Communism	Credited with the fall of the iron curtain
George H. W. Bush	First Gulf War	Prevented the takeover of Kuwait by Saddam Hussein
Bill Clinton	Oslo Accords	A treaty signed between Israel and the PLO
George W. Bush	9/11 Terror Attacks	Prevented another terrorist attack on American soil

Each unexpected war, terror attack, threat, or treaty was a surprise, and it changed the course of each administration and the decisions each president made in some manner. Campaigning for the office of president and actually administering the daily responsibilities are as different as studying four years in college for a career and afterward entering the job market. You will discover that no professor or academic book can actually prepare you for dealing with sudden disruptions and unplanned events, or how to deal with difficult people, the way that a major sudden crisis can.

Administration budgets and agendas never include a section for the unexpected and unwanted events. Yet, there are several possibilities of events that could occur in the next few years that will completely alter and change the landscape of American politics, jobs and prosperity of our citizens, and how the world views America as a nation.

1. A major war in the Middle East

Since 1948, Israel has fought six wars with surrounding enemies and has maintained a continual struggle with internal enemies, such as radical Palestinian homicide bombers and fanatical military organizations such as Hamas. These six wars have involved Egypt, Syria, Lebanon, Jordan, and Iraq, but the largest assembly of nations against Israel is in the future. Identified as the War of Gog and Magog, numerous Islamic nations around Israel will engage the Jewish state in a massive battle on the mountains of Israel in the future.

Since Scripture also predicts that Damascus will be destroyed and never rebuilt (Isa. 17:1), and since intelligence sources see Iran as a future nuclear threat, there may be several wars between Israel and her enemies prior to the major battle predicted twenty-six hundred years ago by Ezekiel (chapters 38 and 39). Any major war in Iran will cause oil prices to rise, and any disruption in oil production or delivery in the Straits of Hormuz would skyrocket the price of the black gold of the desert and bring about an instant global recession, possibly leading to a depression. This is one reason that America has been hesitant to participate in an attack on Iranian nuclear facilities.

2. A disruption in oil from the Gulf

The United States is the world's largest consumer of oil and fuel in the world. Our economic prosperity enables Americans to own their own vehicles, and our state taxes provide a network of roads to travel on from state to state. However, we also depend upon 40 percent of our oil resources (for fuel) to be shipped from the Persian Gulf states, chiefly Saudi Arabia. Fanatical Islamic regimes have targeted both the oil refineries and the House of Saud, the royal family of Saudi Arabia, on several occasions.

Following the 1973 Yom Kippur War in which Israel defeated a surprise attack from Egypt and Syria, the pressure mounted in the Islamic world for the Persian Gulf states to "punish" America's support of Israel through an oil embargo. The embargo, which lasted from 1973 to March of 1974, caused a net loss of four million barrels of oil per day and represented 7 percent of the free world production.[17] The embargo created a panic in many of America's major cities. From that moment, politicians began to cry out, "We must become free from Middle East oil."

Thirty-five years later we have no new refineries and are using more gas than any time in history. When oil spiked to $147 a barrel in the summer of 2008, the cry was, "Drill, baby, drill." After the presidential election in November 2008, the recession was in full swing, and by January 2009 the price of a barrel had dropped to $32.70.[18] As usual, Americans have a short-term memory and will wait for the next crisis to say, "We need to drill here!" Of course, there will be a *horse-and-pony show* on Capitol Hill to make the voters believe their elected official is concerned, and that will cease when the cameras are turned off and things return to normal. However, at some point the point of no return will arrive.

3. The food shortage

In a large southern American city, there are numerous underground bunkers that normally house military weapons, including bombs and missiles. Some time in 2008, the bunker was cleared out. (Much of the weaponry was used in Afghanistan and Iraq.) Instead of bombs, there are now large barrels sealed with food. When a worker on site was asked, "Why are we storing food here instead of explosives?" the answer was short and pointed: "Because we prepare these bunkers for what the next war will be over." There are several reasons why the next major world war could be over food.[19]

Food shortages are caused by natural droughts. In 2008, there were food riots in nations such as Egypt, India, and the Philippines. Reports indicated the people were blaming America for the shortages of wheat and especially rice, as large percentages of land in America were being used to grow corn to make ethanol to add to gasoline.[20]

Food shortages are caused by floods, which ruin crops. In 2008 the breadbasket of America, the Midwest, experienced some of the worse flooding in history. Six corn- and wheat-producing states were under water, and entire crops were destroyed.[21] Tsunamis, hurricanes, floods, and other natural disasters can wipe out entire crops in states and nations, raising the prices of rice and wheat so high that the poor are unable to eat. There is a wheat rust that has been discovered in Africa, Iran, and other nations. This germ destroyed crops years ago and has returned.[22]

Another reason for a lack of food is not just war, but also weapons used in war. With nuclear weapons and the danger of radiation, the ground in some areas may be unable to produce for years. Even in the apocalyptic scriptures of the Bible, John saw a time when a small portion of grain, enough for a small loaf of bread, will cost an entire day's wages (Rev. 6).

Last, but certainly not least, is the possibility of the missing bees. Beekeepers began noticing several years ago that their bee colonies were dying, apparently without cause. One friend from Kentucky saw nearly all of his bees simply die off for no apparent reason. The following two years, this strange condition, called *Colony Collapse Disorder*, continued.[23] Should this continue unresolved, the missing bees could wreak havoc on the global food supply, since the bees pollinate one out of every three bites that we eat in America.[24] Something as small as a bee missing from its natural job of moving from flower to flower and field to field could cause a shortage of one-third of the world's food supply. Interestingly, the visionary John notes that a world famine in the future will affect one-third of the world's food supply!

Thus, the disruption of food, even the disruption that could be caused when truckers are unable to deliver food to the major cities, would create a panic and a sudden crisis that, in reality, no city in America or the world is able to handle.

4. The water crisis

During the past several years, the United States has experienced severe drought from a lack of rain. In 2007, the city of Atlanta, Georgia, experienced a once-in-a-hundred-year scare. The rainfall was sixteen inches below normal. Atlanta receives its water from two lakes: Lake Lanier and Lake Allatoona, which were sixteen feet lower than normal and were drying up! At one point, the city leaders announced that within three months, there might not be any drinking water in the city! The state of Georgia was entering a *water war* with Florida and Alabama and had even discussed annexing a part of the Tennessee River to get more water. The Georgia governor chose to pray for rain, which came shortly after his prayer, to the dismay of atheists and agnostics.[25]

In 2009, not only was much of Texas experiencing the worse drought in decades, which was impacting the farming areas of the state, but also a new threat is emerging from the area of Colorado, Nevada, and California that could post a very serious disaster for all three states in the future.[26] The Colorado River is shrinking at a rapid pace. Water is often provided from the snowmelt from the Rocky Mountains, which lately has been reduced. More than thirty million people depend upon the water, including seven states: Colorado, Utah, Wyoming, New Mexico, Arizona, Nevada, and California. One Western water official described the possible future: "If some of the Southwest's largest reservoirs empty out, the region would experience an apocalypse, 'an Armageddon.'"[27]

In Nevada I saw a large reservoir called Lake Mead that supplies all the water for Las Vegas. The reservoir is half empty. In the Book of Revelation, the apostle John peered into the future and saw no rain on Earth for forty-two months. The drought will become so severe that the mighty Euphrates River will dry up. Some believe this will be due to the lack of rain, and others note that Turkey now has five major dams that can control, or shut, the flow of the Euphrates.[28]

Without doubt, both food and water will be major necessities in the future, and the coming system, which will have both, will control the buying and selling of these to the masses (Rev. 13:16–18).

5. The next terrorist attack

Information publicly available indicates that by the seventh anniversary of 9/11, twenty terrorist conspiracies had been thwarted by U.S. law enforcement.[29] That's just what is on public record. A former U.S. senator related to me that there have been about thirty-five conspiracies and attacks prevented under the Bush administration.

I was personally informed of a plot that involved the purchase of school buses, which were to be filled with explosives and then loaded with children and exploded in front of a public school in the South. In a similar situation, there was great concern when terrorists took 1,200 people hostage in a school in Beslan, Russia. Russian security forces stormed the school, not realizing the terrorists had placed explosives throughout the building, causing a fire that concluded in a gun battle. Afterward, 332 individuals were killed, including 186 children.[30] Perhaps a more frightening report for the United States was released when the laptop of an Iraqi terrorist was seized, and detailed photographs of five schools and their floor plans were discovered in the computer files.[31]

Some Americans believe the war on terror is over now that President Bush has been replaced. In fact, some liberals believe that Bush actually promoted the war on terror and maintained it for his own personal causes and not for the country's protection. However, the danger persists and will continue to persist as long as individuals hate democracy, despise America, and seek a global religious order based upon their private interpretation of their religious dogma.

The clock will eventually strike midnight, and rough dictator-type nations will possess weapons that form the stuff of a sci-fi horror flick. I was informed by two very reputable sources, one outside the country, that intelligence sources believe Iranian scientists have perfected a biological weapon that can be placed in a water supply and kill up to two million people, if it is properly released and distributed. It was allegedly tested on a donkey that died in thirty minutes, and also secretly on a small village near the Iranian border with Iraq with about four hundred people, all of whom died as a result.[32] These types of dangers will increase over time, and it is only a matter of time until America experiences another major attack on its soil that will cause us to forget 9/11 as we view the damage, danger, and threat.

The Islamic holy book, the Quran, makes a strange prediction for the last days. It reads:

> Then you watch for the Day that the sky will bring forth a kind of smoke (or mist) plainly visible, enveloping the people: this will be a grievous Penalty.
>
> —SURAH 44:10–11

An Islamic commentary elaborates more by saying:

> Smoke will appear all over the earth which will cause believers to catch something similar to a slight cold, whereas the unbelievers will be hit harder by it. Finally, a cold wind will come and kill all believers,

leaving only unbelievers on the earth who will then witness the LAST HOUR.[33]

It was reported several years ago that an al Qaeda leader predicted that America would be struck again, and more than one hundred thousand would die in an attack he called "the black wind of death."[34] One of the papers that reported this threat was questioning the meaning of this "black wind." A recent event in Algeria may explain the meaning.

It has been known for many years that terrorists, especially al Qaeda, have sought and attempted to manufacture certain chemical and biological agents, with the main desire being to obtain a valid nuclear or dirty bomb to detonate in a large American city. In January 2009, it was reported that the government of Algeria discovered forty dead terrorists in a forest in Algeria. After examining their bodies, it was believed their deaths were the result of the Black Death.[35] In the 1340s, the Black Death (the bubonic plague) killed seventy-five million in North America, Africa, Asia, and Europe.[36] It is unclear if the terrorist group was experimenting with the plague and something went wrong, or if the plague had been accidentally released. The question now becomes, if a cell of terrorists living in the caves of Algeria have access to such a deadly plague, is it possible that this type of biological agent is already in America? It is no secret that Iran has not only pursued but also has an active biological weapons program.

States have actually been quietly and at times secretly preparing for a chemical or biological attack. In a large southern university town, the Centers for Disease Control and Prevention (CDC) has actually been calling in people late at night and practicing for a major biochemical attack in the area. It was later discovered that many hospitals in major cities and first responders have been told to be prepared at any moment for a sudden attack and the need for masses to be treated within minutes or hours.[37]

When I asked high-ranking officers in both the United States and Israel if it is possible that a major attack will strike America in the future, there was 100 percent agreement that it will occur. The phrase repeated many times is: "It is not a matter of *if* it will happen, but a matter of *when* it will happen." Another attack on the scale of 9/11, resulting in job losses and another military intervention, could push the nation over the economic abyss.

6. A major natural disaster

Hurricanes Katrina and Ike are both history, but the impact of their destructive paths is still evident when visiting New Orleans, Louisiana, and Galveston, Texas. When thinking about a future natural disaster, those living on the East Coast immediately imagine a major earthquake on the West Coast waiting to awaken like a bear out of hibernation. It comes as a surprise to some to learn that one of the most dangerous fault lines in America is called the New Madrid Fault Line, and it stretches throughout the southern and midwestern United States. This fault line produced a deadly series of quakes during three months in late 1811 and early 1812. Four quakes measured 8.1, 7.0, 7.8, and 8 on the Richter scale, damaging houses in Saint Louis and totally destroying the town of New Madrid in Missouri.[38]

There has been concern among many that this fault line is becoming more active and could eventually give way, producing the most destructive quake in American history. The U.S. Federal Emergency Management Agency warned that a serious earthquake in the New Madrid Zone could result in "the highest economic loss due to a natural disaster in the USA." The report named eight states that would be affected: Alabama, Arkansas, Illinois, Indiana, Kentucky, Mississippi, Missouri, and Tennessee. Especially vulnerable would be the cities of Saint Louis and Memphis, with water, transportation, and infrastructure affected.[39]

One area that is seldom mentioned that could in the future create an apocalyptic type scenario is the danger lurking under Yellowstone National Park. It was reported that from December 26, 2008, to January 8, 2009, Yellowstone experienced more than 900 earthquakes—in just one week.[40] Geologist Christopher Sanders posted a report in January 2009 that read: "I am advising all State officials around Yellowstone National Park for a potential State of Emergency. In the last week over 252 earthquakes have been observed by the USGS. We have a 3D view of the movement of magma rising underground. We have all the pre-warning signs of a major eruption of a super volcano—I want everyone to leave Yellowstone National Park and for 200 miles around the volcano caldera."[41]

Others are not as concerned, stating that while the number of earthquake swarms has risen, these swarms are typical, and even that an explosion of the supervolcano could "be of basaltic (non-explosive) magma rather than highly viscous, explosive, rhyolitic magma."[42]

If, as some suggest, the supervolcano in Yellowstone were to build up and erupt, the ash in the atmosphere would darken the sun for several days in and around the area, dropping temperatures and destroying any plant life. The greatest danger would be to the grain harvest in the Great Plains, which would be covered in ash.

While Yellowstone may remain a tourist site for many years, there is indication in biblical prophecies that refers to some form of volcanic activity occurring in the future. We read:

Oh, that You would rend the heavens!
That You would come down!
That the mountains might shake at Your presence—
As fire burns brushwood,
As fire causes water to boil—
To make Your name known to Your adversaries,
That the nations may tremble at Your presence!
When You did awesome things for which we did not look,
You came down,
The mountains shook at Your presence.

—ISAIAH 64:1–3

The fire and smoky vapors and the darkening of the sun may be an allusion to major volcanic activity at the end of the age.

Whether it is a massive earthquake, a water shortage, a food supply disruption, or volcanic activity, any major natural disaster would cause a demise of America—especially since we are now in debt and cannot repay the bailouts!

7. A massive disappearance of people

To those reading this book who have secular knowledge but perhaps little knowledge of biblical traditions, there are millions of Christians of all denominational backgrounds who believe that the Messiah will return again at an appointed time for those who have entered a redemptive covenant with Him. As a Christian, this covenant is made by repentance of sins and faith in Christ. The New Testament gives a promise of the return of Christ for those who believe in Him and are looking for His sudden appearing. The apostle Paul wrote:

> For the Lord Himself will descend from heaven with a shout, with the voice of an archangel, and with the trumpet of God. And the dead in Christ will rise first. Then we who are alive and remain shall be caught up together with them in the clouds to meet the Lord in the air. And thus we shall always be with the Lord.
>
> —1 THESSALONIANS 4:16–17

This event is called by various names, such as the Rapture, the Gathering Together, the Great Assembly, the Catching Away, and the Great Departure. Imagine what would happen, just in America, if suddenly hundreds of thousands or millions of individuals were found missing all at once. How would military bases, ships in the sea, banks, and other industries access computers when those holding the codes are not present?

Any of these seven events, or a combination of them, will have a major impact on America. It is not a matter of *if* but *when* such nation-changing events will transpire. Since any and all of these could affect America, it leads us to ask the question: Is America alluded to in the biblical prophecies? Let us explore numerous opinions, theories, and possible interpretations used by scholars and students to discover the world's greatest End Time empire.

••• Chapter 15 •••

IS AMERICA IN BIBLE PROPHECY?

We shifted from a nation that said "In God We Trust" to "Reality and self we trust." We transitioned from being a land of the free and the home of the brave, to now we are the land of the indebted and the home of the self-indulgent. We also shifted from a land that believes you can be all you can be to now it's get all you can get.[1]

—GEORGE BARNA

SINCE 1776, BIBLE scholars and students alike have pondered the question: Where is America alluded to in Bible prophecy? Is the most powerful Gentile nation that leads the world in financing and propagating the gospel of the kingdom referred to, or at least alluded to, in some hidden, obscure prophetic reference of Scripture?

It has been noted that the majority of America's founders were Christians who viewed themselves in the same manner as the Hebrews who crossed the Red Sea to the Promised Land. The Pilgrims exited their ships on this new continent with the belief that they were fulfilling a divine assignment. Evidence of the Bible's influence is found when examining early American documents, which were based upon the Holy Scriptures. America is full of towns and cities with biblical names: Hebron, Bethel, Canaan, Salem, Zion, Pisgah, Jericho, and numerous other Bible-based names.

When the first pilgrims signed the Mayflower Compact prior to disembarking their ships on November 11, 1620, it read, in part:

> In the name of God, Amen. We whose names are under-written, the loyal subjects of our dread sovereign Lord, King James, by the grace of God, of Great Britain, France, and Ireland King, Defender of the Faith, etc. Having undertaken, for the glory of God, and advancement of the Christian faith, and honor of our King and Country, a voyage to plant the first colony...[2]

By the end of the eighteenth century, America had three main documents: the Constitution, the Declaration of Independence, and the Bill of Rights. It was Harry Truman who said that the founding documents of America were based upon the "Torah, the Book of Isaiah, and the four Gospels."[3] The foundation of our house was built upon the rock of God's Word.

From infant beginnings, America has matured into a full-grown superpower. Founded by people seeking religious freedom, America's shores have beamed the light of the Christian gospel, shining hope to the darkest corners of the earth. Having experienced the leadership of forty-three presidents during our 233 years of *official* history, we have arrived at a time when the foundation of the American house is beginning to shake—not because the foundation is not firm, but because liberal leaders in government, media, and universities from within are pulling the stones of biblical faith out from under the house! As the scripture has said, "Every city or house divided against itself will not stand" (Matt. 12:25). Before the decade of the sixties, most Americans stood upon the same basic spiritual foundation. Today, the house is divided between the liberals and the conservatives, with self-acclaimed moderates caught in the middle. American's *buffet spirituality* now causes individuals to pick and choose their beliefs. If the inspired warnings of the Hebrew prophets offend and are not *politically correct* today, these warnings are rejected, and those on the other end of the house are labeled *religious fanatics* and the *religious Right* because they accept the truth of the Scriptures. Good is now evil, and evil is now good, as biblical truth is twisted to please the readers.

Consider the house divided. The same book our presidents place their hands on when receiving the oath of office is not allowed in public schools. The Ten Commandments may hang in the Supreme Court in Washington, but they are banned from public view of our children and in courthouses in the South. For example, Ohio lawyers for the ACLU set out to remove the motto from the state seal: "With God all things are possible."[4] Armed with the sword of unbelief, a select inner circle of wealthy, self-appointed, God-haters are undermining the foundation of the house in order to promote their godless and faithless agenda.

When the Columbine shootings in 1999 took the lives of innocent teens in Colorado, the question was asked, "Where was God?"

The sad answer is, "In the 1960s, the Supreme Court publicly banned Him from Columbine and every other public school." The only way He was brought into the school facilities was in the hearts of students whose love for God overrode the unbelief of a court decision.

The house of America is shaking, and the foundations are in trouble.

When the Founding Fathers chose the emblem for America, they selected the eagle. This mighty and majestic bird was their visual picture of the potential greatness of America. The eagle is known to rise above the storms and endure much turbulence. Is it possible that prophetic history indicates a nation whose emblem would be an eagle?

The Vision of the Eagle

Near the close of the first century, an unknown Palestinian Jew wrote a story concerning an alleged vision, which was said to have been revealed by an angel of God named Uriel. The vision consisted of seven revelations, one of which includes a strange vision of a giant eagle. The visionary begins by saying:

> Then saw I a dream, and, behold, there came up from the sea an eagle, which had twelve feathered wings, and three heads. And I saw, and, behold, she spread her wings over all the earth, and all the winds of the air blew on her, and were gathered together. . . . Moreover I beheld, and, lo, the eagle flew with her feathers, and reigned upon earth, and over them that dwelt therein.
> —2 Esdras 11:1–2, 5, The Apocrypha, kjv

As the alleged vision continues, it reveals more detail about the eagle. From the midst of the eagle's body, a voice began to speak. One wing begins to reign, followed by another and another. The writer states: "The feathers that followed stood up upon the right side, that they might rule also; and some of them ruled, but within a while they appeared no more" (2 Esdras 11:20, kjv). The vision is written in an almost rambling fashion to describe the wings and the heads. He later writes that the eagle is one of the four beasts (alluding to Daniel chapter 7), and then indicates the eagle is the Roman Empire.

There are, however, some odd parallels when comparing this vision to the political history of America. For example, "The two [wings] went unto it and set themselves up to reign, and their kingdom was small, and fill ["full," rsv] of uproar" (2 Esdras 12:2, kjv). Could this allude to Lincoln and Kennedy, who both dealt with civil rights? Is it possible the Civil War may be alluded to in this statement: "That after the time of that kingdom there shall arise great strivings, and it shall stand in peril of failing: nevertheless it shall not then fall, but shall be restored again to his beginning" (2 Esdras 12:18, kjv)?

Could the deaths of Kennedy and Lincoln be read into this statement: "That in him there shall arise eight kings, whose times shall be but small, and their years swift. And two of them shall perish, the middle time approaching" (2 Esdras 12:20–21, kjv)? Lincoln was shot at the beginning of his second term, and Kennedy was shot in the midst of his first term, or in "the middle time" of their appointed times.

The writer mentions "twelve feathered wings." Could this statement allude to the fact that twelve of America's presidents have served as generals in the military?[5] It has been noted that the eagle's wings were divided on the right and left sides. America has two main political parties divided between the "left wing" (normally Democrats) and the "right wing" (normally Republicans).[6] The three heads of the eagle mentioned in the vision could, by a stretch of the imagination, represent the three branches of government—the judicial, executive, and legislative.

The entire vision is found in 2 Esdras chapters 11 and 12 and is a part of the Apocrypha. The Apocrypha is not in our Bible, nor is it considered inspired Scripture, although it was translated from Greek to Latin and approved as canonical by the Council of Trent in the sixteenth century.

I call your attention to this story to reveal how some individuals attempt to discover the United States in prophecy. Having examined 2 Esdras, a reader can find various possible parallels by pulling out a verse here or there. Our main point of interest is to illustrate that the alleged vision reveals a nation whose emblem is an eagle. America's emblem is the eagle, but the eagle was also the emblem of the Roman Empire. In an earlier chapter I drew many comparisons between the decline of the Roman Empire and America. The Roman Empire finally deteriorated like internal organs rotting with a terminal disease. Although America is strong right now, we should heed the warning in Obadiah 4:

> "Though you ascend as high as the eagle,
> And though you set your nest among the stars,
> From there I will bring you down," says the LORD.

The first nation to place her flag on the moon (among the stars) must be warned in advance of her danger of deterioration from within.

The vision of the eagle recorded in 2 Esdras may contain certain parallels to the United States. Bible-believing Christians must turn our attention to the inspired Holy Scriptures to answer some important questions. Since America is the youngest of nations, is it possible we are not alluded to directly, but rather indirectly, in the Scriptures? Since God hides His revelations in patterns, types, and shadows, perhaps we should search out any possible prophetic patterns that could relate to our nation.

Since the founding of the nation, ministers and scholars alike have pored over the Scriptures in hopes of finding an obscure yet clear reference alluding to America. Several theories have developed, which we will share in this chapter. One such possibility is written in Isaiah chapter 18.

> Woe to the land shadowed with buzzing wings,
> Which is beyond the rivers of Ethiopia,
> Which sends ambassadors by sea,
> Even in vessels of reed on the waters, saying,
> "Go, swift messengers, to a nation tall and smooth of skin,
> To a people terrible from their beginning onward,
> A nation powerful and treading down,
> Whose land the rivers divide."
>
> All inhabitants of the world and dwellers on the earth:
> When he lifts up a banner on the mountains, you see it;
> And when he blows a trumpet, you hear it.
>
> —ISAIAH 18:1–3

Some contend that the land "beyond the rivers of Ethiopia," referred to in Isaiah, is an allusion to America. The nation of Isaiah's vision was a land "shadowed with buzzing wings," or literally *a land with buzzing wings*. The prophesied nation "sends ambassadors by sea." Certainly America, along with many other nations, has ambassadors who travel across the oceans to other nations. The nation Isaiah saw was "scattered and peeled" (Isa. 18:7, KJV). The word *scattered* in Hebrew means to "stretch or to be tall." The word *peeled* in Hebrew alludes to being "smooth or bright." Therefore, Isaiah sees a people who are smooth-skinned and have a bright complexion.

It is important to note that those in northern Africa have a dark complexion; therefore, the nation in Isaiah 18 must be located beyond the area of Africa, as written by the prophet: "beyond the rivers of Ethiopia." Isaiah continued to explain that this nation is "meted out and trodden under foot" (v. 7, KJV). A literal translation would be "mighty and conquering." Other Bible translations read:

> A people dreaded near and far that conquers and treads down.
>
> —BERKELEY TRANSLATION

> A terror far and near; a sturdy race of conquerors.
>
> —MOFFATT TRANSLATION

> Terrible from their beginning and onwards, - nation most mighty…
>
> —THE J. B. ROTHERHAM EMPHASIZED BIBLE

Since this nation is located "beyond Ethiopia" and is well watered by rivers, it is uncertain what nation the prophet was referring to in his day. If one continues to read, a warning is given to this nation, and the prophecy concludes by saying:

> In that time a present will be brought to the LORD of hosts
> From a people tall and smooth of skin,
> And from a people terrible from their beginning onward,
> A nation powerful and treading down,
> Whose land the rivers divide—
> To the place of the name of the LORD of hosts,
> To Mount Zion.
>
> —ISAIAH 18:7

Modern Bible interpreters, after examining this entire passage, are still uncertain of whom Isaiah was speaking in this prophecy. It would be taking needless space to spend time trying to prove this reference is America. Any attempt to "prove" that this is America would simply be speculation.

The Eagle's Wings in Daniel's Prophecy

An interesting story in early American history may indicate that Daniel chapter 7 played a role in selecting America's national emblem, the eagle. A Jewish man named Haym Salomon was a broker who helped finance the American Revolution. In fact, in my personal stamp collection, I have a U.S. postal stamp, *Contributions to the Cause*, with the name Haym Salomon, financial hero. On the back it reads:

> Financial hero, businessman, and broker Haym Salomon was responsible for raising most of the money to help finance the American Revolution and later to save the new nation from collapse.

After the signing of the Declaration of Independence, a committee was formed to design the seal of the United States. According to the *Federalist Brief*, Thomas Jefferson suggested a seal depicting the children of Israel being led with a pillar of cloud by day and a fire by night. Benjamin Franklin picked up on the same theme, suggesting a seal with Moses dividing the sea and the chariots of Pharaoh being swamped under the waters, with a motto: "Rebellion to tyrants is obedience to God." Again the Hebrew thread to our independence was viewed in comparison to the Hebrews coming out of Egypt. Both of these designs failed to make the final seal. A bald eagle was chosen instead.[7]

While there is not historical written record, some have suggested that Haym Salomon may have had input in the design for the American seal. It is suggested that having studied the Book of Daniel, Salomon read where the eagle's wings were plucked from the lion. In this he saw a prophetic picture of how America was being plucked away from the British lion. The eagle, prophetically, would be a perfect symbol for America![8] This seal is printed on the back of every one-dollar bill. Notice that the eagle has arrows in one claw and olive branches in the other. The arrows represent war, and the olive branches represent peace. The eagle faces the olive branches, informing us that America desires peace but keeps the arrows of war available as an option. In modern history, America is not a warring nation but stands ready to defend the peace if necessary. The eagle does not wear a crown as can be found on the many coat of arms found in England and Britain. The crown would represent the royalty of Europe. The crown is omitted, because the new nation would be "of the people and by the people."

Above the head of the eagle are a series of thirteen stars surrounded by a circle of clouds. Notice that these thirteen stars form what is today called the *Magen David*, or the "star of David." There has been much speculation about the symbolic intent of these stars. This design is found on the Israeli flag and is the emblem of the modern nation of Israel.

Christians who emphasize a conspiracy theory often point to the opposite side of the seal with the pyramid, which is also on the back of a dollar bill. I have read various reports of what this occultist seal allegedly represents. It is best to let the journals of Congress reveal the meaning of the pyramid.

> A Pyramid unfinished. In the Zenith an Eye in a triangle surrounded with a glory proper. Over the Eye these words "Annuit Coeptis." On the base of the pyramid the numerical letters MDCCLXXVI & underneath the following motto, "novus ordo seclorum."[9]

It can be added here that Charles Thomson, who served as Secretary of the Congress when the seal was approved, said: "The pyramid signifies strength and duration. The eye over it and the motto Annuit Coeptis allude to the many single interpositions of providence in favor of the American cause."[10] James Wilson, a justice of the first Supreme Court, noted that: "A free government has often been compared to a pyramid...it is laid on the broad basis of the people."[11]

America could very well represent the eagle's wings that were plucked from the lion. If this is so, then it was the Almighty who first plucked the eagle's wings to form a new nation that would certainly become a major End Time Gentile power.

Restoring America One More Time

> But they that wait upon the LORD shall renew their strength; they shall mount up with wings as eagles; they shall run, and not be weary; and they shall walk, and not faint.
>
> —ISAIAH 40:31, KJV

The eagle represents liberty. The powerful wings can glide the majestic eagle to heights of twenty-four hundred feet and can use its wings to carry other eagles to safety. Strong winds enable the majestic bird to fly higher. The incredible eyesight of the eagle enables it to see its prey from a far distance. The eagle mates for life and returns to the same nest on the same rock ledge year after year. It is the eagle that actually teaches the younger eagles how to fly.

No greater emblem could have been chosen to represent America than the eagle. America is the greatest nation on earth. Yet, in the natural, even the strongest eagle experiences a time late in its life where it must experience renewal. This crisis time is called the *molting time* of the eagle. Five things happen to the eagle when it experiences this time of change.

1. The feathers of the eagle can begin to fall out.
2. Calcium builds upon the eagle's beak, thus making it difficult to eat.
3. It can lose its appetite.
4. Instead of flying, it will walk on the ground and become too weak to fly.
5. The eagle's eyes become dry, and it can no longer "cry."

Is our nation presently in the molting period? Just as the feathers are crucial to an eagle and help to guide the eagle in flight, our Founding Fathers created *feathers* to guide us as they incorporated biblical principles in our national documents and traditions. Today, instead of being guided into the path of truth and righteousness, we are being misguided into new paths and ideas that have been proven in history not to work. Hardworking, taxpaying American Christians are being intimidated from carrying a Bible to work, witnessing to a fellow worker, or placing religious pictures on their desks. While the local church still has freedom, in the public workplace and the public schools the mouths of our people (the beak of the eagle) are under a gag rule, forbidden to tell others about the Christian faith. The appetite for spiritual truth is dull in many areas. Many traditional older churches are closing their doors for lack of interest among members. There is a love for the *wilderness* or the *wild things* instead of taking the higher road where the atmosphere is clear and clean. There is a hardness in the hearts of many; we no longer weep when we see death and carnage or hear reports of suicide, murder, and crime.

Has history taught us nothing? Do we not learn from the past? The empires of Bible prophecy have come and gone. The names of the nations are the same: Egypt, Syria, and Greece. Yet their dominion over the world has all but ceased. The mighty Babylonian empire lies in ruins on the banks of the Euphrates. The cities of the Roman Empire are now tourist attractions and the delight of archaeologists.

The voices from the edge of eternity are speaking.

- The Babylonians are saying: "Our wealth could not save us."
- The Medes and Persians, known for passing laws that were never to be altered, are speaking: "All the laws inscribed on stone tablets could not deliver us."
- The Greeks followed, boasting of wisdom. Yet they are speaking to America, saying: "Don't depend upon your pride and your human wisdom. Our empire finally fell, and the wise men could not stop it."
- I can hear the trudging feet of Roman soldiers beating the walls of Jerusalem to the ground, setting fire to the holy temple. See them as they bring Jewish captives from Jerusalem, chained together like sheep marching to their slaughter. Hear Nero as he declares himself as God. Nero conducts another orgy and plans the persecution of Christians. Listen as today, from the lowest pit in the abyss, he cries across the chasm of time and eternity to a proud America: "Your immorality will bring you down and carry you to where I now am!"

Since people pay little attention to history, perhaps this object lesson from nature will reveal the crisis and the way in which to overcome.

The Molting Period

America is in the molting period. Just as eagles during their midlife experience changes, the eagle of America is experiencing changes. When an eagle experiences this moment in its life, it will either renew itself or die in the wilderness.

Many years ago I heard a Baptist minister, Bobby Thompson, speak on the subject of eagles and the molting period. An Indian took Bobby into the heart of the mountains to observe eagles. There the minister saw five giant eagles that were standing on rocks in a deep valley in the mountain wilderness. Their heads were hanging over to the side. Calcium deposits had built up on their beaks, and their heads were too heavy to fly. His Indian friend told him that as long as eagles flew high, the friction from the wind would keep the beak smooth, but when they came down to the floor of this forest and began walking around, the deposits built upon their beaks. No one is certain why the eagles come down from the high places to the wilderness. Perhaps it is curiosity. Maybe they become tired of flying. Soon the eagles lose their appetite and no longer have the strength to fly high and catch their food.

Bobby and the Indian watched as eight eagles began to circle these five birds that were standing in the opening. The flying eagles formed a circle in the sky and began to descend lower, hovering over the five weak eagles. These eight birds had begun dropping fresh rabbit and squirrel they had caught for their companions. It was up to the five birds to reach down and feed themselves. The Indian told Bobby, "If they feed themselves, they will gain strength and live. If not, they will die in a short time."

Bobby returned several days later to discover that three eagles had died. They did not eat. They became so weak that they accepted death over life. Two eagles fed themselves and gained enough strength to fly back to the cleft of the rock. The two eagles hit their beaks against the rocks, thus removing the calcium. This combination of eating properly, going back to its rock, and removing the calcium deposits enabled the eagles to be renewed and fly high again.

Two eagles had *renewed themselves*. Three of the eagles did not, and they died. Let us compare: Empires have come and gone. At the height of their success, they had the attitude of the great ship *Titanic*—"Nothing can take us down. We are unsinkable."

Can America Be Renewed?

How can the eagle of America renew itself in these final days?

1. The nation must be fed the proper diet.

Just as the eagles in the wilderness must eat the proper food to receive strength to fly again, the people of this nation must be *fed truth* in order to gain spiritual strength.

Have you observed the difference between a true Christian and an unbeliever? A true Christian has joy, assists others in need, and is fulfilled through his or her relationship with the Lord and by helping others. The written Word of God is more than information; it is revelation. As this revelation is received into your spirit, it brings illumination and produces inspiration!

When your outlook on life changes, your lifestyle becomes affected. After all, how many atheists do you know who have built an orphanage, a hospital for the poor, or developed a feeding and clothing program in the inner city? I know of none. I do know of many churches that are involved in helping others.

While unbelievers blast Christians for evangelizing others, they often overlook the good Christians do in helping the poor and needy. We do this because we have been fed the true bread of life, the Word of God. Therefore we can drop the Word to other eagles who are in the dry places of life and encourage them that they too can come out of the wilderness and ride the high places.

2. The people of this nation must set their eyes on the "rock."

When an eagle is walking in the wilderness, it forgets the rock on which it was born. Eagles were not created to walk on the ground like a turkey or a chicken; they were created to ride out storms and perch high on the cliffs. In fact, an eagle never leaves the rock on which it was born—except when it is in the molting period.

The Bible teaches that God is our rock (Ps. 62:1–2). David cried out: "When my heart is overwhelmed; lead me to the rock that is higher than I" (Ps. 61:2). America has lost its spiritual direction as secular humanism, evolution, and materialism have replaced faith in God. Today as a nation we are divided and walking around in circles in the *wilderness*. Only when we set our eyes back on the "rock of our salvation" will we be infused with the strength to "lay aside every weight, and the sin which doth so easily beset us" (Heb. 12:1, KJV).

3. We must learn to weep again.

When the eagle goes through the molting period, its eyes become dry, and the eagle is unable to *cry*. When an eagle is flying, a covering over the eyes keeps them moist. Bobby Thompson observed that once the eagle was back on the rock, water flowed from the eyes across the beak of the giant bird.

Due to the affects of the entertainment industry, many of the citizens of this nation have become hardened to the critical needs of those around them. Movies are filled with cursing, crime, rape, and immorality. When a *real* person is murdered, raped, or wounded in the community, many no longer weep over these crimes against humanity. Their hearts are hardened, and the spirits are cold. The media—willingly or unwillingly—have created an environment of cynicism and skepticism, which in return has calloused the hearts of people in this nation. We must learn to "bear one another's burdens" and "weep with those who weep" (Gal. 6:2; Rom. 12:15). This can occur when we are back upon the rock. Weeping is not difficult when your heart is filled with compassion.

In reality, political renewal is only a bandage that will place a temporary covering over the nation's mortal wound. The eagle must experience a spiritual renewal, a reversal from wrong thinking and attitudes of self-destruction. Spiritual renewal begins with the heart and works its way through the rest of the body. We must pray for leadership in the pulpit, the White House, and on a local level that will stand for these basic principles:

1. There is one eternal God who created all men equal.

2. The Holy Bible is the foundation of our nation and should be taught to all children.

3. Biblical teaching is the only way of teaching a value system of what is right and wrong.

4. Prayer is communication with God. Students should be allowed to pray before or after school as long as they do not force their will upon others.

5. Our Christian heritage and history should be restored and taught in the public school system, lest a generation forget the sovereign God who formed this nation.

6. There should be no restraint from the freedom to preach the gospel. After all, this nation was birthed on the truth of the Bible and the preaching of the Word of God.

7. Freedom of religion does not mean freedom from religion.

••• Chapter 16 •••

THE BATTLE OF THE LAST GENTILE EMPIRE

Freedom is never more than one generation away from extinction. We didn't pass it to our children in the bloodstream. It must be fought for, protected, and handed on for them to do the same.[1]

—RONALD REAGAN

A S WE CONTINUE to take a look at prophetic hints about America's future, we will discover that there are many different suggestions about biblical prophetic clues. Some allude to the similarities between ancient Babylon and America, referring to Jeremiah 50–51 and Revelation 17–18 as cryptic clues about the United States. Others point to Isaiah 18, as we mentioned briefly in the last chapter. In this book, I have pointed out the parable of Christ stating that because of Israel's unbelief, the kingdom promised to Israel would, for a season, be given to a nation bringing forth fruit, and I indicated that may allude to a nation like America who has led the nations in declaring the message of the Messiah.

In this chapter I will briefly explore some of these prophetic links. However, after years of study, I believe America's spiritual pattern is linked to Israel and that our political, economic, and governmental patterns are linked to ancient Rome. As we conclude this chapter, I will expand this teaching by revealing many of these patterns through the prophetic images in Daniel 7.

America and Jeremiah's Babylon Theory

Some noted prophecy teachers believe that Jeremiah 50 and 51 are a cryptic reference to America. When one carefully examines the text, it is clear this prophecy is not about America. The Hebrew prophet tells us the prophecy is against Babylon. Since some Bible teachers compare the sins of America to ancient Babylon, it becomes easy to teach that Jeremiah's Babylonian prophecy concerns America. The law of interpretation forbids reading into the text something that is not there.

Look at the words of Jeremiah. The prophet opens by saying: "The word that the LORD spoke against Babylon..." (Jer. 50:1; see also Jer. 51:1). He mentions that Babylon "was a golden cup in the LORD's hand" (Jer. 51:7). He says that Babylon has suddenly fallen (v. 8) and will become "a heap, a dwelling place for jackals" (v. 37). Jeremiah warns God's people to "go out of the midst of her!" (v. 45).

It must be remembered that Jeremiah warned about Israel's seventy years of captivity in Babylon (Jer. 25:11). In fact, Jeremiah gave firm warnings about Babylon throughout his book. If we make America the Babylon in chapters 50 and 51, then we must also make the other references in Jeremiah fit America. This is literally impossible.

Jeremiah's prophecy is connected to the warnings the apostle John gave concerning "Mystery Babylon" in Revelation chapters 17 and 18. Jeremiah, speaking of Babylon, said, "Her waters...will be dried up" (Jer. 50:38). In Revelation 16:12, John revealed that the Euphrates River will dry up. Ancient Babylon was built on the edge of the Euphrates River.

Jeremiah commanded, "Flee...go out of the midst of her!" (Jer. 51:6, 45). John also wrote concerning Mystery Babylon: "Come out of her, my people" (Rev. 18:4). In Jeremiah's vision, Babylon was a "golden cup" (Jer. 51:7). John repeats the same statement concerning Mystery Babylon, saying that she has a "golden cup" (Rev. 17:4).

Jeremiah said "dragons" would dwell there (Jer. 51:37, KJV). The Hebrew word is *tanniym* and can mean "land or sea monster." It probably alludes to some type of desert animal dwelling among the ruins. At times *tanniym* is translated in the original scriptures as "serpent" or "snake." Several hundred years later, John said Mystery Babylon would become a habitation of devils (Rev. 18:2). It is also interesting to note that in Revelation 12, John describes Satan as "a great, fiery red dragon having seven heads and ten horns" (v. 3).

The connection between Jeremiah's Babylon and the Babylon mentioned in Revelation continues. Jeremiah cries out, "Babylon has suddenly fallen" (Jer. 51:8). Seven hundred year later, John prophesied: "Babylon the great is fallen, is fallen" (Rev. 18:2). Because the angel in Revelation 18:2 announced the fall of Babylon twice, with the phrase, "is fallen, is fallen," it could allude to two separate and distinct destructions of Babylon.

The Babylon of Jeremiah's day, built by King Nebuchadnezzar, in time fell into ruins. It was conquered by the Medes and Persians, and then taken by the Greeks and Alexander the Great. Alexander was planning to restore the city to its grandeur, but he died in Babylon unexpectedly at age thirty-three. After Alexander's death, Babylon became the capital of the Seleucid dynasty. The temples were eventually moved from the ancient city, and a new capital was built at the Tigris River. Eventually Babylon became a *ghost town*, but it was never destroyed in the manner that Jeremiah predicted—with a "destroying wind" (Jer. 51:1). In Revelation, John's Mystery Babylon is destroyed with fire in one hour (Rev. 18:8, 10, 17, 19).

Therefore, it seems that Jeremiah was predicting the fall of the Babylon in his day, while projecting into the future when a "Babylon" will be burned and never inhabited again. Since John's vision in Revelation has the same phrases as Jeremiah, then the Old Testament prophet may be alluding to a future Babylon as well as the one of his day. I believe this could be a dual prophecy—a prophecy against the Babylon in Jeremiah's day, which took the Jews captive, and a prophecy concerning a Babylon (which John saw in revelation) that would arise in the future.

It is impossible to rightly divide the Word of God and follow the basic law of biblical interpretation by teaching that America somehow fits into the prophecy of Jeremiah. Some point out the wickedness in America's major cities fit the pattern of Babylon. I would point out there are cities in the world much more immoral than any in America! For example, in Western Europe there are places like Amsterdam, Holland, where prostitution is legal and the government provides hard drugs. Also, ancient Babylon was not noted for its sexual immorality but for its idolatry and its false religious worship.

Daniel's Empires of Prophecy—a More Plausible Prophecy

A theory that seems more plausible is found in Daniel 7:1–7, which is a vision the Hebrew prophet Daniel received while a captive in ancient Babylon. Using the symbolism of animals, the vision reveals several empires that would rule in the future. Some have concluded that one small passage could allude to the United States.

> In the first year of Belshazzar king of Babylon, Daniel had a dream and visions of his head while on his bed. Then he wrote down the dream, telling the main facts. Daniel spoke, saying, "I saw in my vision by night, and behold, the four winds of heaven were stirring up the Great Sea. And four great beasts came up from the sea, each different from the other. The first was like a lion, and had eagle's wings. I watched till its wings were plucked off; and it was lifted up from the earth and made to stand on two feet like a man, and a man's heart was given to it. And suddenly another beast, a second, like a bear. It was raised up on one side, and had three ribs in its mouth between its teeth. And they

said thus to it: 'Arise, devour much flesh!' After this I looked, and there was another, like a leopard, which had on its back four wings of a bird. The beast also had four heads, and dominion was given to it. After this I saw in the night visions, and behold, a fourth beast, dreadful and terrible, exceedingly strong. It had huge iron teeth; it was devouring, breaking in pieces, and trampling the residue with its feet. It was different from all the beasts that were before it, and it had ten horns."

—Daniel 7:1–7

Notice that these "beasts" rule in a succession. The lion is followed by the bear, which is followed by the leopard, and finally the nondescriptive beast with ten horns. Traditionally, scholars point to Daniel chapters 2 and 8 to demonstrate that the four successive empires in Daniel's prophecy are: Babylon, Media-Persia, Greece, and Rome. By this interpretation, the lion represents ancient Babylon, followed by the bear representing Media-Persia, followed by the leopard representing Greece, and the fourth beast that succeeded Greece being the Roman Empire.

History supports this premise: Large stone-winged lions guarded the entrances of Babylon. Large bears roamed the mountains of ancient Persia. The swiftness of the leopard is signified by the incredible conquering ability of the head of the Grecian empire, Alexander the Great. In Daniel's vision the leopard had four wings on its back. When Alexander the Great died, his kingdom was divided between his four generals, signified by the four wings on the leopard. The final beast, with iron teeth, can represent the iron kingdom of Rome. This is clear from the dream of Nebuchadnezzar recorded in Daniel 2 and its image with "legs of iron" (v. 33), which scholars point out clearly represented the Roman Empire.

Yet, there is another nontraditional interpretation relating to Daniel's four beasts. In the text, the angel says: "Those great beasts, which are four, are four kings which arise out of the earth" (Dan. 7:17). Daniel is speaking in future tense. Daniel 7 was written during Daniel's captivity in Babylon. If Babylon is listed as the first beast (the lion), and the four beasts in chapter 7 "shall arise" (future tense), then perhaps the prophet was alluding to a series of End Time empires that would rule in the latter days.

Four Modern Empires of Prophecy

Some scholars teach that these four beasts could represent four modern empires that have arisen to world dominance in the past three hundred years.

1. The lion represents Great Britain—whose "eagle's wings" formed the United States.

2. The bear represents the nation of Russia.

3. The leopard represents the nation of Germany.

4. The final beast represents the final kingdom that will rule at the time of the end.

First consider Great Britain, whose emblem is a lion. Britain was once the mightiest empire in the world. It was said, "The sun never sets upon the British Empire." Britain colonized much of the world, including Palestine (present-day Israel). Notice that the lion had eagle's wings and the wings were plucked or removed. The lion suddenly stood up and was given a heart like a man. While traditional scholars indicate this alludes to Nebuchadnezzar's seven-year nervous breakdown and his recovery in Daniel 4, others believe this speaks of how America was plucked away from the lion of Britain and made to stand alone. America came out of the lion and was given a heart of a man, or a heart of compassion.

If the lion could represent Britain, and the eagle's wings America, then what about the other three beasts—the bear, the leopard, and the final beast? The modern nation whose emblem has been a bear is Russia. Growing up I heard men speak of *the Russian bear*. In Daniel's vision, the bear is lying on one side with three ribs in its mouth. Russia spread its doctrine of Communism toward one direction on the map. The three ribs could represent the three main Communist leaders—Marx, Lenin, and Stalin. The bear "devours much flesh." Countless millions of innocent humans were devoured as the Russian bear clawed his way into nations, tearing apart those who resisted.

The Russian Revolution of 1917 brought about Communism. The next major nation after the rise of Communist Russia was Germany. Germany had a rich history hundreds of years before Communism, but the German influence was felt worldwide with the ascension of Hitler several years after the rise of Communism.

The leopard is the third beast in order, and the German Nazis were the Third Reich. The army of Germany, as did Alexander the Great centuries before, moved with the speed of a leopard to conquer the surrounding nations!

In the Daniel 7 order of empires, another beast, or empire, arises after the leopard. This will be the kingdom of a man called the Antichrist. With the final beast alluding to the last world empire before the return of Christ, this adds some credibility that Daniel 7 may be a dual prophecy: one that alludes to the major empires of Bible prophecy, the theory espoused by traditional scholars, and a reference to modern End Time empires.

It is clear that this next major Middle Eastern empire, which forms in the area of the old Roman Empire, is more than the European Union. In reality the EU is a modern coalition of nations held together by a union of trade and one monetary unit. In their present form, they do not fit the description of the warlike, destructive nature of the ancient Roman beast or the beast revealed in Revelation who is continually "making war" (Rev. 13:4, 7) and beheading all who oppose it (Rev. 20:4). One group that was once a major empire (through the Ottoman Turks) appears to have been defeated, but an Islamic coalition is rising again. I believe the last empire will organize and rule from the Middle East (the same area of ancient Rome) and will be a major Islamic coalition.

We speak about the economic power of the EU and their amassing of wealth; however, it is the oil-producing nations that are swimming in financial prosperity, with billions of dollars in currency and gold in the coffers of Allah. The Gulf oil nation of Saudi Arabia is building Dubai into one of the most completely modern cities in world history and preparing it to become the vacation Mecca of the world. Presently the rich and famous are purchasing man-made islands off the coast of Dubai, and golf courses, expensive hotels, and indoor ski resorts are being constructed. It is literally a city rising from the sea! It is interesting to see the shape of many of the buildings being constructed in Dubai, which are in the form of towering horns. The real wealth has come from the oil from the deserts of Islamic nations. Today, this money is being channeled into the West, not to assist the West, but to purchase prime land, businesses, and mosques throughout the world.

Out of this reforged Islamic kingdom will arise the little horn (the Antichrist), who will seize ten nations (ten kings) and control the global economy. The final kingdom is compared to a lion (Babylon), a bear (Media-Persia), and a leopard (Greece) in Revelation 13:2:

> Now the beast which I saw was like a leopard, his feet were like the feet of a bear, and his mouth like the mouth of a lion. The dragon gave him his power, his throne, and great authority.

The final beast kingdom will actually swallow up the territories of Babylon, Media-Persia, and Greece. Today these are the nations of Afghanistan, Pakistan, Iran, Iraq, Syria, Lebanon, and parts of Turkey, Greece, and the area of Bulgaria (Macedonia). With the exception of Greece and parts of Bulgaria, these areas are predominantly Islamic. If the beasts in Daniel 7 are a foreshadowing of future empires, then the beast kingdom will also impact England, America, Russia, and Germany. The kingdom of the Antichrist will control the economies of the world through a system of buying and selling, using a mark, a number, and the name of the beast. How is this control possible if America is the leading Gentile power in the world? The answer is that there must be a decline in America's power and a removing of America's sovereignty.

America—the Last Great Gentile Empire

Prophetically, the time is coming when nations will lose their individual sovereignty and will unite in various coalitions in order to increase their power and influence, and, I believe, in order to actually survive what is to come. America may possibly be the last great Gentile empire in world history.

Men and women seeking religious freedom, who arrived by ship from Europe, founded America. As the Founding Fathers organized thirteen colonies, America was called *a union*. The U.S. Constitution begins by saying, "We the People of the United States, in Order to form a more perfect Union..."[2] As the government grew into three branches—the legislative, the judicial, and the federal—we were identified as a *republic*, the same term used to describe the governmental form of the Roman Empire. As America continued to expand its influence around the globe, the nations of the world identified us as the United States of America. We moved from a union to a republic to a nation among the nations. I believe that after World War II, America was lifted up beyond a powerful nation and became the lone Gentile empire of the last days.

When studying the past empires of biblical prophecy, there appears to be four common threads woven throughout the fabric of each previous empire: Babylon, Media-Persia, Greece, and Rome. These same four threads are stitched throughout the fabric of America.

1. Military authority

Every previous empire dominated the world through a powerful, undefeatable military machine. The Medes and Persians overtook Babylon by their military. The Greeks, through Alexander the Great, took thirty thousand highly motivated men and conquered more than one million Persians. From that moment, the Greeks appeared invincible. The Roman Army eventually developed into the most powerful army in world history, expanding its influence into many nations previously untouched by earlier empires. Just as ancient Rome was marked with the greatest military, America has become the most powerful fighting force in the world.

Some suggest that Russia is equal to or above America. This is a false assumption. While Russia has in its arsenal dangerous nuclear weapons, the collapse of the Soviet Union brought a division in the Russian military. Many high-ranking officials defected to other nations, assisting in weapons development for pay. Many Soviet troops actually went for months without pay. Russia is still a dangerous force, selling high-tech weapons to rogue Islamic and Communist nations. However, America's advanced technology and discipline among our troops are the envy of the world. The fact that we have the top military is one mark of the American Empire.

2. Economic dominion

Each previous empire controlled the economy of the world in its time. Babylon was rich with gold, while the Persians used silver to pay their taxes. The Romans used the metal of iron for weaponry and for practical purposes. Rome built roads throughout the empire and conducted trade through a large fleet of shipping vessels. Each empire dominated their day through economic power.

Today, each nation in the world has its own currency. Israel uses the shekel; Japan, the yen; England, the sterling and the pound; Germany, the mark; and Mexico, the peso. However, the only currency that is desired and recognized universally is the American dollar. The growth of the global stock markets is so linked to Wall Street in New York that any negative drop immediately impacts global markets. Even dictators like Saddam Hussein had nearly one billion in American currency stashed in hiding prior to the recent coalition liberation of Iraq. As I mentioned in chapter 2, after the 2007 Israeli conflict with Hezbollah, the same Islamic terrorist group that called for death to Israel and the destruction of America handed out $12,000 to each Lebanese who had lost an apartment or home in the conflict.[3] For the past fifty years, much of the world's global economy has been directly linked to the chain of America's currency, the most desirable currency in the world.

3. Political influence

To be a leading empire, you must be the political leader among the nations. Your political clout must extend beyond your own borders and penetrate the hearts of world leaders. This influence of power is the result of each nation's need to cooperate with the empire in charge in order to bring prosperity to its own people. From the earliest days, economic control of gold, lending, banking, and wealth has been the central feature allowing an empire to remain in charge.

During World War I, Great Britain was the leading empire. After World War II, Britain realized it was becoming too expensive to be the guardians of the world. Eventually the British removed their troops from areas like Palestine to make room for the Jewish state of Israel, signing over land and territories to give nations their own sovereign control. This occurred from the islands of the sea to Africa and India and as far as the edge of China. America stepped in to fill the gap, and now the world looks to America to resolve political conflicts and assist in war efforts, including forging peace treaties following conflict. Just as the Roman Empire conducted the Pax Romana (Roman peace), America is called to be the mediator and peacemaker because of the influence and respect it wields.

America—Removing the Final Empire

Most empires of prophecy and history last for a period of two hundred to four hundred years.

- The Medes and Persians ruled for about three hundred thirty years.
- The Greeks ruled for nearly three hundred years.
- The Ottoman Turks ruled for four hundred years.

Columbus was credited with discovering the area of America in 1492; however, America did not build her first colony until 1607 in Jamestown. From the forming of Jamestown until the year 2007 was four hundred years. Mention of this four-hundred-year cycle is found in Genesis 15:13, when God revealed to Abraham that his descendants would live in a strange land (Egypt) for four hundred years, after which God would bring them out of captivity back to the Promised Land. After four hundred years God would use Israel to destroy the Amalekites, a large tribe that had possessed the Promised Land. These tribes were full of immorality and idolatry.

There were four hundred years from the last Hebrew prophet, Malachi, to the revelation of John the Baptist.

A four-hundred-year cycle often alludes to fullness and completion that leads to a major transition. I believe America's "cup of iniquity" is becoming full, and part of the selective judgment God will send to America because of her national sins will be a decline in the great American Empire. This decline can be seen in the warnings God gave Israel concerning breaking His covenant, found in the Torah (five books of Moses).

America and Israel—Parallel Warnings

When the Founding Fathers signed the Constitution, they separated the power of our government into three branches: the executive, the judicial, and the legislative. The president, vice president, and fifteen cabinet departments fall under the executive branch, while the Supreme Court and lower courts are under the judicial. The House of Representatives and the Senate, together called the Congress, are under the legislative branch.

One reason for this separation of power was the founders' desire to erect a wall against a possible future totalitarian rule, which was the manner of control the British were then imposing upon the colonies. This separation of powers created checks and balances. If the president introduces legislation, it must either be approved by Congress or vetoed. If Congress introduces legislation, the president can veto it. Congress has power to impeach the president, as we see with the impeachment proceedings of President Richard Nixon in August 1974.* The Supreme Court can rule on the constitutionality of a law, based on the Constitution, but the Congress can amend the Constitution with a two-thirds majority vote from the states, which has occurred on numerous occasions.[4]

One such example of amending the Constitution occurred after President Roosevelt had been elected for his third term. Congress amended the Constitution to read: "No person shall be elected to the office of the President more than twice, and no person who has held the office of President, or acted as President, for more than two years of a term to which some other person was elected President shall be elected to the office of the President more than once."[5] While the form of our government was based upon a Greek and Roman style rule called a *democracy*, the moral, judicial, and ethical laws themselves found their source in the biblical Torah (first five books of the Old Testament), the Prophets, and the Gospels. Thus, the divinely revealed laws of Scripture were used to forge the moral, judicial, and ethical laws governing the states and the nation.

For example, why do the judicial laws of our land make the following illegal?

- Robbery and stealing
- Bestiality
- Murder
- Abusing children

The answer is because the laws established by God through Moses—the Ten Commandments—established the moral law and revealed the judicial response to breaking the laws. Our national and local laws, which protect the innocent and punish the guilty, are derived from the thirty-five-hundred-year-old writings

---

* The House Judiciary Committee approved Articles of Impeachment against President Richard M. Nixon on July 30, 1974. President Nixon spoke to the nation on August 8, 1974, and resigned from office effective at noon, Friday, August 9, 1974, thus avoiding the impeachment process continuing to the House and Senate.

of Moses penned in the Bible. This is why it is often stated that our national laws are based upon Judeo-Christian concepts.

There are three main divisions of the God code given to Israel to establish a successful, peaceful society that would prosper and live within moral restraints for the betterment of the community.

1. The sacrificial law

The sacrificial code is misunderstood by contemporary readers. In this section of divine instruction, the Israelites were to offer selected animal sacrifices for sin, transgressions, guilt, and fellowship offerings. The blood served as a token for their redemption and a picture of the ultimate and final sacrifice that would come through the Messiah. The meat from the offerings would be eaten by thousands of priests ministering in Moses's tabernacle and later in the temple in Jerusalem. Offering the best from their flocks to God prevented the people from living in selfishness and greed.

2. The ceremonial law

The ceremonial code included the seven yearly feasts, the Sabbath cycles that fell every seventh day and seventh year, and the Jubilee cycles every forty-nine years. These cycles pointed to the future revelation of the redeeming Messiah who would set up His kingdom in Jerusalem. They also served as a practical blessing, giving the men needed time off work three times a year to enjoy fellowship and celebration in Jerusalem. The Sabbath cycles provided much-needed rest for families living in a very difficult time in an agrarian society. Christ fulfilled patterns of the spring feast by dying near the time of Passover, by being in the tomb during the Feast of Unleavened Bread, and by rising again during the Feast of First Fruits. The church was born on Pentecost, and many scholars believe the Messiah will return in the future and fulfill the three fall feasts—Trumpets, Atonement, and Tabernacles.

3. The moral and spiritual law

The moral and judicial code was far different from the ethics of surrounding nations, which included idolatry and unrestrained sexual immorality. By His law, God demanded that the Hebrew parents not offer their children as a sacrifice as other pagan nations did (called *passing your children through the fire of Molech*), not commit adultery and fornication as the surrounding nations did, and not permit sexual relations with members of the same sex. Incest was forbidden, along with bestiality. Other laws included:

- You were not to see the nakedness of nearest kin or family members (Lev. 18:6–18).

- You were not to have sexual relations outside of your marriage (Lev. 18:20).

- You were not to offer your children to idol gods (Lev. 18:21).

- You were to honor and respect your parents and rest once a week (Lev. 19:3).

- You were not to harvest the corners of your field, thus allowing the poor to eat (Lev. 19:9–10).

- You were not permitted to lie or steal (Lev. 19:11).

- If you hired a person for work, you must pay that person the agreed-upon wage (Lev. 19:13).

- You must show respect for those who are deaf and blind (Lev. 19:14).

- You were to honor the older among you and not vex a stranger (Lev. 19:32–34).

- There were cycles of rest every seventh day, seventh year, and each seven-times-seven year (Lev. 25:1–55).

These moral codes were so important that if they were broken, the individual or individuals were punished to prevent others from following their patterns, thereby causing sin to spread like a cancer and corrupt the entire population and thus bringing the disfavor of God upon the nation. The judicial codes revealed the forms of discipline or punishment required for each transgression. Judges and officers were established in every city (Deut. 16:18). It required two or three witnesses to establish guilt in a crime (Deut. 17:6), and judicial leaders were not permitted to receive gifts lest they perverted their decisions (Deut. 16:19).

Christ fulfilled the sacrificial code by His own sacrificial death and observance of portions of the ceremonial code. However, the moral and ethical commandments have not changed, and the same guidelines for moral and social behavior are penned in the New Testament. This is why Christ said:

> Do not think that I have come to do away with or undo the Law or the Prophets; I have come not to do away with or undo but to complete and fulfill them.
>
> —Matthew 5:17, amp

Special blessings were released upon individuals and the nation for obedience to the laws of the Almighty. They were blessed coming in and going out. They would have the ability to lend and not borrow. They would rise high and defeat their enemies during times of war. Their fields would produce, their animals procreate, and their children would be blessed (Deut. 28).

However, disobedience and breaking the covenant would bring strange and negative consequences. When Israel began to trample on the commandments of God, they were warned of impending disasters that would come to their land. These *curses of the Law* are recorded in two main passages—Deuteronomy 28 and Leviticus 26. Just as God allowed certain negative events to occur when Israel was in disobedience to bring them to repentance, we can see these same warnings being given to America.

The Seven Warnings

God said:

> But if you do not obey Me, and do not observe all these commandments, and if you despise My statutes, or if your soul abhors My judgments, so that you do not perform all My commandments, but break My covenant, I also will do this to you…
>
> —LEVITICUS 26:14–16

God then listed seven warnings for the nation that rejects His covenant with them. Let's compare America's recent conflicts with these biblical warnings.

1. "I will appoint over you [sudden] terror (trembling, trouble)" (Lev. 26:16, AMP).

God said He would "appoint" (or visit) you with terror. Since 9/11 of 2001, America has been engaged in a global war on terror. Islamic fanatics entered our nation and orchestrated a well-planned assault inside the security of our own borders. This war has cost billions of dollars, and the attack itself resulted in nearly a half-million job losses in New York City and a loss in wages of $2.8 billion.[6]

2. "I will make your heavens as iron [yielding no answer, no blessing, no rain] and your earth [as sterile] as brass" (Lev. 26:19, AMP).

The Almighty then warns that following terror there would be a lack of rain. Lack of rain has been partially responsible for fires across the nation. Since 9/11, 52.3 million acres have been burned due to wildfires and arson.[7]

The lack of rain created one of the worst droughts in 2007 in the southeastern United States, especially for the state of Georgia and the city of Atlanta.

This popular southern city was warned that without significant rainfall soon, the city of 5.4 million people could be without drinking water in four short months![8] This has never happened in contemporary time to any American city. As a point of interest, Atlanta has become the "San Francisco of the South" and the new capital for the homosexual community.[9] It is also noted that several of the megachurches and megaministries have been caught in unbelievable sexual immorality and scandals. Certainly we have experienced terror and drought.

3. "Your land shall not yield its increase, neither shall the trees of the land yield their fruit" (Lev. 26:20, AMP).

The third progression of warning is that the fruit trees will not produce. A drought would naturally affect the fruits and vegetables. However, in chapter 14 I gave you information about a strange disease called *Colony Collapse Disorder* affecting honeybees that could fulfill this warning. In October 2006, some beekeepers began reporting losses of as many as 30–90 percent of their hives. The first cause was identified as cell phone towers interfering with the internal navigation system of the small bee, which was later rejected. The second theory was that a certain parasite, a small mite, had invaded the colonies and was killing the bees off. The effect of pesticides has also been studied as a possible cause. In May of 2008, the United States Department of Agriculture stated: "The number of managed honey bee colonies has dropped from 5 million in the 1940s to only 2.5 million today." How does this affect us? "Bee pollination is responsible for $15 billion in added crop value, particularly for specialty crops such as almonds and other nuts, berries, fruits, and vegetables. About one mouthful in three in the diet directly or indirectly benefits from honey bee pollination."[10]

4. "I will ... destroy your livestock, and ... your roads shall be deserted and desolate" (Lev. 26:22, AMP).

The next warning is the cattle. Severe weather conditions in recent years—including drought, blizzards, and hurricanes—have created shortages of hay to feed livestock. Shortages have forced many ranchers to sell their livestock.[11] In addition, diseases affecting livestock could seriously impact the United States. The United States Department of Agriculture's Economic Research Service forecast cash receipts from the sale of U.S. hogs and cattle at $14.2 and $49.6 billion respectively for 2005. Experts predicted that the outbreak of just one disease, foot-and-mouth disease, in livestock, "would decrease U.S. farm income by $14 billion assuming a 10 percent decrease in consumption."[12]

As livestock become infected, the next warning appears to allude to travel. God warns, "Your roads shall be deserted and desolate." The word here for roads ("highways," KJV) in Hebrew is *derek,* meaning "a road that is trodden." It is a road for travelers, which is suddenly empty of travelers. How could America's highways become empty? One logical answer would be that the prices of gasoline reached such high costs that it became difficult for the average American to travel beyond places of necessity. In a testimony given by George Soros before the U.S. Senate Commerce Committee Oversight Hearing on June 3, 2008, he reported: "In January 2007, the price of oil was less than $60 per barrel. By the spring of 2008, the price had crossed $100 for the first time, and by mid-July, it rose further to a record $147. At the end of August it remains over $115, a 90 percent increase in just eighteen months. The price of gasoline at the pump has risen commensurately from an average of $2.50 to around $4 a gallon during this period."[13] A major war in a Middle Eastern oil-producing nation would spike the oil prices into costs that could translate into $8 to $10 for a gallon of gas. I think that would make the highways empty.

5. "I will send the pestilence among you, and you shall be delivered into the hands of the enemy" (Lev. 26:25, AMP).

In the New Testament, Christ warned there would be "pestilences...in various places" (Matt. 24:7). The Greek word for "pestilences" can allude to a plague of some sort. In the 1340s, the world experienced the bubonic plague, called the "Black Death," which killed millions. The world has seen typhus, smallpox, scarlet fever, malaria, and other infectious diseases. More recently, concern swept the world as the World Health Organization classified the "swine flu" as a major pandemic.[14] With global transportation through planes and ships, and illegal immigration numbers swelling, it is easy for a pestilence of transmittable disease to pass from person to person. Pestilences are a part of the "curse" for rejecting God's covenant.

6. "... cut off your supply of food ... ration your bread [food shortages]" (Lev. 26:26, AMP).

All along the food chain there are opportunities for terrorists to introduce animal or plant pathogens that would effectively "cut off your supply of food" and "ration your bread." Agriculture is the number one employer in the United States. The U.S. agriculture system is the "most productive and efficient in the world, allowing Americans to spend less than 11 percent of disposable income on food, compared to the global average of 20 to 30 percent." As a part of the global economy, U.S. agriculture "contributes $50 billion annually, making the farm sector the largest positive contributor to the national trade balance."[15] The threat of food shortages caused by food security issues as well as crops being grown to produce ethanol instead of food products is already causing hunger and food riots around the world. Some analysts believe that: "The United States is on the verge of a major economic revolution, a process, which will change where we live, what we eat, and how we view agriculture."[16]

7. "I will lay your cities waste, bring your sanctuaries *[churches]* to desolation" (Lev. 26:31, AMP).

America is already seeing the warning to "lay your cities waste, bring your sanctuaries to desolation" happen. Cities like Detroit and Flint, Michigan, victims of the demise of the American automobile industry, are becoming ghost towns.[17] In addition, at a time when church attendance was already declining and atheism rising, the current economic crisis in America is now affecting churches. A recent report stated: "Americans are now passing on their financial pain to churches and other non-profit organizations by cutting back substantially on their giving during the fourth quarter of 2008. Those reductions—occurring during the most important quarter of the year for donor-driven organizations—will cripple thousands of smaller and less stable donor-supported organizations."[18]

America's national sins are rising up to God in the same manner as the sins of Sodom and Gomorrah. Just as God judged the cities of the plain in the time of Lot (Gen. 19), America is getting ripe for the same judgment.

The Disarray of the Union

We have entered a time in our nation when a powerful group of elitist and self-appointed history changers, many educated in Ivy League schools where they were influenced by professors dominated with a Marxist/Socialist mind-set, are attempting to "institute change in America." The buildings that line Pennsylvania Avenue—encompassing the executive, legislative, and judicial branches of the government—are controlled and dominated by this group. These self-appointed prophets of *change*, instead of protecting Constitutional rights and honoring the American Dream and our Judeo-Christian traditions, are placing their own personal twists and interpretations on our foundational documents.

There are those who desire to *change* or completely amend the Constitution to fit their vision of a new, more progressive (liberal, Socialist) America. However, notice what the wisest man, Solomon, warned:

> My son, fear the LORD and the king;
> Do not associate with those given to change;
> For their calamity will rise suddenly,
> And who knows the ruin those two can bring?
>
> —PROVERBS 24:21–22

The state of the union is in disarray. America began as a union of colonies, then became a republic and emerged as a leading End Time empire. Our founding documents are based upon the Torah—the Scriptures—just as Israel's were, and God holds us accountable for our obedience or disobedience to His divine laws just as He held Israel accountable.

In this section we are going to look at five laws of the Scripture that have been broken, which have placed us in the financial and moral mire that we are presently experiencing in our nation.

1. The abuse of the moneychangers

> If you lend money to any of My people who are poor among you, you shall not be like a moneylender to him; you shall not charge him interest.
>
> —Exodus 22:25

> If one of your brethren becomes poor, and falls into poverty among you, then you shall help him, like a stranger or a sojourner, that he may live with you. Take no usury or interest from him; but fear your God, that your brother may live with you. You shall not lend him your money for usury, nor lend him your food at a profit.
>
> —Leviticus 25:35–37

When the banking and mortgage crisis struck in America, it was a fire stoked by small sparks unseen by the general public. As the winds of interest rates rose to higher levels, the sparks became flames and the flames a wildfire that has burnt millions of people, causing them to lose their dream homes as the homes were foreclosed. The enemy came in the form of high interest rates that raised monthly mortgage payments to levels that could not be paid by the monthly incomes of homeowners. The laws in the Torah are clear about charging interest (called *usury* in the NKJV and KJV), especially when a person is poor and unable to pay it.

In America, any form of money loans or credit is accompanied by some level of interest rate. This is how the lender (bank, credit card company, or mortgage company) makes a profit from the loan. There is, however, a difference in making a living through a nice profit and making a killing through greed. In America, the interest rates vary, depending upon the economy of the nation at the time. Examples of interest are shown below:

The Loan	Average Interest Rate
Loans on cars	1–2 percent
Loans on homes	4.5–7.5 percent

THE LOAN	AVERAGE INTEREST RATE
Loans on colleges	Varied percentage
Loans on furniture	Varied percentage
Credit card rates	7–36 percent

In earlier times, business was often conducted through bartering. If you needed your home repaired, and if I was a carpenter, I would perform the job, and in return you would pay me with food from your farm to feed my family. Eventually, coinage was used—brass, silver, and gold, which was the standard for centuries. Later a paper money was printed, backed by a silver and gold standard. In the 1930s, when the gold standard was removed, the money was backed by the confidence in the government.

In 1913 the Federal Reserve was created to print money and loan it back to the government. The Federal Reserve prints money and loans it to the government—charging interest! This was the very type of system that the early fathers in America, including several presidents, warned not to create.

> We are free today, substantially, but the day will come when our republic will come to impossibility because its wealth will be concentrated in the hands of a few. When that day comes, then we must rely upon the wisdom of the best elements in the country to readjust the laws of the nation to the changed conditions.[19]
>
> —JAMES MADISON

> History records that the money changers have used every form of abuse, intrigue, deceit, and violent means possible to maintain their control over governments by controlling money and its issuance.[20]
>
> —JAMES MADISON

> I see in the future a crisis approaching that unnerves me…wealth is aggregated into a few hands and the republic be destroyed.[21]
>
> —ABRAHAM LINCOLN

After President Woodrow Wilson signed the charter in 1913 permitting the creation of the Federal Reserve, he later wrote:

> I am a most unhappy man. I have unwittingly ruined my country. A great industrial country is controlled by a system of credit.…The growth of the nation, therefore, and all our activities are in the hands

of a few men. . . . We are (now a government) ruled by the opinion and duress of a small group of dominant men.[22]

It is believed that the Great Depression was a situation created by the Federal Reserve. During the roaring twenties, the Federal Reserve released too much cash into the banking system, and then contracted it too quickly in 1929, causing a panic that there would be a shortage of cash and creating a run on the banks. When the mom-and-pop shops failed, the banks stepped in and picked them up for pennies on the dollar. (This is being repeated today as banks are taking homes, land, and businesses back.) Later, a head of the Reserve apologized for helping to create the *circumstances* that led to the Great Depression.[23]

The manipulation of the interest rates is what has helped cause the economic meltdown today. People were given loans at a very low rate, but they did not read the fine print or were not aware of the cost of ballooning interest rates and how they would jack up the price of their monthly mortgage payments. The low loans were sold on the market with the concept that as the interest rates rose, there would be plenty of money to go around. The purchasers assumed that millions of people could pay the increased monthly payments. They were wrong. People stepped out of their homes, filed for bankruptcy, or simply said, "Take this house and do what you want."

In the Torah, the poor among us are *not* to be charged interest when money is loaned to them. If they are poor, they will struggle just to return the money, and even more so with a 5 to 9 percent interest rate added. For example, when the Jews returned from Babylon, the people had left behind homes and farms, which had deteriorated. The grass was not cut, the vines were not pruned, and the tiles of the homes were in disarray. Several wealthy Jews were lending money to the people and charging interest. Nehemiah rebuked them and demanded them to stop the interest charges (Neh. 5:7–11). It was no time to profit from the terrible circumstances of the people.

Today's housing crisis never would have started if first the banks and mortgage companies had avoided lending money to people who had no jobs or income to repay the set payments. If there was an interest charge, it should have been minimal, affordable, and nonadjustable. In this manner, the lender would make a *profit*, and the borrower would have been aware that the rate was set. In the words of Solomon: "The borrower is servant to the lender" (Prov. 22:7).

Government housing and state and local programs, including special ministries through local churches, provide housing and other help for those under certain income levels. But as individuals, we must never forget that Scripture also requires us to help the poor who are poor indeed.

It is evident that greed padded the pockets of Wall Street investors and CEOs of many banks and lending institutions and set in motion an economic tragedy causing emotional suffering, economic suffering in families, and, at times, it has even led to divorce and death. It was the noble idea from the legislative branch of the government that led to the creation of programs to provide homes to those who could not afford them, but it was also those same men and women who seemingly ignored the coming storm caused by the escalation of unaffordable interest rates.

The law of God understood the need for those who are blessed to assist in feeding, clothing, and helping the poor and strangers among us. Ancient farmers were instructed to leave the corners of their fields and vineyards untouched, that the poor could "glean the corners." When the law of the Almighty is broken, then the lawbreakers will experience the repercussions.

2. The perversion of judgment by judges who accepted "gifts"

> You shall appoint judges and officers in all your gates, which the LORD your God gives you, according to your tribes, and they shall judge the people with just judgment. You shall not pervert justice; you shall not show partiality, nor take a bribe, for a bribe blinds the eyes of the wise and twists the words of the righteous.
> —Deuteronomy 16:18–19

The second law given by the Almighty that has been ignored involves judges taking special bribes. In our case, the "judges" would be not only those sitting on the judicial bench, but also those who are passing laws and setting the legal standards for the nation. Moses wrote: "You shall take no bribe ['gift,' KJV], for a bribe blinds the discerning and perverts the words of the righteous" (Exod. 23:8).

There are thousands of men and women who serve corporations as lobbyists, informing the Congress and placing pressure on lawmakers to pass certain laws. It is *technically* illegal for lobbyists to give gifts to their politicians, but it has been pointed out numerous times that *perks* such as golfing trips, private plane rides, special family vacations to resorts and exotic areas, and other *benefits* are at times enjoyed as a *side benefit* for supporting a certain agenda.

While accepting a "gift" from a lobbyist is not permitted, all politicians must have money, and lots of it, to conduct their election campaigns. While the limited amount any one individual can give to a candidate is only $2,500, a corporation or a union can go to its members and suggest they each send the limit in as a contribution for their chosen candidate. Let's face it. Once a person has received millions of dollars, are we so naïve as to believe that the elected official will ignore the gift giver or the contributing corporation's legal needs when a decision is about to be made that either favors or disfavors the supporter? It is for this very reason that a judge is not to receive gifts—it will pervert that judge's judgment. The gift will slant his or her opinions toward those supporters. Thus judgment is perverted, and those who speak truth and righteousness are ignored.

3. Pay it back instead of being locked up

> If a man steals an ox or a sheep, and slaughters it or sells it, he shall restore five oxen for an ox and four sheep for a sheep.
>
> —Exodus 22:1

> If a man delivers to his neighbor money or articles to keep, and it is stolen out of the man's house, if the thief is found, he shall pay double.
>
> —Exodus 22:7

When laws are broken, there is a price to pay. Many crimes include a long visit to a local jail or a prison. I have often said that if we followed God's *law of restitution*, we could prevent certain petty crimes from being repeated. Instead of locking up a person for a few months or years for certain *nonviolent* crimes, instead demand that the person repay the person(s) he or she has wronged or the damage caused. Make these petty thieves work to make physical restitution, or take the money from their paychecks until the damages are repaired or repaid.

This is called the *law of restitution*, clearly outlined in the Bible. A stolen animal required the restitution of five oxen or four sheep in repayment. If a thief was discovered, he had to restore double! If this law was passed in California, I wonder how many carjackings would still occur? Instead of sending the fellow to jail, he would have his bank account emptied or would work under legal supervision to provide a new BMW to the person he stole from!

If the beast of a neighbor ate from the field of his neighbor, that neighbor had to restore the food to his neighbor (Exod. 22:5). If a person set fire to his neighbor's field, he must restore the grain. Here's a good one. If you fight a person and harm him or her physically, you were required to pay for the injured person's lost time and to provide medical assistance to the injured (Exod. 21:18–19).

In America, instead of being provided the opportunity for restitution, people who commit petty theft, damage property, or commit nonviolent crimes are locked up without any opportunity for restoration to be made to the victim. I realize that all the repentance in the world cannot bring back a murder victim, reverse a rape scene, or right other serious sins and crimes. However, applying the law of restitution for general, civil acts of disobedience would send a strong message and, I believe, restrain certain actions and save taxpayers huge amounts of money.

4. Offering our children on the altar of abortion

> And you shall not let any of your descendants pass through the fire to Molech, nor shall you profane the name of your God: I am the LORD.
> —LEVITICUS 18:21

Scripture records two instances when governmental leaders permitted the deaths of newborns and infants. The pharaoh of Egypt demanded that the infant sons born to the Hebrews be drowned in the Nile River (Exod. 1:15–22). Jewish history (Josephus) states that a dream had revealed that the Hebrews would produce a leader who would bring Egypt low. Thus, the king of Egypt legalized an *after-birth abortion* plan and justified it in his mind as protection of his empire. In the New Testament, the magi from Persia informed Herod that a king had been born in Israel. After investigation, the location was determined to be Bethlehem. Herod asked the magi to return to give him a full report following their visit with the future king. Warned in a dream, the magi fled from the area, and Herod, realizing he was *mocked*, initiated a massacre of all infants less than two years of age (Matt. 2:16).

When Israel recaptured the Promised Land, there were heathen tribes that were offering their children to the idol gods they worshiped. One such idol, Molech, was constructed of iron and appeared as a cow from the waist up and a human from the waist down. There was an opening in the belly of the idol where wood and tar were placed and a fire was lit. The entire idol would become hot, and a heathen priest would take a newborn and "pass it through the fire to Molech" (Lev. 18:21; 20:2–5; 2 Kings 23:10). God commanded the children of Israel not to pass their children through the fire of Molech.

> Then the LORD spoke to Moses, saying, "Again, you shall say to the children of Israel: 'Whoever of the children of Israel, or of the strangers who dwell in Israel, who gives any of his descendants to Molech, he shall surely be put to death. The people of the land shall stone him with stones. I will set My face against that man, and will cut him off from his people, because he has given some of his descendants to Molech, to defile My sanctuary and profane My holy name. And if the people of the land should in any way hide their eyes from the

man, when he gives some of his descendants to Molech, and they do not kill him, then I will set My face against that man and against his family; and I will cut him off from his people, and all who prostitute themselves with him to commit harlotry with Molech.'"

—LEVITICUS 20:1–5

Someone may suggest that what we are doing in America by allowing abortion is not the same thing as offering our infants to a burning idol. Some may ask: "How does this warning relate to our time?" The spirit of Molech is identified today with the same spirit that motivates abortion. Many biblically uninformed women make the difficult and heartrending decision each year to have an abortion. Others are so proabortion that they become violent when a person tells them the act is shedding innocent blood and is wrong. Lawmakers are aggressively pursuing the passage of even more liberal laws regarding the killing of unborn infants through abortion.

I do not understand how a Bible-believing Christian can elect a person who is in favor of abortion to a lawmaking position. Some say, "I did not write the abortion law—they did, so I am not responsible." However, the Almighty said that if anyone among His people "hide their eyes" (ignore) when they saw a man offering a child to Molech, God would set His face against that person's entire family! I suggest that there are Christians who for the past forty years have kept liberal, pro-choice legislators in power, and some of these same voters have continued to live in poverty or have seen their children go to prison and can't figure out why the favor of God is not on their families. Could it be that God is displeased with their participation in the shedding of innocent blood? A believer should remember this warning: "Therefore, to him who knows to do good and does not do it, to him it is sin" (James 4:17).

Since the legalization of government-paid abortion on demand with the *Roe v. Wade* decision in 1973, nearly fifty million abortions have been performed in America alone![24] This is nearly fifty times more than all the Americans who have died from the Revolutionary War to the war in Iraq and all wars in between![25]

If shedding innocent blood curses the land, look at the destruction of the land in America the past few years:

- Fires have destroyed millions of acres and thousands of homes.
- Tornadoes in the Midwest and West have flattened thousands of homes and cost hundreds of millions of dollars.

- Hurricanes, such as Katrina and Ike, have wreaked havoc on New Orleans, Louisiana, and Galveston, Texas.

- Earthquakes have shaken the West, along with volcanic eruptions.

- Droughts throughout the United States have threatened our food supplies.

- Floods have destroyed crops, raising food prices.

Many progressive secularists would cringe at my suggestion that there could be a link between our actions of shedding innocent blood and the terrible natural disasters that are costing the government billions of dollars in taxpayers' money to rebuild devastated areas. However, this is one law of God that has been broken. Instead of honoring the miracle of conception and life and the gift of a child, the laws and statutes of our nation are mocking God and dishonoring His name while those sitting in the pew who permit such abominations are dishonoring the sanctuary.

5. Dishonoring the marriage covenant

> And the Lord God said, It is not good that the man should be alone; I will make him an help meet for him....And the Lord God caused a deep sleep to fall upon Adam, and he slept: and he took one of his ribs, and closed up the flesh instead thereof; and the rib, which the Lord God had taken from man, made he a woman, and brought her unto the man. And Adam said, This is now bone of my bones, and flesh of my flesh: she shall be called Woman, because she was taken out of Man. Therefore shall a man leave his father and his mother, and shall cleave unto his wife: and they shall be one flesh.
>
> —Genesis 2:18, 21–24, kjv

After God created man, He created woman to be man's "help meet," which is one who comes alongside to help. In God's original plan, a man would marry a virgin, and the marriage was considered a covenant between the two. When a virgin consummates with her husband, she sheds a small amount of blood as a sign of her virginity. In ancient Israel it was required that there would be evidence of her virginity on the sheets the morning after her "honey-moon" (Deut. 22). This small amount of blood indicated she had entered into a wonderful covenant between herself and one man.

Scripture teaches that because of the hardness of men's hearts, under certain situations God allowed a bill of divorcement (Mark 10:4–5). Throughout history, there were occasions when men and women strayed from the covenant and began to commit sins considered "abomination" and acts that were forbidden in the law of God. For example, in the time of Abraham there were two cities, Sodom and Gomorrah, in which both the young and old men were performing acts of sodomy. Both cities were eventually destroyed by fire in the days of Lot (Gen. 19). Years later, one of Israel's tribes, the tribe of Benjamin, took upon themselves a perversion of same-sex relations with the men in the tribe. The other tribes discussed slaying the entire tribe to revert the spread of the perversion. However, they eventually demanded that the men of Benjamin marry Israeli women, and thus the tribe was spared. Later, Israel's first king, Saul, was selected from the tribe of Benjamin. (See Judges 20 and 21.)

In the New Testament, the apostle Paul warned that men could be "given over to a reprobate mind" if they worshiped the creature more than the Creator (Rom. 1:28, KJV). He spoke of those who had knowledge of God but did not retain their knowledge and instead turned from God and fell into illicit relations of woman with woman and man with man. Paul gave a firm warning about God's wrath, which would be revealed from heaven if such acts were permitted to occur (v. 18).

Destroying traditional marriage

The law of God is very clear concerning these things:

> You shall not lie with a male as with a woman. It is an abomination. Nor shall you mate with any animal, to defile yourself with it. Nor shall any woman stand before an animal to mate with it. It is perversion.
> —LEVITICUS 18:22–23

> If a man lies with a male as he lies with a woman, both of them have committed an abomination....If a man marries a woman and her mother, it is wickedness.
> —LEVITICUS 20:13–14

Today throughout America, millions of citizens have little if any biblical knowledge (or solid teaching in the churches, if they attend), and the new *progressive* leaders are ignorant of the thirty-five-hundred-year-old biblical warnings. Thus they happily pass legislation and give permission to place the title of marriage on relationships that do not consist of one man and one woman. Since marriage is a covenant and divinely established in the Garden of Eden, then when human legislators pass laws that are completely against the covenant that God established, the nation is in danger of the same parallel judgments being poured out that were experienced in Sodom and Gomorrah. The writers of the New Testament bear this out:

> And turning the cities of Sodom and Gomorrah into ashes, condemned them to destruction, making them an example to those who afterward would live ungodly; and delivered righteous Lot, who was oppressed by the filthy conduct of the wicked.
>
> —2 Peter 2:6–7

> As Sodom and Gomorrah, and the cities around them in a similar manner to these, having given themselves over to sexual immorality and gone after strange flesh, are set forth as an example, suffering the vengeance of eternal fire.
>
> —Jude 7

These cities serve as an example. What is it that caused these two twin cities of antiquity to permit sexual perversion that became so violent that the men attempted to break down the door of Lot's house to have sex with the two strangers there (Gen. 19)? As I mentioned earlier in this book, the Book of Jasher, gives us insight. It was the judges, or laws passed, that opened the door to this abomination:

> And the cities of Sodom had four judges to four cities, and these were their names, Serak in the city of Sodom, Sharkad in Gomorrah, Zabnac in Admah, and Menon in Zeboyim....And by desire of their four judges the people of Sodom and Gomorrah had beds erected in the streets of the cities, and if a man came to these places they laid hold of him and brought him to one of their beds, and by force made him to lie in them.[26]
>
> —Jasher 19:1, 3

In the majority of states in our nation, the citizens believe that marriage is defined in our culture as a union between one man and one woman. However, the judges who sit in certain states and courts, giving legislation based on their personal opinions from the bench, are passing legislation permitting alternative marriage, thus making a mockery of the covenant that has been successful for six thousand years. The day we destroy traditional marriage, we destroy the traditional home, the family, and the very foundation of a civilized society.

Various warnings are given by the Lord for breaking His established laws. Many of the "curses" affected crops, animals, and land, and opened the door to Israel's enemies. Perhaps we should take another look at God's laws in His Word. After all, this was the document used to forge our original moral, judicial, and ethical beliefs.

The Divided States of America

The founders established thirteen separate states called *colonies*. The Constitution was written, "In Order to form a more perfect Union..." As more land was purchased from the French, the Spanish, the Indians, and others, the Union was expanded to form the United States of America. During seasons of war and extreme political differences, the Union was divided, and prior to the Civil War it appeared that the South would secede from the Union. Civil War erupted and almost destroyed the "more perfect Union."

But the present situation is far different from the deep division of the Civil War. The United States of America is now the Divided States of America. The division is not just a mental disagreement between opposing political parties and partisan politics. Nor is this split just a liberal rampage trying to drown out a conservative viewpoint. Since 1973 this division has raged between pro-life and pro-choice. Since 2000, the new battlefield is traditional, biblical marriage between a man and woman versus same-sex marriage. Since 2009, new battle lines in the sand now separate progressive Socialists—a new name for old-fashioned, government-controlled Marxism—versus those who believe in the legacy and law of the Constitution. It is the lovers of big government versus those who believe in states' rights. The "tax-them-high-and-spend-more" bureaucrats are battling the "tax-cut" conservatives.

When hundreds of thousands of conservatives took to the streets for a well-organized series of tea parties, protesting a huge multitrillion-dollar deficit and demanding the government to get its greasy hands out of their pockets, the major news networks (except one) painted the entire gathering as right-wing white fanatics, rednecks, and ignorant hillbilly racists.

Just days before the Washington DC tea party protest, the Department of Homeland Security issued a bulletin to police departments identifying possible "domestic rightwing terrorists."[27] Were these "terrorists" fanatics in Islamic mosques? Were they Muslims recently released from prison who planned acts of terrorism such as the New York synagogue attack that was prevented in May of 2009? Or did the list hold names like antiwar liberal William Ayres, whose bombs years ago killed innocent people? No! According to the bulletin, "domestic rightwing terrorists" could be people who take a stand against abortion, who believe in End Time prophecies, and who may even possibly be war veterans returning from Iraq and Afghanistan! Basically, if you live in the

Southeast, express a Christian, pro-life view, and believe in or study biblical prophecy, then you are a possible danger to America! If you are a veteran, your threat level is bumped up an additional notch.

As banks close and Americans lose jobs and file bankruptcy on their dream homes, we hear talk of the system taking over the banks, the auto industry, the medical industry, and preparing to raise taxes to pay for an impossible dream. The *dreams of my fathers* have now become the *nightmare along Pennsylvania Avenue*!

James Madison, Abraham Lincoln, and Woodrow Wilson—who later apologized for helping to create the Federal Reserve—warned us about the danger of a central bank that would manipulate interest rates. We were warned that a government unrestrained could lead to a tyrannical dictator. For this reason, the Constitution ensured the individual rights of every citizen against the abuse of power. This abuse of power was the reason for the impeachment proceedings of Richard Nixon. It was written that a democracy would die when the people understood they could vote themselves generous gifts from the public treasury.[28] I would add...if the people elect leaders who promise to redistribute the wealth.

The America of my fathers is no longer the America they handed to the next generation. Living in the biblical time of the end will initiate changes in the nations of which even the leaders of those nations will be unaware. Previous generations were taught the Bible—including biblical prophecy and the hope of Christ's return. However, today's progressives know little or nothing about the future according to the Bible. Yet they are acting out and initiating activities that fall in line with ancient predictions.

••• Chapter 17 •••

A MESSAGE TO THE CHRISTIAN CHURCH IN AMERICA

---

*Thou would'st take much Pains to save thy Body: take some,
prithee, to save thy Soul.*[1]
—WILLIAM PENN, SOME FRUITS OF SOLITUDE, *1693*

IT APPEARS THAT the United States of America not only patterned its government, including the architecture of the federal buildings in Washington DC, after the patterns of the ancient Roman Empire, but also it is slowly entering an economic, social, and political demise and decline, which Rome, the world's great empire, experienced in the fifth century. There is, however, an interesting *twist* in the downward spiral of the ancient Roman Empire.

That twist is this. As ten major Germanic tribes overran imperial Rome and the Western branch collapsed, the Eastern division of the empire rose to prominence and became a leading empire for nearly a thousand years. This section of the empire was headquartered in Constantinople, Turkey, and became known as *Byzantium*. This empire, the Byzantine Empire, not only continued and expanded its landmasses and dominance in and around the Mediterranean area, but it also coined its own money and built churches throughout Palestine in practically every place associated with the life or ministry of Christ.

When I first traveled to the Holy Land, our group walked through the ruins of ancient cities, and I overheard the tour guide say, "This was once a Byzantine church." The army of the Byzantines provided protection for pilgrims traveling to and from the Holy Land. The Byzantine Empire was more than just another political organization in the East. It was a very religious Christian group that used the Greek language in place of the Latin (used by the West in Rome). One of the magnificent churches in the Europe-Asia region is Hagia Sophia in Istanbul, Turkey. After a thousand years, the Byzantine Empire fell into the hands of the Muslims, and the church was transformed into a large Islamic mosque.[2]

Should America, in years to come, travel the *Roman road* with high taxes, uncontrolled spending, a rush of illegal immigration, and a decrease in production, eventually it could become a hangman's noose on the nation and follow the same pattern of division between the West and East. Once the Germanic tribes began seizing the lands of the Western branch, there was a rise in the power and influence of the Roman Catholic Church through the popes, cardinals, and the bishops. The Eastern branch of the church rose to influence and strength.

When Christ predicted that He would form a living organism called the church, He also added that, "The gates of hell shall not prevail against it" (Matt. 16:18. kjv). Among the original apostles, eleven of the twelve died under persecution and were martyred. Only one died a natural death, the apostle John and author of the Apocalypse. In the first three centuries of the Christian church, there were ten major persecutions initiated by Roman emperors who were threatened by the growth of this new *cult* that believed in only one God and refused to celebrate the pagan holidays. Christians were fed to wild beasts, crucified, arrested, and beaten; some, like the apostle Paul, were beheaded.

The rise of Islam brought a battle between those who believed in Christianity and those who sought to force conversion to Islam. Despite centuries of physical opposition and decrees of death, arrest, and beatings, the Christian faith continued, and the Christian church never, at any time, has ceased to exist on the earth. The extreme threats and persecution from the forces of hell only strengthened the resolve of individual believers who were willing to die for the truth.

The Only Prayer Yet to Be Answered

Prior to His crucifixion, Christ interceded for His disciples. One of His requests to His Father was: "That they may be one as We are" (John 17:11). Nearly two thousand years later, we have seen little *unity* among the numerous Christian groups. The three main branches of the faith are Protestant, Catholic, and Orthodox. Among the Catholics there are conservatives, liberals, and secularists, all with different concepts on moral and social issues. The same is true among the Protestants.

However, history reveals that one thing will always pull the true believers together—persecution. More recently under Communism, Christians living in the Soviet Union or in Eastern Europe (Romania, Bulgaria, for example) lived under severe limitations and verbal and physical abuse. Most churches operated underground and in secret. After the collapse of Communism, the door of ministry opened. I traveled to both Romania and Bulgaria and heard the stories of persecution and hardships and the amazing stories of spiritual growth and maturity of the church living behind the iron curtain. The most impressive element was the large number of youth in each church.

The "Sons and Daughters"

Presently, in many nations outside of America, the Christian church is predominantly made up of young people less than thirty-five years of age. There are massive numbers of young Christians in Ukraine, Latin America, Africa, Singapore, Indonesia, and Europe. This fact is prophesied in Scripture:

> And it shall come to pass in the last days, says God,
> That I will pour out of My Spirit on all flesh;
> Your sons and your daughters shall prophesy,
> Your young men shall see visions,
> Your old men shall dream dreams.
>
> —Acts 2:17

Throughout history, the youth were a significant part of any revolution or social change in a nation. When the Berlin wall was chipped away one piece at a time, it was the younger generation who held the hammers and chisels. Likewise, the new spiritual revolution will be spearheaded by a new generation of young people who will see the "visions" of what should be and act to bring the visions to pass. There is one final generation who will experience the predicted return of the Messiah, and this "chosen generation" will also watch numerous prophecies unfold in their time. Their revolution will not be with guns and bombs in the manner that Islamic fanatics use to attempt to change nations, but their revolution will be with words and deeds.

For example, in the largest Islamic nation in the world, a Christian youth pastor supervised one thousand young ministers who had oversight of twelve thousand young people in one church. He left the security of his leadership position and began living along the riverbank where thousands of poor people were unable to provide food to eat. He set up a feeding program, which for several years has been the source of food for these needy souls. Today, more than 95 percent of the people have received the Christian faith, not through a sword of conversion, but through deeds of love.[3]

Today's generation of youth is *deed oriented*. They are not benchwarmers who enjoy the comfort of older hymns and a one-hour worship service. To them, church is only relevant if you are outside of the building and acting out what you say you believe. If the older believers are the *wisdom* of the church, then the younger generation is the *strength* of the church. Youth can travel throughout the world as the older generation financially supports them and prays for their mission efforts. The coming generation will conquer, but not by the use of a sword; they will conquer through love and the use of the pen, for *the pen is mightier than the sword*. Karl Marx wrote the *Communist Manifesto*, and years later an entire revolution was built upon his concepts. Hitler wrote *Mein Kampf* (*My Struggle*), and his best-selling book unlocked the door for his entry as chancellor of Germany.

America Has Three Syndromes

There are three events recorded in the Scriptures that paint a perfect imagery of three syndromes affecting many Americans. By definition, a *syndrome* is "a group of symptoms that collectively indicate or characterize a disease, psychological disorder, or other abnormal conditions...a distinctive or characteristic pattern of behavior."

1. The Hezekiah syndrome

King Hezekiah was ruling from Jerusalem when he was suddenly stricken with an incurable disease. Through prayer and God's mercy, the king was restored to health and promised fifteen additional years. A delegation from Babylon paid the prosperous king a visit. Hezekiah foolishly opened the treasure houses of the temple, boasting to the foreigners of Jerusalem's wealth in gold. After the Babylonian convoy departed, the prophet Isaiah, under divine inspiration, gave the king a rebuke and a warning of something coming in the future.

> "Behold, the days are coming when all that is in your house, and what your fathers have accumulated until this day, shall be carried to Babylon; nothing shall be left," says the Lord. "And they shall take away some of your sons who will descend from you, whom you will beget; and they shall be eunuchs in the palace of the king of Babylon."
> —2 Kings 20:17–18

If a reputable world leader indicated he had credible evidence that a foreign army would eventually overtake the United States, burn our cities, seize our personal wealth, and sell our children as slaves, would you turn to God in prayer and rise up to ensure the event was prevented? King Hezekiah prayed for his healing when he was dying, but he did not intercede for his city and his grandchildren's future! After the warning, he replied to Isaiah:

So Hezekiah said to Isaiah, "The word of the LORD which you have spoken is good!" For he said, "Will there not be peace and truth at least in my days?"

—2 KINGS 20:19

Hezekiah wanted prosperity in his day, and as long as he maintained his power, controlled the wealth, and had "peace" in his day, he wasn't concerned about the future. After all, he would long be in the grave when the invasion would occur.

Americans, like the Russians, Germans, and the Italians in the twentieth century, are ignoring the signs of terminal economic and social cancer by taking shots of morphine to dull their senses. Most people can't count to a billion, much less a trillion.

Let me give you some mental pictures to explain the scope of $1 trillion:

- One trillion seconds are 31,688 years from the time of the bailout. One bank earned $193 million in one year. To earn a trillion at that rate would take five thousand years.

- One trillion dollars would give every high school student free college for four years.

- If we paid back $1 trillion, paying $1 every second, it would take thirty-two thousand years to pay the $1 trillion debt.

- If we make a stack with $100 bills, $1 million would be 4 feet high and $1 billion would be 4,000 feet high.

- One trillion dollars would stack 789 miles high.

- One dollar is 6 inches long, and $1 trillion laid end to end would stretch from the earth to the sun, a total of 93 million miles.

The Hezekiah syndrome is concerned about the here and now, not the future. It says, "Give me a bailout, give me a raise, and tax the rich. As long as I've got what I want, I'm not concerned about the America my children will see."

2. The Goliath syndrome

The first king of Israel was Saul, a tall, charismatic leader who eventually became more concerned about his perception among the people than approval from the Almighty. In Saul's time there were three economic and social burdens weighing down the citizens. They were in debt, in distress, and discontented (1 Sam. 22:2). With the appointment of Saul, the people expected a positive change, but Saul's pride drove him to make decisions that eventually led to his demise (1 Sam. 15:17–24). Even the Almighty warned Israel that if they selected a king, their new leader would raise their taxes and take one-tenth of their food for his own servants (1 Sam. 8:15).

In Saul's day, the Israeli army was in a war with the Philistines. The battle was stuck and going nowhere, with both sides claiming opposite mountains. A giant Philistine named Goliath stood in the valley between the two camps, taunting Saul and his army. Saul had no heart to fight, and he did not actually respond to the continual verbal harassment from his enemy. His idea appeared to be not to create any more conflict than necessary—sort of, "If we treat them nice, maybe they'll treat us nice." Can you hear Saul saying this? "Fellows, I know the Philistines are terrorists, and historically they have raided our farms, killed our people, and harassed us for many generations. However, this is a new day, and we need a new policy toward our enemies. In fact, let's see if we can sit down at a table and make a peace treaty..."

History has repeated itself. Even the *Washington Post* announced in January 2009 that the war on terror was over with the "stroke of a pen," speaking about the executive order to close down Gitmo prison, which houses numerous dangerous terrorists.[4] Leaders in our generation believe that instead of defeating or destroying those who make threats to annihilate the Jews and use their own nuclear weapons to destroy the West, we should sit down with some good coffee and have a meet-and-greet session. Saul was so concerned about being popular that he was unwilling to create a controversy with his enemies. Does this sound familiar?

3. The Belshazzar syndrome

There was a party going on in the palace! King Belshazzar filled the banquet ballroom of Babylon with the finest wine and foods for the leaders of his administration. In fact, it could be a picture twenty-six hundred years later of the party spirits in America in the roaring twenties prior to the Great Depression.

Jazz musicians sang as the flappers and bootleggers danced the night away in dance halls and honky-tonks from coast to coast. The *hot* stocks were radio and automobile. It was declared that the war on poverty was over, and things would be up from here. Then on October 29, 1929, the stock market experienced "Black Tuesday," often associated with stories of investors and traders jumping out of windows after losing everything. It was a day when stocks fell, followed by a run on banks that eventually led to one-quarter of the American workforce—fifteen million Americans—out of work.[5]

The drunken party life of the roaring twenties came to a sudden halt—just as it did in ancient Babylon. On the night of Belshazzar's party, the hand of

God wrote a final warning on the plaster behind the candelabra, revealing that on that night the kingdom had been weighed and was found wanting, and it would be divided—that very night!

Just like in America, the leaders hoisted their wine goblets and drank themselves into a numb stupor while the enemy was outside the gates, digging under the foundations of the city. America continues to ignore the signs of a crumbling foundation as the party goes on. It was recently reported:

> Since the presidency changed hands less than six weeks ago, a burst of entertaining has taken hold of the iconic, white-columned home of America's head of state. Much of it comes on Wednesdays.
>
> The stately East Room, where portraits of George and Martha Washington adorn the walls, was transformed into a concert hall as President Barack Obama presented Stevie Wonder with the nation's highest award for pop music on Wednesday.
>
> A week before that, the foot-stomping sounds of Sweet Honey in the Rock, a female a cappella group, filled the East Room for a Black History Month program first lady Michelle Obama held for nearly 200 sixth- and seventh-graders from around the city.
>
> Cocktails were sipped during at least three such receptions to date, all held on Wednesdays.
>
> Bookending the midweek activity were a Super Bowl party for select Democratic and Republican lawmakers and a dinner for governors, the new administration's first black-tie affair. It was capped with a performance by the 1970s pop group Earth, Wind and Fire. And a conga line.
>
> The flurry of entertaining is in keeping with the Obamas' promise to make the White House a more open place for everyone.[6]

The Scriptures ask, "If the foundations are destroyed, what can the righteous do?" (Ps. 11:3). In the Old Testament there are seven Hebrew words for foundations. The word used in Psalm 11:3 is *shathah,* meaning "a basis or purpose." It is used figuratively of "political and moral support." The verse is saying, "If the political and moral support is destroyed, what can the righteous do?" The word *destroyed* means to "beat something down." The Hebrew word is *harac,* which sounds similar to our English word *harass!* The foundations are being beaten away by the harassment of liberal leaders, liberal organizations, Marxist-minded professors, and limp-hearted ministers.

Warning: A House Divided

But Jesus knew their thoughts, and said to them: "Every kingdom divided against itself is brought to desolation, and every city or house divided against itself will not stand."

—Matthew 12:25

In Washington, the president lives at the White House. Within the confines of the Capitol are the chambers of the Senate and the House of Representatives. During the time of the Civil War, the Union became divided between the Union and Confederate armies as fathers turned against sons and neighbors against neighbors. Today, the division is a social-moral-political divide that has already divided the House. A recent article in the *National Journal* stated: "Politics has gotten so bad, bipartisanship is now a partisan issue."[7]

Four Reasons America Has Been Blessed

From a strictly biblical perspective, there are four reasons we can trace that have helped America to be a blessed nation.

1. Giving to the poor and needy

Americans are generous people toward the poor and needy. When a natural disaster occurs anywhere in the world, America is always at the forefront in preparing cargos of food, water, clothes, and medical assistance. One of the sins of ancient Sodom was not caring for the poor.

2. Supporting widows and orphans

The Christian community in the United States has for many years been actively involved in assisting widows and orphans. Our concern for the fatherless reaches beyond the homeland, as thousands of Americans spend millions of dollars in adopting children from foreign nations. Missionary organizations have set up orphanages throughout the world that are financed by the compassionate generosity of the public, including the offerings of churches.

3. Supporting the gospel

The believers in the United States have given significant support to the spread of the gospel to the nations of the world.

4. Supporting Israel

A Gallup Poll released in March 2006 stated: "American support for Israel [is] at near-record levels. When asked for their views on the Middle East, 59 percent of Americans say they sympathize with the Israelis, while just 15 percent favor the Palestinians."[8] American churches have raised millions of dollars to send to Israel for the support of many Christian and secular aid programs.

The new administration that took power in 2009 began immediately by saying it would not raise taxes on the majority of Americans. However, the plan was to limit the amount of money a person could give to a charity and deduct from their taxes. This would limit the giving for the gospel, for orphans, for widows, and for feeding and clothing as the people would need their income for the numerous new taxes being demanded by a tax-and-spend leadership.

The Practical Application

Every major transition creates major changes and shifting. What can concerned Americans do from a practical and spiritual level to prepare for the times that may be ahead? "A prudent person foresees danger and takes precautions. The simpleton goes blindly on and suffers the consequences" (Prov. 22:3, NLT).

First and foremost, an individual must have a personal relationship with the Lord and understand the many covenant promises and provisions made available in the written Scriptures. We are promised that God can and will supply our needs (Phil. 4:19).

Then there are some additional precautions that we should be taking:

1. The ability to be independent

The manner in which the economic system is changing in America causes a person to become more dependent upon the government to provide the goods and services needed for personal survival, including health care, Medicare, Social Security, and so forth. The fact is that the more independent a person becomes, the better that person can survive any disruptions originating from the government. Being independent means having your own economic sources set aside through wise investment, limited cash, and even precious metals set in a portfolio.

2. The ability to be self-sufficient

Storms can disrupt power, water, electricity, and the basic necessities we are accustomed to. Often, people are unprepared for natural weather phenomena and end up suffering during long ice storms, floods, or wind destruction. Having additional food storages, water (even a well), and a generator can be a wise investment.

3. The ability to provide your own food and water

This may seem strange in a nation that has convenience and food stores on every city and community corner, but many people are now purchasing parcels of land for the purpose of enjoying planting their own gardens of food, just as their parents and grandparents did in the past.

4. The ability of being debt free

To some extent we will always have some form of debt. It may be the water and electric bills, the cost of food each month, occasional medical expenses, house repairs, and so forth. However, being debt free brings a special inner freedom to a person. In our ministry, our two facilities (70,000 square feet, the digital television equipment, and all contents) are debt free. In our personal life, we owe a mortgage on our home and do not make purchases unless we set aside the money and can pay without creating a debt.

Anyone who travels will need a credit card, since rental car companies, hotels, and airlines prefer credit cards (car rental companies will not accept cash). Thus, a bank card is needed in many instances. When we use a card, we pay the bill on time to avoid the high interest charged. Our nation is in deep trouble due to interest charges on cars, homes, education loans, and other interest-related loans that people cannot repay. A person should seek to reduce debt in every area to bring relief.

••• Conclusion •••

WHAT CAN THE AVERAGE AMERICAN DO?

MAJOR EMPIRES ONLY continue until they become overstretched with their military, overspent in their governmental obligations, overindulgent in their lifestyle, and overconfident that their moral decline will have no repercussions on society. Since the days of the Egyptian pharaohs, all empires either abruptly end when invading armies march on the capital, or they slowly decline and are replaced by a rising nation or ethnic group with stronger armies, better economic advantage, or a personality that is received as a messiahlike figure who can gather the masses under his magnetic charm.

Since 1607 and our first colony, America has continued for more than four hundred years, and the infant of freedom has grown to the giant of democracy—the voice speaking out for oppressed people. The giant has fallen asleep, unaware and unconcerned about men and women in the legislative branch of government who have forgotten the covenant of our ancestors (Lev. 26:45).

When I was a child of five, I had a terrible nightmare of being kidnapped by a stranger. I began crying and screaming as my mother ran into my room and consoled me that it was "just a bad dream." The only way of escaping a nightmare is to wake up!

It is unclear, too early in the game plan, to determine if America and our present leadership will carry us into a Socialist state, limit personal freedoms, and eventually take away freedom of speech and our firearms. It is unclear if our forty-fourth president is a forerunner or a king on the chessboard in these prophetic times. Things can suddenly change and overturn the decisions and plans of a man. However, the time is not too late to stand up, speak up, and pray up!

I suggest the following things for believers to do.

1. Let your prayers be heard.

Pharaoh was a pagan king who rose and "knew not Joseph" (Exod. 1:8, KJV). He initiated a law to abort the sons of the Hebrews immediately after their birth (v. 16). He appointed taskmasters (or tax collectors) to collect the money (v. 11).

The Hebrews spent their time in building the treasure cities, which were the banks of their day (v. 11). Does this sound familiar? We have leaders who have little or no biblical knowledge of the covenant of our ancestors. America has government-sponsored and -funded abortion, is raising taxes, and our money is used to bail out the banks—the treasure cities of our empire.

Eventually the burden became so heavy that the people "cried out unto the Lord," and He heard their cries (Exod. 2:23). Eventually, God Himself initiated a change and a major transition in Egypt as a result of the united prayers of His own people.

Your prayers must be heard for the Almighty to raise up proper leadership, men and women who honor the legacies of the past, including the covenant of our ancestors.

2. Let your vote be heard.

If you refuse or if you avoid voting during an election cycle, your voice becomes a mere echo. You have no justifiable "right" to complain about what you did not make an attempt to change. Voting is one of our basic and most protected privileges in this nation.

3. Let your voice be heard.

I personally know men who have served in the United States Congress. I have asked them, "When a person writes a letter, makes a call, or sends an e-mail to a senator or congressman, does it really matter?" The answer is yes. Each letter sent can actually represent one thousand others who feel the same way but do not take the time to write. When a law has been up for debate, time and again, the protest of the American people placed pressure on the legislator not to pass the law. As a result, the decisions were altered.

We can assume that whatever will be will be and that we have no personal control over events, or we can let our voices be heard through phone calls, letters, and other forms of communication.

4. Let our history be heard.

It has been said that if we do not learn from history, we will repeat it. We must remind the future generations of the high price paid for our freedoms— not just with the Pilgrims, the Founding Fathers, and the major documents that forge the foundation of our house, but also with the wars our soldiers have fought to maintain freedom to peace-loving nations.

We must also teach the younger generation the amazing religious history of our nation. Children attending private Christian schools are taught the wonderful spiritual history of the nation. However, this subject is taboo in public schools, and history has been omitted and revised in modern textbooks. Our children should know America was founded by freedom-loving men and women who came for the purpose of religious freedom and a release from the oppressive government powers of England. If we as Christian parents fail to emphasize our Christian heritage, the next generation will enter historical darkness, and religious freedom will be obsolete.

America is on a collision course with the spirit of ancient empires. The burden of keeping America in God's favor is upon His own covenant people.

> If my people, which are called by my name, shall humble themselves, and pray, and seek my face, and turn from their wicked ways; then will I hear from heaven, and will forgive their sin, and will heal their land.
> —2 CHRONICLES 7:14, KJV

May we wake up, sit up, stand up, speak up, and live up to the dreams of our Founding Fathers and the spiritual covenant of our ancestors. There is still time to stop the nightmare.

••• Notes •••

Introduction: America's Main Street

1. Associated Press, "Russian Scholar Says U.S. Will Collapse Next Year," FOXNews.com, March 4, 2009, http://www.foxnews.com/story/0,2933,504384,00 .html (accessed April 28, 2009).

2. Jon Meacham and Evan Thomas, "We Are All Socialists Now," *Newsweek*, February 7, 2009, http://www.newsweek.com/id/183663 (accessed April 28, 2009).

3. Karl Marx and Frederick Engels, *Manifesto of the Communist Party*, 1848, http://www.anu.edu.au/polsci/marx/classics/manifesto.html (accessed April 28, 2009).

4. As quoted in "Henry George, Sound Economics and the 'New Deal,'" a speech delivered by Charles R. Eckhert before the U.S. House of Representatives, Tuesday, July 2, 1935, http://www.cooperativeindividualism.org/eckert-charles_ henry-george-and-new-deal.html (accessed June 4, 2009).

5. David Goodman Croly, *Glimpses of the Future*, cited in Wing Anderson, *Prophetic Years 1947–1953* (Whitefish, MT: Kessinger Publishing, 2006), 3–4.

6. Ibid., 4.

7. This quiz was created by the author from information gathered from numerous historical references.

8. FOXNews.com, "White House: Obama Opposes 'Fairness Doctrine' Revival," February 18, 2009, http://www.foxnews.com/politics/first100days/2009/02/18/ white-house-opposes-fairness-doctrine/ (accessed April 28, 2009).

9. FOXNews.com, "Dems Downplay Obama's Plan to Oversee 2010 Census," February 11, 2009, http://www.foxnews.com/politics/first100days/2009/02/11/ dems-downplay-obamas-plan-oversee-census/ (accessed April 28, 2009).

10. FOXNews.com, "Washington, Wall Street Buzzing About Prospect of Bank Nationalization," February 21, 2009, http://www.foxnews.com/politics/first100days/ 2009/02/21/talks-nationalizing-banks-spark-debate/ (accessed April 28, 2009).

11. Larry Marsh, "Employee Free Choice Act Drops Secret Ballot in Union Certification," KansasCity.com, March 17, 2009, http://voices.kansascity.com/ node/4031 (accessed April 28, 2009).

12. Pete Williams, "First 100 Days: Assault Weapons Ban," *MSNBC*, April 24, 2009, http://www.msnbc.msn.com/id/30389664/ (accessed April 28, 2009).

13. Charles Hurt, "Obama Fires a 'Robin Hood' Warning Shot," *New York Post*, October 16, 2008, http://www.nypost.com/seven/10152008/news/politics/obama_ fires_a_robin_hood_warning_shot_133685.htm (accessed April 28, 2009).

14. Liz Sidoti, "Overhauling Health Care," TimesLeader.com, March 6, 2009, http://www.timesleader.com/news/hottopics/president/Overhauling_health_care_ 03-05-2009.html (accessed April 28, 2009).

15. Margaret Talev, "Obama's First 100 Days in Office Haven't Been Quiet," McClatchy Newspapers, April 26, 2009, http://news.yahoo.com/s/mcclatchy/ 20090426/pl_mcclatchy/3217776 (accessed June 4, 2009).

16. Associated Press, "Obama Reaches Out to Iran, Looks for Encouragement," FOXNews.com, March 19, 2009, http://www.foxnews.com/politics/first100days/2009/03/19/obama-reaches-iran-looks-engagement/ (accessed April 28, 2009).

17. Dr. Laurie Roth, "Internationalism/Globalism/Obama vs. Sovereignty, the United States and Achievement," CanadaFreePress.com, April 23, 2009, http://www.canadafreepress.com/index.php/article/10497 (accessed April 28, 2009).

Chapter 1: The American President

1. "Washington's Farewell Address, 1796," The Avalon Project of Yale Law School, http://avalon.law.yale.edu/18th_century/washing.asp (accessed April 28, 2009).

2. Bob Slosser, *Reagan Inside Out* (Nashville, TN: W Publishing Group, 1984), quoted in Bob Slosser, "The Prophecy," CBN.com, http://www.cbn.com/spirituallife/BibleStudyAndTheology/discipleship/Slosser_ReaganProphecy.aspx (accessed June 4, 2009).

3. George W. Bush, *A Charge to Keep* (New York: Perennial, 2001), 9.

4. Tony Carnes, "A Presidential Hopeful's Progress," *Christianity Today*, October 2, 2000.

5. Thomas Freidman, "Mideast Accord: U.S. Policy; Clinton Seeks to Buoy Israelis, Saying U.S. Backing Is Firm," *New York Times*, September 12, 1993, http://www.nytimes.com/1993/09/12/world/mideast-accord-us-policy-clinton-seeks-buoy-israelis-saying-us-backing-firm.html?pagewanted=all (accessed April 28, 2009).

6. Asgard14, "Barack Obama's Radical Marxist and Black Liberation Theology Church," Romanian National Vanguard News Agency, February 27, 2008, http://news.ronatvan.com/2008/02/27/barack-obama%E2%80%99s-radical-marxist-and-black-liberation-theology-church/ (accessed April 28, 2009).

7. Barack Obama, *The Audacity of Hope* (New York: Random House, 2008).

8. *New York Magazine*, "Worst Enemy," January 11, 2008, http://nymag.com/news/politics/encyclopedia/worstenemy/ (accessed April 28, 2009).

9. From *The Mike Gallagher Show*, June 5, 2008, transcript viewed at http://thinkprogress.org/2008/06/05/delay-obama-marxist/ (accessed April 28, 2009).

10. From the *Brian and the Judge* radio show, April 14, 2008, transcript viewed at http://thinkprogress.org/2008/04/14/lieberman-its-a-good-question-to-ask-if-obama-is-a-marxist/ (accessed April 28, 2009).

11. Cliff Kincaid, "Obama's Communist Mentor," Accuracy in Media, February 18, 2008, http://www.aim.org/aim-column/obamas-communist-mentor/ (accessed April 29, 2009).

12. Gerald Horne, "Rethinking the History and Future of the Communist Party," PoliticalAffairs.net, March 28, 2007, http://www.politicalaffairs.net/article/articleview/5047/1/32/ (accessed April 29, 2009).

13. Saul Alinsky, *Rules for Radicals* (New York: Vintage Books, 1971, 1989).

14. Ibid., xix–xx.

15. Peter Sleven, "For Clinton and Obama, a Common Ideological Touchstone," *The Washington Post*, March 25, 2007, http://www.washingtonpost.com/wp-dyn/content/article/2007/03/24/AR2007032401152.html (accessed April 29, 2009).

16. *The Socialist Viewpoint*, "Who We Are," SocialistViewpoint.org, September

2001, http://www.socialistviewpoint.org/sept_01/sept_01_20.html (accessed June 4, 2009).

17. SocialistViewpoint.org, "Who We Are," home page, http://www .socialistviewpoint.org/who_we_are.html (accessed June 4, 2009).

18. Michael Dobbs, "Obama's 'Weatherman' Connection," The Fact Checker, *The Washington Post*, February 19, 2008, http://blog.washingtonpost.com/fact -checker/2008/02/obamas_weatherman_connection.html (accessed April 29, 2009).

19. DiscovertheNetworks.org, "Carl Davidson," http://www.discoverthenetworks .org/individualProfile.asp?indid=2322 (accessed April 29, 2009).

20. Karl Marx, "Critique of the Gotha Programme," http://www.marxists.org/ archive/marx/works/1875/gotha/ch01.htm (accessed April 29, 2009).

21. Henry Kissinger, "An End of Hubris," November 19, 2008, Economist.com, http://www.economist.com/displaystory.cfm?story_id=12574180 (accessed May 28, 2009).

22. National Park Service, "Lincoln Home: The Rally," http://www.nps.gov/liho/ planyourvisit/upload/Rally%20Site%20Bulletin%20-%20MHK%20edit%20TT.pdf (accessed June 11, 2009).

23. Daily Herald Staff Report, "How Are Lincoln, Obama Similar?" *Daily Herald*, January 20, 2009, http://www.dailyherald.com/story/print/?id=264901 (accessed June 4, 2009).

24. *Sahih Bukhari*, vol. 9, bk. 88, no. 237, narrated Abu Huraira, http://www .usc.edu/schools/college/crcc/engagement/resources/texts/muslim/hadith/bukhari/088 .sbt.html (accessed June 4, 2009).

25. Information the author heard during a televised speech by Louis Farrakhan in 2001.

26. Bud Simmons, "A New Seal Debuted on Obama's Podium Friday, Sporting Iconography Used in the U.S. Presidential Seal," Associated Press, June 20, 2008, http://bsimmons.wordpress.com/2008/06/20/a-new-seal-debuted-on-obamas-podium -friday-sporting-iconography-used-in-the-us-presidential-seal/ (accessed June 4, 2009).

27. Louis Farrakhan, addressing a large crowd behind a podium Feb. 24, 2008, with a Nation of Islam Saviour's Day 2008 sign, cited in WorldNetDaily.com, "Farrakhan on Obama: 'The Messiah Is Absolutely Speaking,'" October 9, 2008, http://www.worldnetdaily.com/?pageId=77539 (accessed May 28, 2009.

28. *Sahih Bukhari*, vol. 4, bk. 54, no. 429, narrated Malik bin Sassa, http:// www.usc.edu/schools/college/crcc/engagement/resources/texts/muslim/hadith/ bukhari/054.sbt.html (accessed June 5, 2009).

29. Lambert Dolphin, "Allah and the Temple Mount," TempleMount.org, http:// www.templemount.org/allah.html (accessed June 5, 2009).

30. Daniel Pipes, "The Muslim Claim to Jerusalem," *Middle East Quarterly*, Fall 2001, http://www.meforum.org/490/the-muslim-claim-to-jerusalem (accessed June 5, 2009).

31. *Sahih Bukhari*, vol. 4, bk. 54, no. 429.

32. Combating Terrorism Center at West Point, "The Islamic Imagery Project: White Horse," http://ctc.usma.edu/imagery/imagery_nature.asp#whitehorse (accessed May 28, 2009).

33. Muhammad Ibn 'Izzat and Muhammad 'Arif, *Al Mahdi and the End of Time* (London: Dar Al-Taqwa, 1997), 15, quoted in Joel Richardson, *Antichrist: Islam's Awaited Messiah* (Enumclaw, WA: Pleasant Word, 2006), 49.

34. BarackObama.org, "Obama Has Never Been a Muslim, and Is a Committed Christian," November 12, 2007, Organizing for America, http://www.barackobama.com/factcheck/2007/11/12/obama_has_never_been_a_muslim_1.php (accessed June 5, 2009).

35. The information in this section is adapted from an *Israel Insider* staff report titled, "Is Barack Obama a Muslim Wolf in Christian Wool?" posted March 27, 2008, IsraelInsider.com, http://web.israelinsider.com/Articles/Politics/12745.htm (accessed June 5, 2009).

36. Ibid.

37. WhiteHouse.gov, "Interview of the President by Laura Haim, Canal Plus, June 1, 2009, http://www.whitehouse.gov/the_press_office/Transcript-of-the-Interview-of-the-President-by-Laura-Haim-Canal-Plus-6-1-09/ (accessed June 5, 2009).

38. ReligionFacts.com, "Top 50 Muslim Countries," http://www.religionfacts.com/islam/places/top_50.htm (accessed June 5, 2009).

39. Aluf Benn, "Netanyahu Failed to Build Bond of Trust With Obama," *Haaretz*, June 10, 2009, http://www.haaretz.com/hasen/spages/1091720.html (acessed July 29, 2009).

40. *Jewish Tribune* staff, "Obama's Chutzpah: Dictating to Bibi and the Jewish State," *Jewish Tribune*, June 16, 2009, http://www.jewishtribune.ca/TribuneV2/index.php/200906161768/Obama-s-chutzpah-Dictating-to-bibi-and-the-Jewish-state.html (accessed July 29, 2009).

41. David Gardner, "Obama in a Turban: Barack Accuses Hillary of Smear Campaign After Circulating Photos of Him Dressed as 'a Muslim,'" February 26, 2008, *Mail Online*, http://www.dailymail.co.uk/news/article-518585/Obama-turban-Barack-accuses-Hillary-smear-campaign-circulating-photos-dressed-Muslim.html (accessed May 28, 2009).

42. Transcript of Barack Obama interview with Hisham Melhem on Al Arabiya TV, January 27, 2009, accessed at http://www.alarabiya.net/articles/2009/01/27/65087.html#004, on May 29, 2009.

43. Asit Srivastava, "Bowing Before Elders Un-Islamic, Says Deoband Edict," December 17, 2008, TwoCircles.net, http://www.twocircles.net/2008dec16/bowing_elders_un_islamic_says_deoband_edict.html (accessed May 29, 2009).

44. Jim Iovino, "Jesus Missing From Obama's Georgetown Speech," April 17, 2009, NBC Washington News, http://www.nbcwashington.com/news/local/Jesus-Missing-From-Obamas-Georgetown-Speech.html (accessed May 29, 2009).

45. As quoted in Maulana A. U. Kaleem, "The Advent of the Messiah and Mahdi," AlIslam.org, http://www.alislam.org/library/links/00000106.html (accessed May 29, 2009).

46. Ronald Reagan, "Proclamation 5767—National Day of Prayer, 1988," February 3, 1988, http://www.reagan.utexas.edu/archives/speeches/1988/020388d.htm (accessed May 29, 2009).

47. Ronald Reagan, "Proclamation 5018—Year of the Bible, 1983," February 3, 1983, http://www.presidency.ucsb.edu/ws/?pid=40728 (accessed May 29, 2009).

48. Kristi Keck, "Obama Tones Down National Day of Prayer Observance," May 6, 2009, CNN.com, http://www.cnn.com/2009/POLITICS/05/06/obama.prayer/ (accessed May 29, 2009).

49. Hyscience.com, "D.C. Imam Declares Plan For 'Islamic State of North America,'" November 10, 2007, http://www.hyscience.com/archives/2007/11/dc_imam_declare.php (accessed May 29, 2009).

50. Robert Spencer, "CAIR's Congress," FrontPageMag.com, http://frontpagemagazine.com/readArticle.aspx?ARTID=1578 (accessed May 29, 2009).

51. The 30-Days Prayer Network, "Statistics on Muslims in the United States of America (USA)," http://www.30-days.net/muslims/muslims-in/america-north/usa-muslims/ (accessed May 29, 2009).

Chapter 2: The Thunder Over America

1. Robert S. Mueller, "From 9/11 to 7/7: Global Terrorism Today and the Challenges of Tomorrow," speech delivered at Chatham House, London, on April 7, 2008, http://www.chathamhouse.org.uk/files/11301_070408mueller.pdf (accessed April 30, 2009).

2. Associated Press, "Manager: Men Spewed Anti-American Sentiments," *USA Today*, September 14, 2001, http://www.usatoday.com/news/nation/2001/09/14/miami-club.htm (accessed June 10, 2009).

3. HistoryCommons.org, "An Assassination Attempt?" http://www.historycommons.org/essay.jsp?article=essayaninterestingday (accessed April 29, 2009).

4. Ibid.

5. Sebastian Junger, "Sebastian Junger on Afghanistan's Slain Rebel Leader," NationalGeographic.com, http://www.nationalgeographic.com/adventure/0110/junger.html (accessed June 8, 2009).

6. A personal friend of the author made the phone call alerting him to the Web site giving the information about a planned attack on America on July 4. The Web site has since been removed, and this information cannot be verified at this point.

7. WorldNetDaily.com, "Saddam General: WMDs in Syria," Februrary 15. 2006, http://www.worldnetdaily.com/news/article.asp?ARTICLE_ID=48827 (accessed April 29, 2009).

8. Georges Sada, *Saddam's Secrets* (Nashville, TN: Integrity Publishing, 2006). Also available in transcript form at FOXNews.com, "Exclusive! Former Top Military Aide to Saddam Reveals Dictator's Secret Plans," *Hannity & Colmes*, January 25, 2006, http://www.foxnews.com/story/0,2933,182932,00.html (accessed April 29, 2009).

9. "Iraq's Weapons in Syria: Senior Syrian Journalist," January 6, 2004, posted on FreeRepublic.com by RaceBannon on *Free Republic*, October 28, 2004, http://www.freerepublic.com/focus/f-news/1259806/posts (accessed April 29, 2009). See also Mike Evans, "Saddam's WMDs Are in Syria," WorldNetDaily.com, June 29, 2004, http://www.worldnetdaily.com/news/article.asp?ARTICLE_ID=39182 (accessed June 9, 2009).

10. FreeRepublic.org, "Saddam WMD: Findings and Analysis Based on Captured Iraqi Documents (Part 1)," posted by Jveritas on April 23, 2007, http://www.freerepublic.com/focus/f-news/1822157/posts (accessed June 10, 2009).

11. Stephen F. Hayes, "Where Are the Pentagon Papers?" *The Weekly Standard*, November 21, 2005, 2, http://www.weeklystandard.com/Content/Public/Articles/000/000/006/345qrbbj.asp?pg=2 (accessed June 9, 2009).

12. Steve Turnham, "Bill Clinton on Bush Uranium Line: 'Everybody Makes Mistakes,'" CNN.com/Inside Politics, July 23, 2003, http://www.cnn.com/2003/ALLPOLITICS/07/23/clinton.iraq.sotu/ (accessed April 29, 2009).

13. Nancy Pelosi, "Statement of U.S. Led Military Strike Against Iraq," December 16, 1998, http://www.house.gov/pelosi/priraq1.htm (accessed June 9, 2009).

14. USAToday.com, "Clinton Team Jeered During Town Hall," http://www.usatoday.com/news/index/iraq/iraq172.htm (accessed June 9, 2009). Also, quoted in Kathleen Kenna, "Anti-Iraq Show Goes on the Road in America," *The Toronto Star*, February 19, 1998, A16.

15. Hayes, "Where Are the Pentagon Papers?"

16. Jamal Halaby, "Chemical Expert Testifies in Jordan Trial, " June 30, 2005, posted on FreeRepublic.com by WmShirerAdmirer, www.freerepublic.com/focus/f-news/1434136/posts?page=3 (accessed April 29, 2009).

17. Christopher S. Carson, "Saddam, the ATM of Al Qaeda," FrontPageMag.com, May 15, 2004, http://www.frontpagemag.com/readArticle.aspx?ARTID=10600 (accessed June 9, 2009).

18. Associated Press, "Secret U.S. Mission Hauls Uranium From Iraq," July 5, 2008, MSNBC.com, http://www.msnbc.msn.com/id/25546334/ (accessed April 30, 2009).

19. Major General Jerry Curry, "500 Tons of Uranium Yellowcake Moved From at http://209.157.64.200/focus/f-news/2117840/posts (accessed April 30, 2009).

20. Ibid.

21. Story told to me in a personal conversation.

22. Story told to me in a personal conversation.

23. Mark Potter and Rich Phillips, "Six Months After September 11, Hijackers' Visa Approval Letters Received," CNN.com, March 13, 2002, http://archives.cnn.com/2002/US/03/12/inv.flight.school.visas/ (accessed April 30, 2009).

24. Dr. Tatyana Koryagiva, "Will the Dollar and America Fall Down on August 19?" *Pravda*, July 12, 2001, quoted in Dr. Alexandr Nemets, "Expert: Russia Knew in Advance, Encouraged Citizens to Cash Out Dollars," September 17, 2001, http://www.bibliotecapleyades.net/sociopolitica/sociopol_globalbanking09.htm (accessed June 23, 2009).

25. Dr. Tatyana Koryagiva, "Who Will Strike America in Its Back?" *Pravda*, September 2001, quoted in "Russian Economist Predicted Strikes on America," American Patriot Friends Network, November 1, 2001, http://www.apfn.org/THEWINDS/2001/11/prediction.html (accessed June 23, 2009).

26. Tom Z. Collina and Jon B. Wolfsthal, "Nuclear Terrorism and Warhead Control in Russia. (Fear of Theft of Nuclear Weapons by Terrorist)," *Arms Control Today*, AccessMyLibrary.com, April 1, 2002, http://www.accessmylibrary.com/

coms2/summary_0286-67632_ITM (accessed April 30, 2009).

27. Mike Evans, "An Exclusive Interview on Iran With Prime Minister Benjamin Netanyahu," Jerusalem World News, http://myjwn.com/jwn-exclusives/an-exclusive-interview-on-iran-with-prime-minister-benjamin-netanyahu (accessed June 11, 2009).

28. CNN.com, "9/11 Panel: Al Qaeda Planned to Hijack 10 Planes," June 17, 2004, http://edition.cnn.com/2004/ALLPOLITICS/06/16/911.commission/index .html (accessed April 30, 2009).

29. Barna Group, "How America's Faith Has Changed Since 9-11," November 26, 2001, http://www.barna.org/barna-update/article/5-barna-update/63-how -americas-faith-has-changed-since-9-11 (accessed April 30, 2009).

30. Rebecca Barnes, "Latest Barna Research Reveals Increase in Church Attendance—Maybe," April 3, 2006, http://rebeccabarnes1.blogspot.com/2006/04/ latest-barna-research-reveals-increase.html (accessed April 30, 2009).

31. Bassem Mroue, "Hezbollah Rebuilds South Beirut," Associated Press, November 18, 2007, http://www.normanfinkelstein.com/while-the-light-unto-the -nations-destroys-homes-the-axis-of-terror-rebuilds-them/ (accessed June 23, 2009).

32. Edward Gibbon, *History of the Decline and Fall of the Roman Empire*, six volumes published 1776–1788.

33. These cycles have been alleged to have come from Lord Woodhouslee, Alexander Fraser Tytler, a Scottish historian, professor, and author of several books.

Chapter 3: Columbus and His Hebrew Connection

1. Christopher Columbus, *Book of Prophecies*, trans. August J. Kling, who quoted these excerpts in an article in *The Presbyterian Layman,* October 1971, referenced in Restoring Our Heritage, http://www.restoringourheritage.com/ourbeliefs .htm (accessed May 1, 2009).

2. MSN Encarta, "Christopher Columbus," http://encarta.msn.com/ encyclopedia_761568472/christopher_columbus.html, (accessed May 1, 2009).

3. Peter Marshall and David Manuel, *The Light and Glory* (Grand Rapids, MI: Fleming H. Revell, 1977).

4. Samuel Eliot Morison, *Christopher Columbus, Admiral of the Ocean Sea* (London: Oxford University Press, 1939), 356–357.

5. Dr. R. A. Clarke, "Columbus; His Mission and Character," a paper included in *The World's Columbian Catholic Congresses of 1893* (Read Books Online Library, 2007), 26, http://books.google.com/books?id=uA6QXP3aEccC&pg=PA 26&lpg=PA26&dq=columbus+likened+himself+to+moses&source=bl&ots=kqS0h -G7uk&sig=-mjRjrN9uR6DVUlRHWcOco6EyfY&hl=en&ei=xfX6SfzxGsmEtweP 9v27BA&sa=X&oi=book_result&ct=result&resnum=5 (accessed May 1, 2009).

6. Kay Brigham, *Christopher Columbus: His Life and Discovery in the Light of His Prophecies* (Spain: Editorial Clie, 1990), 122.

7. Klaus Brinkbäumer, Clemens Höges, and Annette Streck, *The Voyage of the Vizcaína*, trans. Annette Streck (New York: Houghton Mifflin Harcourt, 2006), 102.

8. Howard M. Sachar, "Destination: The New World," *The Jerusalem Connection*, September–October 2006, 8, http://tjci.org/articles/2006-0910.pdf (accessed June 23, 2009).

9. Robert Chazan, *Church, State, and Jew in the Middle Ages* (Springfield, NJ: Behrman House, Inc., 1979), 319–320.

10. "America's Hebraic Heritage And Roots," http://www.threemacs.org/docs/Americas%20Hebraic%20Roots%20-%20Columbus%20and%20the%20Discovery.pdf (accessed June 24, 2009).

11. Chazan, *Church, State, and Jew in the Middle Ages*.

12. Simon Wiesenthal, *Sails of Hope*, translated by Richard and Clara Winston (New York: MacMillan, 1973), 61.

13. William John Bennett, *America: From the Age of Discovery to a World at War, 1492–1914* (Nashville, TN: Thomas Nelson, 2006), 4.

14. Jane Francis Amler, *Christopher Columbus' Jewish Roots* (Lanham, MD: Jason Aronson, 1993).

15. William J. Federer, *America's God and Country* (St. Louis, MO: Amerisearch, Inc., 1994), 119.

16. Ibid.

Chapter 4: Biblical Parallels in Early American History

1. John Adams and Charles Francis Adams, *The Works of John Adams, Second President of the United States*, vol. 10, "To the Officers of the First Brigade of the Third Division of the Militia of Massachusetts, 11 October 1798," (Boston: Little Brown and Company, 1854), 229, http://books.google.com/books?id=kI08AAAAIAAJ&pg=RA1-PR5&lpg=RA1-PR5&dq=the+works+of+john+adams+volume+ix&source=web&ots=jXBhM_rlRJ&sig=W4STC5KYvU90yQM_o34GzelsnTM#PRA1-PA229,M1 (accessed June 24, 2009).

2. John Parsons, "Bjarni Herjolfsson," *The Canadian Encyclopedia*, http://www.thecanadianencyclopedia.com/index.cfm?PgNm=TCE&Params=A1ARTA0000790 (accessed May 15, 2009).

3. Linn Ryne, "Leif Ericson," MNC.net, http://www.mnc.net/norway/ericson.htm (accessed May 15, 2009).

4. History.com, "Thorfinn Karlsefni," http://www.history.com/encyclopedia.do?articleId=224070 (accessed May 15, 2009).

5. Ronald S. Love, *Maritime Exploration in the Age of Discovery, 1415–1800* (Santa Barbara, CA: Greenwood Publishing Group, 2006), 153.

6. Frederick A. Ober, *Amerigo Vespucci*, "How America Was Named," The Baldwin Project, http://www.mainlesson.com/display.php?author=ober&book=vespucci&story=named (accessed May 1, 2009).

7. Ariel Segal, "The Ten Lost Tribes of Israel: Looking for the Remnants," World Zionist Organization: Hagshama Department, http://www.hagshama.org.il/en/resources/view.asp?id=174 (accessed May 1, 2009).

8. "America's Hebraic Heritage and Roots."

9. Ibid.

10. Norton Anthology of English Literature: Norton Topics Online, "Menasseh ben Israel, *from* To His Highnesse the Lord Protector of the Commonwealth of England, Scotland, and Ireland (1655)," http://www.wwnorton.com/college/english/nael/17century/topic_4/debate.htm (accessed June 24, 2009).

11. Watertown Public Schools, "Encounters in the Americas: The Mystery of Roanoke," Early American History, http://www.watertown.k12.ma.us/cunniff/americanhistorycentral/04encountersintheamericas/The_Mystery_of.html (accessed May 1, 2009).

12. The Avalon Project, "The First Charter of Virginia, April 10, 1606," Yale Law School, http://avalon.law.yale.edu/17th_century/va01.asp (accessed May 1, 2009).

13. Ibid.

14. There are several excellent books on American history. One that I would recommend is *Teaching and Learning America's Christian History*, published by The Foundation for American Christian Education. You can contact them via their Web site at http://www.face.net/default.aspx.

15. Walter A. McDougall, *Freedom Just Around the Corner* (New York: HarperCollins, 2004), 41–43.

16. Jamestown Tinderbox, "A Brief History of Jamestown Colony," http://www.jamestowntinderbox.com/aboutjamestown (accessed May 4, 2009).

17. Sacvan Bercovitch and Cyrus R. K. Patell, *The Cambridge History of American Literature* (New York: Cambridge University Press, 1997), 73.

18. "A Brief History of Jamestown Colony."

19. Ibid.

20. MassMoments.com, "Explorer Gosnold Names 'Cape Cod' May 15, 1602," http://www.massmoments.com/moment.cfm?mid=144 (accessed May 4, 2009).

21. Louise Garfield Bachler and Allison Thurston, "Bartholomew Gosnold (1571–1607): New World Adventurer," *Monograph*, Summer 2007, http://www.cuttyhunkhistoricalsociety.org/monograph/CHS_MonographSpring2007_Gosnold.pdf (accessed May 4, 2009).

22. Rabbi Yitzhak Ginsburgh, *The Alef-Beit* (Lanham, MD: Jason Aronson, 1994).

23. Edmund Carpenter, *The Mayflower Pilgrims* (Chicago: Christian Liberty Press, 2004), 36.

24. The History Place, "The Mayflower Compact," http://www.historyplace.com/unitedstates/revolution/mayflower.htm (accessed May 4, 2009).

25. William Bradford, "The History of Plimouth Plantation," cited in James Stobaugh, *American Literature* (Nashville, TN: B&H Publishing Group, 2005), 23.

26. David O. Beale, "The Pilgrim's and God's Providence," BJUPress.com, http://www.bjupress.com/resources/articles/enews-featured-content/pilgrims-and-god-providence.php (accessed May 4, 2009).

27. Tonda Gainey Siders, "A Special Instrument of Blessing—The Settlement—Part 1," American Destiny, http://www.americandestiny.com/settlement.htm (accessed May 4, 2009).

28. William Bradford, "Of Their Voyage and How They Passed the Sea; and of Their Safe Arrival at Cape Cod," MVLA High School District, http://www.mvla.net/teachers/Estherw/American%20Literature/Documents/The%20Puritans/Bradford_Of%20Plymouth%20Plantation.doc (accessed May 4, 2009).

29. The Avalon Project, "Declaration of Independence, July 4, 1776," Yale Law School, http://avalon.law.yale.edu/18th_century/declare.asp (accessed June 24, 2009).

30. Williston Walker, *The Creeds and Platforms of Congregationalism* (New York: Scribner, 1893), 101.

31. "America's Hebraic Heritage and Roots."

32. Ibid.

33. Cotton Mather, "Nehemias Americanus: The Life of John Winthrop, Esq., Governor of the Massachusetts Colony," http://www.nbu.bg/webs/amb/american/1/mather/winthrop.htm (accessed May 4, 2009).

34. Robert C. Winthrop, *Life and Letters of John Winthrop* (Boston, MA: Little, Brown and Austin, 1869).

35. Cotton Mather quote, cited in Marvin R. Wilson, *Our Father Abraham* (Grand Rapids, MI: Wm. B. Eerdmans Publishing, 1989), 128.

36. William Bradford and William Thomas Davis, *Bradford's History of Plymouth Plantation, 1606–1646*, (New York: C. Scribner's Sons, 1908), 18.

37. Oscar Reiss, *The Jews in Colonial America* (Jefferson, NC:McFarland, 2004), 40.

38. Encyclopedia.com, "New England," http://www.encyclopedia.com/doc/1G2-2536600259.html (accessed May 4, 2009).

39. Marshall and Manuel, *The Light and the Glory*, 193.

40. Michael Togias, "King Philip's War in New England," The History Place, http://www.historyplace.com/specials/kingphilip.htm (accessed May 4, 2009).

41. Samuel Adams Drake, *History of Middlesex County, Massachusetts* (Boston, MA: Harvard University, 1880), 351; http://books.google.com/books?id=hNaAnwRMedUC&printsec=frontcover&dq=History+of+Middlesex+County,+Massachusetts (accessed June 22, 2009).

42. Bryan Hardesty, "Book 1: Discovery and Colonization of the New World (1492–1763)," http://www.history2u.com/book1_discovery.htm (accessed June 24, 2009).

43. Encylopedia.com, "Nathaniel Bacon," http://www.encyclopedia.com/doc/1G2-3404700371.html (accessed May 4, 2009).

Chapter 5: The American Revolution and the Children of Israel

1. Charles Frances Adams, ed., *The Works of John Adams, Second President of the United States: with a Life of the Author, Notes and Illustrations*, vol. 10, "To H. Niles" (Boston: Little, Brown and Co., 1856), http://oll.libertyfund.org/title/2127/193604 (accessed June 26, 2009).

2. Patrick Henry, Address to the Virginia House of Burgesses, March 23, 1775.

3. Charles Assheton Whately Pownall, *Thomas Pownall* (Boston, MA: Harvard University, 1908), 263.

4. Andrew Ronemus, "Minutemen," USHistory.org, http://www.ushistory.org/people/minutemen.htm (accessed May 4, 2009).

5. David Hackett Fischer, *Paul Revere's Ride* (New York: Oxford University Press, 1994), 75–76.

6. Donald L. Hafner, "The First Blood Shed in the Revolution: The Tale of Josiah Nelson on April 19, 1775," Center for Human Rights and International Justice, http://escholarship.bc.edu/cgi/viewcontent.cgi?article=1006&context=hrij_facp (accessed May 4, 2009).

7. Flavius Josephus, *Antiquities of the Jews*, book 8, chapter 8, section 4.

8. Ibid.

9. John O'Sullivan, "The Great Nation of Futurity," 1839, http://web.utk.edu/~mfitzge1/docs/374/GNF1839.pdf (accessed May 4, 2009).

10. *The Boston Gazette*, September 1768, http://www.fbaptistc.org/Boston%20Gazette.html (accessed May 4, 2009.

11. *American Whig*, no. 5, April 11, 1768; begun March 14, 1768, in *New York Gazette*, as quoted in Benjamin Hart, *Faith and Freedom*, "The Making of an American Ideology," http://www.leaderu.com/orgs/cdf/ff/chap16.html (accessed June 26, 2009).

12. Alex Canduci and William Weir, *History's Greatest Lies* (Beverly, MA: Fair Winds, 2009), 125.

13. HistoryNet.com, "Paul Revere's True Account of the Midnight Ride," http://www.historynet.com/paul-reveres-true-account-of-the-midnight-ride.htm (accessed May 4, 2009).

14. Fischer, *Paul Revere's Ride*, 105–106.

15. Press release, "John Parker," The Lexington Minute Men, Inc., http://users.rcn.com/waynemccarthy/LMM2002/media/captparkrpr_08-2.pdf (accessed May 4, 2009).

16. Alan Axelrod, *The Real History of the American Revolution* (New York: Sterling Publishing Company, 2007), 94–95.

17. Captain Levi Preston, interviewed by Mellen Chamberlain, ca. 1843, quoted in Fischer, *Paul Revere's Ride*, 163–164.

18. Fischer, *Paul Revere's Ride*.

19. Herman Melville, *White Jacket* (New York: A. L. Burt Company, 1892), 144, http://books.google.com/books?id=2IDfbljLtXgC&printsec=titlepage&source=gbs_v2_summary_r&cad=0 (accessed June 26, 2009).

Chapter 6: Biblical Patterns in the Nation's Capital

1. Abraham Lincoln, "Address to the 166th Ohio Regiment," August 22, 1864, http://www.nps.gov/liho/historyculture/thankstotroops.htm (accessed June 26, 2009).

2. Rabbi Avraham Sutton, "The Spiritual Significance of the Qetoret (Incense) in Ancient Jewish Tradition," Jewishmag.com, http://www.jewishmag.com/11mag/mystic/mystic.htm (accessed May 5, 2009).

3. Colorado Mining Association, "Coal and Mineral Production," http://www.coloradomining.org/mc_mineralproduction.php (accessed May 5, 2009).

4. Harvey W. Crew, William Bensing Webb, and John Wooldridge, *Centennial History of the City of Washington, D.C.* (New York: Harvard University, 1892), 83.

5. Jason Glaser, *Washington, D.C.* (Mankato, MN: Capstone Press, 2003), 20.

6. Marilyn Prolman, *The Story of the Capitol* (Jefferson City, MO: Children's Press, 1969).

7. TourofDC.org, "The Washington Monument," http://tourofdc.org/monuments/washington-monument/ (accessed May 5, 2009).

8. Eyewitness to History, "The British Surrender at Yorktown," http://www.eyewitnesstohistory.com/yorktown.htm (accessed May 5, 2009).

9. The Patriot Resource, "Continental General Benjamin Lincoln," http://www.patriotresource.com/people/lincoln.html (accessed May 5, 2009).

Chapter 7: A Nation Divided—the Split Between North and South

1. Susan Pendleton Lee, *New School History of the United States* (formerly *Lee's Brief History of the United States*) (New York: Harvard University Press, 1900), 185.

2. Ibid., 105.

3. Ibid.

4. John William Jones, *Personal Reminiscences, Anecdotes, and Letters of Gen. Robert E. Lee* (New York: Harvard University, 1875), 139.

5. Ibid., 143.

6. Ibid., 138.

7. *Soldier of Faith*, painting by Mort Kunstler, text by Dee Brown, Henry Steele Commager, Rod Gragg, Mort Künstler, James McPherson, and James I. Robertson Jr., http://www.mortkunstler.com/gallery/product807_lastcat69.ihtml (accessed June 29, 2009).

8. As quoted in: Robert Underwood and Clarence Clough, *Battles and Leaders of the Civil War*, volume 1 (n.p.: The Century Company, 1887).

9. Robert Lewis Dabney, *Life and Campaigns of Lieut.-Gen. Thomas J. Jackson (Stonewall Jackson)* (New York: Blelock & Co., 1866), 109.

10. Randall M. Miller, Harry S. Stout, and Charles Reagan Wilson, *Religion and the American Civil War* (New York: Oxford University Press, 1998).

11. Dale Carnegie, *Lincoln, the Unknown* (New York: The Century Co, 1932), 219.

12. John T. Woolley and Gerhard Peters, The American Presidency Project [online] (Santa Barbara, CA: University of California [hosted], Gerhard Peters [database]), http://www.presidency.ucsb.edu/ws/index.php?pid=69891 (accessed June 29, 2009).

13. Wayne Whipple, *The Heart of Lincoln* (Philadelphia: George W. Jacobs and Company, 1915), 83–84, http://libsysdigi.library.uiuc.edu/oca/Books2007-07/heartoflincolnso00whip/heartoflincolnso00whip_djvu.txt (accessed June 29, 2009).

14. The Avalon Project, "Second Inaugural Address of Abraham Lincoln, March 4, 1865," Yale Law School, http://avalon.law.yale.edu/19th_century/lincoln2.asp (accessed June 29, 2009).

Chapter 8: The Destruction of America's Families

1. DivorceRate.org, citing Jennifer Baker of the Forest Institute of Professional Psychology in Springfield, Missouri, http://www.divorcerate.org/ (accessed May 6, 2009).

2. ChildStats.gov, "America's Children in Brief: Key National Indicators of Well-Being, 2008," http://www.childstats.gov/americaschildren/famsoc.asp (accessed May 6, 2009).

3. Ibid.

4. Council on Contemporary Families, "Stereotypes Versus Statistics: Data on America's Changing Families," http://www.contemporaryfamilies.org/subtemplate.php?ext=stereotypesedu&t=education (accessed May 6, 2009).

5. Rebecca O'Neill, "Experiments in Living: The Fatherless Family,"

September2002, CIVITAS, cited in "Consequences of Father Absence," FathersForLife.org, http://fathersforlife.org/divorce/chldrndiv.htm (accessed May 6, 2009).

6. Fathers for Life, "Family Violence—Trends, Results," *Common Sense & Domestic Violence* newsletter, January 30, 1998, http://fathersforlife.org/fv/DV_news_letter_980130.htm (accessed July 1, 2009).

7. Joseph Thayer, *Thayer's Greek-English Lexicon of the New Testament* (Peabody, MA: Hendricksons, 1996).

8. Ibid.

9. Quoted in William Jurgens, *The Faith of the Early Fathers* (Collegeville, MN: The Order of St. Benedict, 1970), 74, http://books.google.com/books?id=l62q-d4Wi20C&printsec=frontcover&dq=faith+of+the+early+fathers (accessed July 1, 2009).

10. Tertullian, *On Modesty*, "Chap. IV.—Adultery and Fornication Synonymous," (n.p.: Kessinger Publishing, 2004), 8, http://books.google.com/books?id=kpR7-a9kN-MC&printsec=frontcover&source=gbs_navlinks_s (accessed July 1, 2009).

11. St. Basil of Caesarea, "Letter 217: To Amphilochius, the Canons," NewAdvent.org, http://www.newadvent.org/fathers/3202217.htm (accessed July 1, 2009).

12. Quoted in Catholic.com, "Early Teachings on Homosexuality," http://www.catholic.com/library/Early_Teachings_on_Homosexuality.asp (accessed July 1, 2009).

13. St. John Chrysostom, "Homily 73 on Matthew," NewAdvent.org, http://www.newadvent.org/fathers/200173.htm (accessed July 1, 2009).

14. St. John Chrysostom, *Homilies on the Acts of the Apostles and the Epistle to the Romans*, Christian Classics Ethereal Library, http://www.ccel.org/ccel/schaff/npnf111.vii.vi.html (accessed July 1, 2009).

15. Quoted in Catholic.com, "Early Teachings on Homosexuality."

16. From *Matthew Henry's Commentary on the Whole Bible: New Modern Edition*, Electronic Database. Copyright (c) 1991 by Hendrickson Publishers, Inc.

17. From *Keil & Delitzsch Commentary on the Old Testament: New Updated Edition*, Electronic Database. Copyright (c) 1996 by Hendrickson Publishers, Inc.

18. Marilyn Hickey, *Break the Generation Curse* (Denver: Marilyn Hickey Ministries, 1988), 19, cited in Bob DeWaay, "Are Christians Cursed?" *Critical Issues Commentary*, June/July 1997, http://cicministry.org/commentary/issue40.htm (accessed May 6, 2009).

19. Sacred-Texts.com, "Book of Jasher, Chapter 10," http://www.sacred-texts.com/chr/apo/jasher/10.htm (accessed July 1, 2009).

20. Sacred-Texts.com, "Book of Jasher, Chapter 19," http://www.sacred-texts.com/chr/apo/jasher/19.htm (accessed July 1, 2009).

21. *AMBUSH Mag*, "The 37th Southern Decadence Phenomenon," Southern Decadence, http://www.southerndecadence.com/history.htm (accessed May 6, 2009).

22. Taken from a Southern Decadence promotional flyer for the 2005 event.

Chapter 9: The Trouble on America's Coastlines

1. Flavius Josephus, *Antiquities of the Jews*, book 1, chapter 2, http://www.biblestudytools.com/History/BC/FlaviusJosephus/?book=Ant_1&chapter=2 (accessed July 1, 2009).

2. Flavius Josephus, *War of the Jews*, book 6, chapter 5, http://www.ccel.org/j/josephus/works/war-6.htm (accessed July 1, 2009).

3. Ibid.

4. Ibid.

5. Ibid.

6. Philip Schaff, *History of the Christian Church*, 8 volumes, third edition (Peabody, MA: Hendrickson, 2006).

7. North Carolina State University, "Scientists: Future Atlantic Hurricane Picture Is Highly Complex," *Science Daily*, September 24, 2001, http://www.sciencedaily.com/releases/2001/09/010924062015.htm (accessed May 7, 2009).

8. Martin Wolk, "How Hurricane Katrina's Costs Are Adding Up," MSNBC.com, http://www.msnbc.msn.com/id/9329293// (accessed May 7, 2009); HurricaneKatrinaRelief.com, "FAQS," http://www.hurricanekatrinarelief.com/faqs.html#What%20is%20the%20death%20toll%20of%20Hurricane%20Katrina (accessed May 7, 2009).

9. John Burnett, "'Hell on Earth' at the Convention Center," NPR.org, http://www.npr.org/templates/story/story.php?storyId=4849469 (accessed May 7, 2009).

10. City-Data.com, "New Orleans: History," http://www.city-data.com/us-cities/The-South/New-Orleans-History.html (accessed May 7, 2009).

11. New Orleans Voodoo Crossroads, "A Brief History of Voodoo," 1994, http://www.neworleansvoodoocrossroads.com/historyandvoodoo.html (accessed June 12, 2009).

12. Interesting Thing of the Day, "The Big Easy Does It: Voodoo," February 9, 2005, http://itotd.com/articles/455/voodoo/ (accessed May 7, 2009).

13. "Mardi Gras," http://www.novareinna.com/festive/mardi.html (accessed May 7, 2009).

14. Joe Nickell, "Investigative Files: Voodoo in New Orleans," Committee for Skeptical Inquiry, http://www.csicop.org/si/2002-01/i-files.html (accessed May 7, 2009).

15. Bon-Bagay.com, "Early History: From Freedom to Slavery…to Freedom Again," http://www.bon-bagay.com/History.html (accessed May 7, 2009).

16. W. E. Vine, *Vine's Expository Dictionary of New Testament Words,* s.v. "*krisis*," http://www.antioch.com.sg/cgi-bin/bible/vines/get_defn.pl?num=532#B3 (accessed May 7, 2009).

17. For additional information on Lot's family, see *Matthew Henry's Commentary on the Whole Bible: New Modern Edition*, Electronic Database. Copyright © 1991 by Hendrickson Publishers, Inc., s.v. "Gen. 15."

Chapter 10: Chaos in American Cities

1. See our three-part video series, "The Mystery of Fallen Angels, Giants, and Evil Spirits," Manna Fest 406, available on YouTube.com: Part 1: http://www.youtube.com/watch?v=8Lxc7VmDyuY&feature=related; Part 2: http://www.youtube.com/watch?v=8CpmwCPe-Is&feature=related; and Part 3: http://www.youtube.com/watch?v=PS9jIJEocFo&feature=relatedVideo (accessed May 8, 2009).

2. Allan Moore, *Through Syria and Palestine: A Trip by Canadian Missionaries*, (Wakefield, England: W. Nicholson, n.d.), electronic download available at http://

www.archive.org/stream/throughsyriapale00mooruoft/throughsyriapale00mooruoft_
djvu.txt (accessed May 8, 2009).

3. Rebecca Solnit, *Storming the Gates of Paradise* (Berkeley, CA: University of California Press, 2008), 28.

4. NetState.com, "The Great Seal of California," http://www.netstate.com/states/
symb/seals/ca_seal.htm (accessed May 8, 2009).

5. Steven Sora, *Secret Societies of America's Elite* (Rochester, VT: Destiny Books, 2003).

6. W. E. Vine, *Vine's Expository Dictionary of New Testament Words*, PCStudy Bible 3.0 electronic database.

7. CBS Broadcasting Inc., "Psychic Businesses Booming Amid Economic Downturn," December 2, 2008, http://cbs4denver.com/business/psychic.reading
.economy.2.878383.html (accessed May 8, 2009).

8. "Vintage Wine," http://www.cocaine.org/cocawine.htm (accessed May 8, 2009).

9. Questia.com, "Cocaine," http://www.questia.com/library/encyclopedia/cocaine
.jsp (accessed May 8, 2009).

10. "Cola Marketing History," http://www.solarnavigator.net/sponsorship/coca_
cola.htm (accessed May 8, 2009).

11. DrugRehabs.org, "Alcohol Statistics," http://www.drug-rehabs.org/alcohol
-statistics.php (accessed May 8, 2009).

12. Ibid.

13. Ibid.

14. Ibid.

15. Ibid.

16. Ibid.

17. DrugRehabs.org, "Drug Statistics," http://www.drug-rehabs.org/drug
-statistics.php (accessed May 8, 2009).

18. Ibid.

19. Ibid.

20. Ibid.

21. For more information on the correlation between inner-city culture and drug use, see: Elijah Anderson, "Violence and the Inner-City Street Code," cited in C. Michael Henry, *Race, Poverty, and Domestic Policy* (New Haven, CT: Yale University Press, 2004), 671–701.

22. Quoted from a personal conversation with an anonymous former drug dealer.

23. Karen P. Tandy, "United States Policy Towards Narco-Terrorism in Afghanistan," DEA Congressional Testimony, February 12, 2007, http://www.usdoj
.gov/dea/pubs/cngrtest/ct021204.htm (accessed May 11, 2009).

24. Pierre Thomas, "Rise in Child Abuse Called National 'Epidemic,'" ABC News, April 25, 2005, http://abcnews.go.com/WNT/Story?id=701293&page=1 (accessed May 11, 2009).

25. This information was reported to me after the interview with the pastor, who himself was later killed by the drug lords in Colombia.

Chapter 11: America's Identity Crisis

1. The White House, "Joint Press Availability With President Obama and President Gul of Turkey," April 6, 2009, http://www.whitehouse.gov/the_press_office/Joint-Press-Availability-With-President-Obama-And-President-Gul-Of-Turkey/ (accessed July 2, 2009).

2. William Jackson Johnstone, *George Washington, the Christian* (n.p.: Abingdon Press, 1919), 39.

3. Ibid., 40.

4. Cameron C. Taylor, "The Separation of Church and State," TranslationDirectory.com, http://www.translationdirectory.com/articles/article1693.php (accessed May 11, 2009). Also cited in *Pictorial Encyclopedia of American History*, Volume 2 (United States History Society, Inc., 1968), 96.

5. David Barton, *The Bulletproof George Washington* (Aledo, TX: Wallbuilder Press, 2003).

6. Ibid.

7. Billy Graham Center, "2001 Inaugural Invocation," http://www.wheaton.edu/bgc/archives/inaugural07.htm (accessed July 2, 2009).

8. James A. Smith Sr., "Pastor's Prayer in Jesus' Name Prompts Fla. Politician's Apology," *Baptist Press*, May 10, 2004, http://www.bpnews.net/bpnews.asp?id=18249 (accessed May 11, 2009).

9. Sarah Pulliam, "Gay Bishop Kicks Off Celebrity-filled Event," ChristianityToday.com, January 18, 2009, http://blog.christianitytoday.com/ctpolitics/2009/01/gay_bishop_kick.html (accessed May 11, 2009).

10. BeliefNet.com, "Rick Warren's Jesus Prayer," January 20, 2009, http://blog.beliefnet.com/textmessages/2009/01/rick-warrens-jesus-prayer.html (accessed May 11, 2009).

11. Author's personal knowledge of incident.

12. School Prayer in America, "School Prayer in America," http://www.schoolprayerinamerica.info/ (accessed May 11, 2009).

13. Barna Group, "A New Generation of Adults Bends Moral and Sexual Rules to Their Liking," October 31, 2006, http://www.barna.org/barna-update/article/13-culture/144-a-new-generation-of-adults-bends-moral-and-sexual-rules-to-their-liking (accessed May 11, 2009).

14. Metro Ministries, "About Metro Ministries," http://www.metroministries.org/About/About/tabid/3379/Default.aspx (accessed May 12, 2009).

15. David Barton, *America: To Pray or Not to Pray* (Aledo, TX: Wallbuilder Press, 1988, 1994).

16. Excerpted from the William O'Hair statement in 1999 after the murder of his mother, brother, and daughter, http://www.wjmurray.com/ (accessed May 18, 2009).

17. Ibid.

18. Pierre Tristam, "The Failed Rescue of American Hostages in Iran on April 24, 1980," About.com: Middle East Issues, http://middleeast.about.com/od/usmideastpolicy/a/me090413b.htm (accessed May 18, 2009).

19. The Avalon Project, "Washington's Farewell Address 1796," Yale Law School, http://avalon.law.yale.edu/18th_century/washing.asp (accessed July 2, 2009).

20. Nettie Bates Thomas, "The Monkey's Disgrace," used in John Bava, *Scrapbook of Radiant Gems* (n.p.: n.d.), 34.

21. Avert.org, "Funding for the HIV and AIDS Epidemic," http://www.avert.org/aids-funding.htm (accessed May 18, 2009).

22. UNAID.org, "Status of the Global HIV Epidemic: 2008 Report," http://data.unaids.org/pub/GlobalReport/2008/jc1510_2008_global_report_pp29_62_en.pdf (accessed May 18, 2009).

23. Ronald Reagan, "Abortion and the Conscience of the Nation," *National Review Online*, June 10, 2004, http://www.nationalreview.com/document/reagan200406101030.asp (accessed May 18, 2009).

24. Kerby Anderson, "The Occult Connection," Probe Ministries, http://www.probe.org/site/c.fdKEIMNsEoG/b.4217659/ (accessed May 12, 2009).

25. WorldNetDaily.com, "Most Americans Believe in Ghosts," February 27, 2003, http://www.worldnetdaily.com/index.php?fa=PAGE.view&pageId=17494 (accessed July 2, 2009).

26. *St. Louis Post-Dispatch*, "Court Outlaws Prayer in Schools," June 17, 1963, MSN Encarta, http://encarta.msn.com/sidebar_761594285/court_outlaws_prayer_in_schools.html (accessed May 12, 2009).

27. National Right to Life, "Abortion History Timeline," http://www.nrlc.org/abortion/facts/abortiontimeline.html (accessed May 12, 2009).

28. Huck Gutman, "Supreme Court Issues Watershed Decision on Gay Rights," CommonDreams.org, http://www.commondreams.org/views03/0709-10.htm (accessed May 12, 2009).

29. "Alan Keyes Arrested Protesting Abortion at Notre Dame," InfoWars.com, May 8, 2009, http://www.infowars.com/alan-keyes-arrested-protesting-abortion-at-notre-dame/ (accessed May 12, 2009).

30. PBS.org, "Religious Tolerance in America," *Bill Moyers Journal*, April 18, 2008, http://www.pbs.org/moyers/journal/blog/2008/04/religious_tolerance_in_america.html (accessed May 12, 2009).

31. Richard Kelly Hoskins, *War Cycles—Peace Cycles* (Lynchburg, VA: Virginia Publishing Company, 1994).

32. Nic Fields and Peter Bull, *Ancient Greek Warship, 500–322 BC* (Oxford: Osprey Publishing, 2007), 43.

33. Hoskins, *War Cycles—Peace Cycles*.

34. EyeWitnesstoHistory.com, "The Romans Destroy the Temple at Jerusalem, 70 A.D.," http://www.eyewitnesstohistory.com/jewishtemple.htm (accessed May 12, 2009).

Chapter 12: America—From Producer to Purchaser

1. Vine, *Vine's Expository Dictionary of New Testament Words*, PCStudy Bible 3.0 electronic database.

2. As stated in Trygve's Digital Diary, "How Long Is It?" March 12, 2006, http://www.trygve.com/taxcode.html (accessed July 2, 2009).

3. Cayman Net News, "Editorial: We Are Not the United States of America's Policeman," May 12, 2009, http://www.caymannetnews.com/article.php?news_id=15437 (accessed May 13, 2009).

4. Department of the Treasury, "History of the U.S. Tax System," Fact Sheet: Taxes, http://www.treas.gov/education/fact-sheets/taxes/ustax.shtml (accessed July 2, 2009).

5. Ibid.

6. Ibid.

7. Ibid.

8. Ibid.

9. Ibid.

10. FindLaw.com, "Amendments to the Constitution of the United States," http://caselaw.lp.findlaw.com/data/constitution/amendments.html#f8 (accessed July 6, 2009).

11. Ibid.

12. Department of the Treasury, "History of the U.S. Tax System."

13. Ibid.

14. Ibid.

15. *St. Petersburg Times*, "Joe the Plumber: A Transcript," October 19, 2008, http://www.tampabay.com/news/perspective/article858299.ece (accessed July 6, 2009).

16. Brendan Steinhauser, "Obama: Supreme Court Should Redistribute Wealth," The Conservative Revolution blog, from a transcript of 2001 Barack Obama interview with Chicago Public Radio, http://theconservativerevolution.com/barack -obama/obama-supreme-court-should-redistribute-wealth/ (accessed May 13, 2009).

17. Department of the Treasury, "History of the U.S. Tax System."

18. Jake Tapper, "Obama's Budget: Almost $1 Trillion in New Taxes Over Next 10 Years, Starting 2011," ABCNews.com, February 26, 2009, http://blogs.abcnews .com/politicalpunch/2009/02/obamas-budget-a.html (accessed May 13, 2009).

19. Arthur E. R. Boak, *Manpower Shortage and the Fall of the Roman Empire in the West* (Ann Arbor, MI: The University of Michigan Press, 1955), 39.

20. Ibid., 40.

21. National Right to Life, "Abortion in the United States: Statistics and Trends," http://www.nrlc.org/abortion/facts/abortionstats.html (accessed July 29, 2009).

22. Boak, *Manpower Shortage and the Fall of the Roman Empire in the West*, 44.

23. Ibid., 48.

24. Ibid., 50.

25. Information from a personal conversation.

26. Robert Schoenberger, "U.S. Car Makers Lose Ground in a Hurry to Foreign Competition," October 22, 2007, Cleveland.com, http://blog.cleveland.com/ business/2007/10/us_automakers_lose_ground_in_a.html (accessed May 13, 2009).

27. Tanya Savory, *Houdini* (West Berlin, NJ: Townsend Press, 2008), 7.

28. Federal Reserve Bank of New York, "How Currency Gets Into Circulation," http://www.newyorkfed.org/aboutthefed/fedpoint/fed01.html (accessed May 14, 2009).

29. Federal Reserve, "Money Stock Measures," May 7, 2009, http://www .federalreserve.gov/releases/h6/hist/h6hist1.txt (accessed May 14, 2009).

30. *San Francisco Examiner*, "Examiner Editorial: Get Ready for Obama's Coming Hyperinflation," April 30, 2009, http://www.sfexaminer.com/opinion/ Examiner-Editorial-Get-ready-for-Obamas-coming-hyperinflation-44030232.html

(accessed July 6, 2009).

31. Jeff Madura and Roland Fox, *International Financial Management* (London: Cengage Learning EMEA, 2007), 225–226.

Chapter 13: America—the New Roman Empire

1. History.com, "Rome Founded," This Day in History, http://www.history.com/this-day-in-history.do?action=VideoArticle&id=6874 (accessed May 12, 2009).

2. Harold Whetstone Johnston, *The Private Life of the Romans*, "182. Duties and Rewards" (Glenview, IL: Scott, Foresman and Company, 1908), 114.

3. Tenny Frank, *An Economic History of Rome* (New York: n.p., 1962), 206, referenced in Hoskins, *War Cycles—Peace Cycles*, 19.

4. Ibid.

5. Mark Harris, "Hitler and the Spear of Destiny," http://web.org.uk/picasso/spear.html (accessed May 12, 2009).

6. Ibid.

7. National Right to Life, "Abortion in the United States: Statistics and Trends."

8. Excerpted from a letter from Dutch Sheets, available at http://www.prayerfocusministries.com/eNewsletters/LAGAPN/March/DutchSheetsRelease.pdf (accessed May 12, 2009).

9. Molly Hobaugh-Sorenson, *The Forgotten Virtue*, "The Root Ideas of the Sexual Revolution" (N.p.: Sun West Publishing, 1997), http://www.forgottenvirtue.com/chapter6.htm (accessed May 12, 2009).

Chapter 14: The Future of the West—Told 2,500 Years Ago

1. Excerpted from Perry Stone, *Unleashing the Beast* (Lake Mary, FL: Charisma House, 2009).

2. Agence France-Presse, "Nobel-Prize Winner Backs World Currency," *The Australian*, March 11, 2009, http://www.theaustralian.news.com.au/story/0,25197,25173126-12377,00.html (accessed May 14, 2009).

3. John Irish, Reuters, "GCC Agrees on Monetary Union but Signals Delay in Common Currency," *Arab News*, June 10, 2008, http://www.arabnews.com/?page=6&section=0&article=110727&d=10&m=6&y=2008 (accessed May 14, 2009).

4. IslamicMint.com, "Introducing the Islamic Dinar and Dirham," http://www.islamicmint.com/islamicdinar/ (accessed July 14, 2009).

5. Ron Paul, "What the Price of Gold Is Telling Us," speech given before the U.S. House of Representatives, April 26, 2006, http://www.lewrockwell.com/paul/paul319.html (acessed May 14, 2009).

6. ContingencyToday.com, "Al Qaeda Says Buy Gold, Sell the Dollar," June 17, 2008, http://www.contingencytoday.com/online_article/Al-Qaeda-says-buy-gold,-sell-the-dollar/1315 (accessed May 14, 2009).

7. M. A. Nystrom, "Gold, 1980," December 8, 2005, http://www.bullnotbull.com/archive/gold1980.html (accessed on May 14, 2009); see also The Silver Analyst, "The Great Silver Spike of 1980," May 10, 2006, http://www.safehaven.com/article-5133.htm (accessed May 14, 2009).

8. *Alpha Omega Report*, "NOW's Plans for 1-World Currency Moves Into Media

Spotlight," March 24, 1009, http://aoreport.com/mag/index.php?option=com_conte nt&task=view&id=1181&Itemid=44 (accessed May 14, 2009).

9. Islamic-Word.net. "Islamic World Countries," http://www.islamic-world.net/ countries/index.htm (accessed May 14, 2009).

10. "European Union," http://userpage.chemie.fu-berlin.de/adressen/eu.html (accessed May 14, 2009).

11. Council on Foreign Relations, "Building a North American Community: Report of an Independent Task Force," http://www.cfr.org/content/publications/ attachments/NorthAmerica_TF_final.pdf (accessed May 14, 2009).

12. Judi McLeod, "Debut of the 'Amero,'" *Canada Free Press*, December 14, 2006, http://www.canadafreepress.com/2006/cover121406.htm (accessed May 14, 2009).

13. A video of the Barack Obama Town Hall Event in Lancaster, Pennsylvania, shows his response to a question about the North American Union and can be viewed at http://www.youtube.com/watch?v=id_EvColFzA (accessed July 14, 2009).

14. The CNBC interview with Stephen Previs about the amero can be viewed at http://www.youtube.com/watch?v=_3jdQxDC7pA (accessed July 14, 2009).

15. Mitchell Godfrey Bard and Moshe Schwartz, *1001 Facts Everyone Should Know About Israel* (Lanham, MD: Rowman and Littlefield, 2005), 109.

16. David Muench, Marc Muench, and Michelle A. Gilders, *Primal Forces* (Portland, OR: Graphic Arts Center Publishing Co., 2000), 22.

17. WTRG.com, "Oil Price History and Analysis," *WTRG Economics*, http:// www.wtrg.com/prices.htm (accessed May 14, 2009).

18. Reuters.com, "Iran Says Oil Price May Rise More on China, India," May 14, 2009, http://www.reuters.com/article/GCA-WorldEconomicForum_MiddleEast/ idUSTRE54D35R20090514 (accessed May 14, 2009).

19. This information was given to the author by a source unable to be named. The information is secretive, and the American city cannot be named in this book.

20. BanEthanol.com, "Using Food to Make Fuel Called 'Criminal,'" April 21, 2008, http://www.banethanol.com/2008/04/21/using-food-to-make-fuel-called -criminal/ (accessed May 14, 2009).

21. Rachelle Oblack, "The Midwest Floods of March 2008," About.com: Weather, http://weather.about.com/od/floods/a/MissouriFloods.htm (accessed May 14, 2009).

22. InfiniteUnknown.net, "Airborne Fungus Ug99 Threatens Global Wheat Harvest," http://www.infiniteunknown.net/tag/wheat-rust/ (accessed May 14, 2009).

23. Agriculture Research Service, "Questions and Answers: Colony Collapse Disorder," http://www.ars.usda.gov/News/docs.htm?docid=15572 (accessed May 14, 2009).

24. GreenEarthFriend.com, "Colony Collapse Disorder (CCD): Honey Bees Dying by the Millions!" January 19, 2009, http://www.greenearthfriend.com/2009/01/colony -collapse-disorder-ccd-honeybees-dying-by-the-millions/ (accessed May 15, 2009).

25. Jamie Coomarasamy, "Is Atlanta at Risk of Running Dry?" *BBC News*, November 21, 2007, http://news.bbc.co.uk/2/hi/americas/7104547.stm (accessed May 15, 2009).

26. Brooke-Sidney Gavins, "The Green Report: Drought Conditions Worsen Southwest Water Crisis," March 13, 2009, PopandPolitics.com, http://www

.popandpolitics.com/2009/03/13/the-green-report-drought-conditions-worsen
-southwest-water-crisis/ (accessed May 15, 2009).

27. Joe Gertner, "The Future Is Drying Up," October 21, 2007, *New York Times*,
http://query.nytimes.com/gst/fullpage.html?res=9C0CEFDA103CF932A15753C1A9
619C8B63 (accessed May 15, 2009).

28. Neda Zawahri, "Reconstructing Iraq's Water Supply," paper presented at
the annual meeting of the International Studies Association, Town & Country
Resort and Convention Center, San Diego, California, USA, March 22, 2006
(not available), abstract viewed at http://www.allacademic.com/meta/p_mla_apa_
research_citation/1/0/0/7/7/p100771_index.html, (accessed May 15, 2009).

29. Joseph Abrams and Jonathan Passantino, "Foiled Terror Plots Against
America Since 9/11," September 11, 2008, FOXNews.com, http://www.foxnews
.com/story/0,2933,335500,00.html (accessed May 15, 2009).

30. David Satter, "The Truth About Beslan," November 13, 2006, *The Weekly
Standard*, http://www.weeklystandard.com/Content/Public/Articles/000/000/012/
907jbmkm.asp?pg=1 (accessed May 15, 2009).

31. Ben Feller, "Computer Disc Found in Iraq Contained U.S. School Plans,"
October 7, 2004," USAToday.com, http://www.usatoday.com/news/world/iraq/2004
-10-07-school-disk_x.htm (accessed May 15, 2009).

32. Information given to me in personal conversations with unnamed sources.

33. "Signs of the Last Hour," summary of lecture given by Gharm-Allah El-
Ghamdy, Fall 1991, http://www.msawest.net/islam/fundamentals/pillars/
signsofthelasthour.html (accessed July 16, 2009).

34. Yigal Carmon, "Madrid Bluff?" March 12, 2004, *National Review Online*,
http://www.nationalreview.com/comment/carmon200403121251.asp (accessed May
15, 2009).

35. Peter Goodspeed, "40 Al-Qaeda Terrorists Dead After Exposure to the
Plague: Report," *National Post*, January 20, 2009, http://www.nationalpost.com/
most-popular/story.html?id=1199042 (accessed May 15, 2009).

36. TheScienceExperts.com, "What Causes the Bubonic Plague and How Deadly
Is It?" October 30, 2008, http://thescienceexperts.com/answers/bubonic-plague
(accessed May 15, 2009).

37. Richard W. Niska and Catharine W. Burt, "Training for Terrorism-Related
Conditions in Hospitals: United States, 2003–04," *Advance Data From Vital and
Health Statistics* 380, December 11, 2006, http://www.cdc.gov/nchs/data/ad/ad380
.pdf (accessed May 15, 2009).

38. *The Virtual Times*, "The Great New Madrid Earthquake," http://www.hsv
.com/genlintr/newmadrd/ (accessed May 15, 2009).

39. IDEALS, "Impact of Earthquakes on the Central USA," https://www.ideals
.uiuc.edu/handle/2142/8971 (accessed May 15, 2009).

40. Aly Adair, "Earthquakes Swarm Yellowstone National Park: Dec 2008-Jan
2009," Associated Content, January 10, 2009, http://www.associatedcontent.com/
article/1376733/earthquakes_swarm_yellowstone_national.html?cat=16 (accessed
May 15, 2009).

41. Quote cited in Dee Finney, "Yellowstone Supervolcano Getting Ready to

Blow Its Cork," http://www.earthmountainview.com/yellowstone/yellowstone.htm (accessed May 15, 2009).

42. EarthMountainView.com, "New 3.8 Earthquake Hits Outside of Yellowstone," http://www.earthmountainview.com/yellowstone/yellowstone-news.htm (accessed July 16, 2009).

Chapter 15: Is America in Bible Prophecy?

1. Cited in Michelle A. Vu, "George Barna: America Is Being Destroyed Inside Out," *Christian Post*, May 9, 2009, http://www.christianpost.com/Ministries/Figures/2009/05/george-barna-america-is-being-destroyed-inside-out-09/index.html (accessed May 15, 2009).

2. Pilgrim Hall Museum, "The Mayflower Compact," http://www.pilgrimhall.org/compact.htm (accessed May 15, 2009).

3. Harold L. Willmington, *Willmington's Guide to the Bible* (Wheaton, IL: Tyndale House, 1989).

4. *Sun Star*, "Should God Stay in Ohio's Motto?" June 1, 2000, Ohio Roundtable and Ohio Freedom Forum, https://www.aproundtable.org/library/articles/liberties/godstay.html (accessed May 15, 2009).

5. "Then saw I a dream, and, behold, there came up from the sea an eagle, which had twelve feathered wings..." (2 Esdras 11:1, KJV).

6. "...the feathers that followed stood up upon the right side..." (2 Esdras 11:20, KJV).

7. GreatSeal.com, "First Great Seal Committee—July/August 1776," http://www.greatseal.com/committees/firstcomm/ (accessed May 18, 2009).

8. This theory about Haym Solomon was alluded to in Vendyl Jones, *Will the Real Jesus Please Stand Up?* (Alpharetta, GA: Priority, 1983).

9. GreatSeal.com, "Official 1782 Description of the Great Seal," http://www.greatseal.com/symbols/blazon.html (accessed May 18, 2009).

10. GreatSeal.com, "Explanation of the Great Seal's Symbolism," http://www.greatseal.com/symbols/explanation.html (accessed July 17, 2009).

11. James Wilson, cited in Buckner F. Melton, *The Quotable Founding Fathers* (Dulles, VA: Brassey's, 2004), 116.

Chapter 16: The Battle of the Last Gentile Empire

1. Quoted in Cal Thomas, "Thomas: Reagan Unveiled," *The Washington Times*, June 9, 2009, http://www.washingtontimes.com/news/2009/jun/09/reagan-unveiled/ (accessed July 20, 2009).

2. EarlyAmerica.com, "The Constitution of the United States," http://www.earlyamerica.com/earlyamerica/freedom/constitution/text.html (accessed July 20, 2009).

3. Mroue, "Hezbollah Rebuilds South Beirut."

4. About.com: U.S. Government Info, "The Branches of Government," http://usgovinfo.about.com/od/usconstitution/a/branches.htm (accessed May 27, 2009).

5. USConstitution.net, "U.S. Constitution—Amendment 22," http://www.usconstitution.net/xconst_Am22.html (accessed May 27, 2009).

6. Michael L. Dolfman and Solidelle F. Wasser, "9/11 and the New York City Economy: A Borough-by-Borough Analysis," *Monthly Labor Review*, June 2004, http://www.bls.gov/opub/mlr/2004/06/art1full.pdf (accessed May 19, 2009).

7. National Climatic Data Center, "Climate of 2008: Wildfire Season Summary," http://www.ncdc.noaa.gov/oa/climate/research/2008/fire08.html (accessed May 19, 2009).

8. Jay Watson and Jerry Carnes, "Atlanta Water Situation Called Dire," October 11, 2007, 11Alive.com, http://www.11alive.com/news/article_news .aspx?storyid=104561 (accessed May 19, 2009).

9. Kevin Scott, "Atlanta: San Francisco of the South," January 24, 2003, GayWired.com, http://www.gaywired.com/article.cfm?section=76&id=228 (accessed May 19, 2009).

10. Agricultural Research Service, "Questions and Answers: Colony Collapse Disorder," http://www.ars.usda.gov/News/docs.htm?docid=15572 (accessed May 14, 2009).

11. James Shea, "Drought, Hay Shortage Force Cattlemen to Sell Livestock," December 10, 2007, BlueRidgeNow.com, http://www.blueridgenow.com/article/ 20071210/NEWS/712100325 (accessed May 19, 2009).

12. Thomas Hutton, Thomas DeLiberto, Sheldon Owen, and Bruce Morrison, "Disease Risks Associated With Increasing Feral Swine Numbers and Distribution in the United States," July 11, 2006, http://www.michigan.gov/documents/mda/ Hutton_Pig_Paper_218759_7.pdf (accessed May 19, 2009).

13. George Soros, "The Perilous Price of Oil, *The New York Review of Books*, September 25, 2008, http://www.nybooks.com/articles/21792 (accessed May 19, 2009).

14. Dan Childs, Ammu Kannampilly, and Stephen Splane, "Pandemic 'Imminent': WHO Raises Swine Flu Pandemic Alert Level to 5," ABC News, April 29, 2009, http://abcnews.go.com/Health/SwineFlu/story?id=7456439&page=1 (accessed July 29, 2009).

15. H. S. Parker, "Agricultural Bioterrorism: A Federal Strategy to Meet the Threat," Institute for National Strategic Studies, National Defense University, Washington DC, McNair Paper 65, 2002:x, quoted in O. Shawn Cupp, David E. Walker II, and John Hillison, "Agroterrorism in the US: Key Security Challenges: Vulnerability to the Threat," MedScapeToday.com, http://www.medscape.com/ viewarticle/482308_2 (accessed May 19, 2009).

16. Monica Davis, "How Far Is the US From Food Shortages and Food Riots?" April 12, 2008, accessed at http://www.indybay.org/newsitems/2008/04/12/ 18492403.php, on May 19, 2009.

17. Susan Demas, "Is Detroit Dying?" July 20, 2008, MLive.com, http://blog .mlive.com/capitolchronicles/2008/07/is_detroit_dying_and_other_que.html (accessed May 19, 2009).

18. David Townsend, "Churches Stand to Lose Several Billion Dollars in Economic Downturn," http://afgen.com/churches_lose_billions.html (accessed May 19, 2009).

19. James Madison, cited in Wing Anderson, *Prophetic Years 1947–1953*

(Whitefish, MT: Kessinger Publishing, 2006), 27.

20. James Madison, James Madison Quotes, http://home.att.net/~midnightflyer/madison.html (accessed May 28, 2009).

21. Abraham Lincoln in reply to a letter from a friend in Illinois, cited in Dorus Morton Fox, *The Silver Side—1900 Campaign Text-book* (New York: W. B. Conkey, 1897), 32.

22. Woodrow Wilson, *The New Freedom* (New York: Doubleday, 1913), ftp://ibiblio.org/pub/docs/books/gutenberg/1/4/8/1/14811/14811-8.txt (accessed May 28, 2009).

23. Paul Krugman, "Fighting Off Depression," *New York Times*, January 4, 2009, http://www.nytimes.com/2009/01/05/opinion/05krugman.html?_r=2 (accessed July 20, 2009).

24. National Right to Life, "The Consequences of Roe v. Wade," http://www.nrlc.org/ABORTION/facts/abortionstats.html (accessed May 28, 2009).

25. "Troop Casualties," DoD Statistical Information Analysis Division (SIAD), http://rsrvd.com/mahalopix/ma-troop-casualty.jpg (accessed May 28, 2009).

26. Sacred-Texts.com, "Book of Jasher, Chapter 19," http://www.sacred-texts.com/chr/apo/jasher/19.htm (accessed July 1, 2009).

27. Office of Intelligence and Analysis Assessment, "Rightwing Extremism: Current Economic and Political Climate Fueling Resurgence in Radicalization and Recruitment," U.S. Department of Homeland Security, http://michellemalkin.cachefly.net/michellemalkin.com/wp/wp-content/uploads/2009/04/hsa-rightwing-extremism-09-04-07.pdf (accessed May 28, 2009).

28. Alexander Tytler, cited in Roderick Meredith, "The Future of Democracy," *Tomorrow's World*, volume 7, issue 2, March–April 2005, http://www.tomorrowsworld.org/cgi-bin/tw/tw-mag.cgi?category=Magazine35&item=1109664042 (accessed May 28, 2009).

Chapter 17: A Message to the Christian Church in America

1. William Penn, *Some Fruits of Solitude*, http://etext.lib.virginia.edu/etcbin/toccer-new2?id=PenSoli.sgm&images=images/modeng&data=/texts/english/modeng/parsed&tag=public&part=all (accessed July 20, 2009).

2. Turkey in Photos, "Hagia Sophia," http://www.turkeyinphotos.com/hagia_sophia.html (accessed May 19, 2009).

3. As related to author.

4. Dana Priest, "Bush's 'War' on Terror Comes to a Sudden End," *Washington Post*, January 23, 2009, http://www.washingtonpost.com/wp-dyn/content/article/2009/01/22/AR2009012203929_pf.html (accessed May 19, 2009).

5. MSN Encarta, "Great Depression in the United States," http://encarta.msn.com/encyclopedia_761584403/great_depression_in_the_united_states.html (accessed May 19, 2009).

6. Darlene Superville, "Obama Kicks Up White House Entertaining," March 2, 2009, BreitBart.com, http://www.breitbart.com/article.php?id=D96M09BO0&show_article=1 (accessed May 19, 2009).

7. William Schneider, "For Divided Congress, Making Up Is Hard to Do,"

February 28, 2009, NationalJournal.com, http://www.nationaljournal.com/njmagazine/pl_20090228_6415.php (accessed May 19, 2009).

8. Jeff Jacoby, "America Takes Side of Israel," March 26, 2006, Boston.com, http://www.boston.com/news/globe/editorial_opinion/oped/articles/2006/03/26/america_takes_side_of_israel/ (accessed May 19, 2009).